D1576602

The County Books Series
GENERAL EDITOR: BRIAN VESEY-FITZGERALD

DEVONSHIRE

THE COUNTY BOOKS SERIES

*A Series comprising 57 Volumes. It covers every county
in England and there will be five books on Scotland, two
on Ireland, two on the Hebrides, and one each on Orkney,
Shetland, Wales, the Isle of Man and the Channel Islands*

THE FOLLOWING TWENTY-TWO VOLUMES
HAVE NOW BEEN PUBLISHED

Sussex	*Esther Meynell*
Surrey . . .	*Eric Parker*
Kent . . .	*Richard Church*
Herefordshire . .	*H. L. V. Fletcher*
Staffordshire . .	*Phil Drabble*
Shropshire . . .	*Edmund Vale*
Worcestershire . .	*L. T. C. Rolt*
Gloucestershire . .	*Kenneth Hare*
Hampshire and Isle of Wight	
	Brian Vesey-FitzGerald
South London . .	*Harry Williams*
Cheshire . . .	*F. H. Crossley*
Cornwall . . .	*Claude Berry*
Cumberland and Westmorland	*Norman Nicholson*
The Western Isles	*Alasdair Alpin MacGregor*
Somerset . . .	*M. Lovett Turner*
Ulster . . .	*Hugh Shearman*
Bedfordshire . .	*Laurence Meynell*
Northumberland .	*Herbert L. Honeyman*
Isle of Man .	*Canon E. H. Stenning*
Leinster, Munster and Connaught	
	Frank O'Connor
Warwickshire . .	*. Alan Burgess*
Essex . . .	*C. Henry Warren*

PLEASE WRITE TO THE PUBLISHERS
FOR FULL DESCRIPTIVE PROSPECTUS

DEVONSHIRE

by

D. St. LEGER-GORDON

Illustrated and with Map

London
Robert Hale Limited
18 Bedford Square WC1

First published 1950

PRINTED AND BOUND IN GREAT BRITAIN BY
WILLIAM CLOWES AND SONS LTD, LONDON AND BECCLES

INTRODUCTORY NOTE

The history of any county is an almost inexhaustible subject, and to the "making" of a book in which everything found a place there would, indeed, be "no end." My aim has, therefore, been to concentrate upon matter particularly applicable to Devonshire, avoiding all the old "chestnuts" and endeavouring to present the country and people in a strictly realistic light. The work is not a guide-book, and no attempt has been made at detailed description of towns, villages or individual buildings, except in so far as it served the general purpose.

The task has involved considerable research, and I am much indebted to Mr and Mrs James Pearse, of Pixies' Gardens, Sticklepath, for free access to their valuable library. Thanks are also due to Miss Crighton (Honorary Secretary) and Miss White, of Exeter Cathedral and City Libraries, respectively; to Dr L. A. Harvey (University College of the South-West); to Mr R. Hansford Worth; to my ornithological friends Mr E. W. Hendy, the Rev F. C. Butters and Mr W. Walmsley-White; and to the Editor of the *Estate Magazine* for permission to make use of a previous article upon waterdivining. And finally I would like to acknowledge the help kindly given by Mr H. Wickett, of Willey Farm, Sticklepath, whose unique knowledge of Devonshire agriculture and rural matters generally has been placed at my disposal.

D. ST. LEGER-GORDON

CONTENTS

CONTENTS

ILLUSTRATIONS

ix

ILLUSTRATIONS

ACKNOWLEDGMENTS

*The illustrations above, numbered 1, 10, 11, 13, 14, 15, 16, 18, 19,
21, 23, 25, 27, 31, 34, 35, 37, 39, 45, 46 are reproduced from photographs by Mr J. A. Brimble, A.R.P.S.; 9, 29, 44 by Sport & General;
2 by Eagle Photos.*

*The remaining 25 are reproduced from photographs supplied by Mr
Reece Winstone, A.R.P.S.*

x

CHAPTER I

ONCE UPON A TIME
PREHISTORY

THOUSANDS of years before History begins her chronicle Devon's prehistory was being recorded in the limestone caverns of what is now her southern coast. Then, Kent's Hole, near Torquay, Windmill Cavern, near Brixham, and Cattedown, near Plymouth, where geologists have unrolled the scroll of ages, were caverns upon the edge of a plain stretching away to the Continent.

Northwards across this vast landscape wandered such animals as the mammoth, the woolly rhinoceros, cave bear, lion, reindeer and hyena, and hunting them with primitive stone weapons followed Paleolithic man, to settle in a land now known as fertile Devonshire, but then cold and desolate from a receding Ice Age and practically devoid of vegetation. Amid such surroundings primitive man's only secure or warm refuge was afforded by such caverns, to which he returned after his daily hunting, eventually leaving behind him, under successive layers of rock and soil, the indisputable evidences of his occupancy, unearthed by present-day geologists.

So passed Devon's first human inhabitants with the Old Stone Age of which they were part, and obscurity then descends, filled only by the unrecorded cataclysms of ensuing millenniums. Then suddenly upon the cave floor screen, replacing his more primitive predecessor, appears Neolithic man of the New Stone Age.

Although to us the intervening period presents an utter blank, it was obviously an era of change and progress, for this new human is now living in a land of dense forest, and around him roam, among certain of the former animals such as the hyena and wolf, wild boars, deer of various kinds, oxen, horses; and he is, moreover, attended by the dog. Of Ivernian, Iberian and Silurian extraction, he emerges equipped with the knowledge and use of more advanced weapons and implements of stone and bone, and hundreds of his flint arrow- and spear-heads, together with the stone axes usually termed *Celts,* have been unearthed all over the county. Yet there is nothing to suggest the remains of any domestic dwelling beyond tokens of his presence in Kent's Hole, which is curious in view of the solid stone chambers he erected for the burial of his dead. Only one of these *dolmens* exists in Devonshire—Spinster's Rock, near Drewsteignton, where the heavy covering slab upon its upright supports demonstrates the construction of these family mausoleums. Localities where others once stood are indicated by the frequently recurring name "Shilstone," a corruption of the shelf-stone, or supported slab, once a feature of the vicinity. Nor can Devon produce a single example of the typical Neolithic burial mound—the long barrow raised over bodies or dolmens; and though the destruction of such tumuli is comprehensible among lowland cultivation and buildings, one would have expected some examples to survive upon open moorland.

With two notable exceptions, however, and apart from quantities of flints, largely fashioned from imported East Devon chalk and chert, no Neolithic relics are found upon Dartmoor. The "Shilstones" occur only upon the confines, and taking into consideration the complete absence of anything indicative of dwelling-places, it would seem that, like Paleolithic man, the Neolithic too preferred the lowlands. Yet two of Dartmoor's most outstanding antiquities, Grimspound and Broadun Ring—the largest ancient enclosure upon Dartmoor, covering twelve acres—are attributed by archæologists to this race, not as dwellings, but either as pounds or gathering-places where several hundred people might take refuge together with their cattle should sudden emergency arise; or possibly as temporary camps for herdsmen. Whether the expenditure of so much laborious care upon structures intended only for casual or occasional use would have been worth while, especially upon ground outside their usual territory, may be queried, but cannot now be answered.

In contrast to the dark hiatus which occurred between

2

these two earliest prehistoric ages, the third, known as the Bronze Age, overlapped the Stone Age, probably by several centuries. At some period between 1800 and 1000 B.C. the quietude of the long-headed Neolithic folk was interrupted by the incursion of a round-headed Ugric people, to be followed later by Goidels of a stock akin to the later Celts. They crossed from the Continent, where the discovery and use of bronze had revolutionised weapons, trade and art, and their arrival inaugurated an era of progress and commerce. It was during this period that the controversial *Cassiterides*, or Tin islands, became famed for their Continental or Phœnician trading in this metal, then first being worked in the western peninsula.

Devon is rich in relics of the Bronze Age folk, and as far as can be ascertained from excavation and deduction it is their handiwork that is still seen today, 2,000 years or so later, upon Dartmoor, Exmoor and in many "in-country" districts where the round tumuli survive, though in most instances all trace of the associated stone monuments have here disappeared. A notable group of these characteristic round burial mounds is the Chapman Barrows, upon Exmoor. "Dartmoor and Exmoor," states Mr Hansford Worth, "are the two best archæological museums in the county." The antiquities of Exmoor, however, have suffered even more greatly from the despoiler than those of Dartmoor, for they stand in a district where stone is less abundant, and also less durable, being of a slaty nature. The component stones of the various ancient monuments, therefore, besides weathering badly, were smaller, lighter and so more easily transportable.

Upon Dartmoor, therefore, the numerous comparatively undisturbed relics afford greater facilities for study than elsewhere in the county, but at this immense distance of time controversial and conflicting evidence as to the probable manner of life of their originators is inevitable. These people of the Bronze Age are considered to be responsible for the various stone circles, avenues, kistvaens, menhirs and hut settlements, the latter doubtless utilised by successive generations of shelter-seekers throughout the centuries. Although their occupation must have been concurrent with

3

the time of active tin-seeking, no trace of metal has yet been discovered in any of the many hut circles systematically explored to date. From this somewhat surprising circumstance it has been deduced that the higher moorland population was a pastoral rather than a mining community, grazing flocks and herds in summer, peaceably disposed and needing no defences other than an impounding wall against marauding animals. Fragments of pottery, cooking-stones and charcoal of oak and peat are the most usual archæological finds in the huts, but the scarcity of these articles hardly suggests long or serious domestic occupation. Yet the adjacent memorials erected to their dead were elaborate. Cremation was practised, and the ashes placed in pottery urns which were enclosed in *kistvaens*—miniature dolmens or stone chests formed of rough granite blocks. The kistvaens were then usually covered with the circular earthen barrows or by loose stone cairns.

Menhirs are the single upright pillars, considered to be of a memorial nature, often called "longstones," an exact translation of the Celtic *maen*, a stone, and *hir*, long, as in the Longstone of the Chapman Barrows, and the same primitive conception embodied in the erection of these crude menhirs appears again centuries later in the inscribed Roman pillar, and still survives as the ugly gravestone of our modern cemetery.

Kistvaens, stone rows, barrows and menhirs are found in frequent association, the most comprehensive collection of this nature being the Drizzlecombe group in the Plym valley. One of the three menhirs here has the distinction of being the tallest upon Dartmoor, a height of over 17 feet, and the well-known Bear Down Man is an isolated menhir standing near Devil's Tor. In the Erme river valley, a short distance eastwards, upon Stalldon Moor the longest *parallellitha* or stone row of the fifty or so upon Dartmoor extends for over two miles. The Merivale antiquities are of great interest, and remains of five avenues may be traced upon Shovel Down, near Kestor.

Distinct from the small, compact hut circles and considered to be sepulchral in origin are the "Sacred Circles," composed of tall, upright stones spaced to form a large ring.

Of this type the two restored Grey Wether Circles, with remains of adjacent barrows, near Teignhead, form good examples, the largest being Scorhill Circle upon Gidleigh Common, just above the confluence of the Walla Brook with the Teign.

That such enduring monuments should have been so laboriously erected in the neighbourhood of dwellings assumed to have been only temporarily inhabited, mainly by tribal herdsmen, seems as strange as the building of the two great pounds by Paleolithic man, who also, presumably, had his habitations elsewhere. In each instance one would have expected something less permanent, yet the meagre results obtained after minute investigation hardly support the supposition of the huts having been anything in the nature of settled domestic establishments. There is, of course, the possibility that a succession of families, herdsmen, miners and others, using the same hut-sites with renewed thatchings of reed or ling, and making the most of the little at their disposal in an inhospitable region, would have sought and appropriated any articles that might have been dropped or discarded.

Recent investigations have established that practically every kistvaen and barrow had been rifled years ago, probably in medieval days, as in 1324 a certain Robert Baupel was granted permission by the Crown to seek treasure in such places. Whether this was a pioneer exploration or was undertaken with a knowledge of previous successful search is not related, but the fact may account in part for the scarcity of disinterred relics, while generations of acquisitive miners would certainly have swelled the ranks of Dartmoor's "treasure-seekers."

To summarise, it is remarkable that Dartmoor's ruins, when explored, have shed so little light upon their story, conclusions having been drawn from the absence rather than the presence of dated material. Certainly the occupation of all the hut settlements was not concurrent. The entire Cornish peninsula did not contain so many people. It was probably a roving population shifting its quarters periodically, after the manner of Red Indians or gypsies. If the inhabitants were pastoral, the moors must have been burned from time to time as now, or there would have been no grass, the natural vegetation being heather, and this might have necessitated the vacating of large areas over a term of years, for nothing can live upon burned lands in winter. The settlements, again, may have been summer camps occupied merely by herdsmen without their families, which fact would account for the failure to unearth more evidence of feminine presence in the way of adornments or cooking utensils. The amount of material expended upon the larger enclosures suggests community use, and the real matter for wonder lies in their final abandonment, the upland pastures offering as good a livelihood and probably carrying as numerous a head of stock today as they did three thousand years ago. Nor is there any truth in the convention that cattle cannot remain upon the Moor during the winter. The old rule to that effect is no longer enforced. A great number remain upon the Moor throughout the year; nor would it be reasonable to assume that the tough stock tended by tougher hillmen of old were incapable of similar endurance. Coarse hay as good as that which the American plainsman cuts from the virgin growth of the prairie could doubtless have been made on the Dartmoor marshes in precisely the same manner, and hardy people have existed under harsher conditions than the worst of Devonshire's upland winters can produce.

Man of the Bronze Age, like his Paleolithic and Neolithic predecessors, also wandered into Kent's Hole, leaving behind the pottery and implements which have recorded his presence. But the pictures impressed upon the cavern floor are becoming clearer, and the rapidly widening canvas is now spreading all over the county, the approximate date 500 B.C. linking the close of the prehistoric period with the opening of the early Iron Age.

Once more the Channel waters carried to these shores a fresh incursion from the Continent, this time a Celtic race following Brythons and Goidels, and more akin to the roving Northmen of a still later date. They must have presented a warlike appearance, equipped as they were with iron weapons and tools, which latter they wielded efficiently in the construction of the strong hilltop fortresses which are still familiar landscape features. Possibly the formidable aspect of

6

these new invaders intimidated the settled inhabitants, for
their establishment throughout the countryside would seem
to have been a matter of no great difficulty or bloodshed.
Seizing upon all strategic points commanding coast, river
valley, boundary or trackway, they dug their ramparts and
ditches, and there they settled, becoming the Dunmonii or
Damnonians, the hilltop dwellers, from the Celtic word *dun*,
a hill, afterwards Latinised by the Romans, who found them
thus established.

Thus that part of the ancient kingdom of Damnonia, formerly extending from Cornwall to Hampshire, began
gradually to develop into Dyfnaint, the land of deep, dark
coombes, the Devon of today. Boundaries roughly corre-
sponded, for across the Tamar on the west lay the country of
the Carnabii, while east of the Axe was the territory of the
Durotriges. The Damnonians, therefore, appropriated the
portion between the two rivers, planning their fortifications
to guard the most vulnerable approaches. Thus on the coast
we see their ancient defences on Berry Cliff, near Branscombe; Castle Hill, Dartmouth; the High Peak promontory
between Otterton and Sidmouth; and in the north, those of
Embury Beacon and Clovelly Dykes. The latter camp has
been attributed to the Romans, who certainly may, as in the
case of roads and other instances, have adapted to their own
advantage already existing facilities. Predominant upon their
territory's eastern boundary are Hawk Down, overlooking
Axmouth, and Musbury, now within Devon's boundaries,
but probably then forming one of a rival chain of fortresses
upon the Durotriges' side of the Axe. The great Hembury
Fort is described in the *Victoria History of Devon* as "the
grandest monument of military skill and strategy of the
Britons in the county." Also on this same boundary line are
Membury and Stockland Castles, and Dumpdon Camp
whose crowning clump of trees was for so many years a conspicuous East Devon landmark. Farther west was the Woodbury stronghold commanding the eastern bank of the
approach up the Exe estuary, a function performed by
Cadbury Castle on the western bank.

In the south remains of strong defences may be seen at
Ugbrooke Park, seat of the Cliffords of Chudleigh, while

Milber Down, Coffinswell, is larger in area than any other camp in the county. Many more of these ancient British strongholds command river valleys, such as the three well-known camps above the Teign near Fingle Bridge, Cranbrook, Wooston, and the great sugar-loaf hill of Prestonbury, empurpled in late summer from base to crest with bell heather. In Northcott Camp, six miles from Lifton station, we have an example of a western border camp guarding the Tamar.

For some reason the commanding heights of Dartmoor, with their wide uninterrupted views, did not attract the Damnonians, and the only two hill forts actually situated upon the Moor are Ashbury, on the western bank of the East Okement, and White Tor Camp, above the Tavy, both upon the outermost fringes, merging into the lowlands. No trace of any Iron Age occupation has been found upon Higher Dartmoor, and the few Celtic names that remain are, in most instances, like the camps, found only upon the borders. Considering these facts, in conjunction with the absence of any evidence of tin workings, it seems probable that Dartmoor proper, after the decline of the Bronze Age occupation, once more became depopulated. Some authorities suggest that the thirty-five Ancient Tenements in the Postbridge area, mentioned in a later chapter, had their beginnings during the prehistoric period, as numerous flints and other relics have been ploughed up within their enclosures. Certainly they are of such antiquity that no records or even traditions exist as to their origin. All mention of Dartmoor is, however, entirely omitted from the Doomsday survey of *Deveniscira* (Devonshire), comprising so careful a tabulation of all lands and livestock, and it seems unlikely that such a group of holdings, however primitive, would have been completely overlooked, together with such an important industry as tin-streaming. It may, therefore, reasonably be supposed that the Ancient Tenements were at least post-Norman, and that the high moorlands for a considerable period during the last two or three centuries B.C., until the Saxon invasion, reverted into an uninhabited region encircled by busy British fortresses.

Taking into consideration the fact that 200 of these earthworks are extant in Devon, actual relics of this period again are few. It must be borne in mind, however, that discarded iron soon becomes oxidised and rusts away, and by way of illustration one may cite the remarkable discovery in 1864 of an Iron Age cemetery on Stamford Hill, near Plymouth. Here, in the course of excavations for new gun sites, numbers of graves lined with stone and containing human bones were exposed. Interesting objects of bronze, pottery, glass and iron were also unearthed, the first three substances in such excellent preservation that no difficulty was experienced in assigning them to this late Celtic period. Upon the other hand, the indisputable iron remnants of the same date were so disintegrated that it proved impossible to do more than hazard a guess as to their original shape and purpose. In 1870 a man digging for a rabbit near Holne Chase Camp dislodged instead a pile of iron currency bars and spear-heads; and characteristic Iron Age pottery was found in an exploration of Cranbrook Castle in 1900. It is probable that the ancient iron pits on the Blackdown Hills contributed their earliest yield to this period.

Many of these old hill forts were the original sponsors of the settlements which developed at their feet in more peaceful eras, as, for instance, the villages of Woodbury, Boadhembury and Membury. The Celtic word *dun*, hill, by the way, was later supplanted by the Saxon *bury*, and in the post-Norman period *castle* came to be applied to any stoutly fortified position. Thus, the three different designations are used today to describe the same type of stronghold.

So ends the patchwork piecing of Devon's prehistoric story, and the nebulous curtain through which, so far, we have only been able to peer uncertainly rises at last upon the historical stage, confused and disconnected as many of the scenes will still remain, with the strongly entrenched Britons uneasily watching the passage of the efficient Roman legions along the well-trodden trackways leading into their country from the east. Little resistance seems to have been offered to the newcomers, whose occupation of Damnonia was far less thorough than that of adjacent Dorset, penetration to any extent virtually ceasing with the establishment of the important station Isca Damnoniorum upon the old earthen ramparts of Caerwisc or British Exeter. The Romans were responsible for the first real development of Exeter—their farthest western outpost. The precise date of their entry into the county is uncertain, but is usually assigned to the middle of the first century A.D., and for the next 300 years, until their final withdrawal from Britain in 411, Damnonia became *Britannia Prima*, a province of the great Roman Empire. In spite of such continuous occupation, however, native habits and manner of life were never assimilated with those of the conquerors, as in the subsequent Saxon invasions, but the ancient Devonian remained as British upon the departure of the Roman legions as upon their arrival. In fact, the three centuries of Roman occupation might be considered as purely incidental to the life of the community, which, however, derived considerable benefit from the more efficient methods of its temporary overlords. This influence was not extended to the county west of Exeter, though a limited penetration was made to the north coast in the neighbourhood of Ilfracombe and Clovelly, and larger settlements were formed on the south coast at least as far west as the Teign. In spite of fragmentary evidence, such as road construction and the discovery of pavements and coins, which suggest a more extensive occupation of the county on the eastern side, in general the Roman episode played the least conspicuous part in building up Devon's long history. Britain proved to be a rock upon which the tentacle thrown out by the empire of the Cæsars took little root, and its hold was lightest upon Devonshire—the utmost limit of its reach. In any case, the Roman way was so far from being Devon's way that geography played only a minor part in the preservation of the county's individuality. The Vicar of Bray could not cling to his living with greater tenacity than Devonians to their natural characteristics.

BIBLIOGRAPHY

Devon Association Transactions, xvi, p. 480, W. Pengelly; xxviii, p. 533, Alexander Somervail; xxviii, p. 25, S. Baring Gould; xxvi, p. 101, Report of Dartmoor Exploration Committee; xxvi, p. 185, Robert Burnard; xxxvii, p. 375, J. F. Chanter and R. Hansford Worth; xxiii, p. 25, R. N. Worth.
Victoria History of Devon.
Place Names of Devon, Gover, Mawer and Stenton.

CHAPTER II

DEVON OF THE PAST

IT IS always difficult to specify the period at which the history of a county really begins as distinct from that of the country as a whole. In the earliest records the existence of counties seems to have been established, like that which is "given" in a Euclid problem, and probably represented the area over which a certain tribe had obtained sway or monopoly. It seems, however, that Devon was among the first of the seven shires recognised in the *Anglo-Saxon Chronicle*, where in 851 it is referred to as *Defenascir*; but there exists no record of the date when the county boundaries as such were first determined. The Romans knew the region as *Britannia Prima*, but the mists of antiquity are even denser than those which still frequently envelop the western uplands, and through these the historian has wandered almost as uncertainly as the "pixy-led" shepherd on Dartmoor's wastes. When included in the Saxon kingdom of Wessex, the area annexed terminated with the Tamar, even as it still constitutes a barrier between the Devonshire and Cornwall of today.

It is curious that Devon's eminently historical past is not generally recognised or remembered. The conventional picture that the name presents is peaceful rather than otherwise, a region apart from the turmoils of civil or national strife. Her history is not that which one learns at school. One is taught that William the Conqueror waged a long campaign against Hereward, that he traversed the North with fire and sword; and only from local records is the story of his western expedition in 1068 related. In the old school manual from which my own rudiments of history were unwillingly gathered, Devonshire's part in the Civil War from 1642 to 1649 was dismissed in one curt sentence: "The fall of Exeter reduced the West to peace"; and this summarises upon the whole the inevitable outlook of history books which must necessarily be more general than local. Monmouth's rebellion, although the first action was fought on Devonshire soil, is always regarded as a purely Sedgemoor affair with Taunton Assizes as its grim culmination.

The historian's comparative neglect of Devonshire is not altogether unaccountable, however, since the first and principal scenes in her long drama were of too early a date to be more than touched by the limelight which flooded later events. All the big issues in which the far West figured were decided prior to 1066, beginning when the curtain more or less officially rose upon "England" as such. Before that date the average man has acquired at best a vague idea of the "back-stage" activities which rendered the full drama possible. "Few questions in early English history are more obscure than the chronology of the English occupation of what is now the county of Devon," state the authors of the *Place Names of Devon* in their Introduction, and for the moment this summary must be sufficient. Throughout the Civil Wars the geographical position of the county placed her outside the main sphere of activities. True, no war left Devonshire unaffected, Exeter alone sustaining ten sieges; but these, judged from the standard of main events, were side-shows. No epoch-making battle was fought in the shire, and although William of Orange landed in Torbay, he proceeded eastwards without the occurrence of any important incident to commemorate the county that received him. In like manner, while Devon's most celebrated men—Marlborough, Raleigh, Hawkins, Frobisher and Gilbert—won distinction overseas, connection with their native shire is scarcely remembered. Marlborough is usually associated with his later home at "Blenheim" rather than with his birthplace at Ash House, near Axminster. Raleigh is famous for his colonising efforts and imprisonment in the Tower; above all, perhaps, for the cloak episode, not forgetting the part he played in popularising tobacco. Nor does his name necessarily suggest the old-world village of East Budleigh, where he was born. There was no West-country Montrose to shed his lustre locally, and even Alfred is more renowned for burning cakes on Sedgemoor than for his decisive victory over the Danes at Northam.

Generally speaking, the history of Exeter may be regarded as that of Devonshire as a whole. The city is the Moscow of the West, to which all roads lead even today, and its psychological as well as material importance rendered it one of the main objectives in every war from the first that history records to the struggle between Royalist and Roundhead, the last within our shores which affected the county.

> Many a vanish'd year and age
> And tempest's breath and battle's rage

have swept over Exeter, even as over ancient Corinth, but until the bombs of the Luftwaffe again scarred her beauty with war's rough hand, there was little in her atmosphere to suggest a warlike past. Upon the contrary, when standing today upon the Castle's ramparts, now laid out as the Rougemont Pleasure Ground, it is difficult to imagine the green-encircled city in any other character than as the maternal centre of the varied landscape spread wide around, picturing a peaceful country life the tenor of which might have remained undisturbed not only for centuries but throughout all time.

Yet the story of Exeter, if told from the beginning, is anything save peaceful, and to follow it one must turn back to the first pages of history. The earliest assumption is of a British earthwork erected where the remains of the Castle now stand, and then known as *Caerwisc*, denoting the camp above or beside the water. This was captured by the Romans, probably under Vespasian, who named the fort *Isca Damnoniorum*, to distinguish it from the Welsh settlement of the same name, *Isca* being the Latinised form of the Celtic *wisc*, a derivation which we find again in river names, such as Esk, Exe, Ock (Okement) and other variations, all denoting "water" or, more frequently, the river itself. The same derivation is even found in whisky, or "water of life," sometimes interpreted "yellow water," a most descriptive if less etymologically correct analysis of the modern product.

As we have seen, the Romans were responsible for the first real development of Exeter, where various traces of their occupancy have been discovered. Excavations recently conducted upon bombed premises have yielded additional

13

interesting discoveries of this description. The main west road of their day, possibly part of the Icknield Way, was the thoroughfare upon which the Exeter High Street, or "High Way," now stands. This road traversed the south country from Norwich via Dorchester and Exeter to the Tamar, and entered Devon a few miles east of Axminster, where stretches of its course are traceable, here and there forming part of the route still in use and described in fuller detail later.

With the departure of the last Roman galleys a dark curtain falls again upon western history for a considerable time. There is no record of any serious attempt on the part of the Britons to resist the Saxon infiltration, which, beginning in the sixth century, seems to have been a matter of colonisation rather than conquest during the next two hundred years. Although small sea-borne parties of raiders landed from time to time upon the southern coasts it was along the well-worn eastern land route that the tentacles of serious invasion gradually crept, rolling the limits of the powerful kingdom of Wessex ever farther westwards. They first reached over the Devon border in 568, and finally, under Egbert, stretched across the Tamar to include the suzerainty of Cornwall. Exeter and the eastern parts of the county became anglicised during the latter half of the seventh century. Another twenty years witnessed the subjugation of the northern districts, and that of the whole county was completed by the time Egbert succeeded to his throne in 802.

The history of the old Kingdom of Wessex is of general South-country rather than of Devonian interest, since the attention of its successive rulers, the enterprising Egbert, the persevering Alfred and his scarcely less famous grandson Athelstan, was mainly directed northwards, the more newly acquired western territory being necessarily left in large measure to take care of itself. It must not be forgotten, however, that during the critical period of Egbert's reign Wessex, including Devonshire, was the only kingdom that effectually resisted the Danes, so constituting itself the champion of the nation, the remainder of which had submitted to the invaders.

When the Raven Flag again appeared off the Devon coast

and Exeter fell to the Danes in 876, Alfred, like his predecessor Egbert, rose to the occasion, recaptured the city, and in 878 eventually threw back the invaders, his own kingdom of Wessex remaining once more the only surviving stronghold of the Saxon regime. He paid considerable attention to Exeter's defences, which fifty years later were even more adequately strengthened by his grandson Athelstan, under whom a great deal was effected. This resolute ruler then proceeded to "liquidate" any remnants of the British population by expelling them to the farther side of the Tamar, and thenceforth kept a firmer hold upon Devon generally, which from this time onwards may be considered English in character. This is manifested in various ways, including the preponderance of English over Celtic place-names. So effectual were Athelstan's measures, that when again Danish war-boats penetrated the Exe estuary and attacked the city the siege was unsuccessful, the Northmen being finally defeated in an action fought at Pinhoe, well outside the walls. It is difficult to trace in detail the story of the troubled times that followed, with war in some shape or form the rule rather than the exception. It seems clear, however, that the city was again besieged in 1003 by a more formidable force under the Danish King Sweyn, whom it withstood for two months before its capture and complete destruction. After the withdrawal of the Danes, the indefatigable Devonians again rebuilt their capital and its walls, but not sufficiently well to resist the next assault, made in 1068 by William the Conqueror, to whom the fortress surrendered after a siege of eighteen days. Upon this occasion there was little destruction, the surrender having been negotiated upon good terms, and William restored the city and fortress, employing his own improved methods in rebuilding the Castle, which remained a "strong point" until dismantled after the Parliamentary War.

Nearly seventy years later these defences elaborated by William proved serviceable, when Devonshire, neither for the first nor last time in her history championing a desperate cause, opened her arms to Princess Maude as the rightful claimant to the throne. She took refuge in Exeter, which for three months defied Stephen, and only capitulated upon the failure of the water supply. Upon this occasion again the city suffered little from the reverse, being treated with clemency by Stephen even as by William, and for the three ensuing centuries remained more or less undisturbed by civil or national strife.

When the Wars of the Roses broke out, the county mainly favoured the Lancastrian cause, but Devon lay far apart from the principal areas of conflict and therefore played only a minor part. Exeter was indeed besieged for a short time by Sir Hugh Courtenay, with whose family the city was frequently at loggerheads as a legacy of the old Countess Weir affair, and this adherence to the Yorkist side now provided him with an excuse for more active animosity, several prominent Lancastrians having taken refuge within the walls. The matter was settled by negotiation, however, and when, shortly afterwards, Edward IV approached the city with 40,000 men, in pursuit of Clarence and Gloucester, who like so many others had fled to the West, his entry was unopposed. Throughout this period, as through most of her history, Devon's rôle was that of rigid adherence to the *status quo*, according to her lights or in support of any traditional cause or right, and when Queen Margaret of Anjou landed at Weymouth in 1472, her standard was raised at Exeter, and it was largely Devon men who marched to fatal Tewkesbury, which cost 3,000 West-country lives, including that of the Earl of Devon, the fourth of the line to perish in the Wars of the Roses. With characteristic tenacity, however, the county remained Lancastrian at heart, and it was at Exeter once again that Henry VII was first proclaimed king, nearly a year before Bosworth Field and his actual accession to the throne. This movement was not supported by the city authorities—possibly because the Courtenays had sponsored the proceedings—and when active steps taken by Richard III to deal with the situation brought him to Exeter, his reception was all that even he could have desired. This did not affect Devon's loyalty to the Red Rose, however, after Henry's accession, and Perkin Warbeck found no support when he unsuccessfully invested the city in 1497. It has always been the *people* of the county rather than its administrators who resisted any form of

16

innovation, and this was again demonstrated when the change in the State religion and Prayer-book took place in 1549. This rebellion, if so it can be styled, started in the remote village of Sampford Courtenay, one of the last places where civil disturbance might have been expected, and although it led to yet another siege of Exeter, never assumed any real national importance.

Since the days when Alfred held Wessex and so averted the complete subjugation of the country to Danish sovereignty, the wars of the West, as already remarked, were incidental rather than conclusive, and it was not until the Elizabethan period that Devon again became the storm-centre and at the same time the pillar of the nation. This period, however, is essentially a story of the sea, to be dealt with in the next chapter. The landsmen of the West who "poured to war" upon the memorable night when the beacons announcing the Armada's approach leaped from Dartmoor's heights to "bleak Hampstead's swarthy moor" actually played no part in determining the country's fate. Fortunately they were never required to meet the infantry of Parma, even as those who at a later date rallied on Woodbury Common when Napoleon's shadow stretched across the Channel never encountered the army which triumphed at Austerlitz. Apart from Monmouth's brief march across the south-eastern corner of the county and the skirmish at Axminster, Devon's share of military adventures within our shores closed with the surrender of Barnstaple in 1643, shortly after that of Exeter. This was the longest and last of the ten more or less authenticated occasions upon which War's stern arms embraced the "Queen of the West." When the city was finally taken, the Parliamentary authorities, regarding the shelterer of Queen Henrietta Maria as a Royalist hotbed and potential source of future trouble, dismantled her defences, although the precaution, as it happened, proved superfluous, the tide of war never again setting westwards of the Axe. Often the first to take up arms and quite as frequently the last to lay them down, Devonians none the less cannot justly be regarded as an inflammatory people, easily stirred to revolt. Rather have they always shown themselves tenacious, staunch in support of tradition

2*   17

or ideal, and dour as their own wild hills in resisting encroachment, real or imaginary. *Semper fidelis* was the motto authorised by Elizabeth to be borne upon the City Arms of Exeter, and whether upon points of loyalty, principle or prejudice, the Devon man, once convinced, adheres to his convictions—resolutely or perversely, according to point of view.

One would like to follow the Devon Regiment throughout its long record of service, but the history of a corps is scarcely that of the county from which it derives its name, although one likes to remember that the regiment has borne its part in the two great world wars, having gained battle honours at Bois des Buttes in 1918 and played its part with distinction through the difficult days of Dunkirk, Malta and the Burma campaign during the recent war. The band of the Devon Regiment also had the distinction of accompanying the entry of British troops into Berlin in July 1945. Devonshire, too, took her share in the Napoleonic wars and the Crimea, as well as more recent conflicts. With regard to the Boer War, one must not overlook Sir Redvers Buller, Devon's most famous modern general, whose great effort is seldom sufficiently appreciated, not having been crowned with the success of those who followed him. With far greater forces at their command, the latter undoubtedly profited from General Buller's experience. The first blows of the axe may not fell the tree, but they open a way for subsequent strokes and at least expose the knots to be avoided.

A form of more or less compulsory military service seems to have existed in the county since Norman times, each city, hundred, guild and stannery, as well as ecclesiastical bodies, being required to provide a *muster* of men, according to its special capacity. The officer deputed to equip and organise the training of these little companies was styled a *mustermaster*, and for his services he received in the time of Elizabeth and the early Stuarts an annual "pension" or "stipend" of £6. They must have worked upon the lines of the volunteer or yeomanry forces of a later date, holding a yearly field rally which was also designated a muster, and lasted from one to three days. The men, when on service, were paid 8*d.* a day, which rate seems to have persisted from the fourteenth century until the Napoleonic wars, and considering the standard of the times, compares very favourably with the 1*s.* received by a private soldier in 1914. This money was found not by the National Exchequer but by the town or body which provided the muster, ten days' provisions in advance being also supplied to men called up and awaiting dispatch overseas or to other parts of the country, as when in 1580 "eleven horsemen, well arrayed with their whole Furniture," were sent to join Elizabeth's first Irish expedition "at the sole charges" of the Exeter bishop, dean and chapter. At times of great national emergency the county bore the expense, as when, sixteen years later, Devonshire was required to provide 282 men (94 from each of the county's three divisions) for service in Ireland, a special tax was levied to raise the £1,200 required.

In the case of guilds, which had their little standing armies, an inventory was kept of available man-power, equipment and resources, each member entering the contribution that he was prepared to make. If personally of military age, he enrolled himself under "service." If unable to carry arms, he made a return of any weapons or armour that he could lend, or perhaps an employee who could deputise. Thus in old minutes of the Exeter Weavers and Fullers Incorporation, one entry reads: "A man performed," in other words, a fully equipped soldier. Another registers "a corslet and a gonne," while others merely guaranteed money, one providing 6*s.* 8*d.*, another, "a man performed and 8*d.*," while subscriptions of 4*d.*, representing half a day's pay for a man, were numerous. The character of the equipment, of course, varied with the period, ranging from pikes and such crude armament to "gonnes" and, finally, muskets. The classification of a man was synecdochical, according to the weapon that he carried, a pikeman being a "pike," a musketeer a "shot," in the same manner as a member of a modern shooting party is a "gun."

Apart from privately owned weapons which could be produced in an emergency, parishes and guilds had communal arms, which were stored in some public building, as in a guildhall or village church, these being reserved, presumably, for local defence only. Over the church porch at

Sidbury, South Devon, for example, there is a little room still known as the Powder-room, which once served as the village arsenal, and in old "orders of the day" all men bearing arms were directed to assemble and await instructions in their parish church, such buildings being then used for much the same purposes as the village halls of today.

One of the first levies upon Devonshire for troops to serve outside the county seems to have been made by Edward II in 1318, presumably to help in the quelling of his rebellious barons. Exeter's muster was then 30 men, this being also the number conscribed by Henry VIII in 1512 for his intended invasion of France, although during the Wars of the Roses the assessment for the city seems to have dropped to 20. While Devon generally has provided troops for most military expeditions throughout history, however, it was not until the Elizabethan period that heavy claims were made upon the county. During the Armada crisis Devonshire maintained from 4,000 to 6,000 men under arms, each of the Stanneries then contributing 100, and all the big towns, guilds and hundreds raised as many men as could be equipped. After Elizabeth's day, however, the "muster" system was allowed to lapse until revived by Pitt, when the title of Militia was adopted, and during the Napoleonic wars Devonshire's defence force amounted to about 16,000 men. The county's preparations for observation and defence at that time must in many respects have resembled those hastily improvised in 1940. About 1,780 signalling huts, much after the style of those erected for the use of the modern Home Guard and Observer Corps, were set up on hills conveniently near the coast, and there were organised services to operate in emergency, curiously resembling the arrangements made during the modern crisis. The only essential difference lay in the method of communication to be employed, and whereas the Home Guard huts were sited with a view to telephone facilities, the earlier defenders depended upon the primitive beacons to spread the alarm if necessary. Even in Elizabeth's day there was a special service for this upon the lines of the present Fire Guard, but with rôle reversed, each beacon pile being attended by its own wardens, whose duty it was to keep inflammable material handy and ignite it if required. The old methods were nothing if not thorough, and to ensure that everything should work according to plan, additional guards were posted to watch the beacon-keepers, but whether this should be regarded as advanced organisation or a suggestion of inefficiency is open to doubt.

The curtain has fallen upon many great events and the great figures who immortalised them. During the recent years of trial intrepid men have watched the coast with eyes as keenly discriminating as those which marked the course of "Castile's Black Fleet" or Napoleon's cruising frigates, and many stirring tales remain to be told. Without sentimentalising or any disregard of realities, mention should be made of that masterpiece of effrontery, the L.D.V., or Local Defence Volunteers, nucleus of the later Home Guard, and perhaps the nearest approach to the men who rallied when the beacons flamed that modern Devon has yet known.

By taking the Home Guard to its fickle heart, the Press rendered an unintentional disservice to the Force. Its potentialities exaggerated to the point of absurdity, it became an inevitable target for the subtle humorist, and few people realised that in the comic picture, scarcely overdrawn, lay the real greatness of the men caricatured. When our "Swordfish" planes flew to certain destruction against the German warships passing up the Channel, they made no greater sacrifice than these untrained and practically unarmed countrymen were prepared to face during the first anxious months of the 1940 invasion menace, after the capitulation of France. Far from being the "trained and disciplined soldiers" depicted by the propagandist, there were men and boys in the section of which I had charge who had never fired even a shotgun. Yet they went out by night and day in hourly expectation of encountering enemy parachute troops or landing parties, against whom they stood as much chance as would an elementary village team if required to meet a representative Australian eleven. When at one of our musters I asked an old N.C.O. how, in his opinion, they would fare if suddenly confronted by Panzer troops, he merely ejaculated "My dear sir!" as though that point at any rate had never been in doubt. Indeed, when Conan

Doyle's Sir Nigel faced the bear with a pocket handkerchief, he was as well equipped for an encounter as many a Devonshire farm labourer or carpenter who manned defences, in themselves veritable death-traps, against the expected invader. At one observation post in this district the only weapon available was an old-fashioned bed-post crowned with a serviceable knob, and I frequently lent the iron end of an obsolete walking-stick gun to defenders of the nation going out upon patrol.

Yet neither the humour of its history nor its limitations as a potential fighting force in any way detracted from the merits of the L.D.V., that dauntless assortment of "young lads and drooping elders who might not bear the mail," old soldiers and civilians whose hearts at any rate were in the right place.

As the war proceeded, Devon's ports once again became the centre of great events. Over the wide waste of Dartmoor rolled the thunder of incessant artillery practice and sometimes the distant rumble of more sinister gunfire away upon the Channel. Warplanes droned overhead. Upon the once quiet commons troops manœuvred; military transport roared along the roadways between the red fields and through the white-washed villages. Very different was this display from the preparations to meet Parma or Napoleon and from the early mustering of western men to fight the Danes. What comparisons will be drawn by historians of the future is still to be shown.

BIBLIOGRAPHY

Devon Association Transactions, VII, p. 43, R. J. King; LXIV, p. 75, J. J. Alexander; XXXII, p. 25, Lord Clifford; XL, p. 222, Colonel J. W. Lee; XI, p. 348, A. H. A. Hamilton.

Memorials of the City of Exeter. Izacke.

A short History of the Worshipful Company of Weavers, Fullers and Shearers of the City of Exeter. Beatrix Cresswell.

CHAPTER III

THE SEA SAGA

DEVONSHIRE is in many respects an England in miniature, and like the country as a whole, while producing her soldiers and pioneers of Empire, it is in maritime associations that her greatness has always lain. Even as Nottingham had "archers good," so references to Devonshire in old prose or poetry suggest pictures of bronzed mariners or coastguards with eyes turned ever seawards, watching throughout the ages for the distant sail with its omen of good or ill, the return of the adventurer with his prizes, or the approach of Irish, Danish, Dutch, French, Turkish or Breton raider, as each phase of the sea story brought its potential enemies. There are few people who are not familiar with the fact that "men of Bideford in Devon" manned the *Revenge*, or who are unaware through at least such publicity channels as the B.B.C. or the Aldershot Tattoo that upon a memorable day in 1588 Drake was playing bowls on Plymouth Hoe. Through Drake, the defeat of the Armada has been regarded very largely as Devon's achievement, and from the earliest times to the present day Plymouth has been the western centre and indeed the very hub of Britain's maritime power.

Embarkation point for some of the earliest expeditions to the French wars under the first and second Edward, and notably that of the Black Prince in 1355 which culminated in the successful Poitiers campaign, Plymouth rose from being "the mene inhabitation of fischars" described by Leland to its proud position in Elizabethan days. In 1497, thirty years before what has been termed the "golden age" of the great port's history, a Plymouth seaman had accompanied Sebastian Cabot on one of the first voyages of discovery to the New World.

"For nearly a century . . . the work of western and southern discovery and settlement was carried on almost

23

wholly by Devonshire men sailing from Devonshire ports; while from the waters of Plymouth Sound more expeditions set forth than from all other harbours in the kingdom put together,"

wrote R. N. Worth. Indeed, from 1528, when William, first adventurer of the renowned Hawkins family, set sail for Brazil, to the departure of the *Mayflower* bearing the Pilgrim Fathers to New England in 1620, Plymouth was the starting-point of more than forty voyages, all of historical import. These included those of Sir Richard Grenville and Raleigh to Virginia, Frobisher and Davis in search of the North-West Passage, and Drake's notable expedition to South America, the West Indies, round the world, and his rescue of Raleigh's unfortunate Virginian colonists in 1586. From this port, too, scene of so many triumphant returns, Drake, with Hawkins, embarked for the West Indies on what was to prove the last voyage for them both in 1595. Though Dartmouth had the honour of dispatching the first colonising expedition to the New World, that of Sir Humphrey Gilbert to Newfoundland in 1579, it was from Plymouth that he also set forth on his fatal voyage four years later. The extent of England's debt to these valiant-hearted gentlemen of Devon has been well summarised by the Rev J. Erskine Risk when he states:

"To Plymouth, therefore, and to Plymouth heroes, we owe the origin of our colonial empire under Elizabeth, and we cannot err in coming to the conclusion that the rise of Plymouth as a naval port laid the foundation of Britain's empire of the seas."

It was, indeed, an era of memorable achievement, when the nation's history was emerging from the waters of the Sound in craft which seem to us incredibly fragile and inadequate. The largest trading ship on Devon's coasts in 1572 was the *Christopher*, of 100 tons, and the ocean-going vessels of the intrepid merchant adventurers were little larger, the biggest of Sir Richard Grenville's on his 1585 Virginian expedition being 140 tons. The 190 ships forming England's Grand Fleet, which lay awaiting the Armada in

Plymouth Sound, averaged 160 tons, and each carried a crew of 75 men, yet this assembly of Davids proved its superiority over the Goliaths by whom it was challenged.

Two centuries later the little *Golden Hind* had been replaced by the "line" ships of Nelson, from one of which, the *Bellerophon*, the captive Emperor Napoleon looked across the waters of the Sound on his final journey to St Helena. Today, great ironclads of the Home Fleet, weighing anything up to 35,000 tons, lie at anchorage beside Drake's Island, and as terrible testimony to her undiminished importance it has fallen to Plymouth's share to suffer the heaviest bombardment of any English seaport during the second world war. It would have been consistent with tradition had Plymouth served as the main base for the great Anglo-American operations across the Channel. Geographical considerations deprived her of this privilege, except in the case of the Islands, for which the choice of her port was obvious. The tide of events rendered such an expedition unnecessary, but the little force of 22 men which ultimately landed on Guernsey to receive the formal surrender of the German garrison, 10,000 strong, sailed from Plymouth, while the first U-boat that lowered its flag after the surrender was escorted into Weymouth by two Plymouth vessels.

Plymouth lies at the extreme south-western corner of the county, the eastern side of the Sound being Devon while the western side is Cornwall. Devon has always prided herself upon being the home county of the Navy. For many years Dartmouth has been the cradle of the Naval Executive officers and the R.N. College, Keyham, that of our Naval Engineer officers, while there are large training ships in the harbour at Devonport for young seamen and young engineer mechanics.

Plymouth actually consists of three towns, Plymouth proper, Devonport and Stonehouse, which quarters the Royal Marines, whose barracks have been occupied without interruption since 1783. Devonport, the dockyard member of the trio, lies on the Hamoaze, the estuary of the rivers Tamar, Lynher and Tavy, with an anchorage large enough to accommodate the entire British fleet. Practically the whole of its eastern shore is occupied by naval establishments, beginning with the Royal Victualling Yard at its southern end and extending almost without break for about three miles to the Ammunition Depôt at Ball Point, close to Brunel's masterpiece, the great Saltash railway bridge. Devonport dockyard contains large building slips and dry docks, but by far the largest part is Keyham Dockyard, connected with that of Devonport by a tunnel carrying a railway. During the closing years of the last century Keyham was increased threefold, and contains docks and basins capable of accommodating our largest battleships.

The completion of Plymouth's mile-long breakwater, begun in 1812, transformed the Sound into an immense refuge harbour, but warships only lie in it for a short time before proceeding up to the Royal Naval quarter or going out to sea. Passenger liners calling at Plymouth anchor in the Sound, transferring goods and passengers by tender, as there are no piers or deep-water wharves available for large merchant ships. Standing on historic Plymouth Hoe, the view seaward is magnificent, although any naval man will affirm that the view of Plymouth in the reverse direction on his return from abroad is even finer! On the Hoe appropriately stand several monuments that may be considered national. There we have the beautiful Armada Statue; the Naval Obelisk to the men of the port who fell in the first world war; and Smeaton's original Eddystone Lighthouse, removed from the reef on which it stood for 120 years. There, too, stands the statue of Drake, who, although inevitably associated with Plymouth, was actually born at Crowndale Farm, near Tavistock.

Thus Devon's tradition remains naval rather than military, and this is only as it should be in a county across which the sea winds sweep from shore to shore. The allure of the ocean has always been deeply ingrained in the native temperament, even to be found among men who have never set eyes upon either Channel or Atlantic. The call was always there, fostered in early days by followers of adventurers such as Oxenham, who, returning to their inland homes, brought tales of southern wonders, glory and enterprise, retold over cottage peat fires until the fascination of the sea captured the heart of every imaginative boy. Although Devon has always had her musters, militia, yeomanry and Regiment, it is towards the navy rather than the army that her lads still incline when disposed to enter one of the services. During times of war when general service is required, the position is, of course, somewhat different, the demands of the army upon man-power being greater. Under normal conditions, however, it is the home-going sailor rather than the soldier who boards the west-bound train, and blue is more frequently seen than khaki in the village street when service men are on leave. Before the upheaval of 1914 I was living in a remote village which is as nearly the centre of the county as map and compass can make any point. Its scattered population of about 300 had provided several men for the Home Fleet, but at the outbreak of war the village had not a single representative in the regular army. And this example upon the whole is typical. It applies to all classes, and so strong is the partiality that the boy who is declared unfit for naval service seldom tries the army, even should the choice be open to him.

Devonians, indeed, are seafaring people almost as much as would have been the case had the county been an island, and much of its prosperity is due to its maritime connection. In this the steady development of Plymouth from the *Sutone* of Doomsday Book to the great thriving port of the Elizabethan period was largely instrumental. Plymouth, with its world connection, not only provided an invaluable avenue of commerce but also brought a perpetual flow of new blood as well as money into the county. Commerce brings population and population in general creates trade. It is true that now and again Plymouth and its surroundings suffered from an influx of penniless service men, returned from unsuccessful expeditions and thrown upon the countryside for support. This, however, was more than offset by the landing of crews laden with prize-money and other spoils collected during the French and Spanish wars. At all times money more or less consistently follows the Forces, as the tradespeople of Malta discovered some years ago when, in reply to a "Malta for the Maltese" campaign more or less aggressively adopted, the personnel of all British ships lying off the island withheld their custom for a while—a boycott which quickly restored a realistic view of the position.

As Plymouth's importance increased, that of other ports diminished, particularly as ships grew in size and the construction of the great breakwater facilitated the accommodation of craft too large to enter a shallow harbour. It was this which mainly established Plymouth's ascendancy over the equally fine natural harbour at Falmouth. Along Devon's northern coast commerce was never so extensive, its more rugged and dangerous character discouraging development. The inability of Barnstaple, the main northern port, in former years to admit big shipping further diminished its utility as tonnage increased, although formerly Barnstaple carried on a considerable export trade, mainly of wool, to Ireland and America. While Plymouth furnished seven ships —equalling London's contribution—to fight the Armada, Barnstaple supplied only three, the relative status of the two ports, even in Elizabethan days, being thus demonstrated. Similar drawbacks handicapped the growth of Ilfracombe and Bideford; and although the country of the Grenvilles, North Devon's part in the wars of the early and middle ages was mainly concerned with comparatively minor raids or with the piratical forces which periodically obtained possession of Lundy and plundered the coast or harried shipping on the Bristol Channel trade routes, and more particularly Barnstaple Bay.

Piratical activities were not by any means confined to the northern coast, however, nor to any particular period. They persisted upon the southern and western seas in some shape or form since early history, and a considerable proportion of Devon's manhood was employed either in defending our own shipping or in carrying out illicit expeditions against the property or shores of other countries, for much of the "naval warfare" throughout the middle ages consisted of private or state-subsidised enterprise amounting to little better than piracy. Overrun from time to time by seafaring peoples, it was inevitable that England in her turn should become a maritime race, and with the sea forming her northern and southern boundaries, Devonshire naturally developed this tendency to a greater extent than other counties.

Referring to the Damnonians of the first century B.C., Elton writes:

"It appears from a passage in Cæsar's *Commentaries* that their young men were accustomed to serve in foreign fleets and to take part in the Continental wars. . . . A squadron of British ships took part in the great sea fight which was the immediate cause of Cæsar's invasion of the island, and his description of the allied fleet shows the great advance in civilisation which the southern Britons had attained."

Thus, officially or otherwise, "southern Britons," which in maritime affairs meant largely Damnonians, were constantly at war, and as in the days of "chivalry" when one knight met another they usually fought—or are supposed to have done so—regardless of nationality or party, any ship worth taking was attacked by those of other nations without the necessary pretext of war; and British shipping, always considerable, inevitably suffered to a proportionate extent, even as our long coastline rendered the island particularly vulnerable to attack from the sea.

None the less, it seems curious that a nation whose navy has won so formidable a reputation should have been unable more effectually to guard our commerce, shores and territorial waters. In 1579 the Governor of Guernsey lodged a formal complaint to the effect that "the sea was never so full of pirates," against whom protection was sought. So many ships were lost and their crews either massacred or captured that difficulty was experienced in recruiting men for merchant vessels, while even fishermen hesitated to venture far from shore. The nuisance, or rather terror, appears to have been continuous during the Stuart period, when thousands of pounds were raised in Devon for coastal and trade route defence, and to pay the ransoms demanded for captive seamen upon whose behalf the petition in the Litany for "all prisoners and captives" is supposed to have been inserted. Collections to aid these men were held in churches, and in 1619 a State Fund was inaugurated to equip an expedition designed to suppress Algerian and Tunisian rovers, who were, apparently, the most troublesome freebooters of the period. This fund was a national affair to which the principal ports of the country were required to contribute, each according to its maritime importance and consequent interest in sea-borne trade. Exeter and Barnstaple were each assessed at £500, while Plymouth was required to find £1,000, and protested against the amount since the city had already incurred heavy charges for the defence of the port and the ransoming of many of her inhabitants. The expedition was financed, however, and eventually sailed, but appears to have achieved little, since the trouble continued until more or less effective measures were taken during the strong Commonwealth regime.

Upon the northern coast the difficulties were even greater, since there the authorities had to contend not only with corsairs and their like, but with British robber lords established upon Lundy, which island provided a convenient base for freebooters of every description. This appears to have been the case since an early date, when the place was probably occupied by Danish marauders. There is no direct evidence of such occupation, but it is significant that of all Devon place-names *Lundy* alone is of indisputable Norse origin, and since Norse settlements were established for long periods upon the opposite mainland, it seems only reasonable to assume that the strategic advantages of the island would not have been overlooked. Lundy finds no place in history, however, until the reign of Henry II, when the lordship of the island was held by the Montmorency, or De Marisco, family, the erstwhile representative of which, Sir Jordan De Marisco, embarked upon a policy of robbery under arms, raided the mainland and its ports, and so generally misconducted himself that his holding was declared forfeit to the crown and bestowed upon the Knights Templar with full authority to take possession. With this arrangement, however, Sir Jordan declined to comply, and since the Templars lacked the might to eject, he continued his depredations for the remainder of his life, his son, Sir William, pursuing the same policy until, in John's reign, a tax was levied upon the counties of Devon and Cornwall to provide forces with which to defend the coasts against the marauding exploits of Sir William and his followers. This led to the suppression of the warlike baron, but the family's connection with Lundy did not close until another Sir William De Marisco, great-grandson of the piratical Sir Jordan, was executed in 1242 for an attempt upon the life of Henry III, having vainly sought refuge on the island.

With the suppression of local brigandage North Devon waters seem to have enjoyed a comparative respite from marine raiders for the ensuing three centuries, partly because Lundy was successively held by great families, including the Grenvilles, who supported authority. The island erupted again as a pirate stronghold during the reign of James I, and throughout the seventeenth century was either subjected to pillage or used as a springboard for attacks upon shipping all along the Bristol Channel, which, according to one complaint made in 1625, was as infested with buccaneers as Egypt with caterpillars.

From robbery on the high seas thought turns inevitably to the wreckers who infested the North Devon and Cornish coasts, and were only less dangerous than raiding craft upon account of their limited scope. In part vindication of Devon's record in this respect, one can only remember the marauding spirit of the times, that the wreckers were largely composed of men who had taken part in lawless South Sea exploits justified by popular sentiment, and above all an immemorial tendency to regard the sea as a source of revenue and all that it could bring as legitimate gain. In such matters, also, one is always confronted with the difficulty of distinguishing between history and fiction. The wrecker with his picturesque background provided ideal material for the dramatic story-teller, whose representations in course of time became almost indivisible from real history, and allowance for inevitable exaggeration must be made.

When John Ridd related the misdemeanours of the Doones to Judge Jefferies, that avowed exponent of the short-shrift-and-high-gallows policy not unnaturally enquired why the county authorities did not hang them all, and a similar question must occur to anyone when reading accounts of the more or less traditional but not entirely fictitious robbers of the coast. When wrecking and smuggling were rampant, coastguards and preventive men also patrolled the seaboard, and it seems incredible that the fatal flares which lured ships into dangerous waters could have escaped notice had anything approaching an organised watch been kept, the very wildness of the coast which facilitated malpractices also restricting operations to a few inlets, sufficiently notorious, one would have thought, to ensure a constant watch being kept upon them.

One can only assume that the coastline was inadequately policed; that authority was weak and lawlessness strong; that the lonely coastguard with insufficient men at his disposal preferred to ignore a suspicious-looking ship riding at dusk off Marsland Mouth or Crackington Haven, and more often than not he placed a harmless construction upon a light that blazed above some dangerous cove when a westerly gale raged at midnight. There were doubtless long periods of complete tranquillity when no attempt at wrecking was made and no contraband cargo landed, but even as the story of Robin Hood will through all time people Sherwood Forest with shadowy green-coated archers, so the ghost of Coppinger and his kind will haunt the cruel coast upon which he figured, while phantom buccaneer craft of every nationality lurk in the shelter of Lundy's cliffs or prowl the now quiet waters of Barnstaple Bay.

The pirates, wreckers and smugglers have long since gone, but so has the maritime trade which once yielded them so rich a harvest that it earned for the northern inlet the name of the "Golden Bay." A century ago these North Devon ports still carried on a fair amount of commerce, although, owing to the silting up of Barnstaple Harbour, much of the trade had been diverted to Bideford or Appledore, gradually decreasing, however, as their limitations rendered competition more difficult.

The arrival and development of the big steamship finally established Plymouth as the port of the West, and at the same time completed the effacement of Topsham, which formerly served the Exeter district. In the days of the wooden navy the river Exe carried a considerable amount of shipping, light cargo boats up to about 200 tons, conveying coal from South Wales and timber from Scandinavia, still penetrating by way of the canal to Exeter itself. This ship

Mol's Coffee House, Exeter

canal, constructed in Elizabeth's reign, was the city's reply
to the frequently described erection of Countess Weir, which
had for nearly three centuries impeded the passage of vessels
up the river to her quays. Topsham, however, benefited to
the extent of replacing Exeter as a thriving port, carrying on
a considerable export trade in wool to the Low Countries
during the seventeenth and eighteenth centuries. The ship-
building industry was continued until within living memory,
and by chance I recently talked to a man who saw the last
wooden vessel built at Topsham some sixty years ago. When
Exeter was attacked with such devastating effect by the
Luftwaffe in 1942, the city was described in German com-
muniqués as a "shipping town"—a classification at least a
century out of date. It is a curious reversal of conditions that
Topsham, once famous for its sea commerce, is now known
mainly upon account of its military barracks, as a residential
suburb and a favourite halting-place where pleasure-parties
can be served with tea. Upon the mud-flats of the river which
was once crowded with merchant vessels coots, gulls and
wildfowl assemble in their thousands, while from the quay
alongside which warships once lay a solitary ferry-boat,
sometimes plied by a veritable waterside urchin, conveys the
visitor across the deserted estuary to the farther bank.

Indeed, with the grand exception of the Plymouth area,
the history of Devon's old seaports is much the same. Even
as Hiawatha's song "one burden bore," so the record of
West-country shipping is one long tale of decline, told with
equal eloquence on the empty reaches of the Exe or around
Barnstaple Bay, where during the shipping slump of 1918–
38 one saw derelict steamers a prey to rust and decay, lying
like ghosts of a past not too distant but none the less irre-
vocably gone. Throughout this period officers of the
Merchant Navy were glad to accept posts as caretakers of
laid-up vessels. Yet so far as the life of the people is concerned, it is a matter of change rather than decline. The
towns and villages are more densely populated, and consistent prosperity has replaced the vicissitudes of the old
adventurous days. It is, none the less, a prosperity effected
by yet another complete reversal of conditions. Old centres
of harsh toil and hardy enterprise have been adapted to meet

West front of Exeter Cathedral

the requirements of the pleasure-seeker. Upon the wharves and quays where the hard-bitten mariners of Drake and Grenville lounged and smoked their newly imported strong tobacco, discussing desperate adventures past or to come, lightly clad summer visitors sit around tea-tables or chase ice-cream barrows. The creak of weighing anchors as privateer or royal frigate set sail for some hazardous expedition has given place to the hoot of the charabanc or speedboat horn, announcing another trip. And yet, underlying all, the picturesque past still bears its fruit by virtue of the magnetic charm, the indefinable enchantment of old romance from which these historic ports originally derived their popularity.

Again, apart from the influence of association, it is a significant reflection that the sea, which once provided so much of Devon's prosperity by maritime trade and warfare, brings it still in so different a form, from within the island rather than from without—a dividend from the wealth that the exertions of the county's pioneers established for the nation as a whole.

BIBLIOGRAPHY

Devon Association Transactions, IV, p. 553, J. R. Chanter; XX, p. 312, R. N. Worth; XLIV, p. 630, M. Whitley; XI, p. 175, R. W. Cotton.

CHAPTER IV

LANDSCAPE, RIVERS AND BOUNDARIES

F E W geographical names are more descriptive than Devonshire, or in the original Celtic, *Dyfnaint*, meaning the land of
deep, dark valleys, which were doubtless darker, if no
deeper, in the days when virgin forest stretched from sea to
sea. Dyfnaint is forgotten, together with the primitive people
who trod its wastes, but the "Devonshire" of later times has
acquired a background scarcely less picturesque. To the
modern name, like echoes of old tunes, still cling the music
of those deep, dark valleys, the sound of innumerable
streams, the scent of heather and honeysuckle, the roll of
Drake's drum and the eternal voices of the sea, eloquent all
down the ages.

The mental picture that Devonshire suggests to the mind
of anyone familiar with the West may vary considerably,
according to individual impression or experience, for few
English counties can present a greater variety of aspects.
Here genial beauty nestles in the shelter of stern grandeur;
rich fertility merges almost imperceptibly into wild, wide
desolation. From the agricultural paradise of the "Red
Land" rise the dour clay hills where the beech shadows the
bracken, and overlooking the warm southern seaside-resorts
the grim Dartmoor tors pierce the skyline, rolling back or
gathering their veil of mist, like moody giants inviting or
forbidding approach at the caprice of the moment. Even the
seas that wash Devon's southern and northern shores
differ curiously in character. From the sunny south in-
rolls the blue Channel, to ripple along beaches of sand
or shingle from which the fisherman "sets forth without fear," for harbours are many and dangerous reefs are
few. The red cliffs lack any hint of terror, and along the
greater part of this gentle front have crept the seaside towns,
Torquay, Dawlish, Exmouth, Paignton, Teignmouth, Sidmouth and Budleigh Salterton, with more than the ordinary

amenities. Very different, however, is the story of the northern coast, also bounded conventionally by a "Channel," but upon which in reality the long Atlantic rollers break, driven in by winds that have kissed the Arctic ice or gathered sting from the Devil's Hole—that home and birthplace of the storm far out in mid-ocean. On the northern shore, too, are sandy stretches, but not the friendly little beaches of the south. It is in every respect a sterner, crueller coast, a fron- tier of harsh headlands and jagged reefs over which "the wild sea horses foam and fret" perpetually, and the snarl of the hungry waves, audible far inland on a still night, eloquently expresses the spirit of the shore. Conflicting, indeed, are the ideas of Devon's sea which visitors may acquire, and scarcely less varied are the inland pictures. Widely contrasted as these may be, however, one thing is certain. Whatever the impression, it will be at least dis- tinctive, for in no part of Devonshire could it be possible to imagine oneself anywhere else. Its boundaries and near borders, indeed, contain a little country within itself. Here and there a resemblance to some other county may be traced, but always with the subtle difference which anyone familiar with both cannot fail to recognise. In South Devon, for example, the heather slopes and tall Scotch pines strongly suggest Surrey or Hampshire, but the red soil quickly dis- pels such an illusion. Many of the level cornlands recall a Yorkshire landscape, but the banks and hedgerows are too big, and one misses the sense of wide distances which characterises the broad-acred shire. At times the deep coombes of Dartmoor transport the visitor to Westmorland or Cumberland, but the precipices are lacking, also the loftier summits "which keep till June December's snow." Devon has no natural lakes, her inland water accumulations, which are few, being artificial. It is curious that despite her rich red fertility and reputation as a land of cream and abundance, in Hooker's *Chorographical*, written about 1600, her soil is classified as "very thinne barren and unprofitable servinge to smale use other than for salvages and wylde beastes," and in reality her main characteristic is wild rather than homely beauty, not so much exemplifying England's green and pleasant land as a survival of older conditions.

> Land of brown heath and shaggy wood,
> Land of the mountain and the flood,

wrote Scott of the country he loved and idealised, and in a minor degree the couplet is applicable to Devonshire, for although her mountains are not impressive from a rock and fell climber's point of view, she remains eminently a county of heather-sweeps, precipitous coombes, old oak hangers and wild hill streams the grandeur of which no English county can surpass. Actually Devon is the most uniformly hilly of all the counties and contains the greatest number of rivers, brooks and springs. Indeed, the sound of running water is the constant accompaniment of everyday life. An open stream spanned by frequent foot-bridges threads the streets of many of her villages and towns, such as Budleigh Salterton, Honiton, South Zeal and picturesque little Kilmington, to recall only a few.* "I have yet to see anything that so closely approaches the Highlands" was the recent verdict of one visitor to Dartmoor—an admission reluctantly wrung from one whose partiality for the North was, to say the least, pronounced. However that may be, Devonshire with her hills and coombes, heather and pines, white-washed cottages and dark-haired, dark-eyed people, stands forth among her neighbours as distinct.

Indeed, the Devon country, including in a purely physical sense the north-west corner of Somerset somewhat capriciously thrust into her flank, is as different upon the one side from the chalk undulations of Dorset or the golden ploughland and green vales of Somerset as from the dour stone walls and far less imposing hills of Cornwall upon the other. Even the sheep in their pink-dipped fleeces catch the stranger's eye the moment he crosses the boundary. A passenger on an excursion steamer cruising up the Dart was once heard assuring his wife in all good faith that the peculiar tint was acquired from the soil—presumably an extension of the protective colouring principle.

Less in area than Yorkshire alone, Devonshire covers some 2,490 square miles,† of which in 1938, the last pre-war

---

* Since this passage was written, some of the streams—that in South Zeal for example—have been covered, to facilitate increased road traffic.

† According to the *Devonshire Survey* of 1941.

year before the enforcement of increased ploughing, the large proportion of over 9,000 acres was given up to pastures and rough grazing, including moorland, while 415,118 were arable. The last available woodland statistics, 80,610 acres, were compiled in 1924, since when the six new holdings acquired by the Forestry Commission have considerably increased this acreage,* although war-time felling has to a certain extent counterbalanced this. Also, numerous schemes under consideration would render any attempt at exact figures of little value at the moment. Actually, between rough pasture and moor or wood it is difficult to draw a distinct line, the one often merging into the other without as much as a dividing fence.

The population of the county, at the last census 732,968, or 250 to the square mile, gives a false impression of density, averages in this respect as in most others being merely misleading. Distribution of the inhabitants is very unequal, since apart from Exeter (15,421), Plymouth (208,182), Torquay (46,352), Exmouth (14,591), Newton Abbot (15,010), Barnstaple (14,700) and various minor towns, Devon is one of the most thinly populated of English counties. There are few industries or factories as compared with even Cornwall or Somerset. Exeter herself might be described as a country city, the widely scattered "towns" as mainly market or agricultural. A North-country mining "village" contains as many thousand people as the ordinary Devonshire town its hundreds. Until the arrival of cars upon an extensive scale and tarmac within the past quarter of a century, many of Devon's highways were grass-grown; and as recently as 1914 the main road between Exeter and Okehampton was so rutted that furniture vans found progress difficult. That such conditions have long since changed goes without saying, yet even so the new or, as it might be termed, the artificial population that ribbon development has brought is principally distributed along the main roadsides, away from which all remains as before. One may still walk or drive for miles along a Devonshire byway without encountering a human being, and so few and so well known to one another

* The latest authentic figure of the total area planted by the Forestry Commission in the County of Devon is 8,411 acres.

are the inhabitants that until war brought its influx of evacuees a stranger was an object of interest. It was in a quiet country house near the Dorset boundary that a young housemaid hurried to my mother with the naïve announcement: "Please 'm, there's someone going by in the road, and I don't know who it is."

In the matter of population, it must also be remembered that one of Devon's most congested areas lies in the extreme south-west, where Plymouth, Devonport and Stonehouse crowd together. The western boundary is most pronounced both geographically and psychologically, being formed, with one slight divergence over which local controversy has raged from time to time, by the river Tamar. This area, a few miles north of Launceston, comprising about nineteen square miles, originally formed part of the ancient manor of Werrington. Extending westwards over the Tamar, it has been resentfully described by the Cornish as a finger of Devon poked into their county. In 1929 the Cornish County Council petitioned Parliament for a restitution of the old river boundary; but opposition by the rival Devon County Council proving successful, the encroaching finger has not yet been withdrawn. The village of Bridgerule, on the other hand, formerly Cornish, was exchanged in 1844 for part of Vaultershome, which was returned to the western county.*

Undisturbed through all this, the Tamar, that demurely flowing clay stream, the longest river in the Cornish peninsula with a course of 59 miles, rises within a few miles of the Atlantic. Turning her back upon that tempestuous shore, however, as though it were incompatible with her disposition, she pursues her resolute but leisurely course directly southwards, and absorbing the Tavy and other wild Dartmoor torrents as well as the Cornish Lynher, wanders through marsh, meadow and woodland to discharge her mainly Devonian waters into the great Hamoaze estuary. From source to mouth the dividing line marked by her long, quiet reaches is, with the exception just mentioned, curiously definite. Lying side by side as they do, the two western counties remain aloof with true sisterly antagonism. When

_____
* The latest boundary dispute (1950) concerns the proposed incorporation of Torpoint and Saltash within the City of Plymouth's administrative area.

the lost fox- or stag-hunter on Tamarside seeks information from the native passer-by, he is not told that the hounds have run towards any particular place, but rather that they have "gone away into Cornwall"—or Devon, as the case may be —that is to say into an alien country, quite beyond the informant's sphere of interest. Such an attitude is unusual, if not unique. Anywhere else under similar circumstances the point would be specified without reference to county boundaries, to which the ordinary countryman would attach no importance even if aware of them. In this case, of course, the river, over which bridges are comparatively few, emphasises the demarcation. It is somewhat like the Thames barrier between Middlesex and Surrey, and upon the lower reaches of the Tamar a considerable détour may be necessary in order to pass the Devonian-Cornish frontier.

North of the Tamar the county boundary is marked by the wild little Marsland Brook, entering the sea at the picturesque "Mouth" which bears its name, the home of Kingsley's Lucy Passmore, the witch, to whom the Rose of Torridge took her troubles. Both Torridge and Tamar rise little more than a gunshot apart upon Woolly Moor in Morwenstowe parish, appropriating from the moment of their birth opposite slopes of a little tussocky hillock, bog-encircled. This is a wild, bleak country, the fringe of the great tableland sometimes called the "Plain of Devon," a region where marsh predominates, the home of wading birds, patrolled at night by *ignis fatuus*, that ghostly sentinel of mire and mere, still regarded with superstitious awe among the country-people, by whom it is seldom actually seen, since the will-o'-the-wisp haunts secluded ways, trodden only by the shepherd, the night poacher or the trapper on his starlit round.

From a purely picturesque point of view the greater part of North Devon, as distinct from the coastal area, is not outstanding. The main attraction lies in its rural solitude and its own peculiar quality of wildness, which even cultivation and building have failed to efface. The view seldom conveys an impression of wide spaces, although one may look over twenty miles of country towards the fantastic outline of Dartmoor's peaks, blue or snow-capped, bounding the distance. Through and more or less encircling much of the area loops the indeterminate Torridge, that strange river which after completing its meandering, fifty-mile course, eventually seeks the sea seventeen miles from its birthplace. Flowing southwards almost to Hatherleigh, or until its confluence with the far wilder Okement, as though at the suggestion of that headlong mountain stream, it completely reverses its direction and along quiet and often densely wooded valleys escorts the Dartmoor river back to the Atlantic, to reach which it has chosen so devious a route. This erratic course often proves disconcerting to the stranger. After crossing the impressive tidal flood of the Torridge just below Bideford, twenty minutes' drive brings him to Woodford Bridge, under which passes—as he is told but can scarcely believe—the same stream, here reduced to almost incredible insignificance. When he discovers that the quiet brook—for it is little more—is flowing not seawards but inland, his bewilderment is complete, and recourse to the map becomes necessary for a solution of the riddle. The Torridge is a good salmon river and also contains big trout, although these lack the cleanliness and sweet flavour of fish from the tributary Okement or the only other north-flowing Dartmoor river, the more ambitious Taw.

The Taw rises close beside the romantic Dart, under the western shoulder of mighty Hangingstone, and evincing no disposition to accompany the sister stream, from the outset embarks upon its varied and picturesque run to Barnstaple Bay. Even while sweeping over the lowlands the Taw is eminently a wild river, subject to the moods and quick passions of its mountain birthplace, prone to sudden destructive flood and as rapid subsidence, ever hurrying on, fretful of delay, and singing throughout its course the interminable song of the rocks and the heather, or "crying" as the country-people say, to announce the storm as yet unheard, but brewing far away among the hills, and broadcasting its preliminary mutterings along the widely diverging waterways.

The forty-eight-mile long Taw is North Devon's last link with Dartmoor. Beyond the indentation of Barnstaple Bay, the coast curves north and then eastwards, passing Ilfracombe and scenic Lynmouth to meet the Somerset boundary. Even without personal knowledge of the district and its configuration, the most casual glance at the map suggests that here the eastern dividing line is whimsically and most inappropriately placed. Somerset projects a sharp and quite unnecessary point to embrace country and coastline which, by virtue of general characteristics as well as geographical formation, is most definitely Devonian. Clearly the boundary should run east of Minehead, beyond which the great plain of Somerset, known locally as the "water-country" but generally, though a trifle vaguely, as Sedgemoor, forms a natural limit. Devonshire should certainly include Exmoor and its immediate surroundings to complete her distinctiveness, which at this one point is broken, this time by her neighbour thrusting an elbow rather than a finger unjustifiably into the land of red deer and the storied Doones, leaving the Exe, that essentially Devonshire river, Somerset born, and the ancient town of Dulverton over the border.

The Exe, which figures so conspicuously in West-country nomenclature, follows an even more varied or contrasted course than that of the Taw. Unlike the Torridge, after once turning her back on the Atlantic seaboard, the Exe proceeds steadily southwards, and for many miles threads a long maze of wooded coombes, passing Bampton and Tiverton to enter the wide vale of Exeter, over whose green meadows and grazing-marshes she flows quietly down to her ample estuary fifty-four and a half miles from her source. The history of the Exe, or more specifically of the old-world towns upon her banks, is given in fuller detail elsewhere. Although very largely a river of past rather than of present or future importance, her waters still are utilised, nor does she lack modern appeal. Also, from source to mouth she is rich in interest to the naturalist and sportsman. Along the wood or heather-clad slopes of her higher waters roam the wild red deer. There in autumn stags are belling and the dappled calves are brought to drink from the clear, trout-haunted pools. Further down her flow, but in the same waters, redder Devon cattle or tawny South Hams wade and wallow, and snowy swans float instead of the dippers which flashed along the moorland reaches. Southwards still, the reinforced and now imposing river rolls on to reach at last that ornithologist's paradise the Exmouth and Dawlish Warrens, the haunt of gull, wildfowl and wader, where few estuary-frequenting birds known within the British Isles have not at some time been recorded.

South of Exmoor the line of demarcation between the country characteristic of Devon and Somerset roughly follows the boundary line, with outcrops of the western county more frequently straggling into Somerset than the Somersetshire landscape into Devon. The division is representative in the main, however, until the Dorset border is reached. Then the situation becomes, to say the least of it, involved, and even though the geographical distinction remains as definite as ever, the Devon characteristics in some instances ending as abruptly as though cut off by a hoe, the actual boundary has been subjected to so many variations that even a resident scarcely knows in which county he lives. There are parishes declared Dorset or Somerset for a purpose such as a Parliamentary constituency and under a Devon town for local administration. I remember a controversy as to the legal position of a farmer who pastured a dangerous bull in a field through which ran a right of way. The Devon by-law concerning this point was stricter than that of Somerset or Dorset, but as no positive ruling could be obtained as to which of the three counties the field actually belonged, the existing state of things continued. So mixed up were Devon and Dorset at one time that detached areas belonging to either shire lay well within the other. The parishes of Stockland and Dalwood, lying roughly between Axminster and Honiton, formed a complete "island," classified as part of Dorset until 1844, although entirely separated from that county by Membury and Yarcombe, both large Devonshire parishes. In exchange for these places, as in the case of the Tamar redistribution, Thorncombe and Beerhall were ceded to Dorset. In 1896 a further boundary reshuffle took place, Chardstock and Hawkchurch, formerly Dorset, being incorporated in Devon, while Churchstanton, farther north, passed to Somerset. Conventionally, however, the characteristic division has always superseded the official delineation, and not until he is well away upon the broad, white undulations which could not be Devonian by any stretch of the imagination does anyone consider himself in Dorset.

Judged entirely by the character of the country, the long ridge of Lambert's Castle, whose northern shoulder descends almost like a cliff into the Marshwood Vale, clearly constitutes Devon's main bastion upon this frontier. From the foot of Lambert's Bank and its dependency, Conic Castle, the wide vale marches to meet the chalk, bounded by the vast semi-circle of Dorset's hills stretching from Pilsdon's flat summit to the impressive crest of Golden Cap clear cut against the southern sea. Severed from the Lambert's Castle ridge by one deep valley stands Grighay, Devon's last landmark in the days when Thorncombe, too, lay like an island encircled by Dorset. At one time famous among Westcountry fox-hunters for the gorse-brake which clothed its narrow crown, Grighay "Knap"—as minor or dependency hills are termed in East Devon, being equivalent to a Lakeland "Dod"—for generations constituted an unmistakable landmark upon account of its three beech clumps, locally known as the Devil's Three Jumps. The legend attached to these trees is of the customary type—the hermit of Montacute who wrestled with the Evil One and eventually had recourse to a lusty kick which lifted His Satanic Majesty over miles of country, to land upon Grighay Knap with such force that he bounced twice, the trees springing up to commemorate each impact.

Not far from Grighay stands Thorncombe Thorn, a crossway where once grew the traditional hawthorn under which, as the story goes, the lord of the manor discovered sufficient treasure to build the manor of Sadborough. Below Thorncombe village extends the slowly widening valley of the Axe. Like the Exe, Somerset-born yet eminently Devonian, it meanders over lush grazing country and past roedeer-haunted woodland to skirt old-world Axminster, little changed in character and atmosphere since Monmouth led its inhabitants against the royal troops more than two centuries ago. The Axe, only 23 miles in length, is the most easterly of Devonshire rivers, with only a short expanse of coast separating its mouth from the Dorset cliffs. Within that stretch lies the famous Landslip, so minutely described in guide-books that its story is common knowledge. To the holiday-maker the Landslip has long been a fairyland, and there the botanist and bird observer still find a fruitful field. Incidentally, there have been various minor subsidences along the coastline. At Ladran Bay, for example, fragments of red cliff still stand forlorn and wave-encircled, sole evidence of former promontories now appropriated as ideal nesting-places by the islet-loving gulls. In this bay, however, there is no record of any spectacular fall, and it is rather a matter of slow erosion, to which the cliff-face yields reluctant fragments.

From a geological point of view the cliffs west of Seaton, Devon's most easterly coastal town, into whose bay the Axe flows, possess a special interest. One might almost imagine that Sussex had lent two of her headlands to break the monotony of the long red wall, for the points which hem in the little fishing village of Beer, Seaton's near neighbour, are chalk-white.

Running roughly parallel with the Axe is the bright little Otter, yet another Somerset-rising stream which abandons its parent shire within four miles of its birth and proceeds by quiet ways through the county of its adoption. For its insignificant length the Otter figures conspicuously in Devon nomenclature, like the Clyst and the minute Sid and Kenn, lending its name to almost every village or little town passed in its comparatively short career of 26 miles. Quiet, indeed, are the upper reaches of the Otter through country not only "scarce mentioned in historic tales" but seldom heard of even a few miles away. It is above all a region of rural beauty and peace which has reigned there scarcely ruffled since the Parliamentary army occupied the district and Fairfax established his headquarters at Ottery St Mary. These or similar conditions embrace the neighbouring Culm valley and extend throughout the greater part of East Devon to the Axe Vale, Cullompton farther north, Spryden Forest and the Somerset border. Downstream, swinging wide of Honiton, the Otter enters a more populous district which extends to its outlet at Budleigh Salterton, within personal memory a tranquil little shingle-beached fishing town, to which a three-horse bus from Exmouth provided the sole means of access.

Now it has developed into a popular residential centre, served by rail and motor bus, and except at one point through which the railway passes, linked up with Exmouth by ribbon development. The character of the little river remains unchanged, however. It is appropriately named, being eminently an otter-haunted stream, while its narrow estuary, flanked by reed-beds and an extensive rookery, is rich in bird life. Over the cliff at its mouth the raven croaks, while westwards towards Ladran Bay and Sidmouth is a cormorant colony, where also the peregrine falcon breeds and gulls in great multitudes.

Between Budleigh and Exmouth is Sandy Bay, the resort of numerous oyster-catchers and blackheaded gulls, also of surreptitious human bathers.* Westward again lie the Warrens, with Starcross and Dawlish intervening between the great Exe estuary and its very different neighbour the Teign, not the least spectacular of Dartmoor's waters, with its grand gorges, its daffodil-flushed banks and its many springheads among the mighty hills which nourish the wild sources of the Taw and Dart.

After quitting the bogs and the heather the Teign, leaving Chagford on its western bank, flows for many miles through natural woodland eminently characteristic of the Dartmoor country. This for the most part is little more than tall oak-scrub, but assumes bigger proportions towards Steppes Bridge, where is the principal heronry of the district. It is a valley of wild birds, notably of the rare hobby among others. The stream, which varies considerably in its flow from rapid torrent to long salmon pools, offers an ideal home to dipper or kingfisher, while upon one jackdaw-haunted crag the raven breeds within a few yards of a footpath which threads one side of the gorge, the great nest under the overhanging crag being invisible to the passer-by but in plain view of the opposite slope.

The lower reaches of the Teign are less imposing as, quitting her long gorge, she flows through the still picturesque but more placid scenery that surrounds Chudleigh and Newton Abbot, to which the tidal flow reaches. The

* Until recently prohibited as a bathing place, a large holiday camp is now established here.

river separates Teignmouth from Shaldon, connection between the two places being provided by a ferry and a thirty-four-span toll-bridge erected in 1827.* Siltage has considerably narrowed the estuary, and many of the adjoining grazing-marshes were once covered by tidal waters. Beyond Shaldon the coast stretches on past wooded cliff, bay and headland to merge into the long frontage of Torquay and Paignton, and since guide-books deal exhaustively with these popular resorts, we will return along the 33 miles of the Teign's course to follow her near neighbour, the Dart.

To each of Dartmoor's principal rivers an official "head" has been assigned, but actually the sources are so numerous that the real starting-point of any stream might be considered a matter of opinion. Down every coombe or wrinkle on the upland's furrowed face tinkles a brook, sometimes so tiny that it is little more than a runnel, here appearing, again lost to view as it follows hidden ways under the soil, and so confused is this maze of water-courses that even people familiar with the Moor are frequently uncertain as to the ultimate destination of the water which trickles at their feet. The Dart has probably more heads, or collects more tributary brooks, than any other river, and its headwaters drain a very considerable part of the Moor. Besides its own three "heads" and various nameless streams, it collects the waters of the Black Brook, the Cowsic, the Cherry Brook, the Walla, the Swincombe, the Webburn and the Yeo, and though not as long as the Taw by 12 miles, by traversing a greater expanse of moorland has established its claim to be regarded as Dartmoor's main waterway.

Stealing through the great bogs as though fearful to raise their voices above a whisper upon those lonely silent heights, the countless rills gather volume, spread and cry upon reaching the valleys, until at Dartmeet the main headwaters combine, from which confluence the fine river sweeps on through scenes which students of the beautiful have endeavoured to produce in word and colour picture. All down the centuries the song of the Dart has been accompanied by developments and activities as divergent as

* Freed from toll and taken over by Devon County Council, October, 1948.

imagination could conceive, from the slow growth of Wistman's Wood to the patient labours of the Buckfast monks building and rebuilding their abbey. It sang to the tinstreamers as they cut their leats. It roared in protest round the hardy workmen when they erected the pillars of the old stone bridges; and the famous "cry" is heard today by the picnic party at Dartmeet or Holne Bridge, by the modern salmon-fisher or the moorman seeking his sheep on the hillside, although he hears no music in the sound, but rather the warning of wild weather ahead, for the river's plaint is the stormy petrel of the hills.

The Dart passes no town of any significance until reaching Totnes of Roman association, and once important as being one of the four Devonshire boroughs mentioned in Domesday Book. It is now mainly known as the limit of the tidal inflow and the highest point accessible to the excursion steamer. In Domesday Book the taxes and services required of Totnes were equivalent to those demanded from Exeter with which the place was connected by the Fosse Way, although the precise extent of this ancient track westwards is uncertain. The scenic charm of Dart's ten-mile flow over its tidal reaches, with Stoke Gabriel, Dittisham and Sharpham on its banks, the wooded hills, the quiet creeks and quays, the white-washed cottages—all has been described so often that enlargement would be mere repetition. It is, however, through such enchanted scenes that this most romantic of English rivers carries its now copious flood to the grand finale at Dartmouth—in some respects an anti-climax for waters tossed and fretted by upland boulders, since Dartmouth harbour is famed among many other things for its serene tranquillity. That, however, is merely by the way, and it is only appropriate that Devon, the county of seafaring men, should have the cradle of the navy at the mouth of its most famous river. The great Naval College buildings, completed in 1905, may strike an incongruous note with their somewhat aggressive modernity, but Dartmouth is a place in which the old world and the new combine harmoniously. The selection of the county and the port for the establishment of the college is in full accord with tradition, particularly since Plymouth, home of the full-fledged Navy,

Statue of Sir Francis Drake on Plymouth Hoe

stands around the estuaries fed by other Devonian streams, for it is the privilege of the Tavy, not so famous as the Dart but none the less a river of outstanding beauty and character, to supply, together with her tributary waters, a large proportion of Tamar's flood, which discharges into the Hamoaze and thence into the Sound.

The Hamoaze and Plymouth Bay were described in the last chapter, but even a brief sketch of Dartmoor's streams would be sadly incomplete if it overlooked the Tavy, which, but for the geographical accident in lie of land necessitating its junction with the Tamar, would have rivalled the Dart itself. The twenty-three-mile-long Tavy rises in the heart of the Moor, her two infant arms thrown about remote and beautiful Fur Tor. Wild and grand even for Dartmoor are the valleys which offer the new-born stream a path, and the Tavy loses no time before exploring their recesses. A few uncertain turns she makes to find her feet, and then, like one assured of a purpose in life, she is away with ever-quickening strides. She has not proceeded far in her rapid career before joining hands with the Ammicombe water, an exceedingly picturesque but almost unknown brook, no track intersecting its brief course from its birthplace on the western flank of sinister Black Ridge. Thus reinforced, the Tavy hurries on with great Hare Tor towering ahead, along whose base, bubbling over its pebbles, comes the appropriately named Rattle Brook, plunging into the Tavy's flood with a shout of relief at finding a wider channel and a senior partner after its own hustling heart.

It is characteristic of the tempestuous Tavy, England's fastest river, that she acquires an imposing volume of water far earlier in her wild career than any other Dartmoor stream. Sweeping out a wider channel to accommodate the Rattle Brook, without a backward glance at the wonderful prehistoric villages with whose secrets she was familiar three thousand years ago, she plunges into the magnificent gorge, or *Cleave*, that bears her name, passes the great granite crags at whirling speed, and bidding a hasty farewell to the Moor which she abandons all too soon, rolls on past Peter Tavy and Tavistock, and with power somewhat depleted by leat, aqueduct and canal, but still a noble stream, meets the

Shipping at Appledore, on the estuary of the Taw and Torridge

Walkham at Double Waters. Great woods witness the union, after which, part of her mission now fulfilled, she proceeds at a more leisurely pace to shed all further responsibility into the patient Tamar.

And so the long circuit of Devon's boundaries and streams terminates as it began in the river which of all the inland boundary lines remains the most pronounced. With streams so numerous, space has not permitted a detailed sketch of all. There are, for example, the picturesque Lyd, the Plym, the Yealm, the Meavy, the Bovey, the Erme, the Avon and the Mole, the various Yeos, the Trony with its valley famous for wild flowers, Kenn Brook, the Kennet, Creedy, the Morning Water, the Blackaton, the Little Dart and many more, a list of which would be merely tedious. But one point of interest remains. While various streams flow into this county of rivers, none flow out to seek an alien seaboard, although Devon being a higher county than her neighbours and the main watershed of the West, a reversal of the situation might have been expected. This is a curious natural tribute to the county's magnetic charm, and is general in its application, for while many people come to live in Devon, few leave, and former residents evince an almost invariable tendency to return. To those who know the land of deep, dark valleys this presents no mystery.

BIBLIOGRAPHY

Devon Association Transactions, xxvii, p. 334, W. J. Blake.
Victoria History of Devon.

CHAPTER V

WOODLAND

ONE may safely assume that in a country like England there remains no "virgin forest," that is to say, woodland in which no agency other than the strictly natural has ever been at work. Every square yard has been picked over at some time by somebody, and although in places such as the New Forest or Wistman's Wood on Dartmoor there are trees so old that they may conceivably date from comparatively primitive conditions, these can only be regarded as survivors of the virgin wild, like venerable ruins still preserved in the heart of a modern city. Upon the other hand, it seems more than probable that much of our remaining woodland is natural in so far that it has been self-propagated. Few trees fall without doing their duty to posterity, and a new stock of hardwood has for the most part been ensured by the trees themselves during their period of "occupation."

At one time the deep valleys of Devonshire were certainly dark with forest growth, probably much resembling that which clothes many of the wilder coombes today, the size of the timber varying, as now, with altitude and soil. All the undulating country lying between Exmoor and Dartmoor and extending to the valleys of the Tavy and Tamar was at one time heavily and consistently wooded, being actually the ancient *Donewold*, or Down Wood, broken as now by occasional outcrops of heath. The patches of woodland which still occur intermittently throughout the county may reasonably be regarded as remnants of the ancient forest, since it is obvious that nothing but trees or brushwood of some sort ever covered the ground during the existing era of vegetation. The upper Exe valley, for example, is thick with wood which, extending from Bampton nearly to Tiverton, connects in broken chain of brake and coppice with the more heavily timbered valleys of Cheldon, Lapford, Eggesford and thence up the Taw to Sampford Courtenay and

Okehampton. That the country lying roughly between Oke-hampton and South Molton was once thus heavily wooded may be deduced from the old place-names in which the word *Nymet* or *Nymph*, meaning "intake" or "enclosure," fre-quently occurs. Of these, there are Nympton, Queen's Nympton, King's Nympton and George Nympton, while farther south and slightly eastwards in the Crediton direc-tion the Nymets are more numerous. They include Nichols Nymet, Nymet Rowland, Broad Nymet and Nymet Tracey, the original and infinitely more attractive name for the "redland" village now known as Bow, which designation, although ugly enough, is not as unimaginative as might be supposed, owing its origin in all probability to the *bogh*, or bridge, over the Yeo Brook at the foot of the village. This name is found in Somerset denoting bridges over the reans or "broads," and first occurs in connection with this par-ticular village in thirteenth-century deeds, and is later men-tioned as Nymet Bogh, belonging to the parish of Nymet Tracey. The Tracey connection dates from William de Tracey, who is generally supposed to have built this church as well as those of Bovey and Newton Tracey in expiation of his share in Thomas à Becket's murder. Over the inter-pretation of *Nymet* or *Nymph* there has indeed been some diversity of opinion, but however rendered its connection with woodland remains. The entire Nymet district evidently comprised one large intake, some of it highly fertile land reclaimed from the general waste and originally including Copplestone, which latter, however, was detached about 974 and given its own charter in accordance with its ancient importance. From the limits of this intake heavy woodland extended along the valley of the Trony including Nymph Woods and Spreyton Wood, doubtless linking up with the extensive area still covered in the Teign valley and around Chagford, reaching back via Cheriton Bishop almost to Crediton.

It is probably correct to say that the largest timber of any county stands in its parks of which Devonshire claims about sixty, irrespective of other parkland and numerous smaller estates. Since much of this timber is of alien origin, its interest is purely decorative, and this, of course, applies to the county's conifers, including the Scotch pines, not considered indigenous to the Cornish peninsula. It has certainly propagated more freely than others, particularly on Woodbury which, but for fires, would doubtless have been a fine forest long ago. The little "clumps" of Scotch pine which once provided landmarks such as Membury Castle, Dumpdon Clump, Dishcombe Clump and others were probably planted at some period during the eighteenth century, although for what purpose is not clear. In some cases such as at Membury Castle, these pines formed a ring round ancient British ramparts, and were singularly decorative. Masefield, whose poem *Reynard the Fox* has a distinct Westcountry setting, evidently had Devon's hilltop pines in mind when he described "the Ship" and wrote those realistic lines:

> The moan of the three great firs in the wind
> And the *ai* of the foxhounds died behind.

The roar of wind in those great rocking pines was most impressive, and one speaks of them in the past tense because so many now have gone. The splendid trees on Membury Castle were sacrificed to the national need during the first world war, and Dishcombe Clump followed in 1941. Theirs is the story of many, less conspicuous and therefore causing a less noticeable loss to the landscape which none the less is deprived of a feature, great trees being irreplaceable, at least for so long a time. In the course of years Devon will doubtless possess more conifers than ever before, planting by the Forestry Commission and various Water Boards having been undertaken upon a large scale at many places during the past quarter of a century. The largest afforestations have been at Haldon, Fernworthy, Lydford, Hennock, Burrator, Bellever, Eggesford, Halwill, Hartland and Spryden, to mention a few, the trees planted consisting largely of Scotch and Corsican pine, spruces, Douglas fir and larch. In course of time the county will certainly be "a land where the fir-trees stand," but these will not be the Devon woods of the past, although the sprinkling of indigenous trees, such as birch, may mitigate the alien effect. This is notably the case where old oak woods have been replanted with conifers, although for that matter the fir too has its special Devon association. St Boniface, or Winfrith, of Crediton in the eighth century was, according to legend, responsible for introducing the Christmas-tree into Britain, and this, if correct, might be the origin of firs in the West. However that may have been, the thinnings of the new plantations provide the best supply of Christmas-trees at the moment, those at Burrator having appeared regularly for years in the Plymouth markets.

Birch is a great tree of the Devonshire lowland, particularly throughout the rough country between Dartmoor and Exmoor, and along the river valleys where it mingles with the more predominant alder, or "aller," in the language of the country invariably pronounced "holler," which is apt to be rather misleading. I once asked a farmer whether he could supply me with some poles for fencing. He replied that he had plenty of "holler," and assuming that he meant holly, which makes excellent posts, I hastily compounded for a load. A liberal supply of useless alder arrived, but the mistake being obviously mine, I had to make the best of it. In Elizabethan times all alder along Devon stream banks was reserved for the maintenance of the "lord's mill"—an institution to be considered in those days, as all manors with water facilities at their disposal possessed mills. Alder was, according to an old doggerel, considered more durable when cut in early leaf:

> When aller leaf is as big as a penny
> The stick will wear as tough as any,

and it was also extensively used for tool handles upon the strength of this idea.

Holly grows abundantly in all districts, incidentally giving its name to Holne Chase, Holne being regarded as a variation of *Holm*, the old-fashioned West-country name for holly in general use among the country-people a generation or so ago, although now seldom heard. Another and older name is "Christmas," the connection being sufficiently obvious. It is, indeed, one of the few associations which have survived "enlightenment." Once almost every tree had its place in custom or legend. Green ash was burned on Christmas Eve within my own time. I have seen a huge faggot ablaze on an old farmhouse hearth while hand-bells were chimed by a party of village men as the green brands roared and crackled like volleys of rifle-shots. Elder was never used as firewood, since misfortune followed its burning. Mountain ash could not be broken, or even used for driving a horse. "You mustn't fight (i.e. beat) a horse with a quick-beam (mountain ash) stick," was said to me not long ago by a neighbouring farmer, the inexplicable belief being that after a blow from a mountain-ash switch the horse loses condition. A myrtle bush in the garden brought luck, but may-blossom should not enter the house. Few of these conventions remain. Even the ash faggot ceremony, with its wish and sip of cider as each bond burst, is seldom observed. Modern grates are not adapted to such practices, and I believe that for some years past my own has been the only hearth in this village upon which the traditional faggot has blazed on Christmas Eve. The holly berry has lost none of its attraction, however, and nothing that grows in woodland or hedgerow appeals so strongly to the countryman's heart. I remember two village bachelors, uncle and nephew, blacksmiths, who "did" for themselves in a dilapidated cottage, and led a life which might have been regarded as eminently comfortless, yet the younger of the two on Christmas Eve collected holly with fastidious care to decorate their home, into which no other floral adornment ever entered. So anxious, indeed, are the country-people to secure their berries that they gather them weeks in advance and stick the branches into the earth of their gardens, which proceeding is so appreciated by birds, mice, etc., that when finally required few berries remain and those which survive are so much the worse for wear that a fresh supply is needed. That the trees and woodland birds suffer in consequence goes without saying.

Ash and sycamore, though freely cut, remain plentiful owing to their quick growth and ready propagation by seeding. The juniper, which usually thrives in mountainous districts, has never penetrated to Devonshire, although occurring in Wales. Dartmoor, presumably, lies below its southern limit, although well adapted, one would have thought, to so hardy a shrub.

With the exception of plantations the history of which is usually traceable and which in any case are self-evident owing to the regular growth and species of the trees, most of the Devonshire woodland consists of fragments surviving from the original forest, and here and there still stand individual trees or remnants which doubtless occupied their present positions when the surrounding country was still uncultivated. However that may be, little forest clearance can have taken place within the county before the Saxon infiltration, and nothing upon an extensive scale until some centuries later. According to Hooker, one of Exeter's many old names was *Caerpenheulgoyte*, denoting "the cliff citie in the woods or forests," and until the reign of Henry II all Devonshire was reserved as ground for the royal sport. Prior to that date barely half of the county was enclosed, although the wild part included the heathland, much of which was never covered by timber.

Most trees indigenous to southern England occur in Devonshire upon suitable soil, to the quality of which the timber that it bears is a tolerably safe criterion. There are farmers who will have nothing to do with land upon which beech grows, and the objection is not unfounded, since the tree thrives best upon sandy or gravelly soil and "keeps bad company," gorse and bracken being its too frequent associates. Elm, upon the other hand, prefers a rich loamy soil, and unless expressly planted is seldom seen on poor land. For that matter, the greater number of common elms probably owe their presence to introduction, and the tree's claim to the status of an indigenous species is challenged upon the grounds that it has no representation in the oldest place-names, while its seeds seldom ripen, propagation being effected by means of its "stools." Many names with an elm derivation appear in Domesday Book, however, in proof that the species was well established at that period, and since the tree is common in Germany, the theory that it was of Saxon importation is quite acceptable.

East Devon, the country of gorse and apple-nurseries, is also the home of the beech. One may pass for miles along roads or lanes fenced by hedges consisting of little else—tall hedges, so old that the stumps and "steepers" from which spring the growth are interlaced like an immense trellis-work, presenting barriers more impenetrable than many walls. There the trees attain a great size, providing some of the finest rookeries in the county. They find their way into every patch of woodland, attracting the woodpigeons in spring and autumn to feed on the blossom and nuts. They stand in solitary dignity on the age-old and incredibly wide hedgerows of the district, drive their roots into the great sand-banks, where the badgers and foxes burrow to a vast depth beneath them, and establish themselves upon every hill which rises from the red land itself, climbing the slopes of famous Dumpdon, the highest ground in Devonshire apart from Dartmoor. In the Dartmoor country beech ascends the foothills to well above the thousand-foot eleva-tion and provides the predominant trees around moorland villages such as Belstone and Postbridge, and, indeed, upon most high ground throughout the county where trees grow at all. There when the bitter north-easter rattles through russet foliage, it is usually beech leaves that rustle and crackle with the cold whisper so peculiarly their own.

In every part of the county, however, in wild woodland or in Dartmoor's lonely valleys, in hedgerow, park or on village green, the oak stands unchallenged as Devon's forest king. The ships built in her docks, or those which sailed from her ports were rightly named "hearts of oak," particularly when manned, as so many were, by Devonshire men who grew up in the county where, foremost among others, the oak-tree grows. It is, however, as a forest tree in the old and literal sense that the oak first acquired and still maintains its numerical supremacy. Nearly all the big natural woods are oak woods. Oak clothes the valleys down which the Dart-moor streams sweep from the Moor. It clusters thickly alongside the banks of Okement, Taw, Tavy and Teign, and casts its shadow over the waters of Exe, Axe and Torridge, and perhaps the best tribute to Devon's principal tree was paid when the most essentially Devonian stream received the Celtic name of *Deruentio*, the Oak-tree river, which became the Dart of modern times. The choice of this name was a happy one and peculiarly apt, if not prophetic. The association of the lower Dart with the Royal Navy needs no further emphasising, nor could a more appropriate resting-place be imagined for the sea-weary hearts of oak than the broad surface of the Oak-tree river, flowing gently now, as if, like the ancient Tiber, she realised the situation.

> The troubled river knew them and smoothed its
>   yellow foam,
>   And gently rocked the cradle that bore the fate of
>   Rome.

And so, perhaps, the Dart, recognising the ships that Devon's trees had built and the seamen of Devon's towns and villages, lingers for a while over her last reaches to greet and gently rock her countrymen, upon whom the fate of England still so largely depends.

It is characteristic that while the beech has found a footing upon much of the shallow-soiled upland, Dartmoor has adopted the oak as indubitable first favourite. It is a case of Devon for the Devonian, but without much competition, since few other trees root readily in the growan subsoil from which the hardy oak draws sustenance with little difficulty. The mountain ash is there, sparsely distributed although often effectively placed, as a rule mounting solitary guard over a wild coombe-side or a lonely reach of water. A few hawthorns and holly-trees occur, sometimes in little groups as beside the Fishcombe Water and on Clannaborough Down, and here and there small hoary willows stand, as if captured and held by enchantment, on the fringe of a great desolate mire or upon an insignificant eyot in the bed of a torrent. Over extensive areas no trees or bushes grow. Excepting heather and whortleberry, there is not a bush between Fernworthy and Tavy Cleave, for example, and generally speaking the farther from civilisation the fewer the trees, irrespective of altitude, since birds, the principal propagators, adhere mainly to the fringes of the Moor. Scotch pines growing upon Dartmoor, apart from those in enclosures, could be counted with little trouble. There are a few on the Blackaven. A picturesque little group stands inside a spacious hut circle near Shilstone Tor, on Throwleigh Common, and I once saw a solitary seedling struggling optimistically from amongst the heather near the head of the Lady Brook. The next fire terminated that valiant effort, fires being, of course, one of the main reasons for the scarcity of wood growth except beside the streams which check conflagrations.

Dartmoor's three little oak woods, Blacktor Beare, or Copse, Wistman's Wood and Pike's Copse, have attracted a great deal of attention, particularly Wistman's, being the most accessible. Their principal features rendering them outstanding, if not unique, are great age and the extraordinary manner in which they grow. Taken from north to south, Blacktor Beare lies in the West Okement valley backed by the tor from which it takes its name, that being a shoulder of High Willhayes, and fronting the Slipper Stones with the great heave of Long Ammicombe rising beyond. Wistman's Wood flanks the West Dart, clothing an extension of Longaford Tor, while Pike's Copse overlooks the Erme on the slope of Sharp Tor, each of the three copses facing westwards, and all growing, as few trees grow anywhere except on Dartmoor, in great clitters, with nothing but rocks among which to root.

The mystery attached to these woods lies, first in their existence at all under conditions so eminently unpropitious; secondly, and contingent upon the first, in their limited extent. If trees are produced by natural agency in one spot, why not in fifty others similar in aspect, altitude and main essentials? There is no evidence of a more general distribution of woodland on the Moor, no reason why similar growth should not have clothed every sheltered valley. It is significant, however, that the two clitters on the Okement and West Dart, respectively, in which the woods grow, are the most rugged apart from hilltop excrescences, on the northern half of the Moor, and the selection of these suggests not so much a remarkable freak of chance as natural cause. In other words, to the barrenness and extent of the rock formations the trees owe, if not their existence which remains unaccountable, at least their preservation. The protection afforded by the boulders is evidenced by the failure of any growth to make good outside their shelter. No tree stands in any of the little open spaces which here and there break the sequence of clitters, and whether fires, devastating winds or cattle have been the controlling factor all down the centuries matters little, since, whatever the cause, the effect is indisputable. The problem of heath-fires, conventionally beneficial but actually the curse of Dartmoor, will be discussed elsewhere. That browsing sheep and bullocks destroy seedlings is not questioned, nor can there be much doubt that the bitter winds, together with lack of nourishment, are partly responsible for the dwarfed and grotesque aspect of the trees. Such effects are not confined to the moorland copses, although in their case demonstrated to excess. In Skaigh Warren, on the northern shoulder of Cosdon Beacon, may be seen larches almost as curious. Hedgerows bordering Halstock Down, on the East Okement, display fantastic hawthorn configurations, and throughout any part of the Dartmoor district lying open to the hill wind's sweep, stand thorns, beeches and oaks stunted and warped by the tempest into shapes that would discredit neither Wistman's Wood nor Blacktor Beare.

With regard to the latter again, its story is far from being disposed of by the assumption that the rocks preserve the oaks. The copse itself is little more than half a mile long and perhaps a hundred yards in width upon the average. From its lower extremity, where Beare and clitter end abruptly in heather, the belt of huge, tumbled rock, now devoid of trees for no apparent reason, straggles like a huge grey snake for a further couple of miles up the valley, breaking into irregular patches under Forsland Ledge and finally tailing off somewhat dramatically on the quaint craggy summit of raven-haunted Dinger, beyond which the surface is smothered by the vast peat bogs closing down on every side. One might naturally wonder why, if Blacktor Beare came into existence at all, it did not terminate at Dinger's foot rather than two miles downstream.

The rocks among which the trees stand differ from open clitter in that they are covered, like huge camel-humps, with a thick coating of moss and lichens. These, spreading over the oaks themselves, are largely responsible for their antiquated and, above all, hoary appearance. They look as though the mists in which they are so frequently enveloped had been entrapped in the maze of twigs and there remained petrified into a perpetual veil. In Wistman's Wood, whortleberry growth has actually established itself, like mistletoe, in the massive crotches, and the decay of the ancient little oaks, like that of many forest remnants, will probably be a gradual assimilation with the herbage which their mould has fostered. How old they are is a matter of controversy, and since propagation has proceeded throughout their history, each grove probably contains trees of every age. Their manner of propagation is another much debated question, but in my own opinion most replacements have been effected by means of suckers springing from lateral roots deep down among the rocks. After a careful study of acorns in Blacktor Copse, my own considered opinion is that none ripen sufficiently early to produce fertile seed in the brief moorland summer. Given a season of abnormal fecundity, some might mature, and this would account for the seedlings upon occasions. The general character of the growth, however, resembles that of old hedgerow wood springing from stumps and "steepers" rather than an independent source for each tree. An old document, dated 300 years ago, relates to the sale of Blacktor Beare, presumably for firewood, and the complete restoration of the copse by means of seedlings is improbable. No similar record concerning Wistman's Wood is known to exist, but absence of evidence in no way proves that stroke of axe was never heard within its shade. Upon the contrary, it seems unreasonable to assume that in a region almost destitute of wood its value should have been overlooked by the earlier moorland dwellers, and man may conceivably have assisted natural influences in the control and mis-shaping of the trees. Indeed, their resemblance to many of the old hedgerow stumps already mentioned strongly suggests rough pollarding at frequent intervals, authorised or otherwise, and all considered it would be remarkable if nothing of the kind ever took place. Within living memory a cluster of hawthorns under Ladybrook Tor were cut and dragged a couple of rough miles by an old native—an eminently primitive individual living on the northern slope of Cosdon Beacon—

and the "old men" of the past probably did much the same thing. It may be considered as reasonably certain that amateur pollarding through the centuries has reduced and disfigured the growth of Dartmoor's oaks more than any natural agency.

The identity of the venerable "Wistman," together with his title to ownership of the wood, is debatable. One is probably safe, however, in dismissing him as a myth. The Celtic *Uisg- maen- coed*, or "Rocky-wood-beside-the-river," seems too reasonable and pertinent a solution to be discarded, and while "Welshmen's" or "Strangers'" wood has its supporters, convincing reason for the appropriation of the place by strangers is lacking. The theory that the wood was at one time inhabited by a sage or wise man has also been suggested, but why so sagacious an individual should have selected such a home has not transpired. If he lived in the clitter he must have been a particularly agile old gentleman, confining his activities mainly to daylight, and, however skilful at negotiating rocks, the superfluous exertions to which he subjected himself scarcely suggest excessive sagacity. Possibly, if he were Mr Wistman in person, in his character of owner, he conformed to the "no place like home" theory, or residence might have been essential to maintain ownership. When, as one has seen it, ice seals the Dart's flow from bank to bank and the last dry leaves rasp, wind-driven, through the little wood, Mr Wistman certainly had few competitors for his quarters, and anybody who visited him under such conditions needed wise counsel upon more grounds than one.

Outstanding individual trees on Dartmoor are mostly hawthorn, such as that on the northern Walla Brook. There is also a particularly effective lone mountain ash at the foot of Steeperton Tor, and various others on the Taw, Redaven and East Okement, for example, but less conspicuously placed. "In-country," that is, in Devonshire language, anywhere off the Moor, there are several which have acquired a local or wider fame, and the majority of these are oaks, to which species the place of honour is usually assigned. In this village of Sticklepath, in a meadow near the Taw bridge, stands one which seldom fails to catch the visitor's eye, and is sometimes described as the most beautiful in the county—an ambitious claim.

In some parishes, usually on the village green, there survives a relic of a former giant which in its day was probably a "Gospel oak," near which the parish church was eventually built. The shell of such a tree may still be seen at Brandiscorner, another at Spreyton, and until comparatively recently a third at Newton St Petrock. Perhaps the most famous, however, is that which stands beside the lych-gate in the little village of Meavy. Tradition approximates its age to that of the Norman church in whose close company it has weathered the centuries. Restoration has kept the church intact, but all that man could do for the tree was to provide supports for its failing limbs. It still raises these courageously to acknowledge the call of each successive summer. Props also support the tottering frames of its contemporaries elsewhere, and parishioners watch over these dying giants solicitously—a pleasing example of the value that country-people still set upon tradition. This does not necessarily extend to trees in general, however, towards which the attitude is eminently utilitarian and sometimes even antagonistic. I remember one old village woman who regarded a row of stately elms opposite her cottage with such disfavour that her one ambition, frequently expressed, was that she might live to see them felled. She was always afraid that the wind might bring one down on her roof, so perhaps her animosity was in some degree excusable. Her ambition was gratified, but she only outlived the elms by a few months.

The elm's reputation for instability was also responsible for the pollarding, or rather stumping, of an old "cross-tree" in the village square at South Tawton, not for the first time in its history, since old parish records refer to payments for "steeping the elme upon the Crosse" in 1662. This tree— or possibly its successor, although there appears to be no record of its replacement—which now has a walled-in base, like others of similar designation, occupies the site of an ancient stone cross of which all trace has now vanished. A corresponding elm in Moreton Hampstead, known as the "Dancing-tree" and said to be three centuries old, was blown down in 1904, so perhaps the fears of South Tawton villagers were not altogether unfounded. The tree at Moreton obtained its name from the village custom of making holiday beneath its boughs, which were so sturdy that they once supported a small platform to accommodate musicians, and even one or two dancing couples.

As a curiosity, however, nothing equals the yew which has ornamented the tower of Culmstock church for 150 years. How its roots maintain their hold in the masonry or the tree draws nourishment is a mystery compared with which that of the Dartmoor oaks is simple. The Meavy oak, just mentioned, claims the distinction of being the oldest tree in the West, but antiquity is a point upon which individual priority cannot be established with any certainty. The story of an oak is often so long that while its end is obvious it has no recorded beginning. According to general convention the tree demands three centuries in which to grow, three centuries of mature strength and beauty, and three more are needed for the slow return to the mould which its own leaves have prepared for its reception. It is little wonder that oak-planting is regarded as a long-term policy, compared with which the inducement offered by larch or quick-growing fir appeals to speculators in timber. Few planters want to look as much as one century ahead when quicker returns are available. So the larch and fir are growing beside the stump of the felled oak whose seedlings are rooted up to make way for the alien, and in the future more and more conifers will darken the deep valleys in the place of their indigenous trees, but not before the suns of many ages have set will Devon's oaks have degenerated into a tradition.

Upon utilitarian as well as sentimental grounds the tree is irreplaceable. An oaken beam, an old oak chest, an oaken floor—the word stands for everything good in the way of timber. For a gate-post, granite or oak is the choice if durability is desired. Even as firewood it is unsurpassed. Ash and sycamore burn more brightly, but, whether green or dry, are consumed too quickly in the ardour of their own flame. Beech is good, but requires space, while ever-inflammable larch or pine discharges its sparks too freely over the carpet, or "spits," as the country-people say. Holly is bright but brief; birch, alder or willow characterless; but, as a

64

Shipping at historic Bideford, of Grenville fame

village workman recently remarked, "Give me dry oak."
Once ignited, its flame, like itself, is steady and sure, and
even as it is the longest lived of our woodland trees, so its
stout heart crumbles most slowly into the white ash which is,
in truth, the dust of ages.

BIBLIOGRAPHY

Land Utilisation Survey, Part 92: Devonshire.
Devon Association Transactions, LVIII, p. 299, G. T. Harris.

5   65

Devon's northern coast, looking towards Hartland

CHAPTER VI

HEDGEROWS

A TOPOGRAPHICAL review automatically resolves into two categories, the past and the present, and although Devon's vast hedgerow system is very much a feature of today, it is quite as certainly a relic of past conditions. Nobody erects a hedge now, that is to say, a hedge with a solid bank foundation after the old style. Even when making a new enclosure to surround a building site, for example, the fence is usually of wood or wire, or possibly a wall. A bank, if made at all, is only a diminutive affair to support an evergreen hedge. New field or wayside fences, again take the form of wire-rope or mesh, for the cogent reason that all such substitutes for the natural are more quickly erected and require less attention. In new countries, it must be remembered, there are no hedgerows, only interminable barbed wire, which, while serving its purpose in some respects, has its drawbacks. I remember an occasion in North-west Canada when a mob of cattle stampeded and carried away a quarter of a mile of such fencing in their headlong career. The remainder of the day was spent in shooting the lacerated animals. Colonials regard our hedges as one of the sights of England, and Devon's vast network is probably the most remarkable in the country.

The antiquity of this hedge system is proved by the frequent occurrence of the suffix *hay*, *hayes* or *hayne*, denoting a hedged enclosure, in Saxon nomenclature being mainly applied to old houses or farms rather than villages, which is consistent with the interpretation, since a parish embraces many enclosures. The most famous example, of course, is Hayes Barton, Raleigh's birthplace, both words being characteristic of Devon place-names. Others are Sheafhayne, Pithayne at Yarcombe, North-hay at Inwardleigh, Northernhay and Southernhay in Exeter, Hayne and Broadhayes at Stockland and Westhay at Hawkshead, these being representative of different parts of the county, throughout which numerous similar names occur.

The word *hawthorn* is derived from the same source, being simply the "hedge thorn," and it is interesting to find that country children in Devon still refer to haws as "haggles," "aigles" or "eagles," variations differing but little from the original Anglo-Saxon. By the same rendering a hag was nothing more than an old woman who sat under a hedge, and this is peculiarly appropriate, as Devon, the land of hedges, was also reputedly a hotbed of witches, representatives of which sisterhood were still indicated by their neighbours almost to the present date. But more will be said about them and their ways later.

The reasons for hedges in the first place were doubtless many, some obvious, others inconceivable. The great banks which run in straight lines for miles, although obscured by numerous interlacings, doubtless enclosed the largest intakes, and many of these form the parish boundaries of today. The expressions "single" and "double" banks are literally correct. A single bank is not only narrower but bears only one line of growth along its top. A double bank is several feet wide, with a flat summit along which, as is often said of Devonshire hedgerows, a "putt" or farm cart could be driven. Also, along each "coombe" or edge, a separate growth has been trained with an open space between, so that upon a double bank two distinct hedges grow. Double banks are not necessarily boundary fences, however. Upon some farms they are more or less general, and their original object remains a mystery, since even with labour cheap and plentiful, they serve no purpose that a single bank could not achieve and cover quite an unnecessary amount of land.

The single banks, as already stated, subdivided the larger enclosures and many of the small "plots" or "closes" adjoining the farmhouses were doubtless taken in for the same purposes that they still serve hundreds of years later. One of the most curious things is the irregular course that many hedges take, here and there executing turns, elbows and even hairpin bends for which no reason is apparent. Probably they were made to avoid obstructions such as big trees and rocks, or once formed junctions with other hedges that have disappeared; but whatever the solution, the serpentine effect remains. It is noteworthy that valleys are almost invariably more irregularly fenced than higher ground, the imputation being that the enclosures were made at odd times, which is quite conceivable, since the lower the land, the more thickly wooded. Most of the present woodland covers valleys, and would present clearing difficulties even now. One may safely assume that the more open ground was first taken in, and upon the largest scale. The wooded coombes were doubtless cleared piecemeal, upon the policy of least resistance, where the fewest trees grew, and odd patches were enclosed one by one. Some of the roughest were never cleared at all, but surrounded in time by other enclosures. Hence the patches of woodland which break the monotony of many valley landscapes.

A number of banks have, of course, disappeared within one's own time. At Itton, near North Tawton, I recently noticed a remarkable old hedge of enormous height, containing wood as heavy as much that is cut for timber. It no longer formed a fence, however, every vestige of the bank having worn away. The growth now rises from level ground upon weather-carved supports that once formed the roots, the latter having burrowed more deeply to secure fresh hold. The entire effect is like that of a grotesque and monstrous trellis-work, through the apertures of which sheep and cattle pass at will.

Big roots, needless to say, loosen all banks, thrusting out the soil which heavy rains ultimately wash down, for which reason periodical recasting becomes necessary. Indeed, in the case of those topped with hedges it cannot be said that the existing erections are the originals, except that the same old soil has been used for repairing them all down the generations. Rather, they are like ancient walls or buildings for which new material is occasionally required. While the roots of big wood loosen the soil, however, grass or heather binds and retains it. Upon ground formerly enclosed that has reverted to moor, the old banks may remain for a century or so with little alteration apart from slight subsidence.

As to the origin of banks, they were certainly thrown up or built, like cob walls, with soil dug out upon each side providing the material, the trenches thus formed being the ditches of today, for which three feet is the present allowance when determining boundaries. When ditches are cleaned the soil is still thrown on to the bank, and as an inevitable sequence, the deeper the ditch the higher the fence. The height of the banks above the surrounding level disposes of any question as to other than an artificial beginning, the main point of interest being the growth that surmounts them. Whether much of this was ever actually planted is open to doubt. Assuming the ground to have been more or less covered with coppice when the first enclosures were made, it is only reasonable to suppose that anything which helped to form a barrier or to keep the earth in place was allowed to remain, as it certainly would be by anyone doing the same job today. Also, while a certain amount of method was essential, the original banks could scarcely have been the neat institutions into which generations of careful attention have shaped them. The great idea must have been to build a serviceable barrier, and doubtless roots, stumps, seedlings and even fair-sized bushes, just as they were grubbed up, went on to the bank.

It remained for Nature to do the rest, as she always does. One knows how quickly any artificial mound becomes covered with wild growth, and thus even the big trees which stand upon so many banks originated. Procedure with regard to seedlings varies according to locality. Upon some estates there is a rule that when an old hedge is cut a sapling of some sort must be left at stated intervals. Now that the farmer-owner has become the rule rather than the exception, provision for the future with regard to hedgerow timber is less scrupulously observed. Even so, the preservation of saplings is a convention more or less prevalent among old-fashioned hedgers, and a considerable number survive.

In some highly cultivated districts the claims of agriculture take priority over all other considerations, and trees that border arable fields have either been felled or drastically pollarded. In the South Hams, for example, few trees of any kind are seen, and the fences are kept at the lowest possible level. The presence of so many crab-apple trees in old hedgerows is due in part to an old forest law of Norman times which forbade the felling or even lopping of this species since it provided "food for the roaming herds of deer." The "roaming herds" remain in some parts of the county, although, like the crab-apples, their distribution is now more limited, nor is the same solicitude apparent for either beasts or tree. The present representatives of both are survivals of greater abundance, and doubtless the deer of today prefer the crab-apple's cultivated successor, to say nothing of *pomme de terre*, which is particularly comforting to the cervine palate.

The modern hedge serves many utilitarian purposes probably never visualised by its originators. In those early days, with forest growth abundant everywhere, the idea of the hedge providing timber or even firewood could scarcely have been considered. Now upon many farms the hedges not only provide the only source of both these commodities, but they also supply gate-posts, fencing-poles, hurdle-stakes, "shackles" and material for the wraithe hurdle itself, spargads, bean and pea-sticks, and indeed material for the numerous demands inseparable from the ordinary course of farm and country life. In Devonshire, spar-gads, or sticks from which to make thatching spars, were of special importance when most buildings were thatched, and are still in considerable demand for ricks. Hurdle-wood, too, was frequently needed. Within my own time a Devonshire farm, as a matter of course, produced its own hurdles, which were made, this being highly skilled work, by the special hurdle-maker of the district, who went his round, as the threshing-machine does today, from farm to farm, remaining upon each place until he had completed the quota required. More than a quarter of a century ago I remember a man, then past middle age, but a master of his craft, who was probably the last hurdle-maker of this description in eastern if not in all Devon. He brought his own outfit, consisting of a long and slightly curved beam drilled with holes like the hub of a wheel to hold the hurdle uprights in place, and a small-sized billhook whetted to razor-keenness. He had no measuring apparatus other than his own eye, could "turn," i.e. twist, a stick an inch thick with one flick of his wrist, and used his sharp tool with hairbreadth accuracy. He had the reputation of "never hitting twice to two places."

For wraithe-hurdle making the wood was collected in advance, a considerable quantity being required upon account of wastage. Pliant wood was essential, thus restricting the selection to hazel, willow and oak of appropriate size. Even with all requirements studied, a waggon-load of brush might be required for a dozen hurdles. The pliable kinds are also needed for spars, since each must be twisted into hairpin shape, also again for hurdle shackles or the wooden rings which secure the laths to the stake. The more general use of gate-hurdles, carpenter-made, has removed one essential purpose which hedges served, otherwise their usefulness remains. Even hawthorn, unpopular as firewood, is required for "staddle," material used in making a damp-course foundation for ricks, and the demand is at its highest now that more ricks than ever before are built as more corn is grown. Indeed, as a source of many supplies there is nothing that could replace our hedges, and were the present campaign for their demolition carried to excess, subsequent shortage of many essentials is inevitable.

Without hedges there would be no wild fruits for the ripening of which the woodlands are too shady as a general rule. Appreciation of these revived under war-time conditions. Blackberries, for which 5d. per pound could be obtained, were never so keenly sought, rose-hips being also collected under the auspices of the Ministry of Food, although few country-people nowadays trouble to make use of them. Upon the contrary, sloes, which were freely gathered for sloe gin, have enjoyed a respite, since, in the words of one disgruntled old native who was partial to the beverage, "The bloomin' gin's too dear, yer honour." The age of the spindle-berry has also passed. From it dyes were extracted, red, green and yellow, curiously enough the exact colours of the spindle itself: the yellow seed, its red capsule and green foliage. The wood was also used to make hand-spindles for cottage wool-spinning and for the lace-making bobbins of East Devon.

Of all coppice-wood products, however, it is the hedge or hazel-nut which finds its way most surely to the countryman's heart. The taste is so general that it has developed into a convention, or one of several upon similar lines. The native

Devonian villager picks no wild flower except the "Lent lily," to gather which he will walk many miles. The sweet-pea is the pride of his flower garden, the kidney bean the vegetable over which most trouble is taken and the hazel-nut is the only wild fruit that he ever troubles to pick for himself. These are gathered literally by the sackful, on Sunday mornings as a rule, and every cottage doorstep is as thickly strewn with nutshells during the season as with confetti after a wedding. Each of two famous logan-stones, one in Lustleigh Cleave, the other on Rippon Tor, was known as the "Nutcracker," and to make the great rocks actually serve that purpose was once a favourite game with village youths and maidens who sought a pretext for a quiet walk. The normal Devonian prefers simpler crackers of Nature's own providing, and will willingly sacrifice his last tooth or even new dentures to a big hazel-nut.

The value of hedges for shelter is obvious from the frequency with which cattle avail themselves of it. The difference between the rough and the "loo" side becomes self-evident to anyone when hedgerow ferreting, and during the great blizzard of 1891 sheep which could huddle under high banks topped with beech or holly were left safe and dry upon open pasture, the drifts sweeping over them. In the absence of woodland or coppice, hedges also provide the principal protection to wild life, not only as nesting-places for numerous creatures, from partridge to dormice, but also for roosting cover. The number of conventionally woodland birds that nest in hedgerows is not perhaps fully realised. Magpies and woodpigeons like no place so well as an old hawthorn hedge. The wily carrion crow prefers a large hedgerow tree for strategic reasons, and a year later a kestrel, perhaps, may take possession of his abandoned nest. Sparrowhawk, buzzard and even the raven occasionally favour a hedgerow pine, while fox, badger and the otter at times take possession of burrows in wide banks. Countless small birds roost in holly hedges, which once provided scope for that unspeakable "sport" known as bird-batting which appealed so strongly to rustic youth only a generation or so ago. This was a "three-folk's-job," requiring a simple but specialised equipment. It consisted of a big stick, a bright lantern and a "batting-net," which was upon the lines of a butterfly-net, being a strip of fine mesh attached to two bamboo poles. One held the lantern so that its beams fell upon the net, which another manipulated, while the third beat the bushes on the farther side. The scared birds, attracted by the glare, fluttered straight into the net, to which all comers were fish. It was a simple and effective proceeding, now happily discouraged.

That hedge-banks are largely responsible for the abundance of rabbits in Devonshire is certain. Many are riddled with burrows, and where rabbits are abundant the banks need frequent repair, owing to the tireless excavations of the inhabitants, which if left to themselves would soon demolish their fortress. I can remember single banks which were completely levelled by rabbits within ten years or so. The rabbits kept pace with the subsidence by tunnelling deeper, the hedgerow burrows eventually becoming ground or surface holes, while in each case the top growth, which was mainly bramble, sank with the hedge and degenerated into a line of blackberry scrub on ground level. Even if made eligible for family allowances, however, the Devonshire rabbit must establish new records both for fecundity and industry before he materially decreases the county's vast hedgerow system, to realise the almost incredible extent of which it is only necessary to study a few figures relating to the subject.

The larger the farm the larger the fields, and therefore the fewer hedgerows. In Devonshire, however, really large farms are rare, and even upon these the fields cannot compare in size with those of some counties. In Hampshire, for example, a field, as distinct from a down, may comprise as much as 350 acres. Few Devon fields exceed thirty, and twenty would be considered a fair-sized enclosure, many entire small holdings amounting to no more. Actually, only twelve farms in the whole of Devonshire exceed 500 acres, and there are 162 from 300 to 500. Those between 150 and 300 acres number 1,787. Farms between 100 and 150 total 2,103, but by far the greater proportion of holdings in the county are between 5 and 100 acres, in all 10,536, while to this must be added 2,001 diminutive tenures not exceeding 5 acres.

These numerous little holdings are subdivided more often

than not into tiny fields or plots, and it is estimated that in some parishes a quarter of the enclosures are less than 2 acres in size, while a full third cannot aspire to the three-acre dignity. There are, indeed, moorland parishes of which single-acre plots are a feature. These lie close to the villages, one being attached to each house, and in the case of South Zeal, on the northern fringe of Dartmoor, which is a typical example, their numerous hedgerows projecting from the long straggling street suggest the backbone and ribs of an elongated fish when viewed from any of the surrounding hills. These are known locally as "Burough Acres," being survivals of a system the history of which is, to say the least, involved. It originated in Saxon times, when the borough took the form of an agricultural commune, rather than the municipal centre of today. It consisted of a large area, recognised by charter, and later, in Norman times, was often placed under the jurisdiction of a feudal lord, as in the case of Robert de Courtenay at Okehampton. In that particular division, anyone desiring the full status of burgher was obliged to take a "burgage holding" consisting of one enclosed acre. At Hartland the annual rent of such tenures was one shilling, the tenancy to continue "by the law of inheritance for ever." They were, however, transferable by the payment of a nominal fee, and in course of time changed hands frequently, and have now simply become the property of adjoining cottages, forming either tiny holdings in themselves or in conjunction with other fields. Their main interest in this connection lies in their contribution to the hedgerow system, and as an example of the limited enclosures into which many of the smallest holdings are divided.

A hundred-acre farm upon an average contains about 8 miles of hedges, and, since the proportion increases as the size of the farm or holding lessens, the total length of the county's fences if stretched in one line would encircle the world many times. It has been estimated that the hedges of all England and Wales cover 1,250,000 acres, and Devon's share of this almost incredible total, although difficult to compute, must be considerable. Actually, if compressed, they would constitute a fine forest, particularly if the extensions which they have made beyond their banks are taken into account. Upon semi-wild land or any that has passed out of cultivation, belts of coppice fringe many of the fences, even when the latter are kept sufficiently in repair to maintain boundaries or control the roamings of cattle.

As time proceeds these reclamations by the wild, if unchecked, creep by insidious stages over the gradually reverting enclosures, until the advance from opposite fences meets, and by this means many of our younger copses came into being. Latterly, the emergency demand for wood of any sort, even before the war, has done much to check this natural afforestation. Coppice wood is more easily cut than hedgerow growth and does not involve the necessity of remaking the fence. Enormous quantities have been chopped down in Mid-Devon, and this demand has been responsible for the levelling of much hedgerow growth untouched within living memory.

Once down, many of these old hedges will never be restored. Where banks have sunk the cost of re-digging them has become prohibitive, and when not indispensable their complete removal often facilitates the use of modern implements, such as tractors or hay-sweeps, for which larger fields are advantageous. Indeed, a considerable number have already been eliminated, and in all parts of the county one now sees barriers carefully preserved throughout many centuries being effaced by bulldozers and tractors within as many hours, to meet the changing standards and conditions. A bulldozer, working on a neighbouring farm last winter, uprooted two miles of superfluous hedge, at a cost of £50 to the occupier, who estimates that upon a long-term policy the expenditure will prove an economy, the very considerable problem of upkeep being thus settled for all time.

In the ordinary course of events a hedge is cut every ten years or so, apart from the annual paring or trimming. Once left, the growth is rapid. In the earliest stages three feet would be about the limit of a hazel shoot's growth in one season. Sycamore and ash mount somewhat faster, while beech, holly and oak are more deliberate. As the wood thickens the ascent is less rapid, and of course hedgerow growth that springs from "steeper" or laterals never reaches tree height, saplings independently rooted soon rising above

75

even sycamore or ash "broods" beside which they have developed. After reaching a certain level, the spread is outward rather than upward, and so develop those green tunnels into which old hedgerows, meeting overhead, once converted Devonshire's lanes—an effect now confined to secluded ways outside the scope of by-laws. They were picturesque, those overhung lanes, particularly when they took the form of cuttings between deep banks atop of which rose the pillars supporting the high green arch, so amply roofed that the sunbeams scarcely filtered through. Yet, artistic as they were, the countryside has gained rather than lost beauty through their passing. The deep banks remain, and where once lank grass or ferns alone could grow are now flower-borders, bright with primroses in spring, and tall foxgloves shedding their pink bells over the deeper pink of the soil as midsummer wanes. At this stage they bear a slight resemblance to the Pembrokeshire banks upon which no hedge has ever grown. To anybody accustomed to other conditions such a landscape seems featureless at first glance, like a stone-wall country. The banks of Wales, however, are relieved from monotony, at least during summer, by the profusion of wild flowers with which they are completely clothed, the effect when viewed from a distance or a height being that of a floral net spread over the fields. Devon's hedges even in foxglove time cannot achieve quite so lavish a display, but they possess one great advantage in that their beauty is almost perennial. After the wild roses have shed their delicate petals there follows the honeysuckle, and as the flowers fade autumn flecks the leaves with a light brush, as though to test the shades, applying bolder strokes of gold, crimson and purple, as oak and beech kindle into flame. Then, as the leaves fall, the hips, haws and spindle-berries redden, holding the stage until the holly has donned its scarlet. Even if less brilliant than woodless banks in summer glory, the pageant of the hedges is longer sustained.

Yet even the closely trimmed highways of Devon have not entirely lost their wayside greenery. There are still stretches along which the broad macadam runs between belts of scrub and woodland which have escaped enclosure, although here and there a low bank thrown up indicates an attempt to incorporate the wayside with the adjoining land, the enclosing fence of which stands ten or twenty yards back from the highway. Margins of this description may be seen on the main roads from Exeter to Okehampton, from Okehampton to Crediton, and from Hatherleigh to Bude, the ancient Brandiscorner oak standing, or rather leaning, beside one of these "ribbons" not yet developed. That future road-widening schemes will eventually lick them up is tolerably certain, the only wonder being that they have so long survived.

With regard to wayside legislation, the manner in which history repeats itself from varying angles is curious. In the reign of Edward I the law provided that no bush, ditch or anything that might afford cover to robbers should remain within 200 feet of a roadway. Now space providing clear vision must be allowed to facilitate fast traffic, while in place of the armed bandit is the rabbiting rustic's shotgun, which may not legally be discharged within 100 feet of the highway—a provision proved necessary by an incident within personal knowledge, when an enthusiastic "sportsman" mistook the tweed cap of a passing cyclist for a rabbit running along the hedge-top, and bringing off the best shot of his life, also brought off the cyclist. However, I have forsaken the hedgerow for the highway, which, together with other ways old and new, will require another chapter.

BIBLIOGRAPHY

Devon Association Transactions, LXV, p. 381, G. E. L. Carter.

CHAPTER VII

THOROUGHFARES

1. IN GENERAL

WITH the colonisation of any new country a system of communication develops automatically, access being inseparable from residence if any connection with the outer world is to be maintained. As settlement extends, the problem becomes more complicated. To every place in the world there is some approach, and this being connected with numerous other ways, the intricate maze of high roads and by-roads, lanes, bridle-paths and rights of way gradually evolves.

In the colonies a system of communication *precedes* settlement. When first surveyed for distribution or grant, the country is divided into square sections of 640 acres, between and around each of which is left a "road-allowance" 100 feet wide, which must not be enclosed. In this country settlement was gradual and irregular. Little clearings were made by the first husbandmen wherever ground seemed suitable, and approach to these followed the most convenient lines, avoiding difficult surface and enclosure fences, which, as they multiplied, in their turn followed the tracks for the dual purpose of establishing occupation and preventing cattle from straying or trespassing. So the network of lanes and by-ways developed, more irregular and complicated, but infinitely more picturesque, with their tree and hedgerow growth, than the formal system of the New World. That Devonshire, the home of big-banked hedgerows, should also have become the county of deep lanes with their associations of primroses, foxgloves, red campions and wayside fruits and blossoms, was inevitable, and a walk between these green and flowering banks is the first ambition of the visitor. He often loses his sense of direction in their intricacies, since, owing to the height of the hedges, landmarks are seldom visible. One lane is so much like another; turns are many and have an embarrassing way of bringing a stranger back to his starting-point.

Evidence that a similar difficulty in more serious form confronted wayfarers many centuries ago is found in the old stone crosses which not only marked the moorland tracks but stood at numerous points where in-country lanes converged, and probably indicated direct lines between settlements. Many have disappeared, particularly from the Moor, where anyone in search of granite shafts for gate-posts or building found it more convenient to appropriate something already adapted to his purpose than to split a rough rock into the required shape. Sentiment has preserved a larger number in the lowlands than might have been expected, nor is the temptation to remove them so great where timber posts are more easily available. The important light in which they were regarded, however, is apparent from the fact that the name of a cross that has disappeared usually adheres to its former site, although not necessarily a four-cross way.

In the neighbourhood of Okehampton a veritable maze of by-lanes intersects the countryside round the villages of South Zeal and South Tawton. Practically every intersection has its specific name: Oxenham Cross, Furzedown Cross, Moon's Cross, Spitlar Cross, Dishcombe Cross, Ringholt Cross, Ford Cross; and at many of these, witness to a long-gone age of piety when this emblem was an encouragement to the weary traveller, still stands the old stone cross, sometimes mutilated, sometimes obscured in a tangle of hedge-growth, sometimes carefully trimmed round, according to the outlook of the occupier responsible for the fences.

To describe a few of these, Oxenham Cross, low and solid, stands on the bank of a well-trimmed hedge at the four-lane junction. A quarter of a mile farther on is Ringholt Cross, placed where two lanes converge at the copse end. Moon's Cross—otherwise Mohun's Cross—is a mutilated stump in front of an old barn where lanes from South Zeal and South Tawton join. Half a mile farther again, at the four-way Zeal Head, formerly stood Townsend Cross, since destroyed, and in South Zeal itself a tall cross on a triple-tiered base, the head and arms being of more ancient date than the shaft. At

79

Addiscote Farm, less than a mile again from Oxenham, a small, low cross stands in a hedgerow, and the remains of yet another two are to be seen near the old Manor house of West Wyke, now a farm until recently requisitioned by the Army. All these are to be found within a square mile. Doubtless many more crossroads were formerly indicated thus, as in some cases records only remain of the vanished monument.

Not all the lanes by any means are thoroughfares. Some of the most curious and picturesque merely connect farm buildings with the fields which they serve, and were obviously made not so much to provide access as to prevent cattle driven along them from breaking over the crops on either side. Some of these are only wide enough to admit the passage of a cart, and were clearly intended for home use only. When connected with other equally obscure tracks or where links can be traced with older routes, a right-of-way usually exists, although difficulty in maintaining such has increased within recent times. Now that wheeled traffic has become so general, old field paths have fallen into disuse, and new occupiers of land—naturally enough from their point of view—endeavour to close them whenever possible. Admittedly, when the path invades domestic premises, it constitutes an affront to privacy. A right-of-way at Membury actually passes through a house by means of a "drain-way," or walled-in passage. Presumably the path existed before the house, and recognition of the right took this unusual form. There is also the perpetual nuisance of unshut gates. Lack of responsibility in this respect on the part of the general public is not a "farmers' grouse" but a genuine source of annoyance and even loss. The positive inability of many people to shut a gate which they have opened amounts to mental deficiency, and is scarcely credited except by those who suffer from it. Attempts to close a path, therefore, are not always unjustified, although clearly the remedy should not lie in that direction. In some cases obstructions are erected. In others mere discouragement is tried, as by omitting the replacement of a collapsed bridge, or repairing of stiles in a manner that makes them difficult to negotiate. In Devonshire there have been several recent attempts to close foot-paths, some resisted, others ignored. The legal position appears to be

A typical South Devon cove—Mothecombe

obscure, long usage being no guarantee that the right will be maintained. The county has no equivalent to the North-country "wynd" or "trod," that is, line of flag-stones often extending for many miles, the existence of which establishes right of passage even if somebody's doorstep forms one of the stones.

Disuse rather than closure or indirect opposition, however, has been responsible for the loss of many old ways, and more will disappear in course of time as improved communications are superimposed upon the primitive tracks to isolated dwellings. In this parish is a narrow lane, sunk in places, which passes through and once served a little farmstead, now ruinous. It joins two by-roads, but is never used, being a mere watercourse. During twenty years I have met nobody upon it, apart from the farmer who has taken over the land. If he chose to block it to prevent his cattle from straying, it is not likely that any objection would be raised, and this actually happened upon a somewhat similar track in South Tawton parish, the thoroughfare never being in question, but nobody wishing to use it.

There are many such lanes throughout the county, some-times called "throats," impassable to modern traffic, and in most cases foot-paths have become established following their courses, but inside the adjoining fields. Others that have become obsolete by blocking are the old "druff," drift or drove roads, which can be traced for miles, sometimes forming boundaries between holdings. These are curious ways, wider than ordinary lanes, sometimes, indeed, equal-ling a modern turnpike in breadth, but showing no trace of a prepared surface, and since they run perfectly straight for considerable distances, it seems probable that they were originally ancient tracks dividing intakes, like the colonial road-allowances, which actually they much resemble. A direct connection between these and lanes still in use is often apparent. For the most part they are completely derelict, however, serve no purpose, and have degenerated in long ribbons of coppice. Sometimes they are lost in cultivated land, reappearing in fragments here and there if their course is followed, and constituting a definite system over wide tracts of country.

6*

On the Exe—Topsham, once the thriving port of Exeter

Whatever purpose they served, one interesting feature of the drove-roads is that they are never "sunk" but always proceed on a level, thus differing from most of the old lanes and tracks, the depth of which is a frequent subject of discussion. If one takes the famous lanes of South Devon, with their gully-like banks, for examples, doubtless any excavations that took place were merely for the purpose of reducing gradients, a principle by no means peculiar to the county, although the multiplicity and extreme narrowness of the ways accentuate the effect. With the wear and wash of ages the depth increases, for not only is each lane a channel for surface water, but wheels and feet, which in time hollow a stone step, wear down these tracks as a river hollows its bed, and not until comparatively recent times was much "road metal" expended upon our by-ways. More natural material washed and wore away than was replaced, and deep lanes grew deeper. It is the work not of years but of centuries that must be taken into account, and when one sees the havoc that a few weeks of heavy traffic effects even upon a modern macadamised road, it is not difficult to imagine that the crude vehicles of the past churned the muddy lanes into pits and ruts which the next heavy rains carried downhill. Repair, when attempted, amounted merely to rough levelling of the kind still practised on Dartmoor lanes which extend beyond the liability of local councils. The humps are hacked off and roughly shovelled into the hollows, the way gradually deepening until bed-rock is reached. The gradual macadamising of all parish lanes has corrected further wastage, but anyone who remembers their condition even twenty years ago can picture their history without undue strain upon the imagination.

It is noticeable that old ways almost invariably kept to high ground, and if obliged to cross valleys, left them as soon as possible. This supports the supposition that the ridges were first cleared, or were never so encumbered with forest. Valleys were also unpopular for other reasons in the good old times, being more productive of "incidents." Even in the days of "chivalry" exciting events always took place at a ford. Nobody ever dreamed of lying in wait for the man he wanted on a hilltop, which offered too many chances of deferring an interview. At the bottom of a steep hill withdrawal was not so easy, and one cannot wonder that the users of old tracks disliked such places for many reasons. Very few of the regular ways followed rivers for any distance, although they took advantage of more open depressions, and the unnecessarily direct ascent of many steep slopes suggests a desire to get out of the difficult and dangerous woodland without undue delay.

Admitting provision for unpleasant contingencies, however, it is probable that the character of the ground was also largely responsible for the routes chosen. For example, from this village of Sticklepath the old pack-horse track linking Exeter with Okehampton tops the steep gradient known as Sticklepath Hill at a point 500 feet above the modern highway. To make the latter road, however, it was necessary to blast a passage through a shelf of granite which extends for some distance below the road in the form of a clitter, now obscured by wood growth and therefore unnoticed. The high elevation of the old track was doubtless due to this obstacle.

Effect is often more obvious than cause, and sound reason is seldom lacking for a seemingly pointless proceeding. One may assume that both Briton and Saxon recognised the principle that it is no farther round an orange than over it. Apparently, however, he was also aware that a ridge usually offers an easier path than a valley, being free from the innumerable wrinkles with which the feet of great hills are scored. Also it must be remembered that the primitive tracks made little provision for wheeled traffic, although Britons and Romans used crude carts mainly drawn by oxen. In general, one either walked or rode, and goods were transported mainly by pack-horses. Many of the old stone bridges over Dartmoor streams were built, according to general assumption, for pack-horse accommodation, in which case one can only suggest that the horse of that period must have been a more phlegmatic animal than his descendant, although tradition asserts that the later breed originated in a cross with a Spanish barb, survivor of an Armada wreck. Neither honour, glory nor cash would induce a present-day moorman to ride over one of them, and I have yet to see even a sure-footed mountain bullock essay the venture. Presumably the horses that used them, if any did, were unshod,

but hoofs if wet slip almost as readily as iron on hard sur-
faces, and setting aside the difficulty of getting on to the
bridge at all—an effort calculated to dislodge any load—
were the granite slabs either wet or frozen, the chances of
getting a weighted animal over and down the other side
without mishap do not strike one as overwhelming. For
goats or Scotch sheep—the goat's next of kin—they would
have been eminently suitable, but doubt as to their use by
horses is justified, and one would suggest that the convenience of man, not beasts, was the purpose for which they
were designed. Since the modern moorman and the fox-
hunter use the fords as a matter of course, it seems only
reasonable to suppose that a stolid old pack-horse, whose life
could scarcely have been conducive to excessive skittishness,
was capable of treading the same course, and it seems more
probable that the driver, if averse to water himself, first sent
his team through, possibly pausing on the bank to throw
stones at laggards, and then crossed by the slab bridge constructed for his species.

The pack-horse is the Druid of the ancient trackway, the
conventional user of anything to which no other purpose can
be assigned, and difficult must have been the ways trodden
by that much-enduring animal. Between the parishes of
Stockland and Membury, spanning the little Yarty river,
stands Beckford Bridge, scheduled as an ancient monument
in 1930, to which, when a child, I was introduced with an
assurance that it belonged to this particular category. It
is a narrow affair bestriding the stream like an inverted V,
my youthful reaction to it being awe at its antiquity and
sympathy for the unfortunate pack-horse which, if it did not
stumble on to its knees when mounting the stepless stair-
case, must certainly have accomplished the descent from the
apex in a sitting posture. Now, revisiting the bridge many
years later, it seems to provide an interesting exception to the
nothing without reason rule. Anyhow, whatever reason the
designers saw for its height and shape, other than the picturesque, has vanished with them. The object of an old-
fashioned straight-backed chair was certainly discomfort;
that of Beckford Bridge, maximum difficulty in ascent and
descent. Nor is the reason for its erection at all apparent. It is

too narrow for horse-drawn vehicles, which always negotiated the adjoining ford, where, since 1923, a modern iron structure safeguards the motor engine. A wooden foot-bridge such as that at Westwater, a few miles downstream, would have served the pedestrian, and it is difficult to see why so superfluous a trial should have been placed in the path of the pack-horse. A bridge of half the height would have saved everybody much trouble, and even if the probability of flood were taken into account, a deluge requiring such an elevation would have inundated the entire valley, rendering a bridge of little value, since only a strong swimmer could reach or leave it.

A somewhat similar but less exaggerated example may be seen at Peckisford (Pack-horse Ford) near North Tawton. This bridge, crossing the Taw, admits "one-way" wheel traffic and, though raised sufficiently to reduce the speed of a car to walking pace, was clearly built for general use. The need for this bridge, even in early days, is apparent, since it spans a bigger stream often in spate with Dartmoor water, and at one time doubtless bore much of the traffic to North Devon. The road which it carries also connects with the old highway between Plymouth and Exeter *via* Crediton, and the bridge must have been of considerable importance in the old system of road communications. It also lies upon one of the prospective new routes to link Torquay with the Bideford and Barnstaple district, and its destruction seems probable should this project materialise.

The pack-horse did not entirely pass with the period to which he belonged. Upon the contrary, pannier-work persisted in Devonshire and Cornwall much later than elsewhere. Writing in 1831 Moore in his *History of Devon* speaks of this method of transport as a "remarkable feature of the country," adding that the use of wheeled carriages "is now becoming gradually introduced." In certain remote districts of North Devon, however, where this form of carriage is particularly adapted to the precipitous-sided "mouths" that gash the coast every two or three miles, the pack-horse era survives today in modified form. There are places such as Welcombe, on the Devon–Cornwall border, where the postman still arrives on horseback and where a considerable amount of haulage is done by panniered donkeys. A comparatively new house in which we stayed was built entirely of stone brought by such means, and teams of donkeys at work might be seen at any time.

I remember one particularly picturesque little troop of five, encountered at Speke's Mouth, near Hartland, a few years ago. It was a warm June afternoon with a drowsy ebb-tide slowly receding from a low reef over which oyster-catchers rippled an intermittent chorus. Along the shore a faint blue haze shimmered, and the file of approaching donkeys, slung with panniers to hold sand, might have been a desert caravan proceeding along some sunny southern strand, the rich greenery of the background accentuating the impression. The little procession was in charge of a garrulous teamster, with whom my wife was soon engaged in conversation. The ass-conductor was nothing if not a facile talker, but he happened to be one of those who consider close proximity essential to any interchange of ideas. My wife, upon the contrary, preferred a reasonable space of at least three feet, and being suitably clad strategically backed towards a little tidal pool, followed foot by foot by the donkeyman, and when at last she took refuge in the water I fully expected to see him follow. His advance terminated with firm sand, but not his loquacity, and the conversation proceeded across a watery barrier, as between besieger and besieged, until the disappearance of the donkeys among the rocks eventually necessitated his withdrawal.

The famous Clovelly donkeys, although a survival of an older custom, have degenerated into a more or less artificial feature, like their contemporaries upon almost any populous beach. Upon Dartmoor, also, they are now seldom seen even drawing carts, and not for many years have they been used as turf-carriers, although many people still live who can remember the pollen-dusted processions trooping down from the moorlands in the purple dusk along the turf-tracks, since widened but only slightly, to accommodate the carts which superseded the panniers.

And now, having reached Dartmoor by means of the primitive pack-horse and donkey, it will be necessary to remain for a while in that land of ancient trails, which, if not

Devon's oldest thoroughfares, were busy trade routes long before roads as we know them had reached the West or the recorded history of our island had even begun.

THOROUGHFARES

2. IN PARTICULAR

THE story of Dartmoor's ancient ways does not necessarily begin on the rough tracks which are seen today, and along which a few peat-carts still rumble, although many of them are old enough and in some cases follow far older routes, while still serving present purposes. Little attention is paid to their upkeep nowadays, the modern roads constructed for artillery practice being used when possible, and generally speaking, the better preserved the surface of a track the older its date, since the ancient thoroughfares were often paved or raised to the dignity of crude causeways when traversing bogland.

Possibly "paving" is too ambitious a term for the rough-and-ready principle adopted by the pioneer corps of the past. Sometimes the process involved little more than removing top soil from the naturally flat rock. Even now, when heath fires consume the surface turf one may walk for considerable distances over granite slabs as flat and almost as smooth as the paving upon many primitive causeways, the ground lying between Brook Hill and Cosdon Beacon providing a typical example of this. With the difficulty of transporting material so obvious, it is improbable that much superfluous labour was undertaken. Through peat country most of the tracks run deep, but whether actually "cut" at any time or merely hollowed by use is a debatable point. Anyone familiar with the ranges knows how quickly tracks are worn by cattle daily driven from the danger-zone. They instinctively take the easiest line along the hillside, and the paths which they make sink rapidly. This applies to the crossing of streams or old leats used in the ordinary way. Even sheep make passages which every storm deepens, and one need only observe cattle-tracks through fields to realise the channelling that hooves can accomplish. Teams of pack-horses and tramping companies of men inevitably furrowed the ground over which they passed year after year and century after century. A path once marked was naturally followed, for it is always easier to tread in another's steps, and once a track is made on the Moor it becomes a course for the surface water which sweeps down it in a torrent after every storm. Anyone who has seen a moor track after heavy rain, channelled as it often is to the depth of several feet, ceases to wonder at the origin of "sunken ways." The deepest tracks are always found on gradients, and the steeper the incline the more pronounced the cleft. Along high ground the tracks are comparatively shallow, which discountenances the theory that the ways were purposely sunk to confine driven animals within their bounds. Upon open ground the need for such a precaution would have been greater, nor would it arise upon a rough hillside over which few beasts would evince any disposition to stray.

There are few older thoroughfares than those which traverse Dartmoor in every direction, some still in use today, many lost because not required under changed conditions. It is somewhat remarkable that the main modern roads which now cross the Moor, intersecting at Two Bridges, ignore the routes marked out as the best by wayfarers of long ago. The Great Central Trackway was the principal trade route crossing Dartmoor from Tavistock to Exeter in pre-Roman times, and it has been assumed that a branch from Exeter through Chudleigh connected it with the Romanised Fosse-way. Across this "road," a matter of some 38 miles in all, trudged pack-horse and pedestrian, following the flagstones where visible and, in later years, the crosses or other indications in the way of standing stones set up for guides when snow or mist obscured familiar landmarks. Stepping-stones facilitated the crossing of fords before *clappers*, that is, single slabs or the more recent *cyclopean* bridges composed of two or more spans—the "pack-horse" erections already discussed—made their appearance. The first real stone bridge over the Tavy, the most formidable stream intersecting the route, was not built until the end of the thirteenth century, and wet feet must have been the least inconvenience often suffered. By this way went the streamed tin, sometimes carried, according to tradition, by dog-packs harnessed with minute panniers, to the important tin town of Tavistock, which at a later date was also a centre of wool trading on the western side of the Moor, corresponding with Exeter on the east. Sacks of wool from moorland fleeces passed from interior points to either of these great markets.

Portions of this ancient way, clearly indicating its general direction, have been traced from Heatree Down, in Manaton parish, across Hameldown, through Postbridge due east between the two Dart rivers, eventually emerging round the flank of Cocks Tor to Peter Tavy. It is a curious reflection that the traveller crossing the open Moor in those remote days found it a far more populous region than does the rambler of our own time, for several of the ancient hut villages and enclosures, especially in the neighbourhood of that "ancient metropolis" Postbridge, lay along its route, while tin-streamers were active in practically every valley, and in later centuries probably made use of the huts abandoned by early dwellers.

South of the Central Trackway between the Cistercian abbeys of Buckfastleigh and Buckland ran the Abbots' Way, shorter by some ten miles, yet playing an important part in the central communications of the Moor. It must have been a wild way even in those days of "congested" moorland traffic. Leaving the wooded valley of the Dart, it forded the Walla at its confluence with the Avon, and passing Huntingdon Cross proceeded by a well-defined line to Whitaborough Cairn, where Petres Cross then stood, and thence over the Redlake and the miry waste of Erme Head to Broad Rock, and onwards towards the Plym, before reaching which stream the track divided. The western branch proceeded to Marchant's Cross and over the Meavy to Buckland, while the other diverged slightly northwards by way of Siward's or Nun's Cross to Merivale, forded the Walkham, and keeping north of Vixen Tor climbed the hill to Windy Post or Beckamoor Cross, and so over Whitchurch Down, finally descending the steep incline to the Tavy and Tavistock, which was then a Benedictine settlement.

This route, linking three centres of learning and merchandise, was doubtless freely used and must have been the scene of monastic "ways" in more than one sense. Indeed, the approaches to Tavistock might well have illustrated Tennyson's road to Camelot, along which passed every type of traveller from the worthy abbot on his "ambling pad" to the more ambiguously depicted "curly shepherd lad" or, what is more probable though less romantic, the hillman mounted on his rough cob attended by two or three even shaggier wolfish dogs, man and beasts differing little from their representatives of the twentieth century. One can imagine, too, the little companies of dark-robed Cistercians or russet-gowned Benedictines conducting their sumpter horses laden with rich merchandise, and possibly a little interim refreshment. Along the rough hillsides passed the processions, jovial or solemn according to circumstances, the long, hard way doubtless providing ample opportunity either for meditation or community singing. It must often have been a case of "Amidst the storm they sang," and if the good brothers were as portly as tradition has pictured them, speed was not the main feature of their progress along the Abbots' Way.

This track is also known as the jobblers' or wool-traders' path, which alternative name suggests a more generally commercial than monastic use of the way. The frequency of crosses has no necessary connection with the three religious establishments, some being possibly of earlier date, and Crossing expresses doubt that the Benedictines of Tavistock ever used the Abbots' Way, although suggesting that Siward's Cross was intended to mark the boundary of the Abbey lands. Its antiquity is assured, however, since it is mentioned as a Forest Bondmark in the Perambulation of 1240.

More formidable in every respect than either the Great Central or the Abbots' track was the grim trail known as the Lych Way or Path of the Dead, along which, using Postbridge as the main centre, coffins were borne from any point within the southern Forest boundaries for interment at Lydford, this being the only burial ground within the vast parish, and therefore the only one available to parishioners.

Fearsome almost beyond belief must have been that journey over the desolate and sinister land, with the sphinx-like grey rocks ranged like perpetual mourners beside the trail, age-long recorders of every melancholy procession upon which their cold gaze had fallen; no sound save the raven's croak or the stumbling steps of the mourners "as silent and slow they followed the dead," and before them mile after toilsome mile of rock and mire and flood.

The most terrible part of the journey must have been its length, since even with Postbridge as its starting-point the slow march could scarcely have been accomplished in less than eight hours in good weather and as much as fifteen in bad, when frequent detours were unavoidable. This must often have necessitated setting forth by the light of a flying winter moon, or the even more eerie and less effectual beams of storm-lanterns flashing like will-o'-the-wisps along the way. The most imaginative story-teller, from Scheherazade to Edgar Allen Poe, certainly never pictured a scene more wild and weird, and when the death-white mist crept down from the heights and wrapped the cold wide Moor in its spell of unreality and stillness, all the phantoms of Wistman's Wood must have mingled with the procession, the unearthly character of which no ghostly acquisition could accentuate.

Even when given long summer days and freedom from the mists which are liable to occur at any time of year, the task must have been stupendous. The West Dart, the Cowsic, the Walkham and the more turbulent Tavy intersect the way, and Dartmoor herself, the "cruel Dart's" more savage mother, is seldom kindly. The practice was merci-fully discontinued about 1260, when Bishop Bronscombe, hero of the loaf-and-cheese legend, sanctioned burial at Widecombe as an alternative, being himself, perhaps, no stranger to the hardships of moorland travel.

Besides these main routes, countless by-ways intersect the Moor, the greater number now reclaimed by heath and bog through lack of use. An outstanding survivor is Cut Lane, which connects Postbridge with the Fur Tor area and the wilds of Ammicombe Head. There is also the track which, starting from the northern slope of Cosdon Beacon, skirts Raybarrow Mire and Little Hound Tor, and proceeding

91

along the western flank of Wild Tor, is lost for a while in the peat wastes of Ox Head, but reappears to reach Hanging-stone and the White Horse, there linking up with the Post-bridge and Cut Lane systems. The Kingsway from Oke-hampton to Tavistock *via* the West Okement, Corn Ridge, Great Nodden and the Rattle Brook, is now too broken by intakes and workings to be of much service, and has yielded precedence to a more northerly route from Moorgate along the High Willhayes range, past Dinger, Lints Tor and Great Kneeset to the head waters of the Tavy. This, after leaving the artillery road on Dinger, becomes a formidable path, little trodden except by the moorman's pony, and not recommended to the stranger. Black Lane, threading the bogs of the Plym, Erme and Avon, and so affording access to the grassy Fox Tor slopes, is perhaps the best known of the southern cattle tracks, but these are so numerous in every direction that a comprehensive list would require a special guide-book complete with map. William Crossing describes 81, over the greater number of which the lark now sings unheard, and even this elaborate list would no longer suffice. During more recent years the extension of the artillery-range and military activities generally over various parts of the Moor have blazed new tracks and lengthened old, and with other utility schemes in view the moorways of tomorrow may differ considerably from those of today.

Paths that can be clearly traced from a mountain top frequently fade into the heath when sought at their own level, for which reason a methodical survey from the air might re-establish many lost links. The important part that the Moor and its wild ways once played in Devon country life is manifested by the number of in-country lanes that converge upon it, like the spokes of a wheel upon the hub. Between Okehampton and Chagford, for example, seventeen roads or lanes, irrespective of foot and bridle-paths, form definite lines of approach, each providing its own means of access. Characteristic was a signpost which, until removed for national defence reasons, stood at the junction of one lane with the main Exeter to Plymouth road near Whiddon Down. This post bore not the names of two hamlets through which the lane passes but the somewhat comprehensive ter-

minus "Dartmoor." However, fascinating as are these moorland by-ways, where the heather pollen drifts over "metal"
that man-made tools never laid, I have none the less lingered
too long upon their quiet stretches. The roads by which most
of our traffic crosses Dartmoor today are very different in
character and of a more permanent type, although as yet
they have no history.

The first macadamised road that crossed the Moor, from
Moreton Hampstead to Tavistock, was completed in 1792,
and this, like other great trunks, has since thrown out many
branches. The older roads, bad as they were, and the stage-
coaches which laboured along them, left the Moor severely
alone, although its icy breath must have chilled many
passengers as they met the hill wind's sweep along Whiddon
Down and Firestones Ley. As one of the first Devon General
motor buses drew up alongside the Royal Hotel at Crockernwell, the oldest passenger, a native of Throwleigh, casually
remarked, "Here we used to change coach-horses," and with
the words the years rolled back and the past became the
present. The stage-coach had gone indeed, but the railway
which supplanted it has also seen its heyday and the road was
recovering its own to an extent entirely unanticipated.

Crockernwell was an important posting-house in the days
when coaches carried the mails, the first of which were thus
brought from London to Devonshire about 1785. Prior to
this date, they were carried, like everything else, by post-boys
on horseback, the "through service" from London to Plymouth being conducted in this way. In the second year of
Queen Victoria's reign London mails from Exeter first went
part way by rail, being transferred from coach to train at
Basingstoke. Passenger travel to Exeter was still continued
by road as late as 1841. About this period, immediately
before the general extension of railways, seventy coaches left
Exeter daily for various parts of the country, including one
seventeen-hour connection with London. This mail coach
postal service, when fully developed, was faster than might
have been supposed, being a matter of fourteen hours between
London and Exeter, and thirty-eight hours from London to
Devonport, an interval for the passing of one night in Exeter
being allowed. This was a marked improvement upon the

time schedule of twenty years earlier, when a "machine" plying between Exeter and London required two days for each run. Road services ran prior to the mails, however, two of the earliest recorded stage-coaches being from London to Exeter in 1658, a four-day journey, and another before the end of Elizabeth's reign from Exeter to Plymouth.

Considering the state of the roads, the pace achieved by the coaches was little short of break-neck. The first motor buses in Devonshire averaged little more than 12 miles an hour, compared with which the seven hours required by the coach to reach Plymouth from Exeter seems quite creditable. Sheldon in *From Trackway to Turnpike* gives an amusing account of the two rival coaches *Subscription* and *Defiance* which in an effort to outpace one another on the Exeter to London journey in 1831 attained a record of 13 miles an hour, though *Subscription* ran into a flock of sheep and several horses died from the effects of the race. "Speeding" was not unknown, apparently, even in those days.

Actually, anyone familiar with West-country roads as recently as the beginning of the present century can only wonder that coaches were able to run at all. The roads were better in the time of the Romans than a thousand years later, when their upkeep had devolved mainly upon the monasteries or the lords of the various manors. This state of affairs existed until the reign of Mary, when the work was relegated to the parishes through which the ways passed, the parishioners being required, as a form of rate, to provide the necessary labour. Such conditions must have been very similar to those which prevail on the Dartmoor lanes of today, the farmers who use them occasionally tipping a load of rubbish into a hole which has overturned a cart, or throwing weeds from adjoining intakes over the nearest boundary wall, under the pretext that they will "make surface." Neither the Act passed by the Commonwealth nor any other of the thirty or more executed for road improvement altered the position appreciably, and it was not until Macadam's period that much was effected. So bad had roads become throughout the kingdom generally that the first Turnpike Acts were passed in 1706 as a remedial measure. Although the enterprising Bideford Bridge was increasing its mys-

terious revenues by levying tolls as early as 1712, it was
another forty years before the rest of Devonshire realised its
road responsibilities, and then Turnpike Acts for the various
districts followed one another in quick succession. Progress
was so rapid that the year 1820 found Exeter employing the
great Macadam himself as Road Surveyor, with such beneficial results that within little more than ten years the
seventy coaches were plying along the network of roads
converging on the city.

This doubtless involved an expenditure of labour and
money which, judged by the standard of the times, must have
seemed revolutionary. What the authorities of those days
would have thought of the present road system and its cost
can easily be imagined. In the year 1944 the Devon County
Council presented its special War Economy Road Estimate
of £591,668, coupled with the announcement that a considerably larger figure would be needed to meet the cost of
projected improvements. As to the future of our roads upon
such lines it would be idle to speculate, but one calls to mind
a drawing in *Punch*, depicting a sky black with aircraft above
a vast, empty highway along the centre of which an aged
countryman trundles a wheelbarrow. *Punch*'s caricatures
frequently prove prophetic.

How much Devon's oldest highways owed to the Romans
is a topic of endless controversy. Probably any which they
made followed the line of still more ancient tracks, even as
many new motor roads follow them today, detached fragments of the former thoroughfare remaining here and there,
like guiding lines not yet rubbed out on a design. Upon the
problem of Roman roads such as the Icknield and Fosse
Ways even archæologists of the highest order disagree. The
late Mr R. N. Worth once remarked that the more diligently
he pursued his researches the farther he got from any definite
conclusion, and it is improbable that full agreement will ever
be reached. It seems more or less certain, however, that
Devon was originally served by two trackways which,
entering the county, one from Castle Neroche, in Somerset,
the other *via* Axminster, touched at Honiton, the Icknield
Way diverging to take in Hembury Fort, and swinging back
to resume contact with the more direct road to Exeter at

Straightway Head, near Whimple. From Straightway Head to Exeter they followed a united course until Exe Bridge. Then the Icknield Way proceeds over the Kenn Brook to Little Haldon, where its manifestly British character becomes apparent in many old sunken sections, such as the *Hollow Way*, some of these having certainly been offshoots from the main track. The latter, having reached the summit of Little Haldon, formed a clear connection with the earthworks there and those much farther south on Milber Down, after fording the Teign at Kingsteignton. It then passed along Beacon Hill to reach Totnes, which it crossed from east to west, claiming priority in antiquity over the ancient town itself, preceded only by Exeter and Lydford in order of seniority. This statement remains, of course, open to challenge from other venerable boroughs, each claiming a market-town status while "fuzzy down" still occupied the present sites of its rivals.

The conjectured line of the Fosse Way pursued more or less the same course from Exeter as far as Sandy Gate, where it is thought to have diverged, crossing the Teign at Teign Bridge to reach Totnes by way of Newton Abbot. Mr R. N. Worth held that the Fosse branched near Chudleigh, to mount the high ground and merge with the Great Central Trackway of Dartmoor. A branch is also supposed to have diverged to Axminster and Axmouth, and Joce traces a third north-western line of the Fosse, crossing the rivers Yarty, Otter, Culm, and the Exe near Bickleigh, to Cadbury Fort. From thence it went past the ancient Copplestone Cross, over the Yeo to reach the outskirts of Dartmoor at Fatherford under Ashbury Camp. Hugging the fringe of the Moor to Lifton, the Way then crossed the county border *en route* for Launceston.

As all roads lead to Rome, so most Devonshire roads, ancient and modern, seem to have converged on Exeter as the hub of the western universe. A third Roman or Romanised road, the Port Way, bore down upon Isca Damnoniorum by way of Willand, Cullompton and Bradninch, before pursuing the usual southward course over Haldon across the Teign to Totnes.

Another British way which served the southern part of the

county ran through Stockland, Farway and Chinway in East Devon, and so down to the Teign estuary. Here, about fifty years ago, its existence as an established right of way occasioned a lawsuit, won by the Newton Abbot Rural Council, upon the grounds that the "Way," little more than a mile in length, was an ancient road to which the public had right of access. With this brief revival from the past, the old trackway's route sank once again into obscurity, being with difficulty traced across the lower reaches of Dart, Avon, Erme, Yealm and Plym, at Staverton, South Brent, Ivybridge, Lee Mill Bridge and Plympton respectively, until, true to type, as a deeply channelled lane, it vanishes, as far as this county is concerned, over the Tamar estuary at Saltash Ferry.

By a whimsical turn of Fortune's wheel, with road improvement and its beneficial effect upon coaching conditions, came the railways, to oust the horse-drawn coach from the main roads for ever. It was ironical yet characteristic of Devonshire that the first rail should have been laid upon Dartmoor, mainly owing to the efforts of Sir Thomas Tyrwhitt, whose progressive activities have been applauded or anathematised by county historians according to each writer's point of view. This line ran from Plymouth to Princetown, a distance of 24 miles, and horse supplied the motive power. It must have been little more than a horse-tram, but its opening in 1823 took the form of a triumphal pageant, with band, procession and, needless to add, a gargantuan feed, provided by Sir Thomas upon Roborough Down of all places. This venture preceded the first steam train from Bristol by 22 years, the latter city being then the railway terminus. A year later Newton Abbot's claims were recognised, but nearly another century was required to complete the rail service now in existence, and prosperity had already departed from the railways when the final link between Halwill and Torrington was offered to public patronage.

Two main lines now traverse the county, but even as much of Devon still lies remote from arterial highways, so extensive areas, particularly in the north, remain untouched by the iron way. Of all inhabited districts in England, Hartland is farthest from a railway station, actually 15 miles,

7   97

On the smooth lower reaches of the Dart at Stoke Gabriel

and there are many villages the silence of which has never been broken by the scream of an engine whistle. Employed in this house at the moment is a little sixteen-year-old Devonshire maid who, as my wife recently discovered, has never boarded a train. "But I've *seen* one, madam," she added, anxious to remove any back-number implication. "It came into Okehampton Station when I went to meet my sister, and nearly knocked me down." And even more remarkable instances of village life circumscription might be cited. The same maid happens to be a great-niece of our old carpenter, many of whose sayings and doings find subsequent place in these pages. Their respective homes are scarcely a mile apart, but neither was aware of the other's existence until, meeting over the teapot in our kitchen, the identity of surname led to genealogical research and establishment of relationship. This does not support the convention that country-people are too well acquainted with one another's affairs.

BIBLIOGRAPHY

Devon Association Transactions, XLIII, p. 262, T. J. Joce; XLVI, p. 299, T. J. Joce; XVII, p. 345, R. N. Worth.
From Trackway to Turnpike. Gilbert Sheldon.
Guide to Dartmoor, Part V. William Crossing.

CHAPTER VIII

SANDSTONE, GRANITE AND COB

As MIGHT be supposed in the case of a county whose natural features are so varied, the geological history of Devonshire is almost as diversified as her scenery. Within her boundaries lies the most extensive granite formation in southern Britain, comprising in a broken line Lundy, the great Dartmoor elevation, Drake's Island in Plymouth Sound and the Eddystone Rock. This line intersects the extensive culm area of North Devon and the Devonian rock which bounds the Moor on the south, and occurs again in the extreme north corner of the county.

Along the south coast, roughly from Torbay to the Axe and inland up the Teign, Exe, Otter and Axe valleys, lies the New Red Sandstone, varying in quality according to localities, but comprising upon the whole the finest area of "red-land," as it is locally termed, in England. This extends as far north as Tiverton and Burlescombe, with a tongue some nine or ten miles wide, but narrowing towards the west, thrusting into the heart of the county, where it ends abruptly at Exbourne. West of Torbay, bounded on the north by the granite and lying between the Teign and the Tamar on the Devonian rock—which here, however, is subject to considerable variations—is the eminently fertile district usually defined as the South Hams, covering the county's southern extremity. East of the Axe is soil of yet another character in which limestone predominates with an occasional outcrop of chalk, as at Beer, Membury and Chardstock. Except in the Axe valley this is in the main a hilly country, with shallow soil and excrescences of a white or grey quartz which residents classify under the comprehensive name of "blue flints." These lie so thickly over the fields that they impede ploughing by frequently breaking the shares, while there is land upon which a sheep-fold can scarcely be pitched owing to the difficulty in driving stakes

99

or even making holes with a crowbar. So numerous are these stones that within my own memory they provided the road metal for the district, being bought from the land-occupiers for about one shilling a load. Even so, the supply exceeded the demand, and upon any waste spot one might see huge piles of surface stones which had been gathered off the fields and dumped wherever space permitted, there being no other use for them.

Limestone occurs sporadically throughout the county, but is most abundant in the east and south, Beer, Chudleigh and Oreston being quarries producing the best material, though Oreston is now mainly worked for marble. Limestone is also found in the Ilfracombe district, but only sparsely in central Devon, although extensive quarrying was carried on at Drewsteignton, South Tawton, Meldon and Sourton until about the beginning of the present century. There is none upon Dartmoor, where the granite region covers about 225 square miles, all bordered by the culm—a grit, shale and sandstone composition—which meets the Devonian rock at Tavistock.

Nothing indicates the approach to the granite area more definitely than the villages of grey moorstone, as granite is called when used for building purposes. Typical also are the stone posts of one sort and another there seen in general use. The village of Postbridge is supposed to derive its name from the pillars which support the old cyclopean bridge across the Dart, and anywhere in the Dartmoor country the gate-posts will almost certainly be granite slabs roughly split from the great rocks which strew the hillsides. Until comparatively recent times, or before the matter was taken up by the authorities, many of the old circles and other monuments were depleted for this purpose—a matter upon which Baring-Gould expressed himself very strongly. It was due in a great measure to his efforts that vandalism of this description has practically ceased, and although occasional lapses occur, the slabs are cut for the most part from the crude rock, the ring of crowbar and chisel being one of the most familiar sounds on any accessible slope. When it is a case of buying, granite and oak posts are about the same price, although a hundred years ago oak cost nearly double.

Stone gate-posts, of course, possess the advantage of being virtually everlasting, their one drawback as compared with wood being a tendency to snap at any sharp impact, such as a blow from a cart or lorry wheel. Their advantages are so obvious, however, that in view of improved modern transport and the inevitable scarcity of timber in the near future the demand for them is likely to increase. The easier distribution of these posts was one of the arguments advanced in support of the suggested railway from Okehampton to Bideford in 1831, the first steam line proposed for Devon and actually the last to be constructed about a century later, and even then by a more circuitous route. With rail and lorry service now available to accelerate delivery, however, it is probable that in future quarried rather than surface stone will be used to supply other than purely local demands. Surface blocks not only require detaching entirely by hand labour, but often lie at altitudes or among surroundings unapproachable even by carts, the most accessible having been removed as long ago as about 1790, when granite quarrying first began in the Dartmoor area.

The granite country is also necessarily the district of stone walls and rubbing-posts, which become less frequent as the distance from the Moor increases. These curious old posts, standing like lone pillars or menhirs in the centre of many fields, have outlived the story of their erection, but the extent to which sheep and cattle still appreciate them certainly justifies the effort which sturdy workmen of long ago must have expended upon fixing them. In the case of the old stone walls, one is often impressed at the enormous size of the blocks used. Even if collected in the immediate vicinity, the task of getting them into place must have been stupendous. Slabs weighing five or six hundredweight are not unusual, and since many of them were brought down from the hills where they were first loaded into carts, they speak well for the strength and industry of our village forefathers. Stone shifting, like other rural accomplishments, is an acquired art. Some years ago, aided by an old moorman I was digging a gravel-pit and at the same time extracting rockery stones. We unearthed a boulder so large that I despaired of getting it out, and more to console myself than anything else, pronounced it too big for the rockery. At this my companion's face expressed eloquent disapproval, and with the counter-assertion "He's a *proper* stone, sir," raised it in his arms and, to my astonishment, threw it up from the pit. This art is evidently peculiar to the older generation, however. When, comparatively recently, part of an old wall was temporarily removed for the erection of telephone posts, it was rebuilt by the workmen of today with stones of insignificant size, the original monsters being discarded by the roadside, where they still remain.

The granite formation of Dartmoor constitutes, perhaps, the greatest natural wonder of the West, many of the tors whose quaint structure is so largely taken for granted by the sightseer being in truth fantastic monuments of Nature's carving. Time, aided by the indefatigable forces at his command—the frosts, winds and rains of countless centuries—is a grotesque and versatile sculptor, and whatever appearance the lofty summits of Dartmoor once presented, he has been at infinite pains to fashion the peaks after his own bizarre fancy. The curious lamellar formations which almost suggest deliberate building by giant hands are due to slow weathering of the granite, the softer layers of which waste away with the wear of ages, leaving the horizontal strata and great blocks of perpendicular rock which in their turn either stand in castellated form, or fall, as many must have done, according to the extent or durability of their foundations. The most remarkable example of a vast rock erection which fell from inability to support its height is Fur Tor, once probably the highest as it is still one of the most impressive of Dartmoor's granite excrescences.

Evidence of the collapse is as unmistakable as in the case of a wind-snapped tree at whose base lies the detached top. Once it catches the eye the effect is inescapable, and the grand tor acquires a dilapidated appearance quite unlike the ordinary aspect of a rock pile. That the thunder of the fall was heard by any human ear is improbable. Certainly no pen recorded it, but judged from Dartmoor standards, where time is reckoned in centuries rather than years, one would suggest that the collapse occurred at no remote date. Viewed sideways, Fur Tor presents a striking resemblance to a man's face with peaked cap and short beard, suggesting an old-fashioned sea-captain—an appropriate sentinel to over-look the vast landscape bounded by Plymouth Bay and the southern sea.

A human countenance in rough cast may often be traced upon Dartmoor rock formations. Lints Tor is the Janus of the northern Moor, one stern profile scrutinising the long gorge of the West Okement, while the other keeps perpetual watch over desolate Black Ridge and the great wastes of Cranmere. The grotesque pile known as Bowerman's Nose is topped by a combination in which fancy traces an ape-like jowl, also capped. Vixen Tor offers a remarkable natural representation of the Sphinx, if viewed from the correct angle, and other fanciful suggestions strike the imagination on every side. Waterton Tor, resting longitudinally on its narrow ridge, bears a curious likeness to a battleship, and the four monsters on Staple Tor might be construed to depict almost anything that an imaginative brain could devise. Although outside the Devonshire boundaries, in this con-nection it might be interesting to mention that the famous Cheesewring, near Liskeard, was once seriously regarded as an example of Druid workmanship, representing the god Saturn—yet another addition to the long list of charges brought against a much libelled sect.

The highest elevation reached by the granite upheaval is 2,039 feet, at High Willhayes, upon the great ridge of which Yes Tor with its sharp, craggy summit (2,028 feet) is the most conspicuous feature, not so much from the actual Moor, where intersecting hills frequently obscure higher points beyond, but from North Devon generally, Cornwall and parts of Somerset. From the eastern side great Cosdon (1,799), though surmounted by no tor, is a pronounced landmark, while from the central Moor and Southern Devon, Hay Tor Rock or Rocks, as the double-fanged excrescence should more appropriately be styled, is perhaps the most noticeable as well as the most recognisable point. Hay Tor, though neither high (1,491) nor remote, is one of the most popular of the 160 tors. Once, when disparaging its advan-tages upon account of its publicity, I was corrected by an old lady who assured me that it was "at least ten minutes' walk from the main road." Overrun as it is, however, Hay Tor is an interesting pile, like its neighbour, Hound Tor, whose fantastic array of crags, supposed to resemble canine heads, gave rise to the name. The actual tors, it might be remarked, add comparatively little to the elevation of the hills. Although sometimes precipitous or difficult to climb on account of projections, few reach any considerable height. Mr Hansford Worth, who has added this to his many exhaustive researches, gives the height of Bowerman's Nose as only 26 feet, although previously described as 50 feet, while Vixen Tor, the highest rock pile on the Moor, and classified as 110 feet, he found to be 93 on the south side, facing the slope, and 52 on the north. The elevation of Yes Tor, I might add, has risen within personal experience. Clearly, therefore, statistics are not the most reliable things in the world—at least, one hopes not.

Logan-stones are not numerous, and these in course of time cease to rock, partly from natural causes, such as loss of balance or the silting up of cavities, and in some cases through activities suggested by the tripper's peculiar sense of humour. Concerning vandalism of this kind on Dartmoor my authority is secondhand; but once near St David's Head in Pembrokeshire I found a famous "logging stone" firmly wedged by thin flints, driven so deeply between the rocks that its chance of ever logging again seemed remote. The mentality to which such pranks appeal only suggests that of the touring Yankee who, when shown a candle flame which, he was assured, had not been allowed to go out for centuries, promptly exhaled the lustiest blast of which his lungs were capable, blandly remarking as the light succumbed to the assault: "Guess it's out now."

Somewhat different in motive but similar in effect was the exploit of a young naval officer, who, having wagered upon his ability to dislodge a well known logan-stone on a cliff near Penzance, actually succeeded in doing so, and with such convincing effect that the stone rolled over the edge and fell to the beach far below. The young man won his bet, but was compelled by those in authority to replace the stone, which exceedingly complicated undertaking cost him £500.

Unfortunately, logan-stones which can be wedged or

otherwise tampered with are less common than rock basins which offer little temptation to the tripper or the village youth—a more frequent delinquent in all such cases. He might indeed throw his litter into one, if near, but since he considers no receptacle necessary for this purpose, would seldom take the trouble. The two most famous basins are probably Mis Tor Pan and the far deeper hollow on Kes Tor Rock, which latter lost its artistic effect when railed off as a concession to the nervousness of some farmer who feared that one of his sheep might fall into the "pit"—actually about 30 inches deep. Since the surrounding moors and even the tor itself bristle with real dangers for sheep—bogs, river-bed pools and deep fissures between rocks, to mention only a few—the apprehensions concerning the basin seem grandmotherly at best, and one can only suspect that the farmer who expressed them was merely making conversation, never expecting to be taken seriously. Any ditch contains more potential dangers than this little circular hollow on Kes Tor.

The main interest of rock basins lies in their almost inconceivable antiquity, being, as they are, the results of natural processes so slow that the brain can scarcely imagine them. The much maligned Druid has provided a convenient scapegoat for a great deal that puzzled the antiquaries, the latter in this case somewhat resembling a slow-witted Yorkshire servant in my wife's old home, who, whenever she found cause for complaint in a household utensil, accounted for the defect with the comment: "A man moost 'a' made it." "A Druid must have done it," was the antiquarian's solution of the unaccountable, and for long it provided as acceptable a theory as any other. Even the antiquarian, however, has now accepted the Druid's innocence with regard to rock basins, in the formation of which under the climatic conditions now governing this planet a century has no visible effect. The bird and mountain fable alone suggests the period that would be required for a three-foot-wide "basin-shaft" to bore its way through the largest rock on Dartmoor.

Along the hillsides, sometimes immediately below the great tors, at others flanking minor inclines far from the main elevations, lie the *clitters*, these being accumulations of detached rocks, some of immense size, piled in wild confusion, covering in some instances acres of ground, in others areas no bigger than a tennis-court. Actually, although perhaps unscientifically, clitters can be classified under three headings: (1) heaped accumulations which appear to have been thrown upon the ground rather than to have erupted from it; (2) surface excrescences which look as though the hillside had been slightly lifted, like a gravel path by frost upon a gigantic scale; (3) the flat and far more extensive rock beds which lie little above ground level and might be the exposed granite face of the Moor.

As a general rule, the farther from a hilltop the smaller will be the pile, and in isolated instances, such as Cuttery Clitter on the Blackaven, it seems tolerably obvious that the broken rock constitutes the disintegrated remains of a solitary little tor long since fallen to pieces. Such, one can well imagine, might be the ultimate end of a crag like Ivy Tor on the Taw, or the Coronet of Rocks overlooking the East Okement gorge at the point where the river, running over waterfall and granite slide, passes from Moor to woodland.

Some of the finest clitters on Dartmoor are those which flank the Belstone ridge, particularly on the eastern side, where the ground drops sharply towards the Taw. Belstone Tor itself might be described as one vast heap of granite, and it seems probable that the ridge was formerly crested with huge crags of which the clitters are now the wreckage, the four tors that still stand, Belstone, Higher, Raven and Winter, being fragments of original and far greater formations. Many rock-strewn slopes, the Yes Tor ridge, Tavy Cleave, Stannon and the descent from Hunter's Crag to the Teign, impart the same impression, which is by no means inconsistent with the generally accepted order of events.

There are many cases, however, in which the lie of the rocks suggests an upheaval rather than a fall, and in these one can only attribute the phenomenon to volcanic disturbance breaking up the hillside and leaving a surface too irregular and deeply disrupted for soil to form and so heal the scar. Where the wound was less deep or the upheaval less violent, the great healer has already covered much of the wreckage, particularly where the rocks are of smaller size. Soil has formed over a great deal of Wild Tor Clitter, for example, at least sufficiently to fill up many of the crevices, allowing easy passage around rocks, and even among the most rugged piles the heather finds foothold here and there, also the whortleberry plant, which thrives better among the rocks than in the open.

The "flat" type of clitter, so styled to distinguish it from rock piles, although it usually flanks a slope may extend for a considerable distance and often merges almost imperceptibly into ground apparently covered with heather but pierced by innumerable rock heads. Here the natural question arises whether this ground over which man or beast picks his way with difficulty is old clitter in process of reclamation or moorland whose veneer of soil is wearing through like an old carpet and will soon expose the floor. However that may be, it is a curious thought that upon the face of this wild country, so much of which might in the generally accepted sense be regarded as everlasting, one reads the inescapable story of change, the more eloquent because so much of the old remains to emphasise the contrast.

All around lie ancient hut dwellings, so strikingly reminiscent of a vanished people, and the old workings with their empty leats and heather-covered slag-heaps to provide mute evidence of activities long forgotten. There are the tors themselves in their varying stages of decay, the fallen rocks and the hurrying stream as enduring as the hills, yet symbolising the principle of perpetual motion as their ever-changing waters flow on to "sow the dust of continents to be." Here a sapling is sprouting; there an ancient mountain-ash or oak, dwarfed by the winds of centuries, reaches with bleached limbs over the brook into which its aged body soon will fall. And lastly there is the peat, still in process of formation, yet ever crumbling to decay, and with it untold ages of mountain vegetation that has lived, withered and returned to the soil.

In Dartmoor parlance, the term "peat" is somewhat elastic in its application, being often used to describe any fuel brought off the Moor. Actually, surface turves or "vags" are now cut for this purpose far more extensively than true peat, which can only be obtained far out upon the hills. Much of the soil that covers the Moor is shallow, the rock or growan—decomposed granite not yet consolidated into clay—lying only a few inches below the surface, and while there is not always a definite line of demarcation, the peat veins often end abruptly on grassy slopes like cut banks, although the division is entirely natural. The peat country lies high, usually well above the 1,000 foot level, almost doubling that altitude in certain areas, as around Cut Hill, Forsland Ledge, Dinger and Hangingstone. Its depth, nowhere impressive, can be judged from the cuttings made through some of the principal beds from time to time, mainly for the convenience of riders, from six to eight feet being a rough average upon the great plateaux. It does not lie in a consistent crust, like turf over a field, but is broken into innumerable humps after the pattern of a mud-flat from which the tide has receded. These are intersected by an interminable maze of channels varying in width, usually water-logged or choked with crumblings, only negotiable by a man on foot when frozen hard, and even then presenting endless obstacles. The more remote of these great wastes are inaccessible to carts and have therefore remained untapped, excepting a few spots which were cleared in the now distant days when panniered donkeys conveyed fuel to the villages. Those picturesque conditions have passed for ever. Carts continue to go out, using mainly roads made by the military authorities, but most of the peat cut is now brought in by lorry, and this automatically restricts the field of operations. Thus, accessible veins become depleted, while those which mechanically propelled vehicles cannot approach remain untouched. It has become an uneconomic proposition, and with ever-increasing costs it is improbable that peat fuel will be used to any great extent in the future except by local farmers who can procure it in their own time and with their own "strength." By those who can get it for themselves turf is still freely used, and the scent of peat or, more correctly, vag smoke remains the characteristic and pleasantly suggestive atmosphere of a moorland village. Both peat and vags

are cut in blocks and set up to dry
sheaves, being "turned" occasionally as
The period necessary for the drying p
upon weather, the work continuing thro
if necessary. A Gidleigh moorman rece
the year 1944 he cut and harvested mc
April—that constituting a record for
remaining out as a rule until August or

Peat is, of course, the Dartmoor "coal mentioned in old
records as long ago as 1222, when permission was granted
by Henry III to the tinners to "take coal" for the smelting
of their ore. For this purpose it was usually first carbonised,
100 lb. of peat producing about 36 lb. of charcoal. As compared with coal, crude peat is about 50 per cent or more
lighter, according to its density, and, needless to add, does
not possess the same heat-producing capacity. Attempts to
utilise the Moor's resources upon scientific lines have been
made from time to time. Naphtha works were opened at
Shipley Bridge in 1847, and upon the Rattle Brook in the
Okehampton area an oil-extraction plant is still in being.
Scientists doubt, however, whether the peat accumulations
are of sufficient depth to be developed with satisfactory
results, and the difficulties are sufficiently obvious to anyone
familiar with the country.

The nearest approach to coal ever found in Devonshire
was the lignite deposit in the Bovey Basin—an ancient lake
bed encircled by hills, the wash from which provided the
original composition of the "beds." These were worked from
the latter part of the eighteenth century until about 1894,
the product being known locally as "brown coal," although
at certain depths it attained the uncompromising black of the
genuine article. It undoubtedly possessed greater geological
interest than commercial value, and was unfit either for
domestic or general use, acrid fumes and lack of adequate
heating properties being its principal drawbacks. A certain
amount was sold locally at 2s. 6d. per ton, but it was mainly
consumed in the adjacent pottery works, where it proved
suitable for baking the earthenware. Large amounts were
also conveyed to the Chudleigh quarries and lime-kilns,
loads of limestone being brought back on the return

...ys to the potteries, where it was burned for distribu-
...to the more limeless districts farther north.

This interchange of lignite and limestone between Bovey
and Chudleigh is a typical example of the manner in which
rural industries cooperate to the common advantage. Before
the days of lorries, when draught horses were used for every
form of haulage, Bovey Potteries offered local farmers a
ready market for various products. I remember an old carter
who for many years had conveyed straw from a farm at Kenn
to the works some ten miles away. This straw, bound into
"bunnels," as he called them, was skilfully packed and
roped overnight to form a load of some $2\frac{1}{2}$ tons. About seven
o'clock the following morning he would call at the farmhouse for the special perquisite of the expedition—a two-
gallon jar of cider drawn from the farmer's special tap. Thus
armed, he would start with his three-horse team to mount
the long slope of Haldon, which achieved, he would proceed
at a fine pace—often a full trot, for his horses, too, were the
best—and deliver his straw, for the privilege of unloading
which there must have been keen competition, the fame of
that enormous cider jar being as potent as its contents. That
it always returned empty was not surprising. It is somewhat
remarkable, however, that return it invariably did, with
waggon, horses and driver in as perfectly orderly condition
as when they started.

Operations at Bovey Heathfield are mostly concerned with
pipe and potter's clay, as distinct from the genuine kaolin
or china clay, a granite product formed by chemical dis-
integration of the feldspar. This is not as abundant in Devonshire as in Cornwall, although it underlies the peat bogs in
many places. Upon Dartmoor it is now worked only in the
Torry and Plym valleys, where there are extensive pits on
Heddon Down and Lee Moor. The latter has developed into
a large settlement, drawing its clay by means of pipes from
Shaugh "Lake." At Watcombe red terra-cotta clay is raised
at the head of what was once a picturesque little coombe
between Teignmouth and Torquay, but is now the centre of
a specialised pottery industry.

Although Devonshire does not manufacture bricks in any
quantity, her clay has, none the less, for centuries formed one

of her principal building materials. Cob walls, cottages and farmhouses are still characteristic of the countryside. Rose-red or yellow according to the properties of their clay, these buildings are both decorative and durable, and it is a matter for regret that their period is passing, probably for ever. A century or so ago, cob walling cost about 9*d.* per cubic yard to build, but owing to high labour charges the price would now be so prohibitive that nobody would consider it unless for a whim. That the process was a lengthy one is obvious from the amount of material required. Around my garden is a cob wall 3 feet thick by 10 feet high, and an even greater width was not unusual. Both process and material were simple. Given a stone or brick foundation a foot above ground level, it only remained to apply the clay, which was mixed with straw, preferably barley. The principle was then the same as in rick-making, the builder's eye being the sole guide by which he maintained a perpendicular line. The required height was accomplished by three-foot stages, between each of which a day was allowed for drying and settling, or "quatting" in Devonshire parlance. The rough sides were sheared with a spade, no more being required than to thatch or otherwise protect the top, which precaution remains essential during the wall's long life. For the pre-servation of cob there has always been one simple rule, "Keep its head and feet dry." This observed, the wall takes care of itself, and is virtually everlasting. When pulled down, straw three or four centuries old has been found in much the same condition as when originally incorporated. If allowed to "take wet" it quickly disintegrates, however. As an ex-ample of this, an old cob cottage in this village was recently requisitioned by the Army, but upon being handed over to the Americans, who understood nothing of its principle, the thatch was neglected, wet penetrated, and the whole of a main wall collapsed in consequence. If kept dry, it would easily have doubled its already long life. A second cottage not far distant, abandoned as a dwelling some years ago, lost its roof, and the one granite wall in the building now stands intact, while the remainder, being of cob, has completely disintegrated and disappeared.

For wall fruit-trees nothing equals cob. Not only are

branches easily trained against its surface, which offers no more than the requisite resistance to wooden pegs, thus removing a frequent source of difficulty with stone walls, but it also retains and radiates warmth, like a hot brick. This was a strong point in its favour when used for house-building, thatched cob being ideal for containing fire warmth in winter and excluding midsummer heat. It is also impervious to moisture, thus scoring another advantage over granite, which is eminently porous, as, living in an old granite house, I have good reason to know. One outside wall, indeed, will not even support a paper, which after a hard frost peels off like orange rind, and it has become necessary to line it with matchboard to provide an adhesive surface.

The use of cob was not general throughout the county. Near the Dorset border few traces are seen, for although clay abounds, the "blue flint" always offered a ready-made material of which advantage was naturally taken, grey cottages there indicating the prevailing stone of the district. Over the greater part of the county, however, the white-washed villages conceal, not feet, but frames of clay beneath their veneer, which, though attractive under well-seasoned thatch, sometimes obliterates a far greater charm. In the red sandstone districts, for example, where local clay was used, each village would have harmonised with the surrounding colour-scheme to produce a picture more pleasing than that achieved by any contrast. Where displayed, as at the Rougemont Castle in Exeter, the handsome cruciform church of Crediton, or those of Paignton and Totnes, the delicate natural red of the sandstone has a character so peculiarly its own that even in the form of cob its concealment under any artificial facing seems as regrettable as the whitewashing or painting of old oak beams—a sacrifice too frequently offered to the Devonshire housewife's passion for cleanliness. The stone used for much of the building of Exeter Cathedral was not local but none the less Devonian material, being the white stone for which the quarry at Beer has long been famous.

Architecture, generally speaking, is a matter of period rather than county, although governed up to a certain point by the materials at the builder's disposal. Thus, the long,

Where the Erme River reaches the sea on the south coast

one-room-breadth farmhouses of Devonshire largely owe their design to their suitability for cob and thatch construction, and dwellings of this type can be seen almost everywhere, particularly, perhaps, in Mid-Devon which, as the heart of the county, one might expect to find most characteristically Devonian.

BIBLIOGRAPHY

Land Utilisation Survey, Part 92: Devonshire.
Victoria History of Devon.
Devon Association Transactions, LXII, p. 49, R. Hansford Worth.

Scotch pine, a lone sentinel on the coast

CHAPTER IX

DEVONSHIRE MINES AND THEIR STORY

1. TIN

DARTMOOR'S ancient history can only be described as a volume of problem chapters or reversed limericks to which anyone entering the competition must provide the first rather than the last line. Widely distributed over the Moor's scarred and rugged face are written fragments of stories to which no beginning can be supplied, and this is particularly true of the old tin industry, probably Devonshire's first link with world commerce and, through the West-country, the first step towards Britain's ultimate share in international trade. And thus in the misty dawn of the nation's history, Devon in conjunction with Cornwall turned her eyes towards the sea and to the vast possibilities of maritime adventure.

All Devonshire tin emanated from Dartmoor, and if the earliest products found their way to the Phœnician ships which embarked their cargoes at the crude wharves of the Cassiterides—those isles of mystery whose precise location remains as undetermined as that of legendary Camelot— such metal was worked by the Taw, the Dart and the Erme, to be carried over the heathery tracks which centuries of disuse have failed to obliterate.

Standing now upon the site of an ancient working among the trenches and mounds where ling and whortleberry grow and the ring ouzel nests undisturbed by ghosts of the past, it is not difficult to imagine the tinners at work. If viewed from a sufficient distance to render minute detail immaterial, the picture can have differed little from that presented by a modern gang busy upon the same ground, excavating stone and gravel, or employed upon any of the utility schemes which all too rapidly are defacing Dartmoor. There were the same hills, the same streams, the same slow-motion colour pageant as sunlight and cloud shadow steal across the landscape, and there too were the hut dwellings, abandoned as now and probably as derelict, since all that was perishable in their structure must already have disappeared.

We have already seen that, as far as investigation can establish, the Bronze Age builders of the ancient hut settlements had no connection with the tin industry and, though doubtless a certain amount of use was made of these handy erections, there is no proof that they were ever occupied as dwellings by men of a later period. These miners were probably ordinary country-people living on the confines of the Moor and carrying on work from their homes, as do the whortleberry-pickers and peat-cutters of today. There is no reason for supposing them less capable of walking a few miles than their descendants, although they may have used the huts for shelter or storage of tools, assuming—although admittedly without reason—that honesty was a virtue of the times. The modern peat-cutter would hide *his* tools with excessive care and make a shrewd inventory of his peat.

The actual technique of the earliest workers has been more or less surmised. Few recognisable implements have been found, nor is this remarkable, since no workman necessarily throws his tools away upon the completion of any particular job. The skill lay in separating the metal from the ore, for which purpose rude mortars in the shape of concave stones were probably first employed, and an improvised oaken pestle would have been tolerably effective. Copious washing of the ore was also essential, and for this reason stream-bed deposits yielded the best metal, that being already largely separated by the action of the water. Sifting or winnowing must have been necessary to remove sand, and it is only reasonable to suppose that the workers were familiar with at least some elementary form of the double-handed sieve used by quarrymen of today.

The first attempts at smelting were rough but probably quite effective. A naturally hollowed or adapted stone was used, failing which a sloping trough could always be cut in the turf to convey the molten metal to its receptacle, the principle of packing ore and fuel, in the form of peat and charcoal, differing little from that of the lime-kiln. In course of time, as deeper and more extensive operations required improved methods, the "blowing-houses" developed, these being little stone erections provided with a rough furnace and having a draught-hole, primitive at first but later served by wheel-worked bellows, these in their turn being water-driven by means of leats whose courses still score the Moor's face in every direction. The remains of forty-three blowing-houses have been discovered on Dartmoor, and these, of course, represent a mere residue of a practice which persisted for at least five hundred years. Few valleys escaped exploitation at some time or other, but perhaps the best examples of ancient and extensive operations may be seen at Erme Pits. Evidence of later and deeper workings occurs at Vittifer and Birch Tor Mines, near the Warren House Inn, and it was at Vittifer that the curtain virtually fell upon the tin industry during the last century. The Taw valley also came in for considerable attention, and there too the stream was obviously diverted at various points, either to wash fresh excavations or to remove ore from the original bed.

Behind the earliest Dartmoor tinners there is no historical background, nothing to indicate what manner of men they were, how they lived or whence they came. Were they fair-haired Celts or dark Iberians, or were they Devon men at all? Assuming the Moor unpeopled and that the inhabitants of the hut settlements had faded out with the Bronze Age, follows that the first seekers of tin may have taken the form of prospecting parties from other districts, probably from Cornwall, since the primitive people of the Devonshire lowland would certainly have known nothing about the metal or where to seek it.

With regard to the industry, history accompanies research far enough to establish that Phœnician merchants were trading with the Cassiterides about 400 B.C., but extends no farther, Herodotus, the most responsible recorder, admitting ignorance as to the whereabouts of the islands. Their identity with the Scilly Isles and the Cornish Peninsula has been suggested, although Strabo (first century A.D.) discourages this theory by placing them without precise specification as lying off the coasts of Spain and Portugal, defining them as tin-producing islands with which the Phœnicians had established a trade monopoly. Britain's claim to the Cassiterides is strengthened or weakened, according to point of view, by Diodorus, who, following Herodotus by three centuries, describes western England's tin trade, specifying an island called Ictin as the main port of call. Ictin is represented as accessible from the mainland at low tide, and corresponds in all essentials with St Michael's Mount. Such appears to be the data upon which all theories are founded. The positive identity of the Cassiterides, the most northerly point reached by the Phœnician trading vessels, the period at which the export of tin from Britain began, the extent of Devon's or Dartmoor's participation in the trade of which Cornwall was the centre, still remain matters for conjecture.

The tendency to associate Dartmoor with Cornwall's early tinning operations was inevitable, and there seems to be some justification for the opinion that the moorland workings, as distinct from the actual mines whose history is known, have been considerably pre-dated. By common assumption these are assigned to three periods: (1) the prehistoric streamings, with primitive wooden tools which prohibited anything more than surface operations; (2) the more ambitious efforts rendered possible by the acquisition of iron tools which preceded the Saxon invasion; (3) a thorough exploitation of the ground, which began with the medieval period of blowing-houses and continued until the seventeenth century, when the surface metal became exhausted.

Of these three periods, the last only is corroborated by history. With regard to the earlier efforts the main difficulty in accepting the belief that they ever took place lies in the complete omission of Dartmoor and its potentialities from Domesday Book. As in the case of the Ancient Tenements, it seems inconceivable that the Normans should have overlooked so valuable a source of mineral wealth, in which they were actively interested. They certainly penetrated to Lydford, which was taken by storm in 1068, and had the existence of tin upon Dartmoor been known, the information could scarcely have escaped them. The omission suggests that either no record or trace of previous exploitation existed or that Dartmoor was overlooked, which seems improbable considering its area. The early tinner, indeed, like the hut-dwellers and many of his contemporaries, is a legendary figure who passed into obscurity without leaving any biographical details. None the less, the ancient moorman's autograph is indelibly carved upon many a rough hillside, yet leaving so much to the imagination that now, thousands of years later, controversy continues, while mountain sheep browse over the green mounds which so jealously guard their secrets. Nor will these stores of hidden knowledge surrender much more of their wealth unless fortune proves peculiarly kind, or a brains trust of reincarnated experts could be improvised for the final settlement of questions upon which they alone are qualified to pronounce. Such a trust might consist of a Druid, a Phœnician, a prehistoric tinner, a packhorse, and a hut-circle housewife to deal with domestic problems of the period. For a question-master, experience in Round Table conferences renders King Arthur, complete with Excalibur, the only possible choice, while Puck of Pook's Hill in his dual character of Pixy and medium would certainly be required to announce the programme and introduce the members.

Returning to realities, it is generally accepted that the mineral resources of the county were neglected during the Saxon regime. However that may have been, they certainly revived under Norman control, but not until about 1198 is there positive record of legislation concerning Devonian or Cornish tin. Then Richard I, presumably with an eye to the revenue which he badly needed for his Continental adventures, passed a law to safeguard his royalties, stipulating that all metal should be weighed upon the official scales at Exeter, and prohibiting the removal of tin from the two counties by "man, woman, Christian or Jew" except under special licence, the obvious purpose being to curb profitable smuggling. It is clear, therefore, that the tinning operations had been in full swing for a considerable period prior to that date. It fell to John, whose dubiously interpreted grants still occasion friction in Dartmoor matters, to enact further charters, and finally Edward I applied his hammer—usually reserved for Scottish metal—to the riveting of tin legislation, the apparent object of which was to ensure the maximum amount of mineral by any means, as long as the exchequer, or, indirectly, the royal armoury, benefited.

Under statutes confirmed and revised in 1305, the *Stannery* system became to all intents and purposes a law unto itself. Devon for the first time was dissociated from Cornwall, the tin-producing area being divided into four districts approximately representing the present Forest Quarters, each containing one Stannery town, Chagford, Ashburton, Plympton and Tavistock, standing for north, east, south and west, respectively. In each of these four towns a court was set up to deal with all matters within the area, technical, financial or criminal, so far as the industry was concerned, and the tin-miners were subject to no other jurisdiction. At these centres also, tin produced within the quarter was weighed and *coined*, which process consisted of chipping a corner from each block of metal to test its quality, and if up to standard applying the regulation stamp. Lydford, as capital of the Moor, was granted the privilege of contributing its castle as the Stannery prison, to the exclusion of all other claimants to that honour. That the institution became famous for abuse need scarcely be added. Lydford, incidentally, claimed other distinctions besides its infamous prison. It boasted a population second only in the county to Exeter, and was the centre of all Forest administration, possessing also one of the four Devonshire mints—an honour shared with Exeter, Barnstaple and Totnes. The coinage took the form of hand-made silver pennies, and probably this mint, together with many others, owed its origin to Ethelred the Unready, whose demand upon it, at any rate, appears to have been heavy, since a great number of its coins, paid in Danegeld, reached Scandinavia. Some forty pennies bearing the Lydford stamp may be seen today, I believe, in Stockholm museums.

The combined Stanneries had their own parliament, to which each quarter elected twenty-four members, and this was presided over by an officer of the Crown under the title of *Warden*, the office continuing until the present date and now held by Lord Radnor, who officiates at Truro over the Court of the Vice-Warden, once more representing the united interests of Devonian and Cornish mining, although under very different auspices. The earliest recorded Warden of the Stanneries was William de Wrotham, appointed

Custos in 1197, and since that date in unbroken succession occur such eminent names as the Marquis of Exeter (1533), Sir Walter Raleigh, Lord Dartmouth, and the famous Sir Thomas Tyrwhitt in 1805. The last Stannery court for Devon, as distinct from Cornwall, was held under the wardenship of Lord Granville about 1703, after which a general decline in the industry rendered further sessions unnecessary.

In early days the Stannery Parliament met on Crockern Tor, rough granite seats being improvised to render the "session" literal. Were similar quarters provided for the House of Commons, candidature for election would be less keen than it is today. Whatever defects the assembly hall had, however, the ventilation was good, and presumably the members subscribed to no theories concerning damp seats and rheumatic consequences. It is clear also that legislators of the fifteenth century did not regard the Dartmoor climate in as formidable a light as their descendants—possibly owing to a hut-circle ancestry. At best, since the sessions occasionally opened at 8 a.m. when the mist more often than not must have been waiting to damp their enthusiasm, conditions can seldom have promoted long-winded oratory. Presumably, however, they were no worse than those under which the modern countryman watches hounds from a hilltop in the full stroke of the blast, and is so far indifferent to the discomforts that he would freeze rather than walk about to keep warm any day. None the less, one may safely assume that adjournment to Tavistock, which subsequently became the custom, was a proposal unanimously carried, and knowledge of both Crockern Tor and human nature justifies a suspicion that the practice was adopted at a very early date.

Up to a certain point the Stannery laws worked equitably. There were special provisions against exploitation, speculation or monopoly by monasteries or large private landowners—the principal capitalists of the period. Forest and Stannery officials were also debarred from taking up any fresh holdings. In the interests of the trade, if for no other reason, a high standard of workmanship was enforced, rough-and-ready penalties being imposed for offences such as adulteration of the metal. According to local tradition, any man detected in such practices was compelled to drink a solution of his own compound, and improbable as this may seem, stories of the kind seldom entirely lack foundation.

The early Stanneries from every point of view must have been a unique institution, as picturesque and romantic as any that writers of adventure stories have depicted. It is curious that their potentialities in this respect should have been overlooked. Their only parallel in modern times would be the Dartmoor Commons of the present day, but more of them in their appointed place. To the tinner, however, as to so many figures of the past, distance has lent enchantment, and in his time, it would seem, he was not always regarded in a light either romantic or picturesque. No matter how advantageous the system might have been for tin and tinners, it is not difficult to imagine that gangs of wild men, exploiting a wild country and recognising no law other than their own, scarcely proved an unmixed blessing to the general community not interested in the trade. A demonstration of government by the tinner for the tinner quickly developed, and with virtually complete freedom of action inevitable abuse arose. By a loosely worded clause, the charter empowered tinners to dig for the metal wherever it could be found and to divert any watercourses that might assist their operations. In intent, this obviously applied to unenclosed Crown lands, but the tinners interpreted it as licence to do what they pleased in such matters, and should a neighbour become unpopular, nothing was simpler than to discover tin in his corn-patch or even under his kitchen floor, and failing this, his water-supply could always be requisitioned. Protest availed little. The tinners had picks and shovels with which to argue, if necessary, and they had protected themselves by an ingenious Stannery law penalising anyone who "shall vex or troble" a tinner when hot upon a scent, and in operation the effect of the statute must have been, to say the least, one-sided.

Such practices in the course of time degenerated into the worst form of tyranny—that of the many over the few—and became so intolerable that in 1376 a document was drafted petitioning Edward III for an enquiry into the "many Extortions, Oppressions and Grievances . . . practised by the Tinners and the Officers of the Stanneries," with the request that they should not be permitted to dig in "Pastureland, nor among Woods . . . nor among Houses, nor disturb Waters or any running Waters out of Malice." This was followed by an accusation of favouritism and misapplication of justice at Lydford Prison, tinners "taken for felony" often being "suffered to go at large, from whence much Danger has many times happened."

History records no effective redress. Possibly the Parliament of the day followed the customary procedure of Parliaments by appointing a commission to look into the grievance, but if so the official blind eye was applied to the telescope. It was the old story of revenue calculated to suffer from the imposing of restrictions, and then, as now, from Dartmoor to Westminster was a far cry, and the fire from which the smoke arose burned no fingers that mattered. That abuses had not ceased by the reign of Henry VIII was manifested by the famous case of Sir Richard Strode, who, as M.P. for Plympton and therefore possessing first-hand knowledge, introduced a Bill to control the excesses of the tinners and prohibit their practice of discharging waste into the rivers, even as the Devonian villager of today throws his rubbish into the same convenient tip. In the former case, however, consequences were more serious, the quantity being sufficient to silt up the harbours to which it was carried by the strong flood-waters of the moorland streams. Sir Richard, however, like most would-be reformers, soon found that he had stirred up a hornets' nest, and the four Stannery courts, convened to discuss the situation, immediately found a stick with which to administer correction. Apparently, he had strongly discouraged an attempt to extract tin from his own land, and in the course of a none too amicable interview "trobled a tinner." Summary conviction and the imposition of the maximum fine by all four courts were followed by arrest—such being his first notification of the proceedings. He was consigned to Lydford Prison, where he contrived to exist for a while by out-bribing the jailer, who had been specially paid to make his stay as unpleasant as possible.

Eventually he was liberated by special intervention from Westminster, and further victimisation of the kind was prevented by the Act which established the right of free speech in Parliament—another contribution by Devon to the liberties of the nation. None the less, his Bill, or the two Acts to which it eventually led, proved no more effective than any other law to curb Devonian activities. True, the Stannery Parliament held a chilly emergency session on Crockern Tor and expressed pain at the suggestion that their rubbish could possibly "hurt and quirt" His Majesty's ports, and passed a law of their own constraining every miner to deposit his "Ruble, Gravel and Sands" in "old Hatches, Tippites, miry Places or other convenient Places," away from the rivers, or incur a fine for infringement. This was praiseworthy but optimistic. A local farmer, when hearing of the recent Act to prohibit spring-trapping in the open, casually but prophetically remarked: "I reckon it will be much the same," and anyone who expected the tinners to conform to a merely tiresome regulation was doomed to disappointment. Then, as now, it was "much the same," and it remained for the realistic Elizabeth to put down her foot with characteristic firmness. That the Virgin Queen cared any more than her predecessors for smoke that did not penetrate her own eyes is improbable, but upon law and order, even at the cost of "trobling tinners," she held strong views. Interested as she was in maritime affairs, Elizabeth took prompt action to ensure that the "hurt and quirt" of the harbours should not be merely a matter for deprecation, and by vigorous measures brought the nuisance to an end.

During Elizabeth's reign, and under the wardenship of Sir Walter Raleigh, who did a great deal to improve the general working conditions, doubling the tinners' wages from 2s. to 4s. a week, the industry reached its peak. The Queen encouraged revolutionary measures, and German miners were imported to bring their improved methods to bear upon the various mines of the county. They modernised the existing blowing-houses with larger water-wheels served by skilfully constructed leats, and it was probably in their time that the name "Jews' houses," by which they are still known among the moor-folk, was first applied to these erections.

A hundred years later, however, the surface tin of Dartmoor was practically worked out, and early in the eighteenth century was superseded by Cornish deep mining, only a remnant of the old industry continuing in Devon, although sporadic revivals occurred, but usually of a short-lived and purely local character. Vittifer, near North Bovey, Ailsborough and Whiteworks at Lydford were still working until about 1820, and thirteen mines were producing small quantities of tin as late as 1874. To all intents and purposes, however, the long story of Devon's tin, with its distinctive characteristic background of myth and mystery, closed at the end of the Stuart regime with the final session, already mentioned, on Crockern Tor. From this date, Cornwall's mining industry grew as Devon's declined.

BIBLIOGRAPHY

Devon Association Transactions, VIII, p. 310, R. N. Worth; XXXVII, p. 175, Mrs G. H. Radford.
History of Devon. T. Moore.

DEVONSHIRE MINES AND THEIR STORY

2. MAINLY COPPER

DEVON's mineral wealth was not entirely confined to tin, although the tale of all her metals begins and ends in the past. The silver and lead mines of Combe Martin and Bere Alston operated in the Plantagenet period and, together with the tin proceeds, proved helpful to the Treasury. The reputed Phœnician connection at an earlier date might be referred to the special brains' trust already suggested, but it is tolerably certain that home-produced silver provided the coins manufactured at the four Devonshire mints. The official history of these mines begins with the reign of Edward I, when 360 miners were "impressed" from Derbyshire and Wales to work them, "appeals" to increase output being equally unproductive in those days, even though the King's daughter badly needed a dowry and the hammering of the Scots was an expensive pastime. During the ensuing reign state interest in minerals was not so marked, but with Edward III and the beginning of the Hundred Years War the demand revived. Since the tinners, even when unvexed, could not provide enough, the King granted any Devonian the right to dig for gold or silver upon his own land for the space of two years, reporting success or failure to the King's clerk. Failure would certainly be the answer nowadays, nor would two years be required in which to reach a decision. Excavators of that period appear to have been moderately successful, however, and when the report seemed at all hopeful, His Majesty, who had watched proceedings as a Chinaman watches his cormorant fishing, asserted the royal prerogative in which he specialised and requisitioned the workings. Land-owners lost interest in the search before long, but it had yielded enough to induce the King to commission two officers to search for gold, silver and copper in all his mines—whatever that implied—for the same period, after which he resumed possession and authorised a conscription of labour. The local supply being inadequate, a further contingent was "impressed" the following year from Yorkshire, Derby and Nottingham, but since this only amounted to twenty, they were probably required as instructors to direct the new undertakings. But the principle of forced labour seems inconsistent with a reign during which action at any rate was so "free" that a special law became necessary forbidding the "killing of the Chancellor, the treasurer or any of the judges while in discharge of their duties."

With inevitable fluctuations mining generally continued to flourish, or at least to yield Crown revenue, until Elizabeth's reign, when the renewed need for money to equip the numerous seafaring enterprises induced that canny sovereign to adopt measures to stimulate output, or at any rate augment funds. A *Society for the Mines Royal* was formed under the auspices of Robert Earl of Leicester, Nicholas Bacon, Sir William Cecil, Lord Cobham and Lord Mildmay among others. This company controlled mines all over the kingdom, to the benefit of the exchequer and at no loss to themselves, the only group unaffected being the Stanneries, to which Elizabeth had already applied both the curb and the spur within the limits of their own special sphere.

It seems curious that even Elizabeth in her toothcombings for emoluments failed to ferret out much copper, the possibilities of which were not fully realised until two centuries later. The area lying between the Tavy and the Tamar consists of metalliferous slate, richer in minerals than any other district in the county, as the numerous tin, copper, arsenic, lead and iron mines of the last century testify. During the boom period nearly forty mines were working in the parish of Tavistock alone. As tin declined, copper, the output of which had previously been restricted to a few areas with North Molton as the most outstanding example, largely supplied the deficiency, and in the Tavistock district the first productive lode was discovered about 1817, while the canal connecting the Tavy and the Tamar was in course of construction. The discovery resulted in the Wheal Creabor Mine, and during the next fifty years the ancient Stannery town of Tavistock transferred its allegiance from tin to copper and became the hub of a new mining industry. Wheal after wheal, more picturesque in name than in actuality, developed with the rapidity of a gold rush, and speculators competed for every acre of ground that offered a possible yield. Incidentally, this word "wheal," so frequently connected with West-country industry, is derived from the Celtic *huel*, a mine. The student of mineral history may probe into the secrets of each individual mine, if so disposed, but one wonders what stories, romantic or diplomatic, lie behind such names as Wheal Betsy, Wheal Fanny, Wheal Mercy, the somewhat uninspiring Wheal Josiah, Resolution, Emma, Anna Maria, Friendship, and the Virtuous Lady. Now Betsy, Emma, Anna Maria and the Virtuous Lady, in company with the highly respectable Josiah, have passed with the period which begot them, and by 1901 practically all the Tavistock mines had closed down.

"Far down the ages now" the long history of Devon's minerals extended its epilogue into the present century, during the early years of which the remaining mines throughout the county ceased work. In 1910 only twenty-four mines of any description were operating. The 1920 annual statistics for Devon, issued by the Government in their *Mines and Quarries*, listed small quantities of arsenical pyrites, arsenic and tin ore. In the 1937 equivalent no minerals appear at all. This depressing tale was not entirely due to the exhaustion of the general supply, but in part to increasing difficulties and costs of production, unequal competition with cheap imports, and in some cases to mismanagement. In the Okehampton district, on Copper Hill, Belstone and Ramsley Common, near South Zeal, the remains of two mines which maintained the struggle to its inevitable end rear their dismantled and unsightly shapes, like derelict ships, awaiting demolition by Time's slow hand. In the neighbouring villages are septuagenarians who, as boys or young men, worked in these mines, although few of the old "captains" remain. This title, open to obvious and frequent misinterpretation, was held by the manager of any West-country mine, and, like service rank, once acquired was retained for life. The last captain of the Ramsley mine died in this village nearly twenty years ago. Upon one occasion, when required to establish his identity for the signing of a legal document, a sharp altercation arose upon his claim to the title, the official maintaining that only army and navy personnel were entitled to that status. He stuck resolutely to his point, however, which was eventually conceded.

Concerning the South Zeal and Belstone pits, the more interesting but less productive was the latter, the excavations of which ran beneath the land now generally known as Green Hill. It achieved a maximum depth of 200 fathoms, and the principal working difficulty appears to have been a super-abundance of water, useful for washing the metal but copious enough to constitute a problem. It was pumped from the pit by an enormous wheel, the largest but one in the United Kingdom, measuring 62 feet in diameter. This operated from Belstone Cleave, half a mile away, where the ivy-covered walls of its huge trough still stand, and it must have possessed considerable driving power, since each revolution brought a hogshead of water to the pit's head.

Copper Hill, or Green Hill Mine, employed about fifty men and boys, the latter working upon the surface only, their job being to pound the ore with light iron pestles to release the copper. Women also took part in the more elaborate finishing work, but feminine labour does not appear to have been the rule. A boy in his teens earned 8*d*. a day, from 7 a.m. to 5 p.m. being the regulation hours. A skilled underground miner received £1 a week, while each first grade man had his mate, or "chap," as he was called, usually a youth who acted as understudy and received the lower rate of 15*s*. a week, this sum actually exceeding the agricultural wage of the period for an adult. The method of working in pairs was necessary, one man being required to turn the iron hand-bore or drill which the other drove with a sledgehammer.

Repairing my study window this afternoon was a man, Tucker by name, now aged eighty, who for many years held the post of permanent carpenter at the Copper Hill Mine, where he was responsible for the extensive and highly important woodwork. There being no pit-cages, miners descended the quarter-mile-deep shaft by a succession of ladders and platforms, where one faulty rung or board might involve a fatal accident. Answering emergency calls at any hour of the twenty-four, he has worked, he tells me, on top of the big wheel at midnight, repairing the "launder" or conduit by the light of an uncovered wax candle, the winds which usually sweep down that moorland valley being still for a while, as is often the case at the silent hour when even natural forces appear to sleep.

After Copper Hill closed down, he was employed to erect the fittings at a new tin mine being opened at Hexworthy, on Dartmoor, to which he journeyed every Monday morning with the captain of the closed Green Hill mine, who had also been transferred to the new venture. Both lived in Sticklepath, and for their joint conveyance they were allowed the use of one horse from the mine outfit, and upon this worthy successor of the old pack-horse they slung their provisions for one week. These consisted of food, tea and even milk, for Hexworthy was remote in those days, beyond the reach of local supplies, the operatives being housed in improvised barrack-like sheds which provided shelter and nothing else.

Hexworthy Bridge on the upper West Dart—the "Oak-tree" river

Each man had his own bag, the pair being slung across the saddle, and they accomplished the twenty-mile trek over the Moor by the "ride-and-tie" arrangement, i.e. occupying the saddle in turn, each riding for a mile or two, then tethering the horse and walking on until overtaken, when they again changed places and repeated the process. By this means they made quicker progress than if they had kept company, which would have entailed a walking pace the whole time. Even so, the journey occupied several hours, being broken by a regulation twenty-minutes' halt at Postbridge Inn for a pot of tea, served as a standing order by "crying Emma," as the somewhat melancholy landlady at that period was styled by her customers. Their object, usually achieved, was to start work at 1.30 p.m., remaining at the mine until "Saturday noon," with the exception of a scheduled Wednesday-evening expedition to the nearest farm to replenish their stores with a few eggs or to get the milk bottles refilled. On Saturday afternoon the return journey was made, and week-end comforts must have been appreciated. "I earned four bob a day when I started at Hexworthy," said the old man, "and before I finished there I got 4s. 6d., and thought it master money."

The Hexworthy Mine ran for about ten years, being out-lived for a short period by the Golden Dagger Mine, near Warren Inn. During the mining period Devonshire villages were decidedly cosmopolitan, owing to the influx of work-men from all parts of the country. South Zeal, indeed, acquired the name of "Little Ireland," and according to my old friend the carpenter an exceedingly "vitty" demeanour was essential if one hoped to leave the village after nightfall without a black eye. With the closing of the mines a period of depopulation followed, many of the local men emigrating to the Indian gold mines. Among these was the "captain" who performed the weekly horse-trip with Tucker. He did his best to persuade his old Dartmoor companion to share his fortunes on this longer journey, but when arrangements were almost completed "my missus" intervened, to which Tucker's reaction was: "Now, don't 'ee say no more. I'll bide." And he did.

The actual swan-song of Devonshire mining, however,

Dartmouth Castle guards the river at the end of its long journey was not sung by the coppersmith bird or its British representative. Before the final abandonment of the copper mines, arsenical pyrites had been discovered in many places in conjunction with copper ore, and works to exploit this product came into being, together also with manganese. The latter was raised at Christow, Newton St Cyres and other localities, the chief centre being Milton Abbot, and for a time Devon provided England's entire manganese supply.

Nor can this brief description of the county's former mineral wealth be dismissed without reference to the most widespread of all metal products, iron ore, which has been worked in such widely dispersed localities as the Exmoor district, Haytor, Brixham and Buckfastleigh, the latter among the last to continue in operation. The iron industry, also, had an ancient beginning, very old and primitive pits being in evidence on the Blackdown Hills, obviously excavated to their shallow depth before the age of even the most elementary machinery, and iron mines have outstayed all others, one or two having continued practically until the present day.

The tale of the mines can now be read only in the desolate chimneys, buildings and slag-heaps which impart so forlorn an aspect to their surroundings. Slag-mounds, like disused quarries, indeed, are often softened by time into not unpleasing features of the landscape, but in the case of mundic, the copper-arsenic waste, so large a proportion of the arsenical ingredients remain that they have the same effect as weedkiller in discouraging vegetation, and great piles thrown up fifty or sixty years ago still remain in all their stark ugliness. As long as the mundic retains its properties, these slag-heaps have a certain commercial value, being in demand for gravelling drives and garden-paths—not the first occasion upon which the dust of enterprise has been trodden underfoot.

BIBLIOGRAPHY

History of Devon. T. Moore.
Devon Association Transactions, XLVI, p. 356, Moses Bawden.

CHAPTER X

WOOL

THE West Country has its own rendering of a well-known proverb: "Three generations from hobs (hob-nailed boots) to hobs." This refers to life on the land, where the grand-children of the prosperous *self-made* farmer so often revert to the position of farm-labourers. In general this proves true, particularly when a large family necessitates a distribution of patrimony, and the story of a family often illustrates that of a country or county. As we have seen, the earliest occupation of the prehistoric Devonian was pastoral, particularly in the mountainous districts—the country best suited to sheep in early times—and after the rise and decline of numerous industries, including the once extensive woollen trade, the sheep remains the county's best source of income, and as far as Dartmoor is concerned an exceedingly remunerative pro-position.

The sheep was a domesticated animal in Europe before any historical records, and the date of its introduction to Britain is unknown. Cæsar makes no mention of its presence in his first description of the country, but one of the earliest administrative acts under the Roman regime was the estab-lishment of woollen factories at Winchester for the clothing of three legions, and as the British output quickly exceeded that of Italy, it may reasonably be assumed that the country was already well stocked with raw material. Being imported originally from southern countries, the sheep probably entered Britain by the western ports—the early doors for England's Continental trade. Since the densely wooded coombes afforded poor pasturage, it must have soon found its way to the uplands, the earliest suggestion of its presence being a spindle-whorl found in a hut circle on Legis Tor, in the Plym valley, this supporting other evidence that the Moor-dwellers were familiar with sheep and knew how to utilise fleeces.

Devonshire, however, did not immediately achieve the prominence which she afterwards acquired in the woollen industry. It had to establish its footing and only began to thrive in the county with the arrival of the Cistercian monks at Buckfast Abbey about 1148. This order took possession from the Grey Monks who had been in occupation for twelve years only, and thenceforth merged their identity in that of the more numerous brotherhood. The early history of this ancient settlement remains obscure, but it probably dates from the eighth century and is mentioned as Buckfastre, Buckfasten and other renderings, all being subject to one interpretation: the *Deer fastness*, the suffix *leigh*, from the Anglo-Saxon *ley*, meaning pasturage, and indicating the extensive grazing area eventually acquired by the Cistercians, pioneers of agriculture wherever they settled.

The Savigny grey monks acquired the name from their custom of wearing clothes made of unbleached wool with which product they were obviously familiar. The Cistercians, or White Monks, soon realised the potentialities of Dartmoor's slopes to supply the material for which a demand was opening, and in conjunction with other settlements of their order, notably Ford, Newholm, Torre and Buckland, did much to promote not only the woollen industry within the county but a profitable export trade, which continued until prohibited by measures enacted during the reign of Edward III. Ashburton was probably the first Devonshire town materially to benefit from the monastic activities, and as early as 1236 the abbot and monks of Buckfastleigh were admitted as members to the merchant guild of Totnes, having evidently acquired a considerable commercial reputation.

In some respects the development of the woollen industry coincided with that of tin. It was encouraged by the same monarchs, Edward I, Edward III and Elizabeth, no doubt for the same reasons in each case—the need to stimulate trade and provide funds, and also in part because these rulers were of outstanding character and keenly alive to the advantages of national prosperity. With regard to wool also there is the same absence of early records, and long periods of obscurity during which little reference to the trade occurs in history. In the reign of Edward I skilled operatives from the

Low Countries were invited to England. Edward III, in order to improve English methods, imported further contingents of expert labour, upon the grounds that his countrymen knew "no more what to do with their wool than the sheep that wears it." He also prohibited the export of the raw product, the manufactured article being more profitable to the community and consequently to the exchequer. Elizabeth, again, encouraged the further introduction of skilled artificers by granting protection and charters to refugees from the Spanish Netherlands seeking escape from the reign of terror instituted by the Duke of Alva against the Flemish Protestants, and the influx of these people into the West had a decidedly beneficial effect upon the industry of the county. Many settled in Exeter and other towns and villages engaged in the trade, such names as Stoke Fleming and Bratton Fleming probably owing their origin to the establishment of these Continental colonies.

The word *staple* implies a settled market, and most frequently refers to the wool trade. One well-known Devonshire town which, according to popular assumption, derives its name from this source is Barnstaple, wool being the principal product upon which its position as a great market centre was based. It was certainly applicable in the case of this town, which, receiving the dignity of a borough in the tenth century, carried on so thriving an industry during the next 300 years or so in this particular commodity that for a while it even surpassed Exeter, high as was the standard which the latter city attained and complete as was the supremacy which she afterwards acquired. Barnstaple's trade was already declining before the general boom period, due, no doubt, as in the case of her shipping, to the remoteness of her port and the consequent competitive disadvantages.

There is also a generally accepted convention that the famous Bideford Bridge, across the Torridge, stands—like so much else in Devonshire—upon a "woollen foundation," meaning, of course, that wool fortunes provided the money which built it. Bideford Bridge is a remarkable if not unique erection, not upon account of its architectural beauty, any which it previously possessed having been defaced by innovations, but rather owing to its peculiar status as an institution as distinct from a mere building. Conforming to the true Devonian rule, its definite origin is unknown, also the date of its erection, although Sir Theobald Grenville and other local magnates of the period are given credit for its construction about the middle of the fourteenth century. Since then it has been the recipient of various legacies and endowments, which, administered as trusts for its upkeep, have not only rendered the bridge self-supporting, but actually placed it in the position of a public benefactor, the trustees being enabled to vote superfluous funds for charitable purposes or anything calculated to benefit the town. As a substantial property-owner, it had a voice in all local affairs and has always fulfilled the part of Bideford's good genius, endowing schools, supplying food for the people in times of distress and winding up its good offices by providing a burial ground, thus caring for a section of the populace literally from the cradle to the grave. Nor did it neglect the more convivial side of life, having its own drums for music-making, giving annual feasts, entertaining distinguished guests, and maintaining among other creditable institutions a good wine-cellar of its own, thus never lacking the means with which to make merry when occasion arose. It owned property in many parts of the county, and, one is glad to be able to state, need not be relegated to the depressing list of "has-beens," for Bideford Bridge not only stands today, imposing with its twenty-four arches and 677 feet length of way, but remains a capitalist with an annual income—at least before the 1939–45 war—of about £1,000, still administered by its trustees for charitable purposes.

The famous bridge is far from being the only Devonshire monument provided by the fleeces of her sheep. Another outstanding example is Blundell's School, founded at Tiverton in 1604 on the bequest of Peter Blundell, a wool magnate of the period. In Tiverton also stand three blocks of almshouses, upon one of which are engraved a wool-pack and staple by way of armorial bearings. All these buildings date from the sixteenth century, when the trade was at its height, and during the same period an addition known as Greenway's Chapel was made to the parish church, and dedicated to three saints, including St Blaise, the accepted patron of wool, although his connection with the trade was indirect and purely tragic. Tiverton also was described by James I as one of the main centres, if not the actual hub, of the western woollen industry, and since the same distinction appears to have been bestowed upon Crediton at one time, it may be assumed that each dog had its day or that pride of first place was claimed by a good many towns, which is more than likely. However that may have been, Tiverton's craft certainly reached a high standard of excellence, due in part to the large number of Flemings who settled there with the inevitable advantages of their technical skill and methods. Tiverton, none the less, was peculiarly unlucky, suffering no less than nine destructive fires in the course of her industrial history. Despite these disasters, however, Tiverton had fifty-six fulling mills at work during the reign of George III—a striking proof of her recuperative ability. It is curious that one of her principal rivals, Crediton, suffered in a similar manner, although upon two occasions only, in 1743 and 1769. It would almost seem that wool—the most peaceable of commodities, better calculated to smother than kindle flame—has none the less a distinctly inflammable association, for Barnstaple's declining industry received its quietus also by a destructive fire at the end of the eighteenth century.

Neither the tidal flow of the Torridge nor the fires of Tiverton or Crediton, however, could destroy the woollen foundation upon which so many Devonian and British institutions rest. Great estates and great families were established or enriched, for despite convention the gentry of the middle ages by no means neglected commercial opportunities. Its connection may be traced in old county names such as Woollcombe, in which the association is obvious. Wool provided much of the money which built and manned the ships destined to meet the Armada. Drake and most of his contemporary adventurers were engaged in the trade. The Lord Chancellor and the judges sat and still sit upon wool, and as a characteristic contribution towards England's prosperity, Devonshire was foremost in the field, her share of industry being probably greater than that of any other county.

How great was this share can scarcely be realised today in

a county from which manufacture, except upon a negligible scale, has departed, probably for ever. Yet during its heyday Devonshire must have hummed like a hive. There was scarcely a town without its impressive list of fulling mills and factories; scarcely a stream, however insignificant, which was not driving its water-wheels; not a village and scarcely a cottage in which the whirring of the loom could not be heard. In the words of Hooker, speaking of the industry in his day, which was the end of the Elizabethan period:

"There is no market nor village nor scarse any privat mannes house where in theise clothes be not made, or that there is not spinninge and cordinge for the same: as the daylye travellers can so witnes it for wheresoever any man doth travell you shall fynde at the hall dore as they do name the foredore of the house he shall I saye fynde the wiffe theire children and theire servantes at the turne spynninge or at theire cardes cardinge and by wch comoditie the comon people do lyve."

Barnstaple, Tiverton, Cullompton, Crediton, Axminster, Honiton, Ashburton, Tavistock and Totnes were all thriving centres, with Chudleigh and Exeter already under full headway when first the curtain was lifted upon the county and its way of life. That Defoe when visiting Devon in 1724 should have been impressed by the picture is not surprising. Expecting, perhaps, material for another Crusoe story, he found commercial activity and prosperity unrivalled in his experience: villages crowded not with unsophisticated, gaping rustics but skilled operatives hard at work; while personal acquaintance with Exeter disclosed not the sleepy old cathedral city of his imaginings but a hustling manufacturing town, thronged with merchants and traders from all parts of the world, and possessing a market whose scope and financial turnover was only equalled by that of Leeds. It was inevitable that Exeter, with her central position, shipping facilities and direct overseas connection, should eventually attain complete ascendancy, to the final discomfiture of Crediton, whose birthright and blessing, although in reverse order, she contrived to acquire. Crediton in 1050 was obliged to surrender her episcopal see and in 1538 her prosperous wool-market to her overgrown sister, retaining only her claim to seniority, at best an academic privilege even if conceded, which actually is not the case.

In the early days of mainly manual output, Devonshire's advantage lay in the abundance of raw material. The wool grew upon her own pastures and wide moorlands, finding its way with few transport difficulties to the hands that dealt with it, while abundant water-power to work the mills poured down every valley.

Originally all combing, spinning and weaving was carried on as a handcraft in the cottages, where the necessary implements of the trade, spinning-wheels, carding-combs and hand-looms, were part of the customary household effects, and, as Hooker describes, kept entire families occupied. One wool-comber was supposed to keep eight spinners employed, and wool was either sent to market, and there bought by the more prosperous combers and spinners, or distributed by monks, farmers and flock-masters direct to the cottagers. They returned it spun into chains, these being bought by weavers, formerly also called webbers—a very common Devonshire surname today—in the market or distributed again for weaving upon hand-looms, most of which were hired at a small rental from flock-master or dealer. The weaver returned his work, this time as a piece of rough cloth, and then the clothier or merchant stepped in and took it either to his own or the town fulling or tucking mill—the terms fulling and tucking being synonymous. The first process being a thorough washing, these mills were always situated by rivers or streams in which short wool was dipped in open baskets and long wool wrung out by the use of hooked poles. Cleansing with fuller's earth to remove grease followed, then immersion in the dye vats, after which the cloth was spread upon racks to dry in long, covered sheds. The finishing process was carried out by *burlers*, often women, who with burling-irons, a form of tweezers, nipped out any knots or small excrescences which might be left, and shearers, whose name testifies to their particular tidying-off work. For raising the nap of the cloth, teazels were always used, fields of this plant (*Dipsacus fullorum*) being specially cultivated for the purpose, and though many machines have since been invented to replace this process, it is said that all have failed to effect an improvement on the finish imparted by the old-fashioned method.

Sometimes a master weaver, instead of putting out his work, had several sheds in which he kept apprentices weaving under his own eye. As time progressed this method was preferred—at least by the masters—since it eliminated "wastage" in the form of petty pilfering from the materials doled out, the hand-workers in the villages frequently forgetting to return as much material as would settle their own clothing problems. However and wherever cloth was woven, the final fulling or tucking, dyeing, burling and shearing could only be done at a tucking mill, and there too it was baled and packed by the wool-merchants, either for the great open markets or for private shipment under contract.

Before exportation, however, it was examined and measured by Government aulnagers, or inspectors, on the same principle as tin was "coined," for assessment of royal dues. The necessity for systematic checking can readily be imagined. Every trade has its tricks, to which cloth proved as adaptable as anything else. Even as the strawberry-vendor displays the fattest berries on the top of the basket, so the wool-merchant contrived that the best-quality material headed the bale, too often covering a greater multitude of sins beneath than charity itself. Indeed the modern farmer is not always over-particular about removing impurities which make weight when packing his wool sacks today. Also, being stretchable, judicious pulling of the cloth, to achieve regulation length or ensure a surplus which might be removed for private use, proved a temptation to the unscrupulous, and anyone who has been unfortunate enough to buy a stretched woollen garment can sympathise with efforts made to discourage the practice. Barnstaple cloth, after maintaining a high standard for centuries, acquired a bad reputation, which was unfortunate, since the sins of omission were eventually traced to her near neighbour Pilton, who earned the invocation: "Woe unto you Piltonians who make cloth without wool"; but whether Pilton was actually the arch-offender or merely the scapegoat remains open to controversy. The mischief was sufficiently widespread, however, to necessitate frequent legislation for the suppression of many practices which brought the trade into disrepute.

In the same manner as the Stannery courts legislated for the tinners, so the activities of the wool operatives, masters and men, were strictly controlled by the regulation of their "gilds," the precursors of the modern trade unions. Each town had its own guild, as that of St Lawrence in Ashburton, St Nicholas in Barnstaple and the "Worshipful Company of Weavers, Fullers and Shearmen of the City of Exeter." Each was incorporated by charter and proudly displayed its own arms, usually embodying at least one of the trade insignia. St Lawrence's Guild, for example, bore a teazel, the fullers' badge, as well as the tinners' sun and moon in reference to the town's double trade. Exeter's "Worshipful Company" displayed a regular outfit of tools: two shuttles, a pair of shears and two burling-irons, besides the teazel, being among their armorial devices. In those days a man was proud to wear the livery of his calling, which he donned as assiduously as his descendant scrambles out of it, and even as the stranger visiting Devon today is impressed by the pink sheep of the countryside, so in early times and, indeed, well into the nineteenth century an outstanding sight of Exeter was that of fullers, spinners and shearers, from warden to apprentice, walking about in their green-serge aprons girdled with scarlet wool—the sign of a guild member.

Every well-known merchant also had his private "mark," forerunner, again, of the present trade-mark, with which his bales were stamped in order to facilitate distribution in days when reading and writing were not general accomplishments. The mark of the wool-staplers resembled a long-legged figure 4, round which were entwined his initials or any other individual device. In the same way prosperous merchants, as well as others, such as innkeepers and often private persons, issued their own "trading tokens," a form of coin, usually copper, sometimes brass or lead, with the equivalent value of a farthing, a halfpenny or whatever the coiner liked to fix. Originating in the seventeenth century when trade was booming and small change in payment for corresponding low wages was scarce, these tokens were common and in general local circulation until abolished by a statute of Charles II. In spite of the official veto, however, their sporadic issue continued, one bearing the Exeter Sale Cloth Manufacturers' stamp being dated 1796.

As might be expected, a large percentage of the Devon tokens still extant proclaim their woollen origin. For example, the Ashburton town halfpenny bore the teazel; Exeter and Chumleigh halfpennies depict St Blaise with his carding-comb. A Crediton token has a sheep; Cullompton and Culmstock each chose a wool-pack, and South Molton a stocking. The Mercers' Arms, the Cloth-workers' Arms, a cloth-brush, a fleece, shuttles and scissors—the last belonging appropriately to John Tucker of Moreton Hampstead—are frequent devices on Devonshire seventeenth-century tokens.

Guild regulations were strictly applied and legislated for the pettiest details, such as permission for one worshipful member to sue another if "his pygge do come into the shilhay after satterday next," to the boycotting of "non tradeunionists" in the city, and the financing of two members to journey to Dartmouth and forcibly annex a wool-laden ship, the export of whose cargo was considered detrimental to the "staple" interests. The principles of "peaceful picketing" and trade tyranny inevitably crept into many of the guild's operations, and so powerful was the wool industry generally that in every reign, with two exceptions only, from that of Henry III to George II, special measures for the "benefit of trade" and to the specific interests of the staples were engineered through Parliament. During the Commonwealth period the cause of the guilds appears to have been taboo at Westminster, which is not perhaps surprising, since during the siege of Exeter by the Parliamentary troops wool had made itself conspicuous in a somewhat unusual form, the eminently wool-minded citizens having used innumerable sacks of their principal commodity for barricading the city approaches. Charles II, however, repaired the omission by enacting that nobody should even be buried unless draped in wool, in order to stimulate the market, and although this applied to the country generally, Devonshire, being one of the principal wool-producers, reaped a substantial share of the benefit. Devonshire's profit meant Exeter's profit, and

Exeter in this connection meant the Worshipful Company, which acquired the control of so many threads as time went on that it was able to compel the cooperation of all other guilds within the county. Whatever methods different towns employed in the preliminary preparation of their cloth, Exeter established a monopoly in finishing technique which virtually necessitated all material passing through her fulling mills before it could be rendered saleable, thus placing a valuable trump card in the hands of the guild, the suppression of innovations or any movement detrimental to its own interests being rendered an easy matter in consequence. Indeed, rigid conservatism in adherence to old standards, excellent as they were in many respects, had a great deal to do with Devonshire's eventual loss of trade when variety rather than time-honoured quality became more attractive to the purchasing public. In its day, however, this influential company enforced its will upon the entire wool industry of the county, and thus upon every town, village and remote hamlet, each of which had its mills, many or few, according to size, from the fifty-six already mentioned in Tiverton to one in this village of Sticklepath. Each mill-owner employed his own cottage operatives, one Ashburton firm, for instance, according to the late R. N. Worth, collecting work each week from thirty-eight different parishes towards the end of the eighteenth century. One of the last Chagford serge manu-facturers acquired a spinning monopoly for his mills within a sixteen-mile radius, while Crediton was obliged to range as far afield as Cornwall to find the necessary spinners and weavers.

Each town usually specialised in some particular type of cloth, fashionable in its day but long since forgotten, such as tostocks from Tavistock; narrow pin-white from Totnes; bays and frizados from Barnstaple and Torrington; esta-means, perpetuanos, duroys and saggaties from various centres; kersey stockings from Cullompton; while Tiverton, Ottery and Crediton made kersies, the latter town acquiring a reputation for the finest spinning. Devon kersies were famous during Elizabeth's reign, having a wide Continental market, even penetrating to the Levant and Turkey, which latter country also absorbed a large proportion of our tin exports. Vessels laden with these cargoes set sail in charge of such famous merchant-adventurers as Drake, Frobisher and the Gilbert brothers from all Devonian ports, north and south, returning with French wines and other luxuries, sometimes accompanied by a Spanish ship or two interviewed in the course of the voyage and prevailed upon to place their effects at Britain's disposal.

By the reign of William and Mary Devonshire flocks proved insufficient to provide the fleeces required, and wool therefore was brought from neighbouring counties, also from Wales and Ireland. Imports from the latter country were landed mainly at Bideford and Barnstaple, whence the inevitable pack-horse conveyed them southwards to Crediton, North Tawton, Ashburton, Chagford or any place *en route* which required raw material. Then, having shed its wool the stalwart beast of burden was reloaded with products from the south, luxuries brought in by the trading vessels, these in their turn being distributed upon the homeward journey to any of the prosperous merchants prepared to offer a good price.

Kersey eventually yielded place to serge manufacture, Honiton being one of the pioneers in this departure. In 1660 Exeter's great serge market was established, claiming a weekly turnover of £10,000, a great sum in those days although insignificant when compared with the amounts which change hands at any modern cattle auction held in the same city. I have seen more than one farmer at Exeter market hand a £1,000 cheque to an auctioneer's clerk for a "lot" of bullocks bought as a sideline speculation upon account of their promising appearance. Twentieth-century values, however, bear little relation to those of the early Georgian period.

Cloth was sent in from most Devon towns, North Tawton, Crediton, Tavistock, Buckfastleigh, Ashburton, Cullompton, Tiverton, Modbury, Bampton and Newton Bushel, now a part of Newton Abbot, to name only a few from a list which at one time must have included every village that could boast a mill or a stream to turn it, and in this land of many waters it would be difficult to find one that could not. From Exeter the finished cloth was exported *via* Topsham or loaded upon foreign merchantmen that lay alongside her own quays, accessible to the low-tonnage vessels of those days, arriving from Italy, Spain, Portugal, Holland and France, as well as from the East. It is interesting to note that as Devon owed this great industry in the first place to the enterprise of her old monasteries, so on the crest of her prosperity much of her export trade took the form of dark serge, suitable for the habits of monks, nuns and priests in the Roman Catholic countries represented by many of these foreign customers.

In the nineteenth century Exeter supplied the East India Company with the type of serge known as long ells, of stipulated weight and measurement. Through the Company Devon enjoyed the monopoly of the China trade, for which large consignments of material were supplied annually. Ashburton, South Molton and one mill in the little village of Sticklepath turned out red serge for Indian rajahs' troops, some of which is said to be still in existence.

Devon's serge manufactures outlasted all others and only collapsed finally with the Government's withdrawal of its licence to the East India Company in 1858, and the consequent loss of the county's Eastern trade. The door was thus opened for competitors provided with more up-to-date machinery, which soon out classed Devon's hand spinning and weaving. Although one or two of the more progressive mill-owners introduced the spinning-jenny and other new inventions, in general Devon's initiative proved unequal to the occasion, and the northern factories, having the advantage of steam power and proximity to essential coal supplies, soon established a lead. One or two mills in Buckfastleigh, Chagford and North Tawton continued to produce serge almost down to the present day, but the Crimean War followed by the Indian Mutiny and the consequent liquidation of the East India Company may be regarded as the factors which finally determined the fate of Devonshire's five-century-old woollen industry.

With the industry went the picturesque paraphernalia, the water-wheels, the humming looms, the green-aproned, scarlet-girdled operatives, but the Worshipful Company of Fullers, Weavers and Shearers, alone of the city's many former guilds, exists to this day, and I am indebted for much of my information to one of its members, a former Master and actually a grandson of the last serge manufacturer in Exeter. The guild, now more usually designated the Incorporation, functions, like Bideford Bridge, as a charitable body, relieving within its capacity the needs of a city over whose fortunes it once so jealously presided.

Again after the manner of the Bridge Trust, the funds of the company are largely devoted to educational purposes, such as the conferring of scholarships, and until the second world war the members held an annual dinner, which, however, was not provided out of the funds subscribed for charity but at the expense of "Mr Master," as he is formally addressed, who was thus called upon to supplement his ordinary contribution with another £50 as the price of eminence. Under present conditions the dinner has been suspended, yielding place to an "austerity" lunch of bread-and-cheese and beer —good old-fashioned fare not inappropriate to an old-world survival.

The complete failure of the county's woollen manufacturers affected farmers and sheep-breeders very little, the demand for the raw commodity being transferred rather than lost. Northern trade was booming, the railways had come into operation, marketing facilities continued, and as far as the producer was concerned, the position remained much as before. In any case, from the farmer's point of view the fleece of a sheep is usually a sideline, valuable indeed but not the main source of profit, but whether sheep were primarily bred for wool or mutton, farmers of the Tudor period were certainly alive to the value of fleeces. Big combines to force up prices were not unusual, apparently, and in order to discourage this practice by limiting profits, an enactment of Henry VIII prohibited any individual from keeping more than 2,000 sheep, exclusive of lambs. Sheep, it would seem, in those days were reckoned by hundreds, each of which numbered 120, in the same way as a Devonian hundredweight of potatoes weighs 120 lb. The 2,000 sheep therefore actually amounted to 2,400, an enormous flock at any time, the prohibition thus having the appearance of a "gesture" to meet a complaint rather than an effective restriction. Upon questions of sheep-breeding and the production of fleeces,

Overlooking the Erme valley at Harford—one of Devon's many hedges which will soon disappear altogether

however, one is wandering into the realm of agriculture, and having brought the story of Devon's woollen industry back to its source, the next chapter must deal with the sheep of today, grazing upon the same wild hillsides and upland pastures where their close-woolled, hairy ancestors grazed centuries ago, before the first fulling mills turned or the Worshipful Company of Fullers, Weavers and Shearers assembled to discuss problems and conditions which "Time's wasting hand" has long since borne away.

BIBLIOGRAPHY

Devon Association Transactions, VIII, p. 323, P. F. S. Amery; VIII, p. 797, J. Brooking Rowe; V, p. 90, Sir John Bowring; V, p. 216, H. S. Gill.
Church History. Fuller.
Synopsis Chorographical of Devon. Hooker.
History of Devonshire. T. Moore.
A short History of the Worshipful Company of Weavers, Fullers and Shearers of the City of Exeter. Beatrix Cresswell.

Devonshire's network of hedgerows around Widecombe-in-the-Moor

CHAPTER XI

THE WOOL-BEARER

ALTHOUGH no longer the leader of the woollen industry, being conventionally the "cream county" mainly famous for red cattle and lush meadows, even now in the twentieth century Devon is still a land of sheep. Indeed, when every allowance is made for changing conditions such as enclosure and the encroachment of town upon country, the numerical disparity between the number kept during the seventeenth and eighteenth centuries, when Devon trebled her flocks, and the county's stock in the year immediately preceding the 1939–45 war may be regarded as negligible. The total reached at the height of the woollen industry was more or less maintained, and in 1876 943,542 sheep still grazed in Devon. The agricultural returns for 1938 give the number as 944,361, and although in the ensuing war period the figure dropped by nearly a quarter of a million, the total is exceeded by no county except Northumberland.

In an old *Field Book* (undated) a sheep is defined as "the animal which bears wool," and the evolution of the modern animal in its many guises from this nondescript origin cannot be traced with any certainty. The earliest sheep-breeders paid considerable attention to wool production and concentrated upon the largest varieties of sheep in order to obtain proportionately bigger fleeces. This experiment was not entirely successful, however, the heavier wool, when obtained, proving too coarse to be of much value. In the early days upland sheep were close-fleeced, their wool being hard and matted, overlaid with coarse hair, like moss growing under grass. Its preparation entailed so many difficulties that manufacturers living in the hundreds of Tavistock, Roborough and Lifton during the reign of Edward IV successfully petitioned Parliament for permission to mix flock and lambs' wool with the raw product, adulteration of any kind being subject to heavy penalties if unauthorised. This coat was, of course, the natural covering consequent upon the climate, being a pelt rather than a fleece. Selective breeding eventually produced the long, soft wool subsequently obtained, for an animal's coat, like human hair, is mainly hereditary, otherwise the pelts of Arctic, fur-bearing animals reared in captivity would deteriorate in the course of a few generations. The natural fleece of a mountain sheep is close-fitting and light, like that of the black Welsh variety, in no way impeding the animal's agility. To this rule the Scotch mountain sheep, widely introduced upon Dartmoor within recent years, provides an exception. The unwieldy fleece of this little beast is probably more artificial than natural, however, serving no purpose that would not be equally effected by a close covering and proving a frequent source of danger in water, brambles, or any of the predicaments which beset the path of the upland flock.

Up to date the black Welsh sheep has not invaded Dartmoor in strength, which is curious, since this active, deer-like breed should prove peculiarly suitable to the country. It has as yet failed to capture local imagination, but may eventually supplant the "Scotchman," over whom it has the advantage of size. The "freak" blackamoor, which, despite the proverb, does not occur in every flock, was popular in the days of hand-spinning, his fleece being usually reserved by the owner for family use, since it provided a naturally black wool for home-made stockings and eliminated the dyeing process.

There are four breeds regarded as belonging essentially to the county: the Devon Long-wool, the Dartmoor, the Exmoor and the Close-wool, the latter being seen for the most part in North and East Devon, and is easily recognisable by the distinction its name implies. The Dartmoor resembles the Devon Long-wool in many respects, but has a pied or "smutty" face and legs. The white-faced Exmoor carries a short, straight fleece and is horned. There is also a white-faced variety of the Dartmoor breed, known as the Wide-combe sheep, this being a somewhat smaller but hardier animal, able to live upon the hills throughout the year if necessary. The "Scotchman," unmistakable upon account of its diminutive size, is still regarded as an alien, although numerous upon the Moor, where it is looked upon with disfavour by everyone except its owner. The outstanding characteristics of all the native breeds have become less pronounced within recent years owing to excessive crossing. The object of this was to reduce the size of all sheep as much as possible. Small joints of mutton were in great demand, and the larger the animal, the less ready the market for its carcase. With the introduction of meat rationing, however, and the sale of flesh by weight instead of by joint, the situation was reversed and the big old-fashioned breeds returned to popularity.

Most generally distributed, perhaps, is the white-faced Devon Long-wool, particularly popular upon the clay lands of Mid-Devon, since it does well upon heavy ground, where it also produces the finest fleece. On two adjoining farms in this locality, the one heavy the other light, the weight of wool borne by each ewe differs by as much as 2 lb. in favour of the heavier land. A possible reason for this is that sheep which live mainly upon clay develop more oil in the wool as a natural damp-course, those mainly inhabiting dry ground not requiring and therefore not developing this form of protective covering.

The fleece of a good Devon Long-wool ewe should "tie up" at about 15 lbs., which at the present price of 1s. 4d. per lb. means an average return of £1 per fleece. A Dartmoor or Exmoor fleece is little inferior. A Close-wool seldom yields more than 8 lb., a Scotch about 5 lb., while the sheep peculiar to the South Hams—sometimes reckoned as a separate and fifth Devon breed—much resembling the ordinary Long-wool, but higher upon the leg, carries an equally long but softer fleece, slightly inferior in weight. A good sheep for either wool or mutton is the Improved Dartmoor, a cross between a Dartmoor ram and a Devon Long-wool ewe, a blend which has proved particularly satisfactory in this district.

A heavier Scotch sheep can also be reared upon lowland pasturage, where this naturally minute breed responds to the new conditions, as do many animals or plants when introduced to fresh country. Upon enclosed lands, however, the Scotch sheep is far from popular, being an incorrigible breaker whom no fence, short of a high stone wall, can contain. Where its head can go the rest will follow, and even the trailing fleece seems no handicap to its activities. Quite recently I saw one scale an almost perpendicular bank and crash through a crowning tangle of brambles with the agility and thrusting capacity of a rabbit. Few dogs would or could have negotiated such an obstacle, but the little ewe never hesitated, and although she left handfuls of wool on the brambles, they scarcely impeded her course. Complete must be the entanglement that can hold it, as one who has had the task of extricating a great many knows to his cost. Also it fights the liberator like a cornered deer, and a particularly pugnacious little lady, whom I once found wedged between two rocks, although in a pitiable condition butted so resolutely that I doubt if I could have got her out had not my companion held her by the horns during the operation.

This little animal's capacity for getting into difficulties is unsurpassed even by a hedgehog. It is like a headstrong boy, always requiring somebody to help him out of his difficulties. I have found Scotch sheep in bogs, deep water, marooned on crags, wedged in crevices, hopelessly tied up in barbed wire or blackberry tangles, caught in rabbit-traps and one fighting a large dog in a garden the fence of which it had penetrated. Unlike most sheep, however, it seldom gets upon its back, being too agile. Its one advantage is its hardihood and ability to thrive upon the roughest pastures. In this respect the Exmoor and Close-wool breeds also possess an advantage over either the Dartmoor or Devon Long-wool, both of which require roots or the equivalent during the winter if their condition is to be maintained. The Exmoor, also, is a lighter feeder generally, and there is a Devonshire convention that three Exmoors can be kept for two of any other breed.

But whatever the kind, it all comes back to sheep in the end as the backbone of farm stock. "Sheep is the most profitablest cattle that a man can have," wrote Fitzherbert two hundred years ago, and upon land where sheep can be kept, few farmers would question the assertion. By no means the whole of Devonshire can be regarded as sheep land, however. Dairy and wool farming seldom combine. Calves and lambs are rarely seen at play in the same paddock, and the cream country is not sheep country. Upon the red land, for example, or the great northern plain of Devon, the dairy cow and the store bullock predominate, whereas many hill farmers of the central and moorland areas keep only a sufficient number of cows to satisfy their own needs. There are many mixed holdings, of course, but usually there is a clear distinction between the land occupied by the respective stock. I have in mind one East Devon 400-acre farm roughly halved by a lane below which no sheep were ever seen, above it no cows, the lower land being "unsound" for the one, the higher unsafe for the other.

In the wild state a sheep is a native of high ground devoid of fen or forest, its true habitat being, indeed, above the timber line. Nature, who insists that every creature keeps its place, has rendered it unsafe for the wild sheep to stray below its own domain, the wolf, the mountain lion, the lynx, the leopard and the grizzly bear being ever upon the watch to ensure that boundary laws are rigidly observed. Even the mountain flock could not survive in the regions controlled by the big carnivores, and is therefore restricted to the hardier life and more Spartan fare of the uplands, to which it is constitutionally adapted. The inert, slow-witted animal into which the domestic sheep has degenerated, while surrendering the agility and much of the hardihood that characterised its wild ancestry, has retained all its racial weaknesses, and while unable, with a few exceptions, to subsist entirely upon mountain herbage, has never acquired the ability to withstand the lethal effect of certain grasses produced by permanently wet conditions.

Precisely to define the character of ground that is fit or unfit for sheep would be impossible. The distinction is more easily appreciated at a glance. It is neither entirely a matter of altitude nor of geology, although based upon both. Generally speaking, however, a level field with a clay soil upon which surface water lies is regarded askance, except during periods of drought, when anything is safe. Damp is the real enemy, and particularly the soft grass which long-persisting surface water produces. Much of the danger can be eliminated by draining, however. Along the upper Taw valley lies a strip of clay land differing little in level or composition, but while some of the fields are kept thoroughly drained, upon others nothing of the kind has been attempted. Upon the former sheep graze or lie immune from harm, while disastrous experience has long disqualified the latter as sheep ground. Adjoining these unwholesome pastures, by the way, is one field, lower lying but safe, because drained by natural watercourses and always free from surface accumulations.

Under any circumstances, the man who pastures or, above all, allows his flock to lie overnight on doubtful ground is walking on thin ice. The enemy is always there, and should temperature drop below freezing-point, the sheep, nibbling the rimed herbage at dawn, swallows its death sentence. Again, years may elapse and ground undergo many changes of crop without losing its sinister quality. A Bradworthy farmer recently told me that some old pastures, having proved unsound for sheep, were broken up, tilled with various crops in the customary rotation, drained to the best of the owner's ability and eventually resown with grass. That the ground would be safe after such treatment nobody doubted, and sheep were again tried upon it, all reasonable precautions being observed. "But it was no good," he concluded. "They 'cawded' and we lost most of them."

This incurable disease, to which rabbits also are subject, takes two forms, bacteriologically distinct, perhaps, but classified under the same heading by farmers. In one case the animals lose flesh rapidly and may be written off as a dead loss as soon as infected. In the other, presumably when the liver is affected before the lungs, they fatten abnormally prior to the subsequent decline, and may then be hurried away to the slaughter-house "to save their lives," as the phrase goes. Butchers do not object to "cawded" sheep in the early stages, the flesh being still officially regarded as edible, and farmers who consider that unfit ground requires sheep dressing sometimes stock it with animals intended for early market, selling them immediately they fatten. Once again it is a case of what the eye does not see, but bought mutton rarely appears upon the farmer's own table. "We know too much about it," I was once assured; and it is well not to allow one's imagination too free a rein when the local product appears at dinner-time. When staying once at a primitive little farm on the north coast, we heard that one of the two sheep which the establishment maintained had died a natural death, and for the next few days watched the menu anxiously, prepared to plead loss of appetite or a dining-out engagement should mutton form an inescapable item. Fortunately it did not. Perhaps we also were supposed to "know too much about it."

By choice and instinct sheep are averse to wet conditions, in which respect they differ curiously from other animals. During hot weather the first impulse of a cow or a horse is to get into water. A pig wallows, and even a dog lies in a shallow pool. Sheep seek shade, but always in a dry place. In a sloping field they lie upon the highest ground, and never enter water of their own accord, drinking, when they drink at all, from the edge, while other animals wade knee-deep for the purpose. To cross a mountain stream they never splash through a ford, after the manner of cattle, but choose a place where they can either jump from bank to bank or where boulders provide stepping-stones or, more literally, leaping stages. There are few prettier sights on the moorland than a hill flock crossing a boulder-strewn torrent in long, leisurely file, each animal moving like clockwork with masterly command of hoof and limb, and always without mishap if unflurried. The skill with which their paths are chosen is also worth studying. Not only do they mount the steepest hills at an easy gradient, but a sheep-track is always a dry track. The animals themselves may wander into swampy ground and even the actual bogs when hard pressed for food—often with disastrous consequences—but no path leads through wet places. The beaten way invariably winds round, and whether from the systematic choice of dry footing or owing to the natural drainage of the uplands, the Dartmoor sheep never suffers from foot-rot, which is so prevalent in other parts of the county. One does not see a lame sheep on the Moor unless as the result of accident. In East Devon, upon the contrary, although the flinty soil is generally healthy, lameness either from strip, foot-rot, or the more formidable "lewer"—a core-like growth at the root of the hoof—is very prevalent. There, limping stragglers follow the driven flocks, and the sight of a ewe kneeling to feed is only too common. Possibly the clay soil is responsible for this, but however that may be, the heavier the land the lamer the sheep is a general rule.

A lame flock reflects discredit on the shepherd, although he is not always to blame. Seasons occur when the utmost care proves unequal to the task of keeping a flock sound upon its feet, even as there are summers when the dreaded blow-fly—the worst enemy of sheep—is abnormally busy. The whole-time shepherd, in the West Country even as else-where, is essentially a responsible man who takes pride in his work, regarding the upkeep of the flock not only as a point of honour but one upon which his local reputation as well as his job depends. I always remember the case of a lamb which, being attacked by fly, crept away into thick cover and could not be found until it had reached such a state that a complete body bandage was necessary. After treatment the shepherd scrupulously covered the patient with a piece of sacking very much its own colour, being particularly anxious that it should not be conspicuous and so proclaim to his neighbours or professional rivals that an animal under his care had reached such a condition.

Conventionally at least the shepherd has always been a romantic figure. Outstanding among rural personalities, he has captured the fancy of poet, artist or story-teller all down the ages, and even his modern representative, although shorn of all romantic frills, remains a picturesque character. Upon one farm near Kenn, a quarter of a century ago there still worked a man who would have brought fame to any painter capable of perpetuating him on canvas. Grey, shrunken, crippled with rheumatism contracted during fifty winters in the fields, he still tended his flock with long-prac-tised efficiency. He carried or rather leaned upon a crook which was doubtless an heirloom, and by his side hobbled a bob-tailed woolly dog, also so bleached by "age's frost" that he looked, if possible, more venerable than his master. The old man's voice and the old dog's bark, as they rounded up the flock, rolled back the years, recalling the period of Blackmore or even Thompson, since when the tranquil Kenn valley or the heathery slopes of Haldon had altered very little.

The shepherd, as recalled by memories of one's youth, was always a dignified personage, complete with beard, crook, and eyes which bore a faraway expression acquired by long scanning of rough hillsides. He was always an interesting man, for he saw much in his perennially outdoor life. It was he who could find the best mushrooms or watercress, who knew where the hare nibbled or the covey fed, and even if the genuine man seldom studied Tennyson's "evening star," he had cause to rejoice in a red sunset, for he alone among farm-hands had work to do while others slept.

I have referred to him in the past tense, not because there are none of his calling in Devonshire today—which would be incorrect, although more farmers look after their own sheep than was once the case—but rather because the old-fashioned shepherd, like so many other countrymen, belonged to a type which has passed with his period. He was an institution, a pillar of farm life, upon whose shoulders much responsibility lay, and so deep was his interest in his work that more often than not he spent his entire life upon the same farm.

The first shepherds whom I knew worked for 12s. a week, with cottage, cider, firewood and potato-ground. They also had the perquisite of supplying lambs to neighbouring farmers when one or two were required to replace losses. Should a single lamb die at birth, one of a twin could always be requested from the nearest flock to supply the deficiency, and the price paid, usually about 2s., went to the shepherd. There was no overtime for regular hands in those days, but a bonus at lambing or harvest-time was granted to men from whom extra work might be required. Also, during early summer shepherds supplemented their wages by taking a "busman's holiday" or, in other words, joining forces and visiting each farm in turn to shear the flock.

They worked upon a flat-rate system, pooling their earnings, which averaged about 36s. per week, and it was a festive period to which every man looked forward for months in advance, for besides being highly remunerative, according to the standard of the time, it was skilled work in which all took pride. It was a point of honour that each did his best, and no question of one doing more or less than his share ever arose. That a shepherd should be a proficient shearer was part of the qualifications inseparable from his job, and each automatically took the rough with the smooth in the matter of the sheep which he handled. Work began at 7 a.m. and continued as long as daylight lasted, all meals, and these of a prescribed standard, being provided. "Meat three times a day, sir," a shepherd once assured me when detailing the pleasures that he anticipated on an impending tour.

The hospitality on these occasions was unlimited. Preparations for the annual ceremony upon each farm were necessarily elaborate. They involved the clearing of a barn or "linhay" (waggon-house), upon the floor of which a tarpaulin, locally termed a "wim-sheet," was spread with a tightly packed underlayer of straw to accommodate the knees of the shearers. An easily accessible pen for the sheep was also essential, this being of necessity under cover, since otherwise even a chance shower might suspend operations indefinitely. The requirements also included a table for equipment, such as spare shears, "oil-stones" for honing, a pot of wood-ash for application should a sheep be snipped and the inevitable cider-jug and drinking-horn. A bench for use at meal-times might also be provided. Those were not the days when even elementary school-children must be supplied with dining-halls and "attractive service," and the men were well content to accept picnic conditions as part of the programme.

Each man brought his own outfit, which consisted of shears, stone and white overalls, scrupulously clean at the outset of the tour, and replaced periodically by everyone lucky enough to possess more than one pair. It was preeminently a full-dress occasion, and I never saw a shearer working in dirty boots. I always remember one late arrival who, having other work to do before starting, had forgotten to change his footgear. He noted the omission before entering the shearing-shed, and with a forceful exclamation of horror repaired to the nearest patch of grass for a vigorous, if not entirely successful, clean-up. With each man came his dog or dogs, for wherever a shepherd goes the sheep-dog follows, being as essential a part of his equipment as the carpenter's basket or the navvy's broken clay pipe. These lay around the shed, lolling their tongues in the heat, impatient of inaction, and eyeing one another in bristling neutrality.

The shearer's job was primarily to shear, all supplementary services being provided. Attendant upon the party would be a man—a wool-orderly, so to speak—whose duty it was to bring in the sheep as required, collect and tie up the fleeces and generally wait upon the company, even to the extent of serving refreshment upon demand. If it could be so contrived that every one required a sheep at approximately the same moment, the greater the general satisfaction, particularly if the attendant happened to be one of those mortals whom his fellows delight not to honour but to worry. The ash-pot was never in frequent request, for, as a neglected animal indicts the shepherd, so the cut sheep brands the shearer, and few accidents occurred. Moderation with the cider-jar was also the unwritten law, and upon one occasion only, when the brew, drawn from an old rum-barrel, proved unexpectedly potent, do I remember seeing a party unduly elevated, the unusual character of the drink rather than excessive participation being responsible for that particular lapse.

Smaller farmers whose flocks were insufficient to maintain shepherds worked upon similar collective lines, the procedure being identical in every respect except that the masters, not the men, did the work, and meals were served in the farmhouse kitchen instead of in the barn, the shearers being visitors rather than employees, each man helping his neighbour as the turn came round. Whether owners or shepherds did the work, however, the atmosphere was sociable, and shearing-time an enjoyable if busy event in the routine of rural life. When it was a farmers' affair, old friends often exchanged visits from a distance to help one another over the period, while neighbours whose own work prevented full-time help dropped in towards evening to lend a hand or drink success to the wool harvest. The lure of the occasion was irresistible, and old shepherds or flock-masters whose own shearing days were over would walk miles to "have a look" at the proceedings, to hear the clash of the shears once again, or watch the cloak of white wool slowly slip from the shoulders and sides of each sheep, and comment upon its quality or the skill of the shearer.

Shearing is still an important event, financially at least, but the proceeding has lost the picturesque and social atmosphere. Even before the modern mechanical method was generally adopted, it became customary for each shepherd to shear his own flock at home, single-handed, upon a piece-work basis, while the machine has rendered the working farmer independent of outside help. Employing the new device, one pair of shears can deal with from 50 to 60 Long-wools in a day, as compared with perhaps 35 by the old method. A great deal, of course, depends upon the size of the sheep. A man in this neighbourhood recently wagered that he would remove 100 Scotch fleeces in the course of an ordinary working day, and actually sheared 120. In this case, however, a special effort was doubtless made, nor could such a rate be maintained. As a general rule, 90 would be considered an ambitious target. Discounting spectacular output, a working farmer, helped perhaps by a lad or land-girl, can easily get over a flock of 300 sheep of almost any description in a week, and an old-fashioned shearing party would be as archaic a proceeding as a gang of reapers armed with sickles.

It is, however, pleasant to read that considerable keenness in this ancient craft is still evident among the younger generation, and members of West Country Young Farmers' Clubs have recently exhibited remarkable skill with the clippers, not only in West Country events, but in the more formidable open shearing competitions such as that which, before the war, annually took place in Hyde Park. Sheep-dog trials also have now become an annual institution upon the moors near Yelverton, where Devonshire sheep-farmers compete keenly with those from the northern Fell counties.

In this part of the world, too, some of the ancient "ram festivals" have survived, although in modified and less barbaric form than persisted even a century ago. Thus, May witnesses the age-old ceremony of the ram-roasting at Kingsteignton, and similar observances once took place at Holne and Buckfastleigh at midsummer. Originally, preparatory to the roasting and feasting, a sheep was chased and caught upon the Moor. It was then slaughtered upon a granite boulder and its blood sprinkled over participators and spectators—a clear survival of old pagan sacrificial rites.

Returning to modern times, few Devonshire farms are large enough to maintain great flocks. Upon a rough estimate, the land can support about three ewes to every four acres. In the Dartmoor district many villagers own sheep without occupying any land at all, these being pastured upon the commons or billeted upon farms under a somewhat peculiar system known as "half-crease," the farmer being responsible for the care and "keep," and receiving by way of recompense one half of the lambs and all the wool. A man short of capital is thus enabled to stock his land without initial outlay, but as a long-term policy the arrangement obviously works to the advantage of the sheep-owner, who secures an easy dividend without current expenses. There are also a certain number of Devonshire farmers who, while occupying good sheep lands, keep few of their own but "sell the grass," for which they obtain a considerable price, varying, of course, according to the quality of the land and, above all, the season. Under ordinary conditions, however, grass upon a hill farm should realise about £8 per acre, and the occupier thus gets the benefit of sheep dressing without outlay or risk, and his income is assured. Occasionally sheep or cattle are kept upon grass-land for short periods at a flat rate per head, and I remember one ancestral park, actually just over the Somerset border, upon which sheep were taken to graze at the rate of 4d. each per week, bullocks being accommodated at a charge of 1s. 6d.

As under the half-crease system the occupier is responsible for the care of flocks grazing upon his farm, but the liability is limited, reasonable supervision only being required. There is often a demand for keep when flocks are brought down from the hills in autumn, particularly since many owners of moorland sheep are not farmers at all in the ordinary sense and have no winter accommodation for their animals. Upon this subject, however, there is more to be said, and as we shall meet the Dartmoor sheep again in his mountain home, he may be left for a while amongst the heather and whortle-berry growth until, after the thrusting manner of his kind, he again demands attention.

CHAPTER XII

WATER

RAINFALL AND RESERVOIRS

EVERY country, county or district has its special auditory background, or in other words the predominance of some sound characteristic of the landscape. Around the stately homes of England the rooks hold interminable concourse; in every industrial district the throb of machinery fills the air; and Devonshire's voice is, above all things, the sound of running water. It is heard everywhere, in the "cry" of the mountain torrent, the confidential monologue of the lowland brook and not least in the tinkling of multitudinous rills, audible as one follows any quiet lane or path, although perhaps only subconsciously realised, like the accompaniment of small birds' song to ordinary country life.

An American lady when shown the cascade in Lydford Gorge remarked, "What a waste!" and such might conceivably be the utilitarian reaction to Devon's extensive water-power, unsurpassed by that of any other county, and for the most part unharnessed since cheap coal became indispensable to machinery. Yet Devonshire's streams have not always run "wild and waste," nor was the song of rapids or roar of fall by any means the only story that her waters carried to the sea. As already seen, during the centuries of the industrial boom, there was scarcely a brook within the county which ran its course without paying some toll to the various parishes through which it passed. Insignificant indeed was the force deemed insufficient to turn a mill, and water-wheels of some kind were almost as common upon any in-country stream as foot-bridges. It was not so much a case of water for every mill as mills for every trickle of water. Even today the Taw drives three wheels before crossing a road, and at the end of the nineteenth century it provided the power for two mines in addition. The Ashburton Yeo—formerly known by the infinitely more picturesque name of Ashburn—turned upon an average one wheel for every mile of its brief course, which is actually ten, and there were many other brooks scarcely less hard worked. Even busier, perhaps, were the leats drawn from the Tamar and Tavy, upon whose power depended the copper-mines of the Tavistock district, where in the Wheal Friendship group, to mention a solitary example, seventeen big wheels were kept in motion by this tireless and unpaid natural force. Most of the wheels have long since been dismantled, the mill buildings adapted to other uses. Where serge was manufactured at Sticklepath, for example, the huge wheel which once operated extensive machinery is now reduced to the comparatively insignificant task of grinding pig-corn.

None the less, it seems probable that the vast possibilities arising from Devonshire's water-power will not remain indefinitely overlooked. Before the hurrying Tavy can finally break clear of the Moor, part of her torrent is detained to generate electricity for the West Devon Electric Supply Company, like a tramp required to work for bed and board before proceeding on his way, and it does not seem unreasonable to predict that the county's numerous streams and rivers may yet restore much of the prosperity in which they once played so prominent a part. Devon's lack of coal debarred her from competing with the counties that produced it. Should coal-mining in future prove an uneconomic proposition, repeating upon a larger scale the story of West-country tin and copper, a county which can produce electricity directly by water-power would possess an incalculable advantage, and Devonshire's capacity in this respect is unrivalled. The late R. N. Worth, writing in 1875, remarks: "We find that the total effective power of the rainfall of the county is equal to something like 1,100,000 horses, and expended power equivalent to one million and a half." He proceeds to envisage very much such a coal situation as that already suggested, although scarcely anticipating, one imagines, the problems that have actually arisen.

Water played a great part in Devon's past. Its future contribution may be greater still, but at present a period of "slack tide" prevails. It is notorious that a doctor's family frequently receives inadequate medical attention. One has

Cold East Cross. Modern signposts now indicate moorland ways

known farmers' wives grateful for gifts of rabbits or vegetables, and in Devon it is often a case of water, water everywhere and not a drop to drink. It has been estimated that
Dartmoor alone could supply the average need of 10,400,000
people, yet Devonshire on the whole is badly provided with
piped supplies for domestic and agricultural purposes. The
towns, of necessity, have made their own arrangements.
Exeter has requisitioned the waters of the Exe. Torquay is
served by reservoirs at Hennock and Fernworthy, the latter
recently constructed and impounding the higher waters of
the South Teign; while a conservation of the Wennaford or
Venford water on Holne Moor, made in 1907, supplies
Paignton. Plymouth met her requirements in 1916 by
damming the upper Meavy, Hart Tor Brook, Dean Coombe
Brook and Newleycombe Lake, combining to form Burrator
Reservoir, with a capacity of about 1,026,000,000 gallons
and covering an area of 150 acres. This is the largest sheet
of water on the Moor, and incidentally embraces the sources
of Drake's famous leat, which, originally cut in 1591, for a
long while constituted Plymouth's main outside supply.
Most of the smaller towns have settled their problems by
minor conservations, mostly satisfactory but subject to drawbacks in certain instances, as Holsworthy water supply,
which, being situated near the main road, was much appreciated by tramps, or "wayfarers" as they are euphemistically
termed today, who found it a convenient ablution place for
dusty feet in hot weather. Okehampton's former reservoir on
the artillery range was once used as a rubbish tip by a unit of
His Majesty's forces. Concerning that same supply, now
happily supplemented by new works on the Blackaven, a
townswoman once complained to my wife that "little croco-
diles"—by which, presumably, she meant defunct newts—
got into the pipes, and anyone familiar with the moorland
streams could enumerate "foreign bodies" of a more substantial and disquieting nature. All considered, indeed, there
is much to be said for the primitive well, although these are
not invulnerable, as when selected by a neighbour as a
suitable place in which to commit suicide—an incident
which occurred in this village a few years ago, the constable's
well being the one favoured upon that occasion.

11   161

A relic of pack-horse days at Harford, near Ivybridge

Schemes for utilising Dartmoor's water upon a scale
larger than anything as yet undertaken have been advanced
from time to time, the great basin known as Taw Marsh,
a mile or so above Belstone village, being an area which
inevitably catches the eye of the engineer or company pro-
moter. A few years ago a Bill seeking powers to dam this
valley and pipe a line to other parts of the county was introduced in the House of Lords, but rejected upon various
grounds, practical and æsthetic. The loss of valuable grazing
land was one objection raised by the commoners, also the
interference with water-power upon which local industries
depended, while the question of danger to the inhabited
districts immediately below in the event of accident was
raised in some quarters. As a matter of fact, curiously
enough, several bombs were dropped by German raiders one
night near the site of the proposed dam, and the possible
consequence had the vast reservoir been in existence justified
the fears expressed, as two villages lie full in the path of the
flood that would have been released. The scheme, also, was
considered too ambitious for the purposes required, being
compared by one member of the Devon County Council,
which opposed the Bill, to the cracking of a hazel-nut with
a sledgehammer.

Upon the æsthetic side of the question local and Press
controversy followed the customary channels, some maintaining that the impounded water would further beautify,
others that it would utterly deface one of Dartmoor's most
picturesque valleys. The position was pertinently summarised by Lord Iddisleigh, who, speaking against the Bill
in the House of Lords, remarked that while promoters of
the scheme claimed that the reservoir would look like a
"beautiful lake," in his opinion it would look like a reservoir.
Personally, I have yet to see an accumulation of water, contained by a great dam, that at all resembles a natural lake, the
artificial level being too apparent. Nobody could mistake
either Burrator or Hennock storage for a lake, and by way of
contrast the Red Tarn, under Helvellyn in Cumberland,
could not be mistaken for an artificial reservoir, although
now, like many tarns and lakes, adapted to that purpose. The
difference is hard to define, but perceptible at a glance.

Should the head-waters of the Taw ever be impounded and the great "marsh"—actually a misleading designation—submerged, a fine piece of water might be formed, but a lake never, since its elevation would be false to the natural lie of the landscape. New movements for utilising the Taw water are now on foot and decisions may be reached before these comments appear in print. At present, it would seem, a big reservoir is not contemplated, the flow being considered sufficient to maintain a piped supply by other means. But while projects are discussed, rumours run rife and interested people write to their M.Ps., the fine old river, still unabated, flows down its long gorge, and much more of its flood will reach Barnstaple Bay before its course is diverted by extensive hydraulic experiments.

Within recent years the question of water provision upon modern lines for Devonshire villages has been creeping to the fore. Comparatively few now possess a piped supply and many of the existing arrangements are still almost incredibly primitive. Here in Sticklepath, until 1897, there was not even a central pump. People living at the Okehampton end of the village fetched their drinking water from a public well, the overflow of which was sufficient to maintain a running spout, and this continues to serve a number of cottages within a radius of a hundred yards or so. This, incidentally, is the Lady Well, mentioned in every guide-book together with its neighbour the "inscribed stone," with its almost indecipherable hieroglyphics. Inhabitants of the other extremity of the village, near the Taw Bridge, were less favourably placed, their supply being a furlong down a rough lane where "water clear as diamond spark" gushed from a pipe laid through the hedgerow, its only drawback being its inaccessibility. In 1897, to commemorate Queen Victoria's jubilee, a pipe was run from a spring along the village street with a series of taps from which drinking water could be drawn without such lengthy perambulations. The arrangement does not lack drawbacks. The taps freeze, and if two people go for water at the same time, one at each end of the road, the higher applicant can get none as long as the lower tap continues to run, and as it is customary to leave one's pitcher to fill—and run over—while conducting lengthy business elsewhere, the patience of the person waiting is sometimes strained. Until latterly, when corrosion of the pipes reduced the flow to a trickle, pitchers remained optimistically under the taps for indefinite periods, subject to the attentions of every passing sheep-dog. If one overflowed, anybody who happened to notice it turned off the tap, if so disposed, for the benefit of others waiting above. If left, nobody bothered very much. Each got water eventually, and little bands of hope gathered around a tap were not unusual. As all this happened alongside an arterial road with summer traffic pouring through, care was eminently necessary when carrying the water home. One village character was picked up on the bonnet of a passing car, as a bullock is lifted off the rails by an American cow-catcher engine. He was carried for fifty yards or so before the car could pull up, when he dismounted and stalked off, still grasping his precious pitcher of water, which he had instinctively kept upright during his unwilling ride. This state of affairs continued until 1938, when the rural district council renovated the pipes and took over the supply, which was augmented to provide a pipe-line into any dwelling if required. Even so, out of more than fifty houses and cottages, three only availed themselves of the opportunity, the remaining householders preferring the free product in the road to the payment of 1s. in the £ rate which was charged for the full service. With water flowing all round the idea of paying for it in no way appeals to the Devonian sense of economy, and not long ago when one old cottager was ill he would drink no water unless drawn from the spring in the lane from which he had always fetched it.

There is also the agricultural problem which has latterly received a good deal of attention. Many farms lack adequate water for cattle, as judged by modern hygienic standards. These demand—and rightly, no doubt—water of a high quality for milk production. Here again, however, the would-be reformer is confronted with natural conservatism. Regulation may prescribe and the farmer agree, but the cow remains obstinately unconvinced. "Fair water," as Dickens called it, may be brought into the shippens, but beast, like man, does not always quench his thirst at home, particularly during summer when it lies out, drinks most, and when natural sources of supply have reached their lowest ebb of insanitation. The ditch or brackish hole at which countless generations have drunk, unperturbed by any theories concerning microbes, remains available and seems to be preferred. Few animals are clean drinkers for choice, although often deterred by any foreign substance such as soap-suds in their water. No puddle is too dirty for a dog, and upon the lowlands of Somerset milch cows refresh themselves from the virtually stagnant dykes or *reans*, into which, as a resident once complacently assured me, is discharged "every imaginable thing." The only question with which the ordinary Devonian farmer concerns himself as a rule is whether his cattle will or will not drink the fluid available. If they are content, so is he, and the problem of hygiene never arises.

What the eye does not see causes no misgivings, and the horrors which may be survived unbeknownst are incredible. When living on the eastern border of the county, I found that the spring from which our drinking water was derived had been dammed at its head to provide a pool for cattle, the overflow supplying our little reservoir. The streams which I have already mentioned as flowing through many Devon villages provide household water for most of the cottages on their banks. There is usually a stepping-stone and a little hollowed pool into which the housewife dips her bucket, and if the water is muddy from the activities of ducks upstream or from dogs or cows paddling while they drink, as little dirt as possible is admitted into the bucket. A leat stream running through one village, which I know very well, and which is freely used for every purpose apart from actual drinking, carries the drainage, and far from the cottagers minding, vegetables and clothes are washed in it, and it is used for watering strawberries or lettuce, which are set before and consumed by the unsuspecting stranger. Yet no epidemic of a serious character has ever occurred—and so much for hygiene.

There are few windmills in Devonshire and even waterrams are unusual, the larger country houses being for the most part supplied by wells only. By no means every house possesses as much as a well, however, and it is not uncommon for drinking water to be carried a considerable distance. At the hamlet called Skaigh, near Belstone, for example, two residences, a farmhouse and four cottages were all served by one spring fitted with a perpetually running tap on the fringe of the Moor, a hundred yards from the nearest and double the distance from the farthest dwelling. This is a noted spring, known locally as the Lion's Mouth, with an overflow in which excellent water-cress grows, and possessing obvious potentialities. This state of things continued until a piped supply was installed in 1948. Before then everybody was content, as country-people usually are, there being no hardship in that to which one is accustomed.

The Lion's Mouth spring has so far proved inexhaustible, and similar supplies may be found as a rule even in eminently dry localities. It has been estimated, however, that 80 per cent of ordinary well water is "surfaced," and therefore largely dependent upon rainfall, unless the spring is sufficiently strong to maintain an adequate level during periods of drought. Local as well as general climatic conditions, therefore, essentially figure in all water problems.

The climate of Devonshire varies considerably with locality, owing to the inequality of the altitudes. There is the enervating warmth of the south, as opposed to the bracing air of the northern tableland, exposed to the unbroken sweep of the Atlantic gales, Dartmoor's long elevations considerably affecting both temperature and rainfall. Concerning Dartmoor, Hooker wrote: "And this one thinge is to be observed that all the yere through out commonly it rayneth or it is fowle wether in that more or desert"; and a convention to this effect has always persisted, strangers being invariably assured that the region is the wettest in England, the Lake District alone excepted. Like all conventions, however, this has degenerated into a mere half-truth at best, and over the Dartmoor country generally the rainfall is not excessive, the heaviest being restricted to circumscribed areas. As it happens, the highest ground, that is to say the northern half of the Moor, does not receive the maximum precipitation, for a simple reason. The land rises in a long series of undulations from the Channel seaboard, and depressions approaching from the south-west, the source of most rain systems, are first intercepted by contours which, although lower than many ridges farther inland, are yet sufficiently high to provoke a discharge, the main volume of which is thus expended before the loftier heights are reached. A great deal of rain that passes over the coast-line is thus precipitated over the southern and central Moor, and whereas the mean rainfall at Drake's Place, Plymouth, elevation 12 feet, is 38½ inches, that of Princetown, 1,359 feet at the gauge, is 81 inches. Again, the precipitation recorded on the Paignton catchment area at Holne more than doubles that of the Torquay reservoir area at Hennock, the actual figures being 80 inches as compared with 34—a notable disparity.

The average rainfall over the county generally is 55 inches, but in this respect, as in others, averages are misleading rather than otherwise, since they seldom correspond with the actual amount in any locality. In many districts the depth of precipitation seldom reaches 30 inches, and in the country north of Dartmoor often proves insufficient, although this is seldom realised by the irresponsible section of the populace, among whom the principle of fine weather at any price finds strong if unacknowledged support. The sympathy expressed for farmers when prolonged rain impedes or spoils harvest is seldom apparent when crops suffer from drought, the agriculturist in the latter case being merely the proverbial "grouser." It is curious that rain, actually a most beneficial and indeed an essential provision, should be so universally disliked. "Dirty" is the singularly inappropriate adjective usually applied to it by the country-people, most of whom depend upon rain for their very livelihood. It has been predicted that the day will arrive when the last cup of water upon this planet is consumed. Then will be a "dirty" period in literal truth, but many changes will take place in the world before humanity need concern itself with this possibility.

BIBLIOGRAPHY

Land Utilisation Survey: Part 92, Devonshire.

CHAPTER XIII

WATER-DIVINING

So FAR AS Devonshire is concerned, there can be little doubt
that water shortage, when it occurs, is due to increased consumption rather than failure of existing supplies. This again
is caused by both rising standards of requirements and new
building, the latter not only rendering existing reservoirs
inadequate, but also affecting localities served by private
wells. Where there is no main, each new detached house
requires a storage of its own, and if sunk at a lower level, a
new well not infrequently drains the source which supplies
others by intercepting the vein. The intricacies of the underground water system were demonstrated in this village a few
years ago, when creosoted poles, erected to carry electric
light cables, tainted supplies which, curiously enough, were
farthest away from the line.

During prolonged drought a well that is liable to fail
shrinks even when unused, disappointment being the only
reward of anyone who hopes to increase the storage by conservation. If pumped out, it will recover the level within its
capacity for the time being, but will rise no higher, and the
difficulty begins when the inflow is not sufficiently fast to
meet the demands upon it. There is an old country tradition
that when sinking a well one should go five feet below the
level at which water is found, but this is not always enough.
One sunk upon these premises in 1936—an exceedingly dry
year—seemed equal to any emergency that might arise. The
following summer brought even more pronounced drought,
however. The new well ran completely dry, necessitating an
additional ten feet to ensure a storage.

During that same period Devonshire's springs reached
an ebb unparalleled within living memory. Many
perennial Dartmoor bogs became wastes of sphagnum or
cotton-grass. Spring-head excrescences gleamed white and
waterless on the brown hillsides. Brooks were reduced to

mere runnels, and many in-country wells became empty shafts.

During the first summer, people were content to accept assurances from the oldest inhabitants that such conditions were entirely unprecedented and never likely to recur. When history repeated itself year after year, however, faith in the law of averages weakened. Prospects of future adjustments in no way met present needs, and digging for victory over water became if not the slogan at least the practice. My own well had proved inadequate for some years, and since deepening involved reconstruction in any case, the possibility of finding a better supply on the premises was considered and the services of the local water-diviner requisitioned.

In a Devonshire village the water-diviner is regarded neither as a magician nor even as a particularly gifted individual. He is merely a craftsman specialising in a certain trade, called upon, like a skilled electrician or carpenter, to deal with a contingency that has arisen. A countryman has never heard of rhabdomancy, and in any case would be no more disposed to suspect the water-diviner upon account of old-time impositions than to challenge the qualifications of the doctor because of quackeries formerly practised by charlatans.

In view of obvious effects, it is unaccountable that the practice should be discredited, a little dogmatically, in scientific quarters, and it seems to be a case of an evil name once acquired and never outlived. The disrepute into which it had fallen towards the close of the last century may be deduced from the following expressions of opinion. In the *National Cyclopædia of Useful Knowledge* (1848) the divining-rod is classified as:

"a forked branch, usually of hazel, by which it has been pretended that minerals and water may be discovered in the earth: . . . the rod, if slowly carried along in suspension, dipping and pointing downwards, it is affirmed, when brought over the spot where the concealed mine or spring is situated. The form, the material and the mode of using the divining rod of the modern miners and water finders seem to be superstitions of comparatively recent introduction. Many persons with some pretensions to science have been believers in the powers ascribed to the divining rod."

The Rev. Hilderic Friend, writing in 1883, says:

"This branch of the black arts (rhabdomancy) exists today in China and other eastern countries; it was known to the Romans and is said by some even yet to live on, though it is fast expiring in England."

He proceeds to enumerate the various species of wood employed with the customary preference for hazel, and continues:

"It has recently been asserted that the rod is still slyly employed in Cornwall, although if questioned about it the people would deny all knowledge of such a thing."

Again, in the ninth edition of the *Encyclopædia Britannica* is this definition:

"Rhabdomancy, or use of the divining rod by which the cunning man professes to discover water springs, murderers or hidden treasure. Here it is evident that the decision is arrived at by the diviner himself, not by the twig."

From these comments several interesting points arise. The method is accurately described, but trickery is invariably imputed, the secrecy under which the Cornishmen practised being particularly curious, since considerable publicity is now attached to the proceeding. The implication that the diviner manipulates his rod to suit the occasion is not unusual, being the most plausible solution of the otherwise unaccountable. Upon this point, however, personal observation removes all doubt. The action of the rod is obvious and unquestionable, manipulation a practical impossibility. I have seen a stout hazel-fork, grasped in a man's motionless fists, not only double up but splinter into fragments, and have held his hands firmly within my own while the process was repeated. He certainly applied no pressure, nor could have done so. If anything he resisted the movements of the stick, which writhed and twisted like a captive snake struggling to reach the ground. Indeed, anyone persisting in scepticism after witnessing the genuine process would court comparison with the old lady who refused to believe in the giraffe at the Zoo.

Many natural faculties remain unclassified by science. There is the instinct which guides the young migrating bird upon its first adventurous journey or in building its first nest. There is the sense that enables the badger to locate the rabbit's nest two or three feet underground. The bird finds the land of which it has never dreamed or the prescribed materials for its nest without other instruction than impulse. The badger sinks his shaft straight down upon the rabbits, which he certainly could not "smell," for earth is an effective deodorant, and the divining-rod reacts to the peculiar quality transmitted by means of the hands which hold it.

That some men should possess such a faculty above others is not remarkable. Everyone is not a ventriloquist. There are people upon whom watches will not keep accurate time—a fact, although scientifically denied, the cause being undiscovered. Certain people possess musical or mechanical abilities which others entirely lack, while some are peculiarly sensitive to atmospheric changes. In water-divining, as in everything else, there is, of course, the impostor and, perhaps more common at the present time, the *poseur*, or exhibitionist, but these may be discounted as the proverbial "false prophets" which trouble every age. A typical exponent of the genuine art is the professional "dowser" already mentioned. He is not only a "diviner" but a water-provider, first locating the hidden spring, and subsequently with the aid of his son—in whom, by the way, the ability has not been reproduced—sinking the well and fixing all necessary connections. He only considers his contract completed when the new supply is fully operating.

Beyond a little natural pride in his highly specialised vocation, there is nothing in the least "assuming" about this simple villager, who speaks the vernacular and toils at his well-digging like any ordinary labourer. He is well known throughout the county, being frequently approached by local councils requiring new or supplementary water supplies, farmers whose field springs have failed, or builders of new houses. Quite recently, as it happens, he has been employed by the Devon Council to locate springs in eight districts under the new housing plan, besides being called in to solve private problems arising from the great water shortage (1944). In one place his efforts facilitated the development of a flourishing tomato industry; in another the provision of a swimming pool; and numerous similar examples might be given. He also dowses for minerals, but to find these must hold a fragment of the metal sought in his hand, to supply the necessary contact. This applies also to the location of old "cloam" pipe-lines the precise position of which has been lost, as often happens, when drains have lain unopened for generations. Some years ago a Plymothian, convinced that a hoard of gold was buried on his premises, formerly occupied by a notorious smuggler, sent for New-combe, the dowser, to find it. He failed to do so, but was shortly summoned again, a trap having been laid in the meanwhile to test his ability, and ordered to quarter the ground as before. "I was trying the rod over the yard," said Newcombe, "when down he went, sharp. Before I could speak the old gent called 'Stop,' and took up his gold watch, which I had near stepped on. 'You'm genuine,' he said. 'And now you can go home.'"

Whatever the capacity may be, it is sometimes vaguely ascribed to "electricity" in the body, assumed to be negatived by the wearing of rubber soles. Newcombe, however, being accustomed to country lanes and sodden fields, seldom appears in any other footwear than gum-boots, which have no counteracting effect on his ability. The conventional Y-shaped rod is used, but in this case is fashioned of twisted copper wire, the reaction of hazel in his hands being so strong that the wood merely crumples as already described, necessitating too large a supply of "wands." The equal efficacy of wire is proved by its reaction, which is so violent that I have seen the skin torn from his fingers.

Many people, of course, regard the rod in the same light as the conjuror's hat or the witch-doctor's rattle, namely as a blind serving no purpose except to impress. It is argued that the diviner utilises an intimate knowledge of the countryside to locate invisible water-veins. Taking this par-ticular man as typical, however, the contention is impossible to substantiate. He has received no education beyond that of the village school—considerably less efficient fifty years ago than now. Far from being assisted by any topographical knowledge, it is immaterial to him whether the district in which he officiates is familiar or unknown. Such words as "geology" and "strata" convey nothing to him, and he is unable to classify any rock or stone brought to light in the course of his excavations. With the pride of justification when the shaft is nearing water he will indicate what he calls "watercourse stones"—rocks whose erosion testifies to the proximity of the objective. Beyond that his knowledge does not extend, but the man's faith in his own ability provides, perhaps, his strongest credentials. When a land-owner once demanded in my hearing some reason for assuming that water would be found after undertaking the very considerable expense of digging a well, Newcombe merely replied: "Because I tell 'ee," his certitude carrying conviction which subsequent events justified.

The principle cannot be better illustrated, perhaps, than by a brief description of the process as witnessed upon our own ground. When the water problem arose, application was made to an Okehampton firm dealing in all domestic and agricultural requirements, by whom we were referred to our own local diviner, actually a near neighbour. He arrived one wet morning in rubber boots, an old sack round his shoulders, and with the wire rod in a paper parcel. Grasping the implement with the stem upturned, he embarked upon a comprehensive tour of the premises, indoors and out. Hidden water was registered by the sudden depression of the rod in two of the rooms—one being actually the study in which I write—out through the back yard, across a corner of the walled garden and an adjoining field in a diagonal line. This was tested several times with corresponding results, and other places being tried ineffectually, according to Newcombe there was only one channel upon which to draw. He indicated a certain spot "where the pull was strongest" as the best site for the proposed well, and marked it with a stone. There was nothing to suggest water beneath this particular patch of turf rather than another, the ground generally being of an arid description, entirely devoid of marshy vegetation.

The whole machinery, with its attendant cost, was therefore to be set in motion upon the unsupported assertion of this one little man. Twenty minutes later he was back, complete with pick, shovel and son. With the point of a tool and entirely by eye, a perfect circle was traced in the grass, and the work began.

One of the most convincing circumstances to an onlooker was the assurance with which these two men resolutely plied crowbar and pickaxe through yard after ever more laborious yard of dry, rocky soil, completely confident of ultimate success. The fact that Newcombe is quite unable to forecast the approximate depth at which water will be reached may be cited as further proof that no scientific knowledge influences his predictions. He can estimate by the force of the rod's reaction whether a spring is strong or weak, but nothing further. In this instance water entered freely at 19 feet, but some of his "pits" have been sunk to a depth of 50 or 60, necessitating blasting—an operation also performed by the diviner himself. The entire equipment is eminently primitive, the process of removing all debris from the shaft being effected by means of a crude winch and bucket, worked in turn by father and son. Whatever the depth, ultimate success has always crowned their joint efforts, for Newcombe never digs unless sure of his water. Far from it being a case of manipulation to ensure a contract, the man is completely the servant of his rod, and when this fails to indicate he makes no pronouncement or suggestion. Should the rod remain passive throughout the perambulation he merely pronounces "No water there," inability to find that which is not present requiring no further explanation.

An interesting point that may possibly assist elucidation at some future date is that the water must be earth-covered to permit registration by the rod. Passed over an open stream, trough or pool, no reaction takes place, and it seems evident, therefore, that some peculiarly sensitive bodily trait, acting in conjunction with some unknown quantity in the soil itself, establishes the necessary contact. Regarded thus as a purely physical process, it seems unreasonable to deny its function in certain individuals. Popular scepticism is largely a survival of the inevitable reaction to a period when wands were cut with ceremonial and incantation at certain hours of moonrise or sunset and the entire affair wrapped in an atmosphere of mystery engineered to impress the credulous. Now with all question of "magic" removed from an obviously natural process, its official recognition is probably only a matter of time, and science has certainly made more incredible discoveries than the principle of water-divining is likely to prove if and when it is elucidated.

CHAPTER XIV

DEVONSHIRE VINTAGE

THE dry state of affairs visualised at the end of Chapter XII would not be regarded by the native Devonian as a particularly terrifying prospect. Provided that the customary beverage of the county is available, he could dispense with H_2O, and a dear old countryman once assured me—probably with perfect truth—that he did not know the taste of it. Indeed, the genuine countryman would almost as soon think of eating grass as drinking water, and even as he expects the cultivated products of his soil to provide him with food, so as a matter of course the fruit of his trees supply his vintage.

The crops of any county are, of course, indicative of its soil and climate, and possibly those of Devon are less distinctive than, for example, the hops of Kent, the strawberries of Hampshire, or the flowers of Cornwall and the Scilly Isles. The rich red lands of the Crediton district and the unsurpassed loam of the South Hams produce grain and grass of the best, but nothing that can be claimed as peculiar to the county. It is rather in her apple orchards that Devon specialises, and here she has something of a monopoly, for while Devonshire cream could be made anywhere, being only a matter of preparation, Devonshire cider is the exclusive product of the soil, the apple grown on the red land having a quality unknown elsewhere.

Contrary to convention, the county is the mother of cider rather than of the apple, which, after its conversion from the wild, probably under Roman tuition, wandered about southern England some fifteen hundred years before taking up its headquarters in Devon, where it now occupies nearly 22,000 acres—actually 8 per cent of the orchard area of England and Wales. Cider also was born elsewhere, but drifted west to grow and discover its potentialities, which were first developed towards the close of Elizabeth's reign, when Devon produced so many great things. It was in-

Clovelly donkeys

evitable that the favourite drink of the seafaring county should soon become the favourite drink of the navy. Before long cider casks accompanied the adventurers on their voyages to all parts of the world, doubtless being of assistance in the bargaining for southern produce even as it removes acrimony from modern transactions between farmers and cattle-dealers today. It has always been most popular in Southern and Eastern Devon, the South Hams and Churchstanton districts having the reputation for producing the best brew. Recently the greatest amount has been made round Whimple and Broadclyst, where Whiteway's works were established and large areas converted into orchard, and within the past quarter of a century farmers have found it more profitable to sell their apples and buy cider than make their own.

In a London "daily" a few years ago there appeared a charming photograph of a little girl daintily picking apples into a basket "for cider-making." Having known that particular orchard and its surroundings since boyhood, I was specially interested in the picture and in the attractive fairy-tale that it told. Hand-picked apples gathered by pretty little girls would quench the thirst of few. It would be a most uneconomic and, according to the farmer's lights, an entirely superfluous proceeding. The purpose of hand-picking is to preserve the fruit from bruising, and since apples are crushed in the process of cider-making, precaution against injury would be pointless. No question of hygiene arises. Actually the method adopted upon Devonshire farms is simple. The apples are shaken or poled down, according to the height of the tree, and collected at leisure, to be either bagged or carried loose to the press in a farm cart, into the last use of which no enquiry is made. In either case much of the fruit lies upon the ground for a considerable time, piled into great heaps which are sampled and sifted by foraging pigs, hens, blackbirds, starlings, rats and mice, to mention a few amateur tasters to whose thorough activities I can testify. I knew an old lady who set mouse-traps on her bread-trencher, allowing all crumbs to remain as an additional lure, and a farmer of my acquaintance, acting upon a similar principle, trapped vermin on his cider-apple-heap.

Cyclopean Bridge across the East Dart at Postbridge

Fortunately, as in the case of water-supplies, unsuspected dirt causes no misgivings, nor does it, as a rule, harm anyone. With cider, conventionally at least, impurities work off during fermentation. Anyhow, by the time the apples reach the grinder the worst is over. Troughs and buckets have usually been washed, if only superficially, and the straw, as decreed by convention, is by curious contrast scrupulously clean.

Nothing could be simpler or more elementary than the process. The grinder is worked upon the more primitive farms by the old-fashioned horse roundabout, which in more progressive establishments is replaced by the petrol engine. Apples are emptied or shovelled from the cart into the pan which feeds the grinder, like meat into a mincing-machine. The pulp slides down to its own special trough, tub, or other receptacle, and this is scooped up and passed on to the man at the adjacent press—the cheese-maker—who packs it into the straw. This should be the longest obtainable, as its purpose is to hold the pulp in place, and layer by layer the "cheese" rises like a little rick, four or five feet square, according to the size of the press and the material available, and may be perhaps six feet high. Above the cheese is suspended the press, a great slab weighted with a beam, the whole being controlled by two screws turned with a crowbar, upon the principle of a spanner. This is lowered upon the cheese and screwed as tightly as possible, the juice oozing from every part of the great "apple-cake" and trickling by means of a runnel and spout into the tub. Renewed pressure at frequent intervals is necessary, and as the cheese flattens the sides are pared off with a hay-knife, the trimmings being piled upon the top and squeezed afresh. This process is continued for two or three days, during which time the body of the cheese shrinks incredibly, leaving at last only a dry residue from which the utmost pressure can extract no more. The tub is periodically emptied into waiting casks, and the juice, if tasted, is sweet and rich but far from being cider as yet. The real making is the next and final stage, known as *racking*.

The better the soil the better the apples, and the best apples, as a matter of course, yield the best cider. Farmers who pride themselves upon a good drink to offer their friends often reserve certain trees of a particularly choice little orchard for private brewing. The juiciest apples in the world cannot do justice to their juice, however, unless it is carefully racked. This means removing the fermenting liquid into a fresh cask at the psychological moment, in the precise determination of which lies the cider-maker's skill. Upon farms where a considerable quantity is made, a man is kept in perpetual attendance, sometimes for two or three months, his business being to watch the newly filled barrels and, when scum oozes from one of the bung-holes left open for the purpose, to transfer the contents to another cask. This is "racking," and while the juice continues to "work" or ferment, racking also continues and may become necessary at any hour of the day or night during the fermentation period. Even as an epicure is supposed to watch over his ripening pears, sitting up all night if necessary to eat them as they reach perfection, so the keen cider-maker mounts guard over his casks. I have known hard-worked farmers rise during the small hours to inspect their vintage and rack if required.

It is, of course, the fermentation and not the racking that transforms apple-juice into cider. The change is effected when left in the same barrel, as long as an outlet for the impurities is assured. Unracked cider, however, is usually both sour and flat, and old hands at the work always declare that a caskful which is allowed to "go back," that is to say when the scum subsides again in the same barrel, is a cask of cider spoiled. Judicious racking removes the musty flavour which is otherwise liable to occur, and imparts an almost champagne-like quality which a connoisseur recognises at the first sip. Cider of this quality can scarcely be improved upon as a drink, although at one time a certain amount of illicit distilling to produce a potent spirit or cordial was practised in certain districts, remote Hennock being the unsuspected and therefore highly suitable centre of this craft. It never reached serious dimensions, however, and little has been heard of it during the past half-century. It may therefore be considered a lost trade, the tricks of which have passed into oblivion with those who practised them.

In many a Devonshire village there is still to be seen, close to its parent church, an ancient "church house," such as that which exists at South Tawton or Kilmington. Its monastic exterior to some extent belies the activities formerly carried on within, for although the building might be considered in general the ancestor of the modern parish room or "victory hall," it was here that churchwardens of the fifteenth and sixteenth centuries solemnly brewed the "parish ale" for sale and distribution to the residents. Here, too, the latter, many of whom had walked long distances to attend service, gathered afterwards to eat their refreshments, supplemented by a decorous draught—doubtless under the strict surveillance of some highly respectable churchwarden.

The South Hams for several centuries and until quite recently produced, in an atmosphere of mystery, its own special drink, commonly known as "white ale." With this the stranger professed himself duly impressed, although in retrospect he might venture the opinion that its enjoyment was an acquired taste. Actually, when an enterprising and somewhat sceptical enquirer finally procured an analysis in 1877, the ingredients of the unique beverage were found to be a compound of ground malt, hops, flour and eggs, the only mysterious element consisting of the yeast-like substance used to promote fermentation and known locally as *grout*. In the composition of this grout lay the great secret, jealously guarded for generations by a few and, finally, a single family, which thus acquired at one and the same time a reputation, a monopoly and a steady source of income. Taste and therefore demand for white ale have now declined, and the ordinary countryman, whether he lives in the South Hams or elsewhere, prefers cider to ale of any sort, or even draught beer. Even in Devonshire, however, there are confirmed beer-drinkers whom cider will not satisfy, although—and probably because—it is a lighter drink and generally admitted to be more beneficial to health.

At one period, however, this was not the case, for, beginning about the year 1724, when Devon's apple crop was said to be the heaviest ever known, cider was held responsible for a prevalent complaint known as Colica Damnoniensis, or Devonshire colic, the obvious alternative interpretation being doubtless more frequently applied in those "bluff and hearty" days. This was a serious disorder eventually traced not to the innocent apple, accused once again for the downfall of man, but to the manner of cider production. In those days juice from the pulp ran into granite troughs, the joints of which were sealed with lead, cement being then unusual, and Colica Damnoniensis was finally proved to be nothing more than lead poisoning. This being remedied by replacing the old "moor-stone" troughs with the wooden tubs since used, cider became the drink that cheered without other ill effects than inebriation, and instead of proving a source of illness, gradually acquired a reputation as a panacea for all complaints, from thirst—most prevalent of all and often chronic—to scurvy. As a provision against the latter disease, during the seventeenth century cider was officially provided for the fleet, the only difficulty being to obtain enough, and this supply continued until lemon juice was eventually substituted about 1796.

The country-people of today drink cider as a cure for colds and measles, a hot pint-mugful being the prescribed dose—to be repeated at frequent intervals. Indisposition is not needed as an incentive, however, any excuse serving. Its cooling effect is urged during hot weather, its warming qualities when the Frost King reigns. It prevents chills when one is wet through, and failing all else, work in field, barn or garden produces thirst—the best justification of all. Indeed, in old-fashioned farmhouses it provided a constant solace or refresher. In the days of open kitchen hearths upon which three-foot logs blazed during winter evenings, the conventional pint-mug, stationed at correct warming distance from the fire, was as much an institution as the kettle, and to this all members of the old-fashioned long family had access. Modernisation has produced nothing that quite equals the primitive comfort of an old-world Devonshire kitchen hearth, with benches fitted into the ample chimney corner. Macaulay surely had such a picture in mind when he wrote the closing stanzas of *Horatius*:

> When the oldest cask is opened
> And the largest lamp is lit,

the atmosphere which he creates approaching perfection

When young and old in circle
Around the fire-brands close.

Even the chestnuts glowing on the embers are not out of
place, only the cider-mug being needed instead of the kid on
the spit to transfer the scene from the Apennines to Devonshire.

Memory retains many such impressions, the only difference being that the "goodman," who was usually a farmer,
ex-gamekeeper or country-inn landlord, instead of recount-
ing the deeds of Horatius told endless stories of the fields
and woods, old poaching affrays, village life, sport and
characters of long ago. Then old times, old scenes and old
faces came to life, the cider-mug acting like a magic crystal
while the firelight illuminated the screen upon which each
picture was projected. True, the settles were hard, the wood-
smoke got into one's eyes, and evidence that the spaniels and
sheep-dogs did not scratch entirely for amusement was seldom lacking. Still, when someone rose to replenish the logs,
kicked the dogs out of the way and repassed the mug, minor
inconveniences were forgotten, and it was with invariable
reluctance that those chimney-corner gatherings eventually
broke up.

Then, it must be admitted, the difficulties sometimes
began. There was the farmer-guest who, after a good day's
rabbit shooting and a subsequent fireside "tell," was piloted
to his pony-cart and set upon his homeward way. Once
started, however, he composed himself at the bottom of the
cart for a nap, leaving the rest to the horse, the plan succeeding until the first sharp corner was reached. Fortunately the
crash was heard; man, ferrets, dogs and other impedimenta
being retrieved from the road without much damage. There
was another who started to walk home along a moorland
track, upon the first rough stones of which he deposited self
and gun, with sobering effect to the former and considerable
detriment to the latter. Such were rare occurrences, however,
nor must the Devonshire countryman be regarded as intem-
perate. He could, and still can, consume a great deal of cider
with little effect—certainly in these days when the drink is
thinned almost beyond recognition. Even when diluting was

unknown there were men upon whom it had no intoxicating influence. I remember one who, for a bet, drained a peck measure filled to the brim—not at a draught, but at a sitting —and showed no sign of drunkenness.

Upon farms where it was made, cider was always a recognised perquisite of the employees, sometimes taken into account on the wage bill. Every workman had his little wooden keg, or "firkin," which held two quarts, that being the day's allowance. Sometimes a firkin held three pints only, this being an advantage rather than otherwise, since it provided occasion for claiming the balance, and more often than not the keg got refilled, particularly if the farmer's wife or daughter, upon whom the job of replenishing usually devolved, happened to be amiably disposed. The original filling was always the master's or bailiff's job, done first thing in the morning when the men assembled to take orders for the day. Where several were employed, a row of firkins could be seen hanging, each on its special nail, by the cellar door awaiting treatment. At harvest-time, or upon other special occasions, there was no restriction, within reasonable limits, to the amount consumed, nor was an additional mug refused at ordinary times unless the applicant was obviously drunk. The Devonshire farmer is nothing if not generous with his cider. It is freely given to all callers at the door, and there is no surer way of giving offence, or at least of creating a strained atmosphere, than to decline it if offered. There was one queer old character who carried hospitality in this respect to excess, compelling any stranger who accepted his offer of "a pint" to drink incredible quantities under threat from his shotgun.

His farm in East Devon is still famous for many things besides the eccentricities of its former occupier. It stands among grand trees with a historic rookery upon either side, possesses excellent dairy ground and two of the finest orchards, from which at one period a hundred hogsheads of cider were made annually upon an average. The district is also the centre of the apple-tree producing industry, almost every farm as a matter of course having its "nursery" containing young trees in all stages, from "grubbles," or grafts, to planting size. For this the soil, which contains a certain amount of lime, is well adapted, while the growing trees are kept thickly bedded with a constant "muckling" of young gorse, which heats to form a rich but light mould, almost as fertile as decayed leaves.

It is a great country of gorse, the springtime gold of which is almost comparable with the late summer pink of the heather lands, and here, if not cultivated, it is at least utilised, quantities being cut every year for the apple-tree nurseries. For this purpose a short, close growth is preferable, and it is usually cut in strips, which at the same time provide "rides" through the brakes, to facilitate shooting. Thus a constant supply is also assured, for gorse if allowed to grow unchecked soon reaches maturity, from which stage decay is rapid, nor does a brake necessarily repropagate itself, more often than not dying out completely, to be succeeded by bramble growth and bracken. Many gorse-pods will snap, however, and many petals drift down the breeze before the nursery-men run short of muckling furze, and reversible beyond belief as public taste undoubtedly is, the most revolutionary change yet witnessed must needs take place before demand ceases for young trees destined to produce Devonshire apples and Devonshire cider.

BIBLIOGRAPHY

History of Devonshire. T. Moore.
Devon Association Transactions, XVII, p. 324, Frederick Willcocks.

CHAPTER XV

PRIMITIVE AGRICULTURE

A STORY-TELLER's main difficulty lies in finding a suitable beginning, but surely an account of Devon's agricultural life could not start more appropriately than beside the sea, where everything Devonian begins. In this case it was the southern sea, rolled slowly inshore by a light breeze, and the eastern corner of the county, with Devon's last headlands jealously screening the Dorset coastline, the precise spot being Weston Mouth, which name may suggest little to most people, for it is a lonely little beach approached only by a deep chine down which no modern vehicle can pass.

To greet the sunshine the bright May morning had assumed her gayest colours, and over all had spread a blue veil which softened contours and mellowed distance. In the bushy hollows, where the scent of gorse and sea-breeze mingled, the blackcap was singing. Herring gulls drew silver threads against the terra-cotta cliffs or the vivid green of birch and willow-splashed slopes. Where the brushwood yielded space to velvet rabbity turf the rare blue lithospermum (*L. purpureo-cæruleum*) gleamed as though reflecting the general hue of sea and sky; and on a little terrace, like the first attempt at cultivation made by primitive man, was the potato-patch upon which the fitting representative of old-world, West-country husbandry had been at work.

We met him, or rather his donkey, at a turn of the path, for here, as at Speke's Mouth in the north-western and therefore diametrically opposite corner of the county, the panniered donkey still transports all commodities along the cliff paths. The donkey's owner was not far behind. Round a big rock he stepped out of the past, grey, sturdy, sun-tanned, and, but for one or two minor details of dress, differing little —or so it was easy to imagine—from the man who originally cleared the little patch and planted the first potato two or three hundred years ago.

185

Like his representative on the Cornish border, he too was ready to talk, as men who work in quiet places always are, and soon my wife, the old man and I were seated on a flat boulder, with the cliffs above, the sea spread wide before us, while the donkey grazed, the gulls wheeled overhead, and like a slow-motion picture old Devon returned to life in the story of seventy years and the changes they had witnessed.

Throughout his life, the old man had worked on the cliffs, planting the same little potato-plot that his father and grandfather had tilled before him. From those remote oases of cultivation, facing the sunny channel and unaffected by the frost-laden northern gales, came the famous early Branscombe potatoes which yield priority only to those of the Scilly Isles. His story was typical of Devonshire industry, the almost invariable record of decline which would have been depressing from its monotony but for the individual interest inseparable from reminiscence of picturesque bygone conditions. In his grandfather's time and within his own memory, many of the less precipitous slopes, now abandoned to birch scrub and guelder-rose, grew tons of early potatoes which found their way to Exeter market by means of a conveyance that would attract considerable notice if it appeared in the High Street today. It was a light waggon upon which 15 cwt. would be loaded, and twice weekly during the early harvest this load was drawn into the city by four donkeys, which tackled the hills with characteristic resolution, the slow but sure equipage eventually arriving after paying toll at the four turnpike gates which then existed between Exeter and Branscombe.

Leaning on his long stick, like a bushman from Sir Percy Fitzpatrick's tales, his feet planted solidly and heedlessly among the trailing blue lithospermum, the old man's conversation ranged from potatoes to potentates, from wild nature to world affairs. He told realistic tales of contraband cargoes conveyed by starlight up the deep chines so ideal for the purpose—stories which are merely trite when recounted in a guide-book, but vivid with living atmosphere when related by one who spoke from first-hand knowledge. They were fishermen too, those early cliff husbandmen, and as they wielded mattock or scythe keen eyes frequently wandered

186

seawards, ever on the watch for the wheeling cloud of gulls which indicated an approaching mackerel shoal beneath the steel-green surface. At the first intimation of a shoal off-shore a shout went up, echoed from ledge to ledge along the cliff-face. Tools were downed, and a general scramble ensued to launch the boats moored upon the little beaches below in readiness for such a contingency. Now the fish, together with the busy cultivation and the old methods, have vanished from this quiet little corner of Devon, the shoals dispersed by "night-drifting," the primitive agriculture superseded by changing standards and conditions. But still the old donkey and the older man were tramping the cliff paths so fraught with memories. Still the donkey carried and the man planted the same brand of potatoes, competing with jackdaws and the few wild pheasants for the early crop, tackling the same difficulties and mastering the same problems with which he had contended throughout his long life, but now alone.

As compared with others, Devon is not a great potato-growing county. The culm is too heavy, and it is in circum-scribed areas such as the Chagford and Moreton Hampstead districts, Combe Martin and parts of the Exe valley that a speciality in this line has developed. The suitability of the Chagford soil was discovered at an early date in the potato's history, and this led to the establishment of an open air market at Two Bridges, which enjoyed a considerable trade during the eighteenth century. That pack-horses conveyed the produce goes without saying, and Two Bridges of old upon market-days must in some respects have curiously resembled the modern Two Bridges upon hunting days, although if each assembly could view the other the difference would doubtless seem more remarkable. One can imagine the envious glare with which the much enduring pack-horse would regard the glossy thoroughbred which follows the Dartmoor hounds, while the up-to-date fox-hunter might well imagine himself in peculiar company and would require no admonishing red ribbon on the tails of the pack-horses to make him keep clear of their hoofs.

The old market must have been as picturesque an assembly as the pink-coated concourse of today; and the hotel, had it then existed, would have done even better business, for genuine thirst, keen bargaining and free exchange of money could not fail to bring trade to any bar. Buyers were in constant attendance from Plymouth, Tavistock and all the moorland villages, for potato production was not encouraged in South-West Devon, tenant farmers, indeed, being prohibited from growing more than they needed for their own consumption, or to supply their employees. Actually, this is not as arbitrary a provision as it might seem, and at the present time similar restrictions often prevent the sale of hay or straw unless consumed upon the holding, the idea, of course, being that crops grown for outside markets require no stock upon the land, which suffers in consequence. Without any prohibiting clause the modern farmer seldom grows very many, and even the present war subsidy of £10 per acre cannot tempt him to spare ground which might be more profitably and less laboriously cropped. Upon the culm 4 tons per acre is about the yield that a hill farmer expects, as compared with double that quantity in good districts, while the labour of planting, hoeing, digging and sorting is considerable—also the risk. Every labourer on a Devonshire farm has the privilege of growing potatoes for himself in the field assigned for the purpose. All are planted in one communal piece, each man marking his own row or rows. The planting is done by the staff generally at the expense of the farmer, who provides the necessary equipment and manures, the employee merely bringing whatever seed he wishes to plant; and the same principle applies to the harvesting of the crop.

As to the actual potatoes grown, there is no outstanding variety peculiar to the county, such being mainly a matter of individual preference. Growing conditions vary with each locality, and since the official list contains 158 recognised varieties, scope for selection is not lacking. A potato remains a potato, and the crop depends more upon season and cultivation than the sort planted.

Comparatively speaking, small-holders are more extensive potato-growers than the genuine farmers, and this applies particularly to moorland districts, where little rough intakes, unsuitable for other crops, form a feature of the hillsides. Most of these are owned by the occupiers and throughout the county generally the farmer-owner has become the rule rather than the exception. Whether this is an advantage or otherwise in the main remains an open question, since the removal of restrictions, which are seldom imposed without a reason, does not necessarily improve the standard of farming. Again, much that a lease requires of both landlord and tenant is liable to lapse when the characters are merged in one individual upon whom no positive obligation rests. Repairs are deferred, fences neglected, and while an industrious man is naturally encouraged to do his utmost for his own, lordship of the soil does not ensure that immediate profit at the expense of the land will not be preferred to a more beneficial long-term policy. Everything, of course, depends upon the man. A good farmer improves the land whether he owns or rents it; a bad farmer in either case has the reverse effect; but a bad owner, if also the occupier, is more undesirable than a bad tenant, being in a stronger position. One has seen a useful farm thoroughly exhausted by an owner-occupier who had concentrated upon cereals to an extent that no tenancy agreement would have allowed.

Many Devonshire agriculturists under present national conditions are confronted with this same problem of land exhaustion. Certain soil after bearing three successive corn crops has been taxed beyond its fertility, and as one experienced farmer recently remarked to me, "Now we've got to pay for it." He was faced with the necessity of resowing with grass at a cost 50 per cent in excess of the £2 per acre subsidy originally paid for breaking it, and considered the transaction far from profitable. Similar predicaments are common today, "bad farmering" being the agriculturist's frequent, and not always unreasonable, comment upon the policy required of him. The circumstances are, of course, exceptional, but the practical farmer, assuming that he is efficient, should be the most competent judge of his land's capacity and the crops which experience has taught him that it will produce most profitably. Every farmer, if at all original, develops his own line with experience, but there is a natural tendency to adopt local methods or to use fertilisers that are most easily procurable. Owing largely to the abundance of lime, this has always been a popular dressing, and

possibly upon account of its extensive use in the past much
of the soil is sufficiently supplied with calcareous ingredients,
as recent analyses have proved. Its use, according to Risdon,
dates from about the middle of the seventeenth century,
rapidly becoming general as new quarries were opened in
many parts of the county. No product of the kind has ever
been in greater demand, and Sheldon remarks that a hundred
years ago "lime carts were so numerous that they broke up
the surface of the roads." This is quite credible since even
within my own time lanes approaching the great workings at
Tolsis, near Axminster, were deeply rutted, while the
quarries at South Tawton were thronged with vehicles from
all the surrounding country. W. H. Gamlen, writing of the
early 1880s, describes the queues of carts and waggons which
formed wherever lime was procurable, and also records the
manner in which boys mounted on "fore-horses" went
ahead to secure a place in the queue, upon the same principle
as the employment of messengers outside theatre doors.

Later, distributing centres were established, Exeter,
Babbacombe and Bampton being among the most important.
Rural districts mainly depended upon local supplies, particularly in East Devon, where every available outcrop was
worked. Indeed, upon any farm one may still see the remains
of old kilns which fell into disuse, either owing to the
increasing facility with which lime could be procured "ready
made" from a distance or to the introduction of artificial
manures. However obtained, lime has always been in great
demand among western farmers, and as long ago as 1829 it
was provided in one of the Turnpike Acts that no toll was to
be levied on any vehicle "carrying or conveying on the same
day any lime to be used for manure."

Formerly, East Devon farmers regarded it more as a
soil-lightener for clay lands and a grub-deterrent than as a
fertiliser, although its general utility was always recognised.
Whether suitable or otherwise, however, owing to a scarcity
of alternative manures large quantities are being used at the
moment. Great white heaps, deposited by lorries, break the
green of the landscape, sometimes completely blocking the
gateways in true Devonian style. Last winter I was told by a
visitor that snow lay thickly on the cultivated slopes of the

East Okement valley, bordering the Moor, and took the trouble to investigate the phenomenon, none having fallen on the nearer hills. As one might have guessed, the fields were white with lime and gleamed from afar with a hoary and distinctly snow-like effect—a typical example of the need for checking even first-hand information.

The whitening of the Devonshire landscape not by artificial dressings but through the conversion of so much grass-land to corn is an inevitable feature of present conditions. In the days when partridges were abundant, sportsmen would have rejoiced in the extensive "arishes," as stubbles are always termed in the county, and for lack of which coveys frequently forsook the grazing farms in favour of those where pickings of grain could be found. Comparatively little of the stubble's wealth is claimed today, however, either by wild birds or any other, although the farmer's wife occasionally manages to move a fowl-house on to fields before the all-too-rapid tractor forestalls her. It was formerly the custom to drive Michaelmas geese to the stubble to "finish them off," even as cattle are removed to the Exe marshes for the same reason. Geese not provided with grain are known as "green geese" and seldom reach the same size as their better-nourished fellows.

The green goose was the conventional "poor man's goose," which, being self-supporting, not only at one time figured conspicuously upon the countryman's festive board but also provided a very profitable sideline—with a little judicious fattening—for the Christmas and September markets, the Michaelmas goose being a stout survival in Devonshire among eminently old-fashioned people. For the most part, however, he has seen his day, the modern poulterer preferring the larger, corn-reared bird, and although general shortage at the moment has created a new demand, the green goose more strictly belongs to the donkey and cliff-potato-patch period, and he therefore strikes an appropriate note upon which to quit the subject of primitive agriculture.

BIBLIOGRAPHY

Devon Association Transactions, xxxvii, p. 168, Robert Burnard.

CHAPTER XVI

LIFE ON THE LAND

1. MAINLY CONCERNING STOCK

As mentioned at the end of the last chapter, the face of agricultural Devon has once again changed considerably with the exigencies of war. Much permanent pasture has been retained as such because unsuitable for grain, in the production of which Devon as a whole has never excelled. She reached her peak in arable acreage from 1870 to 1888, since when, excepting the first war period, the amount steadily decreased for fifty years, the figure falling from 602,912 acres under the plough to 415,118 in 1938, for which record neither bad husbandry nor the wheat slump can be held entirely responsible.

The second world war and the period immediately following it did not bring the farmer the same fortune that he reaped in 1914–18. Big prices, of course, were realised, top-grade barley, for instance, fetching more than 30s. per cwt. in 1949. Much of the apparent prosperity, however, can only be described as artificial, being largely due to substantial state subsidies and the general inflationary trend which can scarcely continue indefinitely. These payments flowed in from wheat and potato acreages, the ploughing of old pasture, calf-rearing and moorland cattle. Subsidies, like the price of grain, however, are subject to frequent revision, and several are actually due for withdrawal in 1950.

Grain prices, of course, affect agriculturists in varying degree, according to the crop in which each locality specialises. The red land of Devon, the Tiverton district, and above all the Culm valley, are particularly suitable for barley, a yield of from 50 to 60 bushels per acre being expected in a normal season, whereas two-thirds of that amount would be considered good upon the clay soil of the central and

Countisbury Hill, above Lynmouth—one of Devon's steepest roadways

northern areas. The red loam, on the other hand, is not so good for wheat, of which 40 bushels per acre may be grown upon the Mid-Devon clay lands. In the production of oats there is little difference upon either soil, the clay yielding upon an average 50 bushels to perhaps 55 on the red land.

Since the war the farmer's profits have been further controlled by higher costs in every department. Wages, which still show a tendency to rise, already exceed the highest figure reached from 1914–18 by 100 per cent. Even a set of shoes for a draught horse now costs £1, whereas far more durable shoes were once supplied for eightpence each. The price of artificial manures before subsidisation increased by £10 per ton, £37 being paid for blood manure, while superphosphates mounted from £2 2s. to £7. Lime indeed was subsidised at 60 per cent, the farmer therefore paying the pre-war price of £3. These rates particularly affect the hill farmer, whose harsher land requires more liberal dressing. Much of the red land, for that matter, is less self-sufficient than is commonly supposed. The heavier vein which penetrates as far west as Exbourne has a local reputation for "eating manure," and often proves difficult unless "caught exactly." If Devon clay, red or yellow, once reaches the set condition which countrymen define as "sour," a week's labour may be necessary where a day should suffice to render it fit for sowing. The cost of cultivation upon adjoining farms may differ immeasurably.

To offset this, returns generally are also high. Cider apples realise £14 per ton, as contrasted with £3 before the war. Milk and eggs, as considered throughout the year, have never been more expensive, butter alone remaining at the comparatively low figure of 1s. 6d. per lb. The standard rate of prices received for cattle is also good, a fat beast making £5 9s. per cwt. live weight. A good Devon bullock should turn the scale at anything from 10 to 12 cwt. About £46 would therefore be a satisfactory price for a store beast. South Hams are larger cattle, ranging from 13 to 14 cwt. These are not suitable for all districts, however, preferring a light soil, and whereas they can subsist upon Dartmoor despite the contrast between mountain pasturage and that of

Haytor Rocks—Dartmoor's best-known granite pile

their rich southern habitat, they lose condition rapidly on the culm, even if provided with the best grass that the land can produce. They appear to possess a tubercular tendency which develops upon the yellow clay, and South Hams cattle introduced to this particular area have, almost without exception, failed to survive the experiment.

Milch cows at the moment fetch better prices than other cattle, comparatively speaking. A Devon heifer together with first calf should be worth about £50. Once, incidentally, I bought the equivalent for about £13, from an old country-woman, and was given a receipt for £31—a document which for original phrasing and spelling should have found its way into the British Museum. A Shorthorn heifer and calf may fetch as much as £60 or £70. This beast has not penetrated far into Devonshire, however, being only seen east of Exeter, where Friesian cattle have become popular during the past few years. A farmer at Whimple recently paid £1,200 for five of this breed, evidently foreseeing a future demand for it. Upon the moorland the black hornless Galloway has proved, in the main, best adapted to the hard conditions, but throughout the county as a whole the Devon predominates, a somewhat finer variety, known as the "Red Ruby," being reared north of Okehampton. All told, in 1928 Devonshire's head of cattle totalled 339,175 beasts, and during the war years this number has been exceeded by another 30,000.

The value of cart-horses on the other hand has declined considerably, a good animal now being worth only £40 or £50. The horse, undoubtedly, has seen its day in agriculture partly because the tractor is proving less expensive and more practicable than once seemed possible, and partly because the modern farm-labourer will not adopt old methods. Farmers complain that they cannot get a young man to work a horse, and even waggoners of the older generation no longer undertake the duties which formerly fell to their lot, now expecting to resign responsibility for their teams when the actual field work is over. Formerly, a waggoner's hours of duty differed from those of other workmen. He arrived at the same time, 6.30 a.m., but half an hour was allowed in the stable for tackling up his horses and giving them an initial feed. The day in the field was divided into two halves, from

7 until 11 a.m., and from 1 until 5 p.m., a two-hour break being taken to rest man and beast. While others went home at five, however, the horseman remained to bed and feed his charges, the time occupied in this process depending upon the man and the amount of care that he voluntarily bestowed. Once, the charge of his horses was the waggoner's pride and often his main joy in life. This interest was even more pronounced than in the case of the shepherd, being more personal. There was never any fear of a good carter ill-using or over-working his beasts, his great aim being to spare them whenever possible. He was like a solicitous old nurse, jealous for the children's interests and reputation, and upon farms where more than one waggoner was kept each man had his own stable, whenever feasible, to avoid perpetual friction. I once heard a farmer of sixty years' experience declare that he would give nothing for a carter who was not prepared to steal for his horses, and I have yet to meet a first-class man who would not do so. If an old-fashioned ploughman grumbled when ordered to turn up a field in a manner that involved taking a stiff gradient, it was wholly upon account of the extra work placed upon his team, and he always schemed that the horses should lie in as long as possible, even though doing so meant an avoidable continuation of his own evening duties. "Master ought to have the same bed these poor toads have got tonight" was the disgruntled remark of an old waggoner as he led his three darlings out one wet May evening, and if told to keep them in he would have been delighted, even though the order necessitated fetching straw and fodder and the addition of an hour to his day's work. Another old "specialist" was so particular about the appearance of his horses that when they lay out he made a practice of taking them in on Sunday afternoons to give them a thorough grooming. The horses evinced their appreciation when released by rolling in the dustiest place they could find, while the farmer called the old man a fool for his enthusiasm, which none the less remained impervious to any discouragement.

A valuable workman's attachment to his team was a constant source of embarrassment should the question arise of selling an animal or effecting any redistribution among the other carters. There was one ardent horse-lover—incidentally bearing the not inappropriate good old Devonshire name of Beer—who when drunk, which was his sole failing, enlivened the homeward walk from the village pub with a loud monologue upon the superior merits of his charges and an avowal that he would seek fresh employment if deprived of them. Anger at the treatment of one of these horses, which another man was using in the harvest-field, once nearly cost him his life. An altercation led to blows, and in the end he was knocked down with a pitchfork, sustaining concussion. He recovered, however, which was also fortunate for the other man, who had been arrested, and so escaped the charge of manslaughter.

No waggoner willingly consented to another using his horses, but there were occasions when he was obliged to surrender his privilege in the ordinary routine of farm duty. By one of the many curious conventions that still prevail, it has always been the head carter's job to sow the seeds. Since the introduction of the drill this has, of course, involved horse-labour and therefore no transfer of responsibility. In the days of hand-sowing, however, the horseman scattered the seed while a deputy followed with harrow or roller, for which reversal of the customary order there appeared to be no logical reason, since the other man might just as well have done the sowing.

Procedure upon West-country farms is largely governed by similar customs. In the harvest-field it is usually the waggoner's job to load, although boys are sometimes employed to take the loads in—a curious departure, again, this being responsible work. A shepherd is usually the rick-maker, or "minds sacks" when threshing, and there are prescribed jobs which the farmer himself may or may not do. As might be supposed, it sometimes falls to him to fill a vacancy. When the shepherd went upon his annual shearing tour, the employer took over the sheep, pitching the fold and doing all the hard work himself. Upon no account must he plough, however, or do any horse-labour, and should a waggoner be absent, another employee must be found to deputise or the job stands over. He never delivers any ordered goods in person, although his son may occasionally do so when other hands are particularly busy. Again, although the contrast seems unaccountable, it is quite in order for him to milk. This is the more curious since milking is generally barred by employees. Indeed, modern advertisements for farm-hands frequently contain an undertaking that such work will not be required. That the master should be obliged to do it, however, is not regarded as in any way incongruous, and as a matter of course the task falls upon him or members of his family.

Another recognised part of a farmer's personal duty is the charge of the bull. If he does not own one himself, it is incorrect for him to conduct cows to a neighbour's beast for stud purposes, any odd hand being requisitioned to act as escort. To receive all such visitors is his special department, however, and few employees grudge him the privilege. The management of a bull is not anybody's job, being fraught with considerable danger, which the countryman for the most part takes as a matter of course. At a menagerie he would regard the man who enters the carnivore's cage with admiring awe, nor would it occur to him that he takes a greater risk himself when he unchains the great ruminant which stands placidly chewing in its stall. A bull is a most formidable animal, temperamental and at best unreliable. In the fields he is always treated with respect by the passer-by, but as laws for the protection of the public are strict, particularly in Devonshire, where no bull may graze upon pasture crossed by a right of way, nobody is seriously incommoded. Of the many accidents, fatal and otherwise, that I have known, the victim has always been a man in charge of the animal. However harmless a bull's record, he is liable to a sudden change of mood, particularly in stall or yard, where he does not wait to indulge in the preliminary admonitions which usually presage a charge in the open, thus enabling the object of his resentment to expedite a retreat.

When confined, his onslaught is sudden and devastating, as evidenced by a long tale of fatalities. I knew of a yardsman who, rather than carry water to the stall, habitually released a bull to drink from a trough. Warned of the danger, he expressed contempt for the bull, and indeed his ill-usage of the animal was a scandal upon the farm. Then came the occasion when the bull struck in his turn, and to such terrible purpose that the man, when found, was a mangled heap, his clothes shredded to rags, the body tossed behind an iron barrier which alone saved the remains from complete obliteration.

This tragedy, by the way, proved the cause of another accident which fortunately had a merely humorous termination. The bull was removed to another farm and conducted along the highway by the staff, rope and armed attendants which were customary at the period—more than thirty years ago, when cattle-vans were unknown. The cortège happened to meet a carriage and pair containing two old ladies driven by their coachman, who, recognising the approaching bull as the recent homicide, gave it so respectful a berth that the near wheel took the bank, the carriage overturned and the old ladies rolled out upon the road almost under the nose of the bull, who fortunately was in no position to take action, even if so disposed. As it happened, nobody was hurt, although the coachman ever after disliked any mention of the male bovine in his presence.

A bull when grazing with cows at times finds his harem insufficient, and occasionally breaks in order to cultivate fresh feminine society. In a neighbouring lane the other day I found one atop a bank exchanging pleasantries with ladies of his race in an opposite field. Suggestions that he should return to his own quarters being completely ignored, I preferred his contempt to more active resentment and interfered no further. On the Somerset border, where restrictions were lax, I remember a huge beast who sometimes abandoned his own herd at nightfall and patrolled the lanes in search of amorous adventure. To encounter this great bison-like apparition round a dark corner was most disconcerting, but he never attacked his fellow travellers, who were only too well content to grant him right of way. Particularly rampageous bulls are occasionally handicapped by a pole suspended from the neck to impede their activities over hedges. When fierce, a blindfolding board over the face to render a direct charge difficult was not unusual, although this must have proved an additional irritant. A beast so veiled once attacked the farmer's son, who, being armed with a stout stick, stood his ground, aiming a terrific blow at the bull's head as it blundered towards him. The board received the shock and split in two, thus providing the bull with a clear field of vision. "I never runned so fast in my life," the man assured me. "And serve you right," was his father's comment, "for if you hadn't hit the board, a crack like that would have killed the bull, and I should ha' been sorry to spare he."

No farmer readily admits that his bull is "surdly," which stands for dangerous in the vernacular, and oddly enough the beast is usually upon his best behaviour with the boss. This is not always the case, however, and a neighbour was recently obliged to get rid of an animal which had taken an inconvenient exception to himself—"to the right one" being the verdict of his family, to whom the bull had long been a source of terror. I remember a woman farmer who refused to part with a herd autocrat which had gored one of her daughters. Another insisted that ill-treatment of her Jersey bull was the cause of its "sauciness," which incidentally cost her the services of two successive employees, the first deciding that enlistment, even during war-time, provided a safer livelihood; the second taking refuge in matrimony and removal to his wife's home at a distance.

Upon large dairy farms a yardsman is still sometimes kept, but even this functionary becomes rarer every year. In 1943 we stayed at one such place, where about thirty cows were milked by the modern mechanical method. The farmer and his son did the work, however, and this is now the rule rather than the exception. It was once the custom upon a large mixed farm for the dairy to be let off as a separate department, and many of the older holdings include a "dairy-house" more or less attached to the premises. Here the dairyman lived and took complete possession of the milch herd, for which he paid an annual rent per cow, all profit from this being his property. The "dairy" also included the right to keep a stipulated number of pigs—to consume superfluous milk. The farmer took all risks and was responsible for replacements, also for the upkeep of land to which the cattle had access. Special arrangements were also made with regard to hay, litter, mangolds and other requirements, and a certain amount of overlapping took place unless, as was the case upon some of the largest farms, the dairy occupied a site of its own with separate yard and outbuildings. With its various advantages and drawbacks, this system still prevails in some localities, although gradually dying out. The chances of loss lay too heavily against the farmer, who had no effective remedy in the case of mismanagement or defalcation, and I have known instances of the owner being obliged to take over the herd himself, his rent too often failing to materialise. If satisfactory, upon the other hand, it was a solid contribution towards a tenant farmer's rent realised without much outlay.

The dairy-land of Devon enjoys an almost world-wide reputation, and Sheldon records that formerly, in springtime, inleading roads were blocked with droves of calves brought in from neighbouring counties for summer keep. The reputation perhaps exceeds its merits, since the 710,000 acres of which the county's enclosed pasturage consisted prior to the war is composed of the best and the worst, much of it falling far below the luscious standard of "golden cream" association. For dairy produce, indeed, there is magic in the name of Devon, and I have heard it proudly used in praise of her butter by a farmer's wife whose cows seldom tasted other than rough moorland grass with which the pasturage of any other county might compare favourably. Devonshire cream, by the way, is merely the product of local custom. Its preparation is simple and might be imitated anywhere with similar results.

The above grass acreage includes neither the uplands nor the in-country "moors" and "marshes," these being rushy enclosures of varying sizes found upon almost every farm. Officially designated *Molinia Moors*, from the type of coarse grass prevalent upon them, they cover more than half of the agricultural area of the county, and in central or North Devon frequently comprise the greater part of a rough grazing farm. They are covered with boggy growth of every description, often including willow and alder scrub, and one may wander through mile after mile of this prairie-like country, over which the curlew ripples in early summer and which for the remainder of the year is abandoned to a silence entirely foreign to the general idea of an English landscape.

In East Devon more of this land is gorse-covered, but it varies little in general character throughout the county and visitors from more fertile areas naturally wonder what purpose it serves or what profit can possibly be derived from it. As rough pasturage it is more useful than might be supposed. Cattle accustomed to the conditions, even though wallowing for the greater part of the year hock-deep in mud, not only contrive to live upon it, but do tolerably well, and when occupied by a tenant farmer the rent is low.

Land values in Devonshire have risen even as elsewhere, although subject to the contrasts inseparable from a county of such diverse conditions. Rents, which had altered little during the past century, range from 50s. an acre for a rough farm on the culm to £6 in South Devon or upon the red land. In localities well placed for dairy farming, such as the upper Taw or Torridge valleys, small farms—always more expensive by comparison—may let at from £7 or more an acre, and in this neighbourhood good meadows, let off independently, bring in about that amount.

The saleable value of land is too elastic for generalisation, the prices obtained during periods such as the present or the years immediately succeeding the 1914–18 war being no criterion as to its real worth. From 1917 to 1920 holdings rented at £70 per annum when auctioned realised as much as £3,000, and speaking for the near future at any rate, the value of a farm will be the amount that its owner can get for it. When discussing the price that a holding might fetch, I heard a practical farmer remark, "There's fools about: it may fetch anything," he being a man who was sold out twice during the 1914–18 war rather than pay a figure which he considered merely fantastic. He waited his time and when prices slumped eventually bought a 175-acre hill farm for £2,000—a bargain which he has since turned to profitable account, as the price included timber which realised £500 and an additional house.

From 1917 onwards many farmers suffered from the necessity—as an alternative to ejection—of buying the land which they occupied at a figure which the subsequent fall in prices rendered entirely uneconomic, and the extent to which history repeats itself remains for the future to decide. That the situation cannot recur upon the same scale is tolerably certain, since, as previously remarked, the tenant farmer is now the exception rather than the rule, and it is probable that a great many older men will seize the opportunity to retire from business while values are high, and in stock exchange language "take their profit." If anyone suffers, it will be the amateur who buys during the boom and eventually finds that he has made an uneconomic investment. This, however, introduces another aspect of the case and an opening for a new section.

BIBLIOGRAPHY

Land Utilisation Survey: Part 92, Devonshire.

LIFE ON THE LAND

2. MAINLY CONCERNING FARMERS

THERE is a well-known saying that no gentleman ever made money at farming, and life-long acquaintance with the land and its occupiers certainly bears out the convention. Apart from the proverbial but usually short-lived luck of the beginner, I have yet to meet the permanently successful amateur farmer. For this one can advance no positive reason. The professional may work no harder, he may be no better business man, his knowledge of up-to-date methods may be inferior, as often as not he has less capital at his command. Yet the man who farms as a matter of course, because his father and grandfather did so before him, rarely fails to make a living, whereas the man who chooses it as an occupation, preferring country life to one of the professions, almost invariably loses money, and unless entirely independent is obliged to try something else. The curious point is that the landed estate-owner who retains a "home farm" always *expects* to lose upon it. A well-known West-country M.P. in such a position once told me that for him the best season merely minimised the inevitable deficit. I remember another Devonshire squire who farmed about 700 acres of his own land upon which he had been born. He knew his subject and every yard of his ground, but lost £400 a year as a reward for his efforts. Late in life he handed it over, rent free, to a nephew, also bred in the district. The younger man had just left Cambridge, where he had studied agriculture. He was keen, competent, knowledgeable, and yet, even though relieved of both tenant's and landlord's financial responsibilities, his uncle remaining responsible for rates and upkeep, he could do little more than clear expenses, allowing nothing for the cost of a household, which in his case did not arise, since he lived with his parents. Under ordinary circumstances, with rent to pay and a house to maintain, the failure would have been complete.

Again, by way of contrast, the most consistently successful farmer known to me started life as a blacksmith, being, incidentally, the same man who surrendered two farms rather than buy at a disadvantage. He possesses a distinct flair for agriculture, inherited by his sons, each of whom specialises in a line of his own. Neither of them likes farming, yet they possess the secret of turning it to account, and this applies to more than one whom I know of the younger generation. Disliking it, they still make it pay, whereas others in a different social position, choosing the life because it appeals to them, fail to make both ends meet. The only parallel that occurs to me is a homely one, also agricultural. In local country-house gardens this spring there was an unaccountable dearth of white broccoli: heads no larger than cricketballs were the rule; but in any *cottage* garden gleamed discs with the circumference of dinner-plates. The cottager, the squire, the doctor and the vicar adopted similar methods, planted similar seedlings, yet for some inexplicable reason failed to achieve similar results.

In practice the case is simple after all. There are vocations to which certain classes of the community are better adapted than others, and the genuine farmer is certainly one of a class apart, although his social status varies with the district to which he belongs. Farming runs in families. Until quite recently, at any rate, the farmer's son automatically became a farmer in his turn. It was the one vocation to which he was considered qualified, and upon the land he remained.

In the agricultural classes there are at least three definite distinctions: the farm-labourer and the small-holder, who differ little, since the latter acts in the former capacity most of his time; the working farmer, the usual occupier of the 100 to 200-acre holding; and the large farmer, conventionally but not quite correctly defined as the "yeoman," who is better off and usually inhabits a different type of house by the quality of which the potentialities of the farm and the status of its occupier can generally be estimated. It follows automatically that the wealthier type of agriculturist predominates on the good land, the working farmer in the less prosperous districts. The relative positions somewhat resemble those of the Harley Street consultant and the general country practitioner, the main distinction being the funds at the disposal of each, and the effect of the financial position upon their respective families. On a rich Devonshire farm, whether owned or rented by the occupier, it is customary for the youngest and not the eldest son eventually to step into the father's place, his elder brothers having already received their patrimony by being established upon land of their own. In the working farmer's household the same rule obtains, with the significant difference that the father is seldom in a position to finance his elder sons, the farm providing a comfortable living but allowing no surplus. The young men are therefore constrained to strike out for themselves, and either become small-holders, eventually mounting higher in the scale, or in some cases, when the family is too large, merely labourers.

The latter step does not necessarily involve any social descent, since members of a working farmer's family mix with employees upon terms of complete equality. Communal meals are taken in the kitchen and all save the farmer and his wife are addressed by their Christian names. The farmer is not "Somebody" but simply "Maister," his wife being "Missus," and the same appellations hold good among friends as well as employees. Farmers always call one another "Master," and when referring to the occupier of any holding a villager never speaks of him by name but as

"Maister to Somewhere," after the manner of a Scotch title.
For instance, my good farmer-neighbour Mr Wickett of
Willey is simply termed "Maister to Willey."

There are few harder or more industrious lives than that
of the West-country working farmer. His week is a seven-
day week, his day never long enough for the work to be done.
Again, almost every measure designed to ameliorate the
farm-labourer's lot means an additional burden for his
employer. When the man who looks after the horses or
store beasts is exempted from week-end duties, "Master"
must do the work himself. When, as is now the case, three
men are required to accomplish anything which two would
have done a few years ago at half the cost, it falls upon the
employer to make up the deficiency as best he can. His work
is never finished, his worries multiply, and the wonder is not
so much that he grumbles as that he carries on. Actually he
does more than carry on. He makes good, and as compared
with other "trades," in the course of long experience I have
known very few instances of a good farmer being sold up.
Even when financially pressed he takes his difficulties philo-
sophically. "Never worry if you owe anybody money. Let
the man you owe it to do the worrying," was the attitude
prescribed by one practical-minded agriculturist, and the
logic seemed unanswerable.

At the best of times there is little luxury or even comfort
attached to the working farmer's life. Bountiful fare, according to his own standards, goes without saying. "I like to live
well, yer honour," an old Devonian once assured me, using
a quaint form of address peculiar to himself. He was a
mountain of a man with an absurdly high-pitched voice,
and his portly appearance testified to the truth of his assertion.

"'Twould be a poor job, sure enough, if you had to live
on your rations," was the topical pronouncement of another,
to whom, apparently, it had not even occurred that millions
of people were constrained to do so. Even so, the standard of
the ordinary farmhouse table does not represent the fat of the
land to the extent that might be supposed. The meals are
taken upon the American three-a-day system, with little
variation of menu. Not counting the inevitable cup of

early-morning tea, swallowed by candle-light during the greater part of the year, there is no breakfast, in its place a ten o'clock or ten-thirty "fried lunch" being served. This is followed by a midday dinner, about one-thirty, of meat, vegetables and cider, but without any sweet course or "afters," as it is called. And about six o'clock, when milking is finished, comes "tea," at which ham or meat pasty is provided, with cake or perhaps a fruit tart. Cream is a great feature of this final meal, but it is eaten without jam on dry bread. If neighbours are being entertained for nap—the great card game in farming circles, cold meat and cider are served about midnight in the dining-room, which remains unused except upon such social occasions. Normally the kitchen is the feeding and general living-room for both family and any employees who "live in." There is seldom a comfortable chair, the family sitting upon benches or settles, and anyone who wants to read must sit at the table, the lamp-light seldom being good enough to allow him to do so near the fire. As a class they are great readers, mainly of newspapers and particularly the locals, every column, paragraph and advertisement of which is scanned. Indeed, nothing escapes the farmer-reader, and comments upon my own work by neighbours are frequent, particularly when some statement concerns their interests.

That two of a trade should talk shop is inevitable, but the extent to which farmers talk "farmering" whenever and wherever they meet has few parallels—except perhaps in clerical circles. It is not only their work but their outlook and their very nature, this being, perhaps, the main secret of their general success. If one consults a legal or scientific expert upon some point, he can seldom supply the information off-hand but is obliged to "look it up." Indeed, a recent B.B.C. Brains' Trust definition of an authority was one who does not necessarily *know*, but has ready access to the required data. The born farmer, upon the other hand, has no bibliography other than life-long experience and that of his fathers before him, but it is not possible to ask him a question concerning land or stock which he cannot immediately answer. And yet, with few exceptions, he is always upon the look-out for new ideas, since as my friend Farmer Wickett remarked only a few days ago: "I've had more than fifty years of it, and here I am still learning."

The character of farm work has undergone so many changes even during the past quarter of a century that old-fashioned methods, general not long ago and now only practised upon primitive hill farms, will soon be regarded as antiquated survivals, akin to Okehampton "Giglet Fair" or the Helston Furry. It is only within comparatively recent years that the self-binder came into general use. As a youth I tied many sheaves behind the now virtually obsolete reaping machine known as a "trapper," and can remember when many fields were cut with scythes for preference. Now, the price of labour, even if obtainable, would prohibit such methods, and few young men of the present day could either bind a sheaf or use a scythe. The tractor with its three-to-one output is fast replacing the horse-plough, even upon small-holdings. The farmer who possesses one can not only save £1 a day when breaking up his fields, but can get over the ground quickly when it is in the most suitable condition instead of being so often caught by weather before the work is completed. Nor is the tractor the only contrivance relieving the horse today. A neighbour frequently uses a light motor-van for conveying artificial manure, seed, or anything that can be easily manipulated to the field where it is needed. Even dung-heaps are "carted" by lorry when possible, and it is not difficult to visualise a day when motor-power for all purposes becomes universal on the land.

A wider adoption of mechanical methods appears to offer the only, or at any rate least hopeless, solution of the labour problem. It is not so much a question of inadequate payment, as the almost fantastic wages offered by despairing employers conclusively proves. It is the hard manual toil that lacks appeal to the "nation on wheels" into which even rural England has developed, and speaking for this locality, which is probably as representative as any, scarcely one village lad in a hundred, when leaving school, chooses a life upon the land. When I remarked to one farmer that I could not imagine who would do the spade work in the future, he, literal-minded after the manner of his kind, replied: "No, nor the ploughing neither." Another, when discussing the same problem, said: "You can get a man to sit on a seat and drive round a field, but to dig a hedge or clean out a pig-sty —no!"

The reply made by Jorrocks to the fastidious applicant for his huntsman's post, "I does all the dirty work myself," was regarded, when written, as an exquisite piece of irony. It would now be a rendering of the actual, as a glance down the advertisement columns of any newspaper would testify. Permanent women land-workers are as a rule less fastidious and, comparatively speaking, more efficient than the younger men, largely because they adopt the work for choice. The land-girl has never been a feature of Devon farm-life, and when encountered is usually the farmer's daughter. Such women, subject to their physical limitations, are equal to the best men, and in the case of some personally known, even better, particularly in the care of animals. Upon the nearest large farm—that of Mr Wickett—is a twenty-four-year-old daughter of the house, who certainly does the work of two present-day employees, male or female. Nothing is too technical for her, from tackling a difficult lambing case single-handed to the making of a rick. She is a first-class trapper, can use a scythe, take a man's place on the thresher or in the harvest-field, can manage a bull, and is often the only one who can get the best work out of a difficult sheep-dog. Her hours are identical with those of her father—from dawn till dusk during the greater part of the year. She is the mainstay of the 600-acre farm round which she proceeds at a loping trot which carries her from point to point with the utmost economy of time; her one weakness, if so it can be termed, being inability to reserve her opinion of an inefficient workman. Were her all-round ability more generally distributed, it would ensure the future of Devonshire agriculture. Women, incidentally, when obliged to farm upon their own responsibility almost invariably make a thorough success of it, and I have more than once heard the suggestion that a farmer and his wife might exchange their customary functions to the general advantage.

We hear a great deal nowadays about small-holdings for all and communal farming. The former is an old slogan, a hardy periodical, and since legislation for the acquisition of

208

land has existed for the past thirty years, an agricultural millennium is unlikely to develop in that direction. Communal farming, or a system much resembling it, has always more or less existed in primitive Devon, and to a large extent still operates. The old sheep-shearing institution already described was one example; the combined planting of potato-plots and even gardens another. To tackle half an acre of potato-ground single-handed is a formidable undertaking. Companionship lightens labour, however, and when friends combine to do a job toil becomes a pleasure. A quarter of a century ago one rarely saw a small-holder or a labourer working in his plot alone. Even as each flock of sheep was sheared in turn by joint effort, so each potato-plot was planted and dug by a party of neighbours helping one another.

Upon the same principle, harvest was a parish affair in which everyone participated according to his ability, and usually without any question of payment, except in the case of regular employees. To help in the hay or corn-field was considered a pleasant diversion from the routine of ordinary work, and during the long midsummer evenings when "saving" continued until dark, the ordinary farm staff was supplemented by volunteers who hurried to the fields as soon as their own duties were accomplished. Definite as well as casual cooperation was also the custom. The village carpenter would lend his men to pitch hay or bind oats, in return for which farm horses would be provided for hauling the carpenter's timber; or, again in recognition of lusty help at harvest-time, the innkeeper or blacksmith would get his stock-in-trade transported by farm waggons.

At the beginning of the present century only the larger farms possessed any mechanical equipment or "strength," and the man who had a self-binder or a seed-drill usually did a great deal of work for his neighbours, who helped with his crops in return. The first man to possess labour-saving contrivances in this district tells me that he wore out his earliest machines upon "other folks' fields." Now, most of the smaller farmers have acquired outfits of their own, and the attractive old system—which, of course, had its drawbacks as well as advantages—has become less general. Up to a

14*   209

The Erme Valley

limited point it still exists. There is a great deal of mutual help, particularly at threshing-time, when the procedure is identical with that of the old sheep-shearing days—the organised tour of a district, the joining of forces, the lavish hospitality. There are, indeed, many survivals of past conditions, but in the words of my old moorman friend John Bennett, "It bain't a bit the same as it was years agone," and survivals merely emphasise the change.

With regard to tools and general outfit, the Devonian's sense of property has always been, and still remains, peculiarly Devonian. When making a census of such things for war emergency purposes, the difficulty in establishing the ownership of implements was incredible. It transpired among other things that a waggon used for many years by a small-holder did not belong to him at all. He had borrowed it from the local smithery and thenceforth appropriated it as his own, ignoring every demand for its return. The case is typical of a list too long to be enumerated. Once acquired, a tool as often as not becomes the property of the borrower by right of hanging on to it. Action for recovery is never taken, the deprived party getting as good or better from someone else. I once lent a saw to a neighbour, and after a year had passed without bringing its return, tactfully enquired whether he had finished with it. His dismay at the bare idea of surrendering the saw was so manifest that it was presented to him on the spot. Those who live in glass-houses must throw no bricks, however. Some months ago I tried to buy a sledgehammer from our Sticklepath Foundry. Nothing of the kind was on sale, but I might *borrow* one "with pleasure." It is still in my wood-shed.

A certain amount of interdependence there must always be, and this is desirable in the common interest, but those with the longest experience of the land and its problems consider that the future offers the best prospect either for the small-holder who can rely mainly upon his own efforts or for the "big business" of the industry, the five or six-hundred-acre farmer who works upon wholesale lines and is of necessity provided with labour-saving plant and all the means for economic production. For the average Devonshire farmer, the hundred to two-hundred-acre man, the outlook is not so good. The cost of work not directly profitable, hedging, weeding, draining and the general upkeep of the land, is likely to prove too great a tax upon his returns. Machinery, manure, seed, everything that he is obliged to buy will be too expensive, and unless the prices of produce are maintained at an artificial level, he can scarcely hope to balance his budget. The advantages of any collective system, so widely advocated of late, have yet to be tested. Upon Devonshire commons the principle of publicly owned land has long been in operation, but that is a subject which will be discussed in another chapter. There is a wide distinction, however, between common land where every man does what he likes and land owned and administered by the state, and the closer one's acquaintance with the entire agricultural situation the better one realises the difficulties with which it bristles. In no direction can the realist see an agricultural millennium, unless state subsidies become permanent.

In state farming, as we have seen it upon requisitioned land, little hope lies, and with it would pass all incentive to endeavour. The reasonably good farmer automatically got the most from his land for his own sake, but when profit or loss is immaterial, output usually suffers. Seldom indeed has a profit been shown upon land managed by a bailiff or agent, and there is no reason for supposing that the state would be more fortunate than the private land-owner who suffers annual loss upon his home farm. Nor can one visualise the large collective farm successfully administered by a democratic community unaccustomed to regimentation. The varying standards of ability and industry immediately present not only problems but sources of inevitable friction. Anyone who has organised even a country cricket-club knows how different is the attitude adopted towards privilege and work, nor is it conceivable that the industrious man would for long be willing to share the fruits of his labour with another who provided only the minimum of effort.

The "three-acre-and-a-cow" slogan is too old a red herring to attract a large following. The answer is surely self-evident. Wilder Devon is a land of small-holders few of whom can exist without their bigger neighbours. To a country community the large farm, like the large estate, is the goose which lays the golden egg—of little use when broken up and divided. The land of the county, equally distributed, would provide everyone with ground upon which to starve but not to live, and the main source of employment would have disappeared. The Parliamentary candidate who presented the Socialist heckler with a half-penny as the share of his property to which the man would be entitled under a wealth-distribution scheme demonstrated the position upon the land today.

In Devonshire no question of land monopoly arises except, oddly enough, upon the commons, where the lord of the soil is not the offender. Throughout the county there may still be seen an old-world rural community, picturesque and prosperous. Change is here, as elsewhere, and it seems strangely inconsistent that while every effort is made to present "this England"—which means the England known and loved—in the most attractive setting, the same influences are at work to wreck everything which constituted old England's charm. As Mr Churchill would express it: "I am not one who holds the view" that England of the past was pernicious. If it were so, why do we set such store upon survivals? Rather, one clings to the hope that good old ways, old figures and old times have not "gone for aye."

CHAPTER XVII

THE COMMONS OF DEVONSHIRE

BEING a county of extremes, in climate, soil and general conditions, Devon's harvest is spread over many months. In the warm south the earliest potatoes are actually lifted before the latest are planted on the hills; and whereas on the red land, or areas such as the Kenn valley, all the corn has sometimes been "saved" by the end of July, the harvest moon gilds many sheaves still out upon the uplands, where the ingathering of potatoes and bracken may extend into Indian summer. Then "fern" may be cut and loaded straight upon the waggons, although it has lost quality and is more brittle than when cut in the green state. Bracken is still used freely for bedding on hill farms as a substitute for straw, but has its disadvantages, being a medium for conveying wire-worm to the land, and is considered unsafe for young calves, upon whom it has a purgative effect if eaten. Under present conditions there is, of course, no dearth of straw, for which, indeed, there is little demand, owing to the greatly increased quantity grown and the rapidly declining number of horses —once the chief consumers. At the moment it is actually being burned in considerable quantities, which seems incredible in view of its former high price. Only a few days ago I saw a great pile of beautiful wheaten bundles ablaze, fine material for thatching reed, which not so long ago, if combed, would have realised about £8 per 100, and now amounted to nothing more than waste matter for which neither the owner nor anyone else had the least use. Even neighbouring hill farmers, who would gladly have fetched it under ordinary conditions rather than cut bracken, found the cost of transport greater than that of harvesting the material near at hand, and so the seemingly uneconomic situation remains.

The steady encroachment of bracken within the last few years has become a serious problem, not by any means confined to Devonshire, since it appears to be more or less general. It has been estimated that about 2½ million acres of land in England and Scotland alone are under bracken at the present day. A large proportion of this is what might be termed natural waste ground, though most "wastes" of this description are utilised for grazing.

Bracken unfortunately cannot be regarded with the same equanimity upon hillsides, commons and moors as heather. The latter provides food in the young stages of its growth, and when allowed to form large bushes, adequate shelter and shade both to grouse and other small birds as well as to sheep and cattle, besides possessing the great advantage of affording protection in winter. Banks thickly covered with heather prove the salvation of many a flock in winter snow-storms. Upon the other hand, bracken is shunned by all grazing animals, and receives therefore no check by this natural means. As pasturage it has no value. It provides a little shade to sheep in hot weather, but in winter, when shelter is more essential, nothing remains of it but a decaying mass of leaves and stalks.

Science has experimented and effective means of eradication have been found, but they are both long and costly. Cutting the young stalks twice a year is one method; treatment with lime or basic slag another; while spraying with various chemicals has also answered the purpose. Yet another, but entirely unscientific, remedy for a bracken-infested area is to introduce into it a herd of pigs, whose deep and persistent rootings prove a decided deterrent to the rootstocks—as well as to everything else. While these methods may be adopted in comparatively small enclosures, however, they are impracticable upon large areas. Bracken-cutting machines are now obtainable, but these are useless upon steep or boulder-strewn ground.

Various suggestions to account for this rapid spread are advanced. Natural conditions have probably been partly instrumental in fostering its growth, for *Pteris aquilina* is a lover of dry ground, and not for years has land been so thoroughly drained of natural moisture through a succession of dry periods as at the present time.

Extensive burning of gorse-brakes and moors is another

contributory cause, for on all waste places and hillsides heather and bracken wage constant warfare for supremacy, heather obtaining mastery in hard, compact soil, where its shallow roots find a firm hold, bracken prevailing in ground of a drier, more friable character into which its deeper roots penetrate with ease. Repeated fires sometimes smoulder away the peat itself to a depth of several inches, completely destroying the surface-spread roots of heather and grass, but leaving those of the bracken untouched below. Potash from burned vegetation is an excellent fertiliser; thus the bracken, besides being freed entirely from the competition of its rival, receives an added stimulus, and so springs and spreads with renewed vigour.

Even when fire does not burn deeply enough to destroy roots, it has the effect of loosening surface soil and providing those conditions which encourage bracken and check heather. It seems plain, therefore, that two factors, the constant firing of moors and brakes and a cycle of abnormally dry years, are at any rate partly responsible for the extension of *P. aquilina*. One cause is artificial and therefore remediable. The other, as yet, is beyond human control, but the problem is becoming serious enough to warrant Government attention. The entire matter is but an instance of the old adage that one may have too much of a good thing, for to country-lovers and dwellers it is matter for regret that a plant of such beauty and wild association should come to be scheduled as a "pest."

Bracken, however, is far from being the only problem presented by the commons of Devonshire, some definition of which is perhaps desirable before proceeding any further with the subject. The term embraces the outlying expanses of Dartmoor and southern Exmoor, Woodbury and numerous smaller areas, of which the best example is Torrington, whose common lands include certain communal enclosures over which all parishioners have rights of pasturage. Somewhat similar is Sticklepath Moor in Sampford Courtenay parish, being an area of some thirty acres upon which any villager may graze cattle. There is also Hatherleigh Moor, locally computed to contain as many acres as days in the year, although officially scheduled as 430, or actually, from the varying estimates given, covering as much ground as anyone cares to make it. Most interesting of all, perhaps, is Braunton Great Field, roughly 350 acres in extent, the 500 strips into which it was divided before the war being a relic of Saxon communal husbandry. A long list of smaller unenclosed spaces might be compiled, several having been requisitioned and cultivated by the D.W.A.E.C. through the exercise of their emergency powers. After the expiration of hostilities, most of these were re-grassed and restored to their former use, which, except in the case of large areas, is slight under modern conditions. The main interest centres in the great Dartmoor commons unaffected by war-time measures, and for a long while presenting difficulties to which official attention must sooner or later be directed.

Common rights vary considerably according to the circumstances under which the land was acquired. If originally granted by charter or, in later times, bequeathed, the extent of the rights conferred is usually specified, and there are many areas in Devonshire classified as "common" but actually carrying no privileges except to occupiers of adjoining land. In many respects the great Dartmoor commons are differently placed from all others, and one doubts whether a similar situation exists elsewhere. To all intents and purposes they form part of the great Royal Chase, from which they were officially separated by the Perambulation of 1240, which defined the area still to be reserved as "Forest," but left the boundaries unmarked by any visible barriers.

This was undertaken at the royal command by twelve knights, duly appointed and sworn, and is probably the most famous "perambulation" ever made in England, or at any rate in Devonshire, and it has certainly caused the most controversy. For this reason it strikes one as matter for regret that it was undertaken at all, or if it had to be, that it did not embrace the entire Moor, which, apart from various encroachments since made, must have covered very much the same country that it does today. In general use, the distinction between Forest and commons is little more than nominal, nor would anybody be much affected were the entire area classified under one heading or the other. Be that as it may, assuming that the object of the circuit was to mark out a special reserve, it must have been an exceedingly careless piece of work, since it failed to include much of the best ground, nor can the imagination suggest any reason for leaving so wide a ring of waste land around the Royal Chase, as it was certain to constitute a future source of friction. It must be remembered, of course, that the situation which has since arisen was certainly never anticipated or even visualised during the Norman regime. Again, the precise purpose of the perambulation is open to question. That it was intended to indicate the area excepted from the general disafforestation of the county there can be no doubt, but whether the line actually ridden by the twelve knights who made the round was designed to mark a boundary for all time is quite another question. It seems as likely that they merely made a tour or survey of the country scheduled for reservation, taking an inner and easy route—as they certainly did in some instances—and that no question of definite boundaries ever arose. Otherwise it seems incredible that the final indications of divisions, to which considerable importance was attached, should have been so cursory. If worth doing at all, it was surely worth doing properly, and if boundaries over which trespass would be an offence were intended they would scarcely have been purely "lineal," or unmarked. Reason suggests either that the perambulation was a mere "token" march, the significance of which has been exaggerated, or that the full story of the division, if it took place, is unknown.

A circuit of the imaginary line is clearly beyond the scope of this work, and in any case it serves no present purpose other than a rough guide in matters which concern the special interests of the Duchy as opposed to those of the commoners. It took precisely the course which any mounted party making a tour of the Moor and resolved to get back by dinner-time would take today. Outside its limits lies a wide belt of moorland indistinguishable from the official "Forest," and this is the ground specially classified in early writings as the "Commons of Devonshire," although seldom referred to by the old name nowadays. Over this area of about 80,000 acres anyone resident in Devonshire, excepting parishioners of Barnstaple and Totnes, has the right to pasture sheep or cattle, but this privilege is limited to pasturage, and differs from *venville rights* which extend to *turbary*, these entitling the holders to turf, peat, surface granite, or "anything that can do them good" except "vert and venison"—another elastic clause, since "venison" is held to apply to game generally.

As compared with questions arising upon the history, extent and interpretation of Moor rights, the problems which ordinarily puzzle antiquarians are simple, and the more closely the entire situation is studied, the more obscure it becomes, like a misty landscape viewed through binoculars. Even the origin of venville rights, for which most of the moorland parishes paid a small annual acknowledgement until comparatively modern times, is uncertain. They are supposed to date from fines imposed upon the *vills*, or early manors, for trespasses upon the royal forest, the assumption being that in course of time the vill, and subsequently the parishes which supplanted them, found it less expensive to pay the fines in form of a rent—actually damage in advance —and so evolved the venville parishes which still claim the full rights, although two only, Belstone and Sheepstor, continue to pay the nominal yearly fees. It seems clear that any rights possessed by parishes were previously vested in the more ancient manors. In old farm deeds one may find clauses conferring Moor privileges upon the occupier or owner, and these must certainly date from a period when such rights were at the disposal of the manors or their lords, and could either be leased or transferred by sale. It is significant that clauses of this description are limited in the licence which they bestow. The owner of Willey farm in Sampford Courtenay parish, for example, is entitled to pasture "sixty sheep on Dartmoor," and this is interesting as Sampford Courtenay has no "common rights," as they are now generally, although, perhaps, not quite correctly understood, upon the assumption that such are vested in certain parishes, to the exclusion of others.

The evolution of the parishes is as difficult to trace as everything else. Evidently they succeeded the vills, which they gradually absorbed, although in some cases the old manor survived, at least officially, more or less corresponding with the "village" which now bears its name, the connection being obvious. The establishment of the churches as parochial centres doubtless contributed to the dissolution of the vills, and as each parish developed, it gradually acquired a monopoly over adjoining common land, and moor rights became a parochial rather than a manorial concern.

How the monopoly was established in each case or the division originally made can only be conjectured. Parish boundaries, no doubt, formerly coincided with those of the vills they incorporated or represented, changing with fresh acquisitions, but beyond this their development is hard to follow. It seems improbable that any such boundaries existed upon Dartmoor while the whole remained a Royal Chase under the Manor of Lydford, and one would rather incline to the view that the commons were gradually acquired upon the same principle as the old intakes—by the metaphorical, or in some cases literal, staking of claims by parochially minded people.

Upon the Moor "stakes" usually take the form of granite slabs about the size of gate-posts, which mark most lineal boundaries, whether Forest or inter-parochial, and once in every seven years the inhabitants of each moorland village march around the parish confines as indicated by these posts, the proceeding, which is taken very seriously, being that known as "beating the bounds." It is accompanied by a certain amount of ceremony. When a boundary stone is reached, for example, the oldest man in the crowd must lift the youngest boy and stand him upon his head on the top of the stone, the object of this proceeding being either to hammer its precise location well into the juvenile brain or to symbolise perpetuation. Should any coveted asset, such as a gravel-pit or watercourse, lie on the wrong side of the boundary, the landmark is adjusted accordingly, only to be replaced by the rival claimants when their own perambulation is made, parish boundaries, like everything else on the Moor, being controversial. All that can be done to assert a "right" is done, and the proceedings are crowned with a public meal of bread and cheese and cider, brought by cart to some accessible point, this being the only part of the ceremony concerning which I have never heard any altercation.

Sometimes a parish common merely consists of the unenclosed ground lying between the Forest boundary and all cultivated land within that parish. There are cases, however, in which the common of one village considerably encroaches upon the frontage of another. Belstone has a larger moor front than South Tawton, but possesses about half the amount of common. Sampford Courtenay, again, though actually touching the Moor, has no common at all, and in such cases one may be confronted with the anomalous position of men occupying adjoining cottages, one enjoying, the other debarred from full venville or common rights. There was the aggressive "commoner" who, under those precise circumstances, objected to a neighbour collecting a barrow-load of surface stone for repairing a garden-path. The incident occurred in this village, and some interesting questions arose when a few years ago the parishioners of South Tawton endeavoured to prevent some gypsies from picking whortleberries on the Moor. The ground being common, the crop wild and the gypsies, in this respect at any rate, ordinary members of the public, the villagers' claim to monopoly might have proved difficult to sustain. The gypsies, however, reacted by buying a plot of ground, so establishing a residential qualification, of which, as it happens, they have made no subsequent use.

Together with many others, I have long urged that the entire position should be classified and set forth upon an explicit up-to-date basis. The uncertainty and friction which have persisted for centuries over the extent or limitations of "common" privileges are so interminable that most people seem to regard them as a necessary evil, but while the undesirability of the situation remains clear to all, so does its absurdity. Almost every law or code of laws governing private property or individual action has needed periodical revision. Even concessions granted to the highly privileged tinners required constant adjustment, and it is ridiculous to maintain that procedure upon the Dartmoor commons should be governed by charters as antiquated as the early Stannery statutes, and granted under circumstances which have changed no less completely. Even this ancient form of "rule" can only be regarded as nominal, since the old regulations—many of them beneficial—have for the most part ceased to operate, and upon ground where the interests of many are involved a measure of law and order is surely more desirable than upon private property where action is controlled.

Officially, procedure is subject to the ordinary laws of common and turbary, together with additional privileges claimed under the old charters. Ancient Dartmoor law, however, contained also provisions and regulations to prevent abuses and inequalities, and it is perhaps inevitable that in course of time the privileges should stretch, while anything in the shape of restriction is treated with increasing disregard. Also, the legal position, through long controversy, has become so obscure that the commoner is genuinely ignorant as to the scope of his rights and has for long adopted the simple course of being a law unto himself. The liberty of the subject is an excellent thing, but the individual who construes freedom into licence soon becomes an offence to his neighbours. There was the man who exterminated a colony of jackdaws, which were regarded as an interesting feature of a Dartmoor crag, because in his opinion "they warn't no good." There was another who fired pasturage upon which his neighbour's sheep grazed, not because he expected to derive any benefit from doing so, but merely in assertion of his "right to swaley." And worst of all today is the big flock or herd-owner who drives another man's beasts away from the grass which he wants for his own cattle.

These might be regarded as typical examples of situations which repeatedly arise and which, although deprecated, are usually accepted as inseparable from conditions that cannot be altered, rights conferred under King John's charters being urged in justification of almost any abuse. I have many times heard villagers bring up the name of John in the endless arguments that arise, and incredible as it may seem, even intelligent people do not appear to realise that King John is more dead than Queen Anne. If legislation of so remote a date is still extant, then witches may be burned and wives beaten today.

King John or no, for the obviously remediable there is always a remedy, and in the case of Dartmoor there need be no insuperable difficulty. If the commons are indeed common, the mere accident of residence upon one side of a hedge should not deprive a man of privileges which he is in a position to use, and to which in bare justice he is as fully entitled as his neighbour who enjoys them. Public property, again, is not the property of any individual. No man should have the right capriciously to destroy that which more responsible people—joint owners—wish to use or enjoy, and certainly there should be no private monopoly of common land.

The latter is a point which must be faced soon or late. A "commoner" is officially classified as a rate-payer, of which, perhaps, there might be a couple of hundred in a moorland parish. All of these are entitled to benefits from the common, the main wealth of which is probably reaped by two or three whose cattle appropriate the best pastures, often crowding the little flock or herd completely off the Moor. Even without proceeding to high-handed or lawless extremes, monopoly can be exercised merely by heavy stocking. It was doubtless to prevent such situations that the clauses in old leases limited the number of beasts that a farmer might pasture on the hills, and indeed the Forest laws, which should be in force today, still prohibit any man from running more cattle than he can winter upon his own land.

Upon this subject there is scope for endless controversy. That the Moor should be utilised nobody will deny, and circumstances render some people in a better position than others to take advantage of its resources. At the same time, a great common over which hundreds of people hold equal rights ought not to become to all intents and purposes a private ranch under the domination of one or two big cattle-owners who pay no more for the privilege—and often less—than other parishioners who derive no benefit from the Moor at all. One could name men making a substantial four-figure income solely by running cattle upon common ground the use of which they actually deny to other people whose rights are less questionable than their own.

That everyone is not in a position to take advantage of common rights goes without saying. None the less, even as each householder must contribute his or her share towards local expenditure, so all are entitled to a dividend upon a public asset. When an individual or a company acquires state land for exploitation, a price is paid to the state, and the same principle should surely apply to common land when turned mainly to private account.

In the *Estate Magazine* a few years ago I proposed the skeleton of a plan under which Dartmoor's resources might be more equitably distributed. It would involve no material change and little more than a restitution of reasonable control, which should never have been allowed to lapse. One would suggest that any rate-payer, as now, should be entitled to pasture a limited number of animals upon Devonshire's commons, irrespective of parish; reasonable proximity to the Moor, without which nobody could look after his beasts, being the obvious and certainly the fairest qualification. Anyone who desired to exceed this number should be at liberty to do so upon the payment of a prescribed rate per head, an expressly defined right held by any commoner who could not use it being also purchasable. The receipts would be treated in the same manner as compensation now paid to certain parishes for interference caused by the artillery range, that is to say, either distributed equally among the parishioners or credited against the local rate. In the case of a general scheme, a county basis rather than a parochial might be preferred, all moorland assets, if extensively appropriated, being taken into account. As matters now stand, fuel, except at a prohibitive price, is only obtainable by those who possess means of transport, and I do not propose here to enter upon the controversial topic of sporting rights—worthless under existing conditions and covered by another scheme of which more will be said later.

There remains only the problem of heather-burning—a hardy annual concerning which much has been already written. Indeed, the strong feeling expressed upon this subject from all quarters during the long drought of 1938, when destructive conflagrations were so prevalent, forcibly emphasised the need for some measure of long overdue reform. With the outbreak of war it was hoped that black-out regulations and the serious view taken of night fires by the military authorities would check the trouble, at least "for

223

the duration." Actually, neither official orders nor the fear of Nazi bombs proved the slightest deterrent, except during the first year, after which, surreptitious igniting leading to no police action, open disregard of the regulations soon followed. Now and again the National Fire Service called out the Home Guard or the inmates of village inns to extinguish fires which were blazing unchecked on the hillsides, but, incredible as it may seem, no proceedings were ever taken, and apart from a little grumbling at the effort involved, nobody seemed to mind. According to Devonian ideas, to live near a gorse or heather bush without putting a match to it is inconceivable, regulations to the contrary being generally treated as nonsense.

In Scotland since 1773 the position has been regulated by a law which entirely prohibits "Muir burning or heather burning" between April 11th and November 1st, subject to a slight extension upon application, and if this provision is necessary upon land much of which is privately owned and where method and discrimination are observed, no remarkable intelligence is required to realise the far greater need in country where no rule is recognised other than the whim of the moment. The Devon Agricultural Committee have now inaugurated a demonstration scheme upon moorland segregated for the purpose, the idea being to educate the moor farmer in the principle of scientific "swaling." The plan is excellent, since it will provide definite data in support of argument. The difficulty, however, has always lain in convincing the man who desires nothing so little as conviction. Here again one must get down to reality, which is this: to produce pasturage is the ostensible purpose of burning heather, but there are few countrymen who, if allowed an entirely free hand, can resist burning for burning's sake. There is no argument so strong as inclination. I have heard a Dartmoor man admit that he had fired too much heather in the past, and that his sheep had suffered from winter shortage in consequence. Yet the following spring he would be at it again, setting alight to anything that would "run," having persuaded himself that "it was better swaled off to get rid of the old sour stuff," although experience had taught him that even "sour stuff" was preferable to none. The bad economy

224

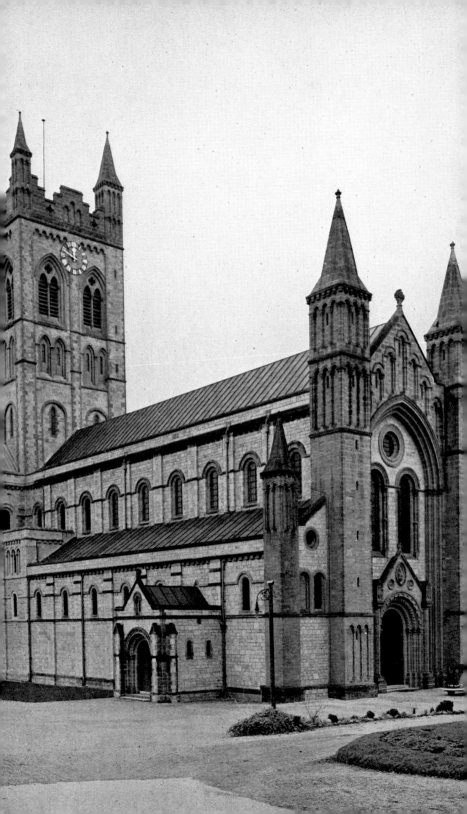

of the indiscriminate policy has been repeatedly demonstrated. It was recognised in the old Forest laws, and it is difficult to believe that any man can be so foolish as not to realise it in theory, although he disregards it in practice. The pipe-lover knows that his pocket will benefit if he refrains from smoking, but he burns his tobacco as the sheep farmer the moorland pasturage, and for the same reason. The production of grass may be the excuse, but it is certainly not the motive that prompts gangs of village youths to set the moorlands ablaze during the long summer evenings. Were such their purpose, it would be better served if each lad carried a scythe or hook and cut off the bracken heads—a proceeding for which they have not yet discovered the necessity.

A few years ago, when describing the complete disregard of the Game and Wild Bird Protection Acts in one of my previous books, I was charged with exaggeration by critics who do not live in Devonshire and naturally, therefore, *could* not believe that such a state of affairs existed. In like manner, visitors from Scotland or the Yorkshire moors, when told the story of Dartmoor's heather, cannot conceive such a situation possible. They assume that the conflagrations seen during midsummer or at the height of the nesting season must be accidental, and the idea of school-children or irresponsible youths being allowed to ignite a destructive blaze purely for amusement, or even an adult deliberately to start a fire which may spread for miles without any effort at or possibility of control seems too preposterous. The position, as more or less officially interpreted at the moment, is that the "commoner" cannot legally be prevented from doing much as he likes, but he may not authorise anyone else—even a member of his own household—to light a fire. Thus, children or youths have no lawful justification whatever, but, strange as it may seem, convention is on their side and they are supported by their parents, whose one idea is to assert and maintain "common rights." The Duchy of Cornwall, it should be added, have always forbidden burning on the Forest side of the boundary, but fires are as rampant there as anywhere else. In a sentence, the entire position once again calls for strong legislation.

So far, appeal, protest, argument have proved equally

The famous Bideford Bridge

ineffective, and one can only hope that importunity may at last extort action from weary authority, always reluctant to face direct issues. A country rector was once waited upon by a deputation of parishioners requesting a new sermon, since he had preached one only for many months. He promised compliance with the demand when he saw the least sign of the much-repeated exhortation bearing fruit. That is the answer to anyone who complains that he has heard too much about heather-burning on Dartmoor.

BIBLIOGRAPHY

Guide to Dartmoor, Part V. William Crossing.
Perambulation of Dartmoor. Samuel Rowe.
Devon Association Transactions, XIX, p. 377, W. F. Collier.

CHAPTER XVIII

MOORMEN AND BEASTS

FOR grazing purposes Dartmoor Forest is divided into four
Quarters, each under the wardenship of one Moorman, who
receives the low charges made for pasturing animals upon
the Duchy land under his special jurisdiction. Flocks or
herds running upon the commons inevitably extend their
range over the Forest boundaries, and for this the commoners to whom the greater number belong pay a nominal
rate in proportion to the number of beasts they own. Cattle
from outside areas are also sent to the hills for summer keep,
and one may often see breeds quite alien to the district, such
as South Hams and even Jerseys, picking a temporary living
off the moorland herbage, especially upon wet ground where
soft young grasses grow around the spring-heads or moss-
hags. These places prove a constant source of danger to all
beasts, even those accustomed to the country, particularly
early in the year, when cattle are out of condition. Tempted
by the superior herbage, they venture too far into the dangerous ooze and are soon engulfed. Many sink no farther
than belly-deep, but, unable to extricate themselves, perish
from exhaustion and chill. Others sink completely and may
never be seen again. There was a recent tragic instance of a
valuable hunter which in the course of a run with the Mid-
Devon hounds galloped into a mire. The rider, a lady, unfortunately alone, extricated herself, but the horse went
down, and before help could arrive had sunk so deeply that
only its ears were visible.

The risk from disease, apart from chill, is not as great on
the hills as might be supposed, the land being "sound" in the
main. Even red-water, the scourge of cattle transferred to
inferior pasturage, is less prevalent on the Moor than on the
poorer culm, which goes far to prove that infected soil is
responsible for more trouble than the actual quality of land
or food. Few lowland cattle can stand the Dartmoor winter,

however, and when the moorland colours fade to russet and grey, when the ring-ouzels pack in the valleys to enjoy their farewell feast off the mountain-ash berries before final departure, the summer herds return to the lowland, some to winter quarters on in-country farms, others to the grazing-marshes beside the southern rivers, there to complete their qualification for the inevitable end—the primary purpose of bovine existence.

Although the Moor loses her summer population after her brief season, the genuine hill cattle, the black Galloways, a few of the hardier Devons, the ponies and the mountain sheep are always with her. The inky silhouettes of the Galloways are conspicuous upon the snow-covered hillsides, and many of these beasts, which have ranged the uplands for generations, in some respects are almost wild. One finds their minute calves nestling like fawns in the ling, sometimes startling a stranger at whose feet they spring up and scamper away vociferating or, to use the expressive Devonshire phrase, "blaking" for their mothers, grazing with the distant herd. Upon such occasions the cow quickly arrives, clearing the long heather in her stride, like a hind, and a close approach is not always advisable, the Galloway being the one Moor animal likely to charge a human being. So cunningly are the calves concealed in deep ling that moormen have considerable difficulty in finding them when required, the only way at times being to withdraw and watch from a distance until the mother eventually approaches the spot, when the slim black calf arises from its form like a peat-sprite to greet her, subsiding again a moment later without leaving the slightest hint of its whereabouts.

From time to time the long-haired, longer-horned Highland cattle have been tried upon Dartmoor, shaggy beasts of ferocious mien but placid disposition. They are picturesque additions to the moorland scene, with their bison-like appearance and quaint little hairy calves, which, though not as studiously concealed as those of the black cattle, are shy of an intruder, at whose approach each little oddity seeks shelter behind his mother's ample robe, like the old-fashioned child behind the once voluminous skirt of its nurse, and the skill with which it maintains this screen is comical and at times provoking, as when one is attempting to take its photograph. These beasts are never likely to become general upon the moor, however, as for some reason they do not take as kindly to the country as the Galloways, and show a curious aptitude for getting into trouble in the bogs, to which their hill ancestry should have rendered them naturally wise. In Scotland the Highland bull has a formidable reputation, but upon Dartmoor he has no opportunity of indulging any such propensity, as full-grown bulls, being classified as uncontrolled animals, are denied the free range of the moors—a necessary provision from all points of view. Now and again one is seen with a herd, but he is usually an "escape," broken out from some intake, the loose stone walls of which always appear singularly inadequate to contain any beast resolved upon breaking.

When picnicking at Knack Mine, overlooking lonely Steeperton Ford, we once saw two visitors, a man and woman, who believing themselves alone in that wild place were enjoying a bathe in the river Taw, nudity being considered safe under the circumstances. Unfortunately they had chosen a spot too near the crossing, at which two mounted moormen suddenly appeared escorting an old Galloway bull. The couple submerged and hoped for the best, but their Cairn terrier proved an unlooked-for complication. The moormen shouted for its removal in case the bull should take action on his own account. Exciting developments seemed probable, but the woman was equal to the occasion. Arising from the water like a naiad, she arrayed herself in a towel with which she was fortunately provided, grabbed the dog and retreated among the rocks, while the bull acknowledged the concession by passing on quietly.

A large number of black cattle winter on the moorland, helped by a bare minimum of artificial feeding on the fringes, towards which they gravitate, like the ponies, at the approach of hard weather. The ponies are sometimes represented as indigenous to the high ground and quite independent of outside aid. Actually they work as far down as possible in winter, and it is probable that in the days before enclosures more or less isolated the country now known as

Dartmoor, they migrated to the lowlands with the first frosts or general worsening of conditions. All cattle seek shelter when necessary, and there is every reason for assuming that when much of the in-country was down and woodland, the same wild mountain animals wintered at lower altitudes. The origin of the pony or the date of its introduction to Dartmoor is unknown. Like many of the old Devon families, he seems to have been at home when the Conqueror called, and is such an institution upon the hills that the heather slopes would be incomplete without his little dark form silhouetted on the ridges, or the picturesque family groups that can be watched for two or three years, each colt from the minute foal to the four-year-old marking one stage in the moorland pony's growth. He is, moreover, such an engaging, sturdy little beast and so "honest," to use the localism, that all animal-lovers regard the possibility of his passing as something of a calamity.

Yet, general favourite as he is, there is reason for fearing that, apart from a temporary revival under war-time conditions, the Dartmoor pony's day is drawing to a close. Indeed, it might be argued that to some extent he has already become a figure of the past, since the greater number are no longer true to breed. The hill pony of today is seldom a real "Dartmoor." The ancient stock, though still retaining many of its original characteristics, has long since been intermixed with fresh blood of almost every type, with the result that nowadays pony-fanciers could gratify any taste when making a selection from the upland droves, while still purchasing an animal from Dartmoor.

The numerical decrease is more marked than the loss of type, however, for the pony has to a large extent outlived his usefulness. The substitution of electrical power for horse labour in so many of the mines has considerably affected the pony market, while the passing of the "jingle" in favour of the small car has involved the virtual disappearance of light pony vehicles from the roads. So far as England is concerned, the stout little animal from the hills is required for riding only, and since his usefulness in this respect is obviously limited, it is not difficult to understand that the demand for the Dartmoor pony has dwindled.

The lot of the moor pony has never been enviable, for even at the height of the trade's prosperity the fate of the animal for the most part can only be described as pathetic. Reared in the breezy freedom of the hills with unlimited space at their disposal, a destiny more tragic than the darkness and drudgery of the pits could scarcely be imagined. Now, however, a great number find their way to slaughter-houses, being sent overseas for this purpose before the war, and as this practice will doubtless be resumed, one cannot but think that extermination would be preferable, if this is the only alternative.

However one regards this aspect of the situation, as an edible animal the pony has at the moment acquired an artificial and, as compared with prices prevailing from 1930 onwards, an entirely disproportionate value. A number recently sold in the Okehampton district realised as much as £27 apiece, the former price of a mare and foal being at one period only 30s.*

The periodical pony-drifts which continued, although upon a reduced scale, until the beginning of the recent war formerly constituted one of the most picturesque events of moorland life. On an appointed day all the ponies then grazing upon one Quarter of the Forest were rounded up, the owners being required to assist the Duchy officials and the Warden of the Quarter in one big drive to a central enclosure, where the ponies were impounded for a general stock-taking. Each animal was identified, claimed, and upon payment of the Forest dues, released, to return at leisure to its special pastures unless driven back by its owner. Unbranded ponies automatically became the property of the Duchy, were impounded and subsequently sold. Like everything Devonian, the institution has or had its social side, a meal of bread and cheese and cider provided at the Warden's house near which the final function took place invariably winding up the proceeding. The last Dartmoor pony-drift was held on the northern Quarter in August 1940, but owing to shortage of drivers and difficulties arising from the

* The Dartmoor Pony Society is making a great effort to preserve and restore the pure breed, but the difficulties are increased by the fact that mongrel stallions are now allowed to range the Moor.

national situation, could not be regarded as representative, and subsequent fixtures were cancelled.

The revival of the practice will doubtless depend upon the post-war status of the pony upon the Moor. In any case, latterly the proceeding had lost much of its significance, the number of ponies assembled being negligible in comparison with the impressive droves of former days. At one time a drift, without exaggeration, resembled nothing so much as a round-up of mustangs or range-cattle in the Wild West, the only difference being that the slopes were carpeted with heather instead of sage-brush, with the great tors for background to break the wide distances which upon the prairie stretch interminably into the purple-blue. Otherwise the proceeding was quite as picturesque and scarcely less romantic. Although privately owned and branded, the unbroken little Devonian is as independent and ungovernable as any broncho that ranges the plains of Montana or Texas, and as much skill is required to steer a madly galloping troop into a primitive Dartmoor enclosure as to pen any Western drove in a corral.

Even upon the reduced scale to which it had degenerated, a drift had not entirely lost its spectacular effect. At one moment black cattle and ponies graze undisturbed as yet upon the summer moorland. Then from afar come faint sounds swelling in a scarcely perceptible crescendo, until from the indeterminate murmur the hoarse barking of range collies and the cracking of whips become distinguishable. The heads of the grazing cattle are now erect. The ponies break into a trot and bunch. Stragglers emerge from the hollows whinnying in their anxiety to find their fellows. Then upon distant ridges midget forms appear, waver along the skyline and plunge into intervening coombes, to break into view again as they breast nearer eminences, while the barking, the yodelling cries of the drivers and eventually the thunder of galloping hooves swells upon the still air like a coming flood. Soon the entire panorama is visible—the careering droves heading inwards from every direction, the riders hovering upon the rear and flanks, intercepting efforts to escape or collecting stragglers. Ever in attendance, marshalling, steering, or singling out, bound the tireless wolflike dogs, displaying almost incredible discrimination between the animals which they are herding and the cattle or sheep, bunched upon every hilltop but realising, as animals usually do, that the upheaval is no direct concern of theirs. When the first arrivals have been piloted into the enclosure, which is a little walled-in field, the main difficulty is surmounted, the remainder entering more readily, while each converging troop brings more helpers into a circumscribed area. The actual drift may take three or four hours, and as midday approaches the company is swelled by farmers and cattle-owners who have taken no part in the active proceedings, arriving to claim any animals that may have been caught in the round-up, or to pay outstanding dues, drift-day being also rent-day. The final assembly of semi-wild ponies, shaggy dogs and men that differ little from their prototypes of medieval days, has no modern equivalent. The setting—the Moor, the tors, the rocks which pierce the turf of the enclosure; the walls themselves are probably unchanged since the first drift took place, and unless the chapter is already closed, will doubtless so remain until the end, for Dartmoor institutions, like the Moor itself, do not offer much scope for innovation.

Similar to the drifts up to a certain point is the work of the range-clearers, picturesque figures whose existence is scarcely realised even a few miles away from Dartmoor. Occasionally a summer visitor to the Okehampton or Belstone district might meet a maroon-coated horseman, pollen-dusted, jogging homewards towards the close of day along some moorland track, the bronzed rider, his pony and the gaunt dogs loping astern all imparting the impression of having covered many miles of swamp and heather under a sun which browns the face of man and bleaches the hide of beast. Enquiry elicits the information that the man is a "range-clearer," whose duty it is to remove cattle from any part of the artillery ranges upon which shells are likely to fall.

Formerly range-clearing was a summer job, lasting perhaps from early May until September; for the rest of the year His Majesty's gunners were well content to abandon Dartmoor's windswept ridges to the golden plover and any animal, wild or domesticated, hardy enough to remain there.

Since the outbreak of war, however, the wilds of Cranmere, the Brimbrook and the Blackaven have known no respite from an all-round-the-calendar bombardment, and the range itself has crept outwards upon all sides, bringing new areas under the ban. Until 1942 red flags flown from Yes Tor, Watchet Hill and Hangingstone enclosed the danger-zone in a comparatively limited triangle. Later they stood upon Cosdon Beacon, Waterton Tor and Fur Tor, while other extensions have been claimed in the Willsworthy and Postbridge areas. Even as I write here in my study on the fringe of the Moor, down from the hills rising beyond the Taw river, which bounds my garden, rolls the intermittent boom of artillery fire, and if I climbed about a mile to the crest of the first ridge I should hear the range-clearers at work, as they have been day after day with few intervals since the war years.

The area from which cattle must first be removed and debarred from re-entering while firing is in progress depends upon the range used. As a general rule it extends from Halstock Down in the extreme north along a rough line around Wild Tor and Waterton to the Dart. It is bounded on the western side by the West Okement and the Ammicombe water, roughly embracing Cranmere and all the wild ground north of Fur Tor and the Teign—indeed the greater part of the northern Forest Quarter. It is only appropriate, therefore, that the Warden of this section is also Warden of the Ranges, the supervision of which has been in his hands for the past quarter of a century. He is tenant of Hartor Farm, the property of the War Office, situated actually upon the range, the house being provided with a bomb-proof shelter in which the family were compelled to take refuge when short-range guns were in action. It is still occupied, the warden with his wife and children having lived there for many years and his father before him, the children riding on ponies along moor-tracks to Sticklepath, the nearest school, their parish being actually Lydford, many miles away across often impassable moor. It was here, incidentally, that the northern pony-drifts were held, among surroundings peculiarly adapted to such an assembly.

Near this remote homestead, one of the loneliest in England, is White Bridge, a crude wooden structure spanning the short but picturesque Blackaven, and here the range-clearers, drawn from the neighbouring villages, have always met, often at grey dawn before summertime became the custom, to take their orders for the day. Each mounted on his sturdy moor cob, wearing the maroon riding-coat which is the uniform of his calling prescribed by Government, and followed by one or two of the indispensable cattle-dogs, they form a workmanlike and probably unique party. Before them lie several hours of strenuous work, for it is necessary to toothcomb every hollow, and while the mists of the morning veil the Moor little groups of cattle, particularly when couched in deep ling, may easily be overlooked, to prove a source of trouble if not actual danger later in the day. Each man may have an area of perhaps two or three thousand acres from which every animal must be driven before a gun can be fired, and even when this very considerable task has been accomplished the range-clearer's work is far from done. For the remainder of the day he must keep the movements of the grazing herds under constant supervision, and at the first indication of any tendency to wander back over the shell-swept country it is a case of mounting and galloping perhaps a couple of miles to divert the movement. How great the need for this constant vigil can only be realised by those who have witnessed the rapidity with which moor cattle move. The slightest cause may set a herd in motion— the bark of a sheep-dog rounding up a flock is more than enough to stampede ponies, which, indeed, sometimes gallop considerable distances for no apparent reason other than *joie de vivre*. Again, the activities of flies render cattle restive, and when grazing in the ordinary way even sheep are ever upon the move, passing from one patch of herbage to another and so from hill to hill in a shorter space of time than might be imagined unless one has watched their movements.

During the long hours when the range-clearer is at his post his yodelling cries or the hoarse voice of his dog may be heard intermittently along the ridges which he patrols at frequent intervals. A good observation point is essential, and each man has his recognised stand, commanding a wide view and usually connected by telephone with the Warden's post.

When bitter winds sweep the hills there are more desirable places for man and horse than the crest of a bleak Dartmoor ridge, and where no other cover is available a rough shelter which provides at least a measure of protection against cold or rain is sometimes built. Failing this, the lee of a tor from which great rocks project is made to serve the purpose, and I have seen a range-clearer crouching with his pony and dogs in a little hollow where nothing but heather and whortle-berry growth broke the north wind which had lost little of its sting since sweeping the ice-fields round Newfoundland or Labrador.

Unlike most moormen, the range-clearer has no ancient or romantic history, no place in old Dartmoor literature, being by a curious and inconsistent freak of circumstance a modern product, although at the same time the most picturesque and old-world figure seen on the hills today. One can only compare him with the Western cowboy, and it is more than singular that the artillery range, in many respects the most devastating innovation that Dartmoor as yet has known, should have produced its most unique and in some respects most primitive institution.

Riding the moorlands at all seasons are the cattle-men or sheep-owners, less spectacular than the range-clearers, because lacking the maroon coat, but constituting a more representative figure of the landscape, since as long as cattle and ponies have ranged the upland these riders, probably some of the first horsemen that England knew, have been upon the hills. Each rides the rough cob of the country, and, as a girl visitor exclaimed when she saw a range-clearer without his distinguishing coat, "is just an ordinary man," usually a farmer from one of the neighbouring parishes, who has followed the wandering of his herd or flock since child-hood, knows their favourite pastures and the easiest way to reach them. Every man, or rather his pony, has a special path which remains open during his time, and when he grows old or abandons his activities on the hills, gradually disappears. Within the past quarter of a century I have known many such trails to each of which the name of its user might have been given, but which the Moor has since reclaimed, and the same may be said of old turf tracks, still discernible here and there, but along which no wheels are likely to pass again. Change of path is also partly due to change of pasturage, certain slopes being more favoured than others by cattle over periods of years, according to the condition of the herbage.

The Scotch sheep, although a new importation, has taken kindly to the country, where it is hard to believe that it is not indigenous, so perfectly does it assimilate with its setting. The shaggy, greyish-white form so closely resembles the low, lichen-covered rocks that it offers as perfect a picture of camouflage as even Nature can show, and it is as much at home on the high tors as the mountain fox himself. This sheep more closely approaches the goat, or perhaps the chamois, than any other member of its race, and sporting dogs which take no notice of lowland sheep almost invariably fall for the little mountain sheep when first they meet it, for the breed is very near the wild.

A Government subsidy of 7s. 6d. a head is now paid upon all hill sheep, including the Scotchman, this being something of a windfall to owners of Dartmoor flocks, which cost no more to keep now than before the war. One local farmer —who, by the way, owns none himself—pertinently remarked that the common interest would be better served were they taxed rather than subsidised. Admittedly, along the Moor boundaries the Scotch sheep is an unmitigated nuisance. Miles out upon the wastes, where he can eat nothing but heather-shoots and the after-growth of burned lands, he bothers nobody; but when nearer civilisation the sweeter grass of the foothill meadows attracts him as clover draws the bee, and erect must be the wall or tough the fence that keeps him out. Occupiers of adjoining lands are responsible for the common boundary fences, but this regulation preceded the Scotchman's arrival, and barriers which would have turned any ordinary animal presented no obstacle to him, and he has profited from the rule which relieved his owner from the obligation to fence against him. Wherever there is good grass he finds it—even on my tennis-court, which he reaches by scrambling along the bank of the Taw river at its base.

There is nothing prettier upon the hills than young

Scotch lambs, which arrive in April when the first green tints soften the austerity of the prevailing grey, when the cuckoo is finding its voice and snipe are drumming. Then the tiny white lambs with their jetty extremities frisk among the rocks or scuttle through the heather like mountain leverets at the earth-shaking approach which one had thought so cautious, and watching them play, with all the awakening moorland world around, one regrets that any young animal should ever grow up, and decides that mint is a herb which nobody possessing any æsthetic instincts should grow in his garden.

Chapter XIX

DARTMOOR'S APPEAL

DARTMOOR is no longer the land of complete mystery that it was even a century ago. There is a current convention that the road constructed in 1792 from Moreton Hampstead to Tavistock "opened up" the country, and the building of the prison in 1806 brought a measure of publicity to an area until then completely remote. The foundation-stone of the original building was laid by Sir Thomas Tyrwhitt, to whose indefatigable energies the development, agricultural and otherwise, of the Princetown district was almost entirely due. The original purpose of the institution was the accommodation of French and American war prisoners, and while used as such Princetown became the centre of very considerable commercial activity. The presence of some 9,000 men offered unprecedented opportunities for local trading, and an open market was held weekly within the prison confines. To this, dealers, farmers, their wives and daughters from all the surrounding country flocked with every saleable commodity, many people settling in the district to exploit the exceptional advantages. One cannot but contrast these conditions with those of the moment, when, in spite of incalculably improved facilities, prison employees receive special compensation for the alleged hardship of living amid such isolated surroundings.

With the departure of the prisoners of war this artificial prosperity automatically declined, and comparative solitude returned to Princetown until, in 1850, the present convict settlement was established there. It is undoubtedly the most unpopular penal institution in the country, and judging by the trend of present-day sentiment it seems probable that history will repeat itself and that Dartmoor prison before long will become a thing of the past.

Despite Sir Thomas Tyrwhitt, the Prison, the main roads, hotels, charabancs and motor tourists, much of Dartmoor still remains comparatively unknown, although so universal is the general knowledge of wilder England today that there can be few people who have not obtained a superficial impression of the country. Even local knowledge extends little further, the majority of Dartmoor people being familiar only with their own area, which they utilise for some particular purpose—grazing beasts, cutting turf or picking whortleberries. As a general rule, those who spend most time upon the Moor are not residents but visitors, and in most cases the impressions obtained by the latter are perfunctory, for Dartmoor's appeal is subtle, appreciated only by those susceptible to its indefinable influence.

A year or two ago upon a remote shoulder of High Willhayes we came upon a party at the extreme end of the new artillery road. Around stretched a vast panorama, extending from coast to coast, but for which the strangers, apparently, had no eyes. Having driven their car as far as possible, they were standing about at an obvious loose end, eating their lunch and broadcasting their litter. They enquired if they were anywhere near the Prison, and when informed that a detour of some thirty miles would be necessary to get there, immediately disclaimed any intention of making it. Since the prison was on Dartmoor and they were also there, they assumed that they must be somewhere near the prison; that being one example of the visitors' outlook and the Moor's appeal.

I have almost invariably found when conducting friends upon a maiden pilgrimage to Cranmere Pool that, even if forewarned, they are either disappointed or remark that it is not at all the type of place they had anticipated. Upon one characteristically unsatisfactory occasion I acted as guide to a young sister-in-law who was anxious to make the trip. It chanced to be one of those perfect summer days which are all too rare upon our bleak and misty uplands, and as I chose the easiest route, we arrived without any of the expected adventures. So, too, had a charabanc party, with the result that the scene rather resembled a sordid village fair than a lonely spring-head on High Dartmoor. My young charge was bitterly disappointed, and refusing to observe the conventional ritual of letter-posting and signing the Visitors' Book, forswore the place for then and all time.

240

Exeter Guildhall

The pilgrimage to Cranmere, by the way, acquired an unparalleled popularity during the years immediately preceding the war. The rough tracks originally made for artillery practice were so appreciably improved for the convenience of the lorries which superseded the old horse-drawn military vehicles that the ranges became a system of good motor-roads, and it was possible to drive within little more than half a mile of the "Pool" itself. Visitors became so numerous that the primitive posting arrangements evolved by James Perrott, the Chagford guide, during the '80s no longer met the case, and in 1937 under the auspices of the *Western Morning News* a little pillar-box of moor granite was erected. Its construction was the work of Aubrey Tucker, the old Copper Hill and Hexworthy Mine carpenter often mentioned in these pages, the box being formally unveiled by my wife in the presence of a company gathered from all parts of the county for the ceremony. The *Western Morning News* has always supplied the Visitors' Book, kept first in Perrott's and later in Tucker's box, and the frequent necessity for renewal testifies to the popularity of the expedition.

The Cranmere trip by car, as conducted today, bears no comparison with the old Cranmere trek on foot, neither does it give any idea of the hills as trodden by the real moor-habitué. When once the prescribed routes and beaten tracks are left behind, desolation is the essential spirit of Dartmoor. Upon all sides is a silence, sinister and impressive, which weighs upon the stranger with a tangible presence. Once when crossing the great bog above Tavy Head with a man from Nairobi, he remarked that never, even in the African jungle, had he encountered such utter solitude. There, he said, one at least occasionally met an old negro herding his goats or came upon a native village, but here was nothing as far as eye could reach to suggest human life or activity. One might be upon a dead planet or a world forsaken. Again, when following the "wild ways of Dart" with a friend, she suddenly exclaimed: "*Thank goodness* there's a pony!" Not a living thing had gladdened her eyes for at least two hours, she assured me, and the appearance of this one little animal evidently proved a genuine relief.

16*   241

Scotch sheep, now the principal "wool-bearers" on Dartmoor

When once the outskirts of Dartmoor are left behind one sees little life, wild or domesticated. Grazing animals are always there, but swallowed up in the big landscape, and a thousand beasts may escape notice among the numerous coombes and undulations. Few birds are seen. The occasional meadow-pipit starts up at one's feet, or perhaps once in the course of a day's walk grouse are flushed. In early summer, of course, there is always the skylark's song, as inseparable from British moorland as the drone of bees over a clover field. Throughout the greater part of the year, however, an atmosphere of utter lifelessness envelops the Moor, manifested in a complete absence of sound. If Dartmoor has a voice, it is Devon's ubiquitous song of the streams, which rises from every valley, and which, when heard in solitary places, is one of the most desolate sounds on earth.

Since one walks upon Dartmoor mainly for pleasure, to ensure which good weather is essential, the Moor is usually explored under such conditions. Few save hunting people or moormen visit the remote parts during winter, and even hunting is largely dependent upon weather. Yet anyone who would know Dartmoor really well should also study her winter aspect, which, after all, is her true character. Then she has shed her brief summer veneer of warmth and fragrance and stands forth in her true colours, stern and wild, welcoming no guests other than the storm wind and the bitter frost and snow, to which she clings as the most appropriate companions of her solitude. Deep snow brings complete isolation to Dartmoor. The few tracks, being mostly sunken ways, are buried in drifts, while the clitters and crevices, being invisible, render the ground dangerous for horses. Any sheep or cattle left out are marooned, although they tend to gravitate towards civilisation at the approach of hard weather. None the less a considerable number perish, and towards the close of the severe winter of 1946–7 the rate of mortality among ponies particularly was high. Then the melting snows told grim stories of things which need not be tolerated. That is the seamy side which the Devonian mountain system conceals beneath its cloak of dazzling beauty.

The spectacular effects of Dartmoor under arctic conditions have never been fully appreciated because seldom seen. It is not a country of winter sports, the snowy periods being too irregular and not sufficiently prolonged. The hillsides also are unsuitable for tobogganing or ski-ing owing to streams and clitters. Long walks involve an amount of exertion only within the capacity of the most hardy, although the experience is worth almost any effort. Away in the heart of the Moor, from which no trace of civilisation is visible, a more perfect picture of utter loneliness could not be conceived. Except for one's own muffled footfall there is no sound in the land. Even the streams are frozen, and the absence of their "cry" creates a tenseness like that of a room in which the clock has ceased to tick. One is conscious of the unnatural stillness without necessarily analysing the cause. Away upon every side stretches the untrodden snow. moulded into fantastic effects by the storm-wind which brought and carved it. Harsh outlines are softened except where a great tor, whittled clear by the blast, stands black and grim, like a presiding giant, inscrutable, unapproachable. If there is sunlight, the frozen waterways gleam like polished silver, and when the wonderful phenomenon known as the *ammil* sheaths all the upland vegetation in a glittering ice casing, the diamond-bright splendour of each wild hillside baffles description. Then the twigs of lone mountain-ash or willow become transformed into a natural lustre, or wind-glass, through which the bitter nor'easter plays the cold rattling tune specially reserved for his own skeleton fingers, and beyond the capacity of other musicians and other instruments to produce.

The ammil does not occur with every frost, but is more frequent than commonly supposed. It is produced by a renewed freeze-up after a partial thaw, usually occurring upon high ground, where as often as not it escapes notice. When trees are dripping on the lowland, I have found every twig sheathed in ice at the 1,500-foot level, above which one may encounter iron frost when comparatively mild conditions prevail in-country. Upon Dartmoor proper one always finds the deepest and most enduring snow farthest from civilisation, quite irrespective of altitude. Heights such as Cosdon Beacon or even High Willhayes may be clear, apart from drifts, while Cranmere and the wilds of Tavy Head are still deeply covered, although at a lower elevation, the reason probably being that the outlying slopes are more directly affected by damp winds from either sea. Actually, if one can face the effort of reaching them the peat-veins can be traversed with greater ease during hard frost than under any other conditions. The natural dykes which intersect them in every direction, and are usually choked with peaty mud and water, then offer an easy surface upon which to walk, if the snow is not too deep, and one is independent of the few artificial cuttings the use of which is almost indispensable under ordinary conditions.

The peat-veins which extend over a great part of the northern Moor constitute a vast maze in which a stranger is more likely to lose his way than find it, unless he adheres rigidly to prescribed routes, which are blazed with white stones at frequent intervals. Divergence ends either in a *cul-de-sac* or interminable windings, which bring the pedestrian back to his starting-point if they do not land him among the waterways and peat-holes through which he must wade, perhaps knee-deep, or jump and scramble from hummock to hummock—a most exhausting proceeding. When iron frost binds peat and water alike, however, this difficulty at least is removed, and one may wander for hours through the strange, silent land, where one ceases to wonder at the fantastic tales which emanated from ancient Dartmoor.

Perhaps the secret of Dartmoor's loneliness lies not so much in its solitude and absence of life as in its lack of *connection* with life as one can visualise it. Anyone who walks far along the by-paths of the New Forest now and again comes upon an ancient tree, far exceeding in girth and spread all its surrounding fellows. There it stands, a venerable monument whose gnarled limbs may have given shade to Plantagenet kings as they hunted the deer, or even sheltered the sturdy bowmen who lined up at Crécy and Agincourt. There it is not difficult to people the ancient scene with picturesque figures which imagination readily calls to life, but the spirit of old Dartmoor is not so easily recaptured. Its date is too remote and seems to belong, not so much to another period as to another age. While an old tree is like a feudal castle, a relic but still inhabited, Dartmoor is a vast ruin, not of a building but an era, and even as an abandoned dwelling is always more desolate than the virgin wild, so there is no solitude to equal that of the derelict world of which Dartmoor is a symbol.

One cannot visualise those barren hills, themselves unchanged in the minutest feature, thickly populated, as they must have been, with busy human life. Standing now within the circular walls of Grimspound or beside the even more picturesque ruins that overlook Tavy Cleave, it is hard to imagine the quiet hillside more populous perhaps than an ordinary country village today. Beautifully situated was that settlement nestling upon the slope not far above the point where the Tavy and Rattle Brook meet. Down the long gorge the wild river dashes headlong over the same boulders from which those fishermen of long ago must have angled for the trout whose descendants dart for cover under the dark hovers at one's approach. From the grassy slopes of Hare Tor comes the sheep-dog's bark. What dogs were barking, one wonders, when the owner of the hut in whose doorway one stands looked down that same long valley perhaps thirty centuries ago? One would like to know so much more of those dim, distant days and the primitive Bronze Age folk whose hands reared those identical walls which have stood throughout the years, mute testifiers to conditions which one might otherwise almost regard as fabulous. One assumes that these sterile hills were inhabited from necessity rather than choice, and it is a curious thought that country which now provides the final refuge for our wildest beasts and birds against humanity should then have been occupied by man because affording protection against forest beasts or even fiercer tribes of his own species. Will the slow wheel of the ages again rotate, one wonders? Will our highly developed artificial life again revert to the primitive, and is it for this that the aloof, immutable hills are waiting?

But the thought is too big to be captured. Obscure in its past, inscrutable at present, and assured of its future in the serenity of irresistible might, the Moor remains, as indifferent to man's reactions as the Sphinx to the insects which alight on its face, and remote problems which defy solution may be abandoned for the moment.

Plans for the utilisation of Dartmoor are frequently discussed, but the answer to all questions upon this head becomes self-evident with increasing knowledge of the country. It is too sterile and too exposed to be utilised for any agricultural purposes other than those which it already serves. The limited success of afforestation, the tendency of the land already enclosed to revert to the wild, the failure of various commercial enterprises provide sufficient examples, and concerning the frequently advanced proposal to convert the Moor into a National Park, the outcome is of little real importance. To all intents and purposes it fulfils that need already, and one can suggest no change in the general position that would benefit the community as a whole. Latterly, doubt has been expressed in certain quarters as to the public right of access to Dartmoor. The area, it is suggested, is not covered by the *Law of Property Act*, and right of entry for "air and exercise" might at some future time be denied. This has never been officially challenged, however, during centuries of enjoyment, and it would hardly be in the interests of anybody to raise the question now— even if tenable. There is no area in Great Britain where the public on the whole cause less annoyance or commit fewer offences. Indeed, no material harm is done by visitors and, so far as they are concerned, no measures of "control" are necessary. Regulations as to camping and such matters are already in force, while the litter nuisance is covered by by-laws. It is rather by residents that abuses are committed, to deal with which a revision of the entire position has already been suggested.

With further reference to the National Park idea, I have always urged the advantages of Dartmoor as a wild-life reserve. One would like to see the entire area, both Forest and commons, established as a sanctuary for all animals, but birds at least should be given absolute protection. Admittedly Dartmoor is not altogether ideal for this purpose, mainly upon account of its altitude, barren character and climate. None the less, it possesses many advantages which other areas lack. The most favourable asset is its great extent.

As a general rule, bird sanctuaries in particular are far too circumscribed to be of much real value. Their limits are so narrow that birds pass on without discovering that freedom from molestation can be enjoyed, whereas the Moor not only offers ample space, but also contains excellent breeding-places for species which are harried elsewhere.

It is true that bird life generally is not prolific on the high moors, but this is largely due to the destruction wrought by indiscriminate fires during the nesting months. Presumably, the conversion of the Moor into a National Park would entail suitable measures of control in the matter of this and other abuses, and one may also assume that a National Park would embrace the dual purpose of a wild-life sanctuary. There are several points, however, to be considered.

Is it proposed, for example, to embody the entire area officially known as "Dartmoor," which comprises both Forest and commons—in all, some 130,000 acres? Otherwise the scheme could scarcely prove successful, since, as stated in the last chapter, boundaries are elastic, being only indicated by crude landmarks, sometimes miles apart, and any attempt at defined divisions in the form of fencing could not be made without detriment to the character of the country. The latter consideration must always be borne in mind, since upon it are based the most serious objections to the scheme as a whole.

It must be remembered that the main charm of Dartmoor today lies in her primitive quality; her immense loneliness and wild austerity; her wide spaces and utter remoteness from anything approaching civilisation. Rob the Moor of these features and her character is gone, and with it all that constitutes her attraction to the real nature-lover. The great wild hills should certainly be as free as air to all who can enjoy them, but the very charm that they now possess renders it imperative that their atmosphere should be maintained.

Dartmoor today is a grand natural monument, representative of vanished ages, vanished peoples and vanished conditions. Intersected and besprinkled with modern "amenities," such as light railways, camps, hostels and rest-huts, public telephones, bathing-places, garages, petrol-pumps, tea-rooms and every erection that "progress" demands in the interests of public recreation, she would degenerate into a mere dreary wreck of her former self, a dumping ground for one section of the community, for whose benefit, real or imaginary, so much has already been sacrificed.

Should the proposed scheme materialise, one can only plead for no desecration of the places where even today "solitude and silence reign"; that the construction of all facilities necessary for accommodation and entertainment shall be rigidly restricted to those areas into which civilisation has already penetrated and where every reasonable purpose and requirement may be served. By this means nobody need be the loser, and the few wild and unspoiled districts that still remain in our overcrowded little island may be preserved, not only to posterity, but to the very considerable number of people who appreciate their charm today.

CHAPTER XX

PLANT LIFE OF THE MOORLAND

DARTMOOR's plant life is of the usual heath, bog, peat and grass-moor type, but lacks the alpine species found upon our northern hills. Its actual flora, to use the word in its narrower interpretation, is less interesting to botanists than the varied *cryptogams*—ferns, mosses, lichens and liverworts—whose growth and variety are fostered by the ideal habitat provided by natural physical features. A hundred years ago, Rowe, in his *Perambulation of Dartmoor*, gives the number of cryptogamous plants as 660, but G. T. Harris, writing in 1917, considers the true total to be more than double that figure. Towards the end of the last century Edward Parfitt expressed the opinion that Devonshire was one of the richest counties in the United Kingdom for lichens, producing 500 species and varieties. Twenty different lichens were collected by Miller Christy in 1922 in Wistman's Wood alone. In addition, 345 species of moss are listed for the county by the *Victoria History of Devon* (1906), and it is therefore unnecessary to point out that the specialist can readily obtain access to detailed information on all these subjects elsewhere.

Brief mention may, however, be made of one or two plants from this category which may attract the attention of the interested but unscientific observer. Common upon many dry, peaty slopes, the papery tufts of *Cladonia rangiferina*, the reindeer moss, form a grey carpet between the stems of heather and whortleberry, together with another attractive *Cladonia*, the hoary, scarlet-lined "pixy cups" (*C. coccinea*).

Before the discovery of aniline dyes, various lichens, especially from Dartmoor, were used for colour extraction, and Moore in his *History of Devon* states that during a six-year period from 1762, 100 tons of the *tartareus* lichen were collected for purple dye, and quantities of *parellus* also gathered for a similar purpose in the Okehampton district. When one considers the feather-weight consistency of most lichens, to amass 100 tons by hand may be considered a notable achievement! When chemicals replaced natural dyes and the lichen industry died out in consequence, whortleberries continued to be used up to the present day for the rich Tyrian purple they afforded, and this unique harvest of the hills will be described a little later.

Returning to the cryptogams, it may be mentioned that the striking stag's-horn club-moss (*lycopodium*) occurs sparsely in the northern section, which can also claim the first British record for the famous "luminous" moss (*Schistostega osmundaceæ*), first located—surprisingly, to those who are familiar with the road today—in the lane leading from South Zeal to South Tawton. Growing in dark rocky crevices for preference, the light reflected by its cells renders this moss conspicuous when search has been re-warded, but it is certainly uncommon, though not confined to Dartmoor, occurring also in the Barnstaple, Torquay and Honiton districts.

Tracts of spongy sphagnum mosses are characteristic of the peat bogs. In hot summer weather when the shallower mires and spring-heads dry out these great green sponges, com-pletely drained, wither and disintegrate, detached fragments from their dry skeletons lying about like whitened bones in the sunshine. Except to a botanist, the dozen or more different species, sub-species and varieties of sphagnum are confusing, but several kinds, including *S. acutifolium*, a *plumosum* variety, and *S. cymbifolium* are quite common. The latter in August, when its round-headed capsules are ripe, resembles nothing so much as a giant pincushion stuck with brown-headed pins. Very arresting also are the compact round pillows of some of the *rubellum* varieties, forming vivid red cushions here and there among the other greener spreading sphagna in large boggy tracts.

Associated with sphagnum as a distinctive feature of the bogland are the nodding white heads of the two bog-cottons, *Eriophorum polystachion*, the narrow-leaved cotton-grass, and *E. vaginatum*, sheathing cotton-grass. The former of these sedges, recognised by its drooping umbel, is the more common, though the sheathing sedge, with its one compact tuft, is also plentiful, but upon the Dartmoor and Exmoor bogs only, seldom being encountered in-country. Its fluffy white tuft has earned it the name of "hare's tail," and both are impartially designated "pixy flags" by moorland folk, in reference to their traditional propensity for "pixy-leading" the unwary to their undoing in a bog. Here, too, may be found the erect spikes of bog asphodel (*Narthecium ossifragum*), the yellow flowers being later replaced by tawny pointed capsules.

Of the three sundews, *Drosera rotundifolia* is most common. The oblong-leaved (*D. longifolia*) also occurs, but should not be confused with *D. anglica*, the English sundew, which it somewhat resembles in the shape of its leaves, but which is mainly confined to one or two spots in the eastern part of the county. Pink-flowered bog pimpernel (*Anagallis tenella*), marsh pennywort (*Hydrocotyle vulgaris*), louseworts or red rattles (*Pedicularis*) and in spring the pale, purple-veined marsh violet (*V. palustris*) are abundant. The latter little blossom is long-lived, for coming first into bloom in early spring, its moist habitat, combined with cool upland winds, prolongs its flowering season well into July and often later. Marsh hypericum, woolly of leaf, with pale yellow blossoms, although preferring the lower marshes, may also be found upon higher altitudes. Pale butterwort (*Pinguicula lusitanica*) is not uncommon in sphagnum bogs, but occurs less frequently in the northern part of Dartmoor than elsewhere. Most attractive of all, perhaps, are the fairy-like bells of the tiny, blue ivy-leaved campanula (*C. hederaceæ*), which threads its slender branches in and out of reed clumps and ranker marsh vegetation. Sweet-gale, or bog-myrtle, the botanist's *Myrica gale* and the Devonian's "scented withy," is a fragrant feature of much of Dartmoor's marshy ground, climbing above the 1,100-foot contour line. Damp heathland, where standing bog water usually dries out in summer, is a favourite habitat of the pink cross-leaved heath (*Erica tetralix*).

The two other prevalent species of heather, *E. cinerea*, generally known as bell-heather, and the common ling (*Calluna vulgaris*) prefer drier ground and occur abundantly everywhere. The ciliated and Cornish heaths (*E. ciliaras* and *E. vagans*) have both been reported from Dartmoor, but were probably introduced, and whether, like the red grouse, not being indigenous, they ever become really established remains to be seen. Ling displays considerable variation in colouring and growth, and according to my own observation, apart from the true white heather, there are three distinct shades: the common mauve, sometimes so pale as to be almost "off white"; a decided pink; and least frequent, an attractive deep red. On an arid, windswept area such as Dinger Plain, *Calluna* plants are stunted to a height of perhaps a few inches only, with seared, rusty leaves and few blossoms. By contrast, single floriferous sprays of a foot in length may be gathered from a borderland molinia moor at a lower elevation. In spite of such diversity, however, there is but one species of ling, but with many variations. White heather, contrary to general belief, may be found without much difficulty—provided one knows where to look. There are certain slopes which will produce a good-sized bunch year after year; others upon which it is useless to search. Cosdon Beacon, for instance, provides a dependable supply on a high south-eastern arc of its circumference, but little or none on its lower contour lines and corresponding north-western arc. My own experience is that the most likely spots for white heather are among newly established young growth upon a deeply burned-out area, or where the ground has been pared for "vags." It is seldom seen as a large plant of woody growth—possibly because its conspicuousness would invite removal, whereas low, young sprays are easily over-looked.

The blossoming of ling in August among the compact golden bushes of the autumn-flowering gorse—*Ulex nanus* or *U. Galii*—whilst mountain-ash berries redden along the streamsides, combine to paint Dartmoor in her gayest colour-scheme of the year. Both heather and gorse sometimes act as "hosts" to the parasitic lesser dodder (*Cuscuta epithy-mum*), which smothers large tracts beneath its pink clusters, though in certain northern districts it is never encountered. Speaking from personal knowledge of a fairly large local area, I know of only one small patch, and that in a marsh on the extreme outskirts near Throwleigh.

But while heather bushes are still darkly green, other

small blossoms open between their stems in spring and summer. Earliest of these is the milkwort (*Polygala vulgaris*), a flower of many colour variations, white, pink, mauve and every shade of blue, but, again, only one species. From the date of its first blooming about Rogationtide, when intercessory processions for blessing crops and, later, parochial beating of bounds took place, the plant became popularly known as the "Rogation flower," in the same way as West-country children today still call the greater stitchwort (*Stellaria holostea*) "whitsuns," connecting its appearance not with Whitsuntide but with "White" or Low Sunday, following Easter. It is interesting to note that for the newly appointed "Farm Sunday" of the 1944 war-time period the old Rogation Day has been appropriately selected.

Other common and lowly plants of the dry uplands are the yellow-flowered tormentil (*T. potentilla*), heath bedstraw (*Galium saxatile*) and eyebright (*Euphrasia officinalis*), only mistaken by the veriest neophyte for white heather, though upon several occasions I have been asked for a verdict upon this point. Here, too, grows the little sheep-sorrel (*Rumex acetosella*), and one appreciates its presence at 2,000 feet, in contradistinction to the intense dislike with which one regards the same plant in the garden, where after years of active discouragement its yellow, thread-like runners still continue to enjoy the unabated hospitality of my gravel paths and herbaceous borders. Later in the year one associates this small sorrel with that scabious-like campanula, sheep's-bit (*Jasione montana*).

Speaking of campanulas, *C. rotundifolia*, the harebell, so abundant on the downs, moors and upland pastures of other counties, is, like the cowslip, a rare plant in Devon. Upon Dartmoor, with the exception of one or two border localities, it is entirely absent, its sparse occurrences being mainly in the northern area of the county, approaching the Exmoor borders. Fragrant wild thyme (*Thymus serpyllum*), usual companion of the harebell upon other downs and heaths, occurs plentifully in some Dartmoor districts upon lower slopes, and is not found upon others, the same applying to cathartic flax (*Linum catharticum*), whilst juniper, so familiar a feature of northern uplands, is a

complete absentee from Dartmoor, owing to the non-cal-
careous nature of the soil.

Dartmoor's only gentian—using the term as popularly
applied to the "true blue" species—is *G. campestris*, formerly more plentiful in southern districts, such as Roborough
Down, and also on the northern lime-containing soils round
Meldon quarries, near Okehampton, than is now the case.
Exmoor, again, as with the harebell, is in a somewhat
stronger position. Other plants belonging to the gentian
order occurring upon the Moor are the pink-flowered centaury (*C. umbellata*), abundant upon the lower rough
pastures, though not found upon the granite areas, and bog-
bean or buckbean (*Menyanthes trifoliata*), which grows
plentifully, though locally, in swamps. The yellow centaury
or yellow-wort (*Chlora perfoliata*), common upon Braunton
Burrows, where it consorts with distinct dwarf varieties of
C. umbellata and the two rare gentians, *anglica* and *amarella*,
is not a moorland plant, though found in certain calcareous
districts elsewhere, notably in East Devon.

The general advance of bracken (*Pteris aquilina*) has
already been described in Chapter XVII, and it only remains
to add that upon Dartmoor it seldom ascends above 1,400
feet or extends to the true peat, which therefore serves in
some measure as a natural check to its rapid infiltration.

The cranberry (*Oxycoccus quadripetalus*) and cowberry
(*Vaccinium vitis-idea*) have been recorded from Dartmoor,
but only as of rare occurrence, nor is the bearberry (*Arcto-
staphylos uva-ursa*) to be found at all, and the abundant
whortleberry (*Vaccinium myrtillus*) is, therefore, the sole
representative of the wild fruit crop. Borderland woods,
tumbled clitters, streamsides, dry slopes and island banks
elevated above bog or stream, all afford foothold to this
lucrative plant. In the first of these habitats the bushes cover
acres of ground beneath the trees, sometimes among oak, as
at Fingle Bridge and Halstock on the East Okement; sometimes between pine trunks, as at East Hill near Ottery St
Mary and on Shute Hill near Axminster. As might be
expected, where timber is dense the plants bear little or no
fruit, but in clearings and open spaces, berries, though
inclined to be small, ripen earlier than in more exposed

situations upon the open moor. Nowhere are finer fruit-bearing bushes found than in the clitters, where, after the manner of the oak-growth of Wistman's Wood, Blacktor Beare and Pile's Copse, it enjoys the protection from fire and cattle afforded by the great granite slabs. Here, by scrambling over tumbled rock, one may sit and strip bush after bush of berries that surpass the cultivated black currant in size. Heathery mounds rising from swamps usually produce fine fruit for much the same reason, the wet ground proving an equal deterrent to sheep and fire. There are, in fact, few situations on Dartmoor where whortleberries in small or large quantities cannot be gathered, small plants, checked by close grazing, intermingling almost everywhere with heather and even amongst bracken, as upon the Small Brook banks below Metherel.

During July and August, when the whortleberries are ripe, there is scarcely a rocky valley within walking distance of a roadway where parties of men, women and children may not be seen working with unceasing diligence throughout the long summer days. Proficiency is not easily acquired by an amateur, to whom the skill of the native often seems miraculous. The whortleberry-picker of the last generation could gather as many as 20 quarts in a day, that is to say 30 lb., for which he seldom received more than 5s. Now the output has considerably declined, but the remuneration exceeds the old Moorman's "dreams of avarice." I know many people who once picked for 1d. per quart. The price paid in 1942 was 2s. 6d. for the same amount, but during the following seasons was controlled at 9d. per lb., and the output declined proportionately. One villager naively remarked to me that control was merely tyrannical, since it deprived the public of a useful fruit supply. Apparently it had not occurred to him that the reduced price in no way prohibited anyone from continuing the supply, and that if the consumer had a grievance it was rather against those whose services were only purchasable at a fancy figure.

In the *Field* two years ago I remarked that a Dartmoor tor covered with whortleberry growth is literally far more profitable than good cultivated land of a corresponding acreage. This is true even under normal conditions, and during the boom described, fruit to the value of anything from £1 to 30s. might be gathered by a single picker in a few hours without great difficulty. Such was the lure of the high prices that people flocked from miles around, even coming by car for the purpose. The crowds seen upon the hills far exceeded those of normal times, when the village schools were closed for the whortleberry season—an old custom rendered necessary by the alternative of empty benches.

Until the recent war years, pickers carried their fruit to the house of the nearest receiver, this perhaps involving a walk of several miles with a good load. The demand increased so greatly during the boom, however, that competing dealers drove their vans on to the Moor itself, and so intercepted the harvesters as they returned. Some of the women wheeled perambulators long distances, the hardihood of the mothers being only equalled by the patience and endurance of the babies, constrained to spend a long day on the open hillside, often under conditions far from congenial. Inclement as these were, however, pickers considered the game well worth the candle, its value being illustrated by the achievement of one man, a gardener, aged seventy-four, who, during the summer of 1942, claims to have picked 400 quarts during out of work hours. Estimating his earnings upon an average at 2s. per quart, the profitable character of this "sideline" needs no emphasising.

Double summer-time certainly helped the whortleberry-pickers on the northern area, as later arrivals had the advantage of access to the artillery range, which nowadays monopolises a considerable part of these moors until late in the evening. In affected localities pickers might be seen pursuing their peaceful old-world occupation along a valley upon the farther side of which machine-guns operated or heavy artillery hurled screaming projectiles across the wide sky-scape. Firing seldom continued until dark, however, and the lowering of the official red flag which marked the danger-zone was the signal for enterprising gatherers to work farther afield. At this stage soldiers released from their military duties frequently joined the outgoing parties, the opportunity of considerably augmenting their pay being too good to lose. The most picturesque part of the proceeding

Some of Devon's unused water-power—River Dart between Buckfast and Totnes

has always been the return. As dusk falls every path is dotted with little processions, descending the winding ways by twos or threes with heavy baskets on their arms, fingers and clothes stained with purple juice. The whortleberry-picker is dressed for the part, however, empurpled aprons and trousers being all in the day's work.

Whortleberries are not the only plants to flourish in the deep-creviced clitters, for these, together with damp rock faces and boulder-strewn stream banks, produce, as might be expected, a wealth of ferns. The *Filices* family is well represented upon the Moor and its immediate outskirts, while 32 species out of a British total of 37 occur throughout the county generally. Unfortunately, many of the rarer ferns are disappearing, particularly the grand Royal Osmunda, about which, actually, the same statement was made seventy years ago. One complainant of the last century even attributed its destruction to "young ladies and curates, who by its sale sought to eke out slender incomes." That these decorous pilferers were not the only offenders is testified by the frequency with which *Osmunda regalis* is seen in moorland gardens. An old lady who died a few years ago in this village, at the age of eighty-seven, always exhibited with the utmost pride two great osmundas, which stood one upon each side of her garden gate, she herself having planted them as a young girl. The house has now passed into other hands, but the osmundas, now also getting well "up along," as they say in Devon, still upthrust their green crosiers, commandeering year by year an ever-increasing area of the garden. In May their great roots present the curious aspect of a flourishing lily-of-the-valley bed—a fortuitous but happy association, for the lilies reach maturity unshaded by the fronds, which later cover with their spreading greenery the aftermath of withering plants at their feet. As the old lady herself explained: "It is considered *very* unlucky to transplant lilies-of-the-valley." So the first intruders remain, and with their hosts have continued from strength to strength in a policy of mutual convenience.

I am unable to state the record life of a Royal Fern, but it is an odd reflection that a plant of the type usually labelled "delicate" should have outstayed the generation that saw its planting, and in so doing will defeat attempts at accurate recording of its age when, at length, its life-span too is ended.

BIBLIOGRAPHY

Devon Association Transactions, xxxviii, p. 270, C. E. Larter; xlix, p. 51, W. P. Hiern.

    British Flora. Bentham and Hooker.

    Flora of Devon. Martin and Fraser.

CHAPTER XXI

VILLAGE LIFE

CONVENTIONALLY the West-country villager is reticent towards and suspicious of the stranger, and it is difficult to imagine how this entirely erroneous idea arose. In reality he is communicative and eminently friendly, and far from being antagonistic to all "foreigners," does not know the word as he is reputed to use it. During the past few years a considerable number of troops have been billeted in this area, but I have yet to meet the service man who did not seem genuinely sorry to leave it. The story was always the same. In no part of the country had they been made so welcome, and they had little hope of meeting such friendliness or hospitality elsewhere. Speaking from personal experience, I think this applies to any eminently old-world population. If one enquires the way from a native of primitive South Wales, he is not content with elaborate instructions, but personally conducts the stranger to a point beyond which he considers mistake impossible. Devonshire people are not always quite so assiduous, although upon one occasion an old Exmoor farmer, at least fifty years my senior, could not be deterred from piloting me across a part of the moor along a way which was exceedingly hard for him and which I was fully capable of finding for myself.

That was typical West-country courtesy, which is deeply ingrained in the people. It comes as naturally to the Devonian as repartee to the Cockney. It might be called suavity, and although sometimes compared unfavourably with the bluntness of the Yorkshireman, it by no means necessarily denotes insincerity. Even as the northerner is inherently downright, so the Devonian is innately courteous or "vitty," as expressed in the vernacular.

The unstudied ease with which a Devonian says the correct thing is enviable. "He kept the place very nice, as you do," said the village postman when commenting upon a previous occupier of my house. On another occasion I was at a loss for an appropriate rejoinder when an Okehampton bookseller gravely enquired: "What do you consider the best Dartmoor book, next to yours?" There is never a hint of sycophancy in such touches. They come as readily as "please" or "thank you," and appear to be quite as spontaneous. A farmer friend, to whom I am indebted for many a good day's sport and other services, contrives to remove any sense of obligation with an inborn tact that no training could cultivate. Indeed, in the Devonshire farmer one often finds Nature's gentleman, possessed of a quiet dignity and freedom from embarrassment unsurpassed in any circle. I remember once when assembling for a meal in a farmhouse kitchen after a day's shooting, the party was joined by an employee who had not been with us. He enquired: "What sport?" but some diversion arising at the moment, got no answer. A few minutes later, when the other matter had been settled, the farmer pointedly turned to the man, whom everyone else had forgotten, and gave him an account of the day.

When a farmer says "Never mind yer 'at" as one enters his house, the headgear must on no account be removed, the invitation to retain it being a compliment—a gesture intended to confer the freedom of the house and place the visitor at his ease.

Village manners may not be those of Sir Roger de Coverley, even as the vernacular, though pure of its type, scarcely resembles the court language of today. None the less, rural etiquette is most punctilious within its own limits. When a party of youths assembled at the local "Fools' Corner" disperses for the night, individual leave-taking between all members is the rule. The long list of "good-nights" is like a roll-call conducted by each in turn. An acquaintance when met must always be acknowledged by name, although two in company are sometimes greeted by old-fashioned people under the joint terms of "both." I remember an old waggoner who when he met me walking with a friend would pass us with the brief salutation "Sirs," while friends often merely exchange names—the main essential—without "passing the time of day."

Codes of behaviour, as covered by that comprehensive term,

"the proper manner," are numerous and involved. When a West-countryman goes to view a farm, house, cottage or holding advertised "to let," he must formally enquire whether the occupier has finally decided to close the tenancy or would like to reconsider his previous decision. This question, asked and positively answered, confers a mutual obligation, upon the applicant to withdraw if desired; upon the outgoing tenant to make no new offer for the holding. In all business transactions, customary rather than legal procedure is observed. A bargain or a deal is concluded by "touching flesh," and even in the letting of property other than farms, where precise definition is necessary, a written agreement is dispensed with as often as not. One might naturally conclude that little business could be conducted under such informal conditions, but actually the lack of formality makes no difference. In any case, the legal position is seldom considered, and if inconvenient or contrary to custom, merely ignored. Should a man wish to abscond or evade his obligations, a scrap of paper seldom prevents him from doing so. Every defalcation within my experience has been in defiance of signed agreements, and the Devonian custom of dispensing with such superfluities has a great deal to commend it.

When a farmer land-owner lets his shooting, it is almost invariably by word of mouth. The only man I knew who "ran word" had signed an elaborate agreement drawn up by a well-known Exeter solicitor, to whom he had let his entire sporting rights. He had actually sold them to three people at the same time, but in true Devonshire fashion escaped prosecution, neighbours being reluctant to give evidence against him.

In the letting of shooting a curious convention exists. A gentleman tenant is entitled to the best bag he can secure, the best of sport is not grudged to him, but he must make no profit out of it. If a professional trapper is the sporting tenant—a common case nowadays—a substantial margin for himself is taken for granted. The one is supposed to make a financial sacrifice for his sport; the other to make a profit. When a farm labourer is granted the privilege of catching rabbits, a somewhat similar principle applies. He is welcome to as many as he can use, but must not "make a sale of it." Few farmers, again, object to villagers picking blackberries or mushrooms for home consumption, but not for market. The former is permissible household economy, the latter "scrounging." When permission is given to shoot, fish or take produce such as turnips, greens or pea-sticks, it involves an unspecified but recognised obligation to call at the farm "in the proper manner" when the privilege is exercised. "Quite a nice gentleman, but he forgot his way to the house" is a criticism which anyone who takes advantage of a Devonshire farmer's hospitality is well advised not to incur.

In every genuinely rural district there remains a definite sense of class distinction, also of *noblesse oblige*. Well within my own time it was considered correct to "honour" the parson or squire by charging him a higher rate for all saleable commodities. So much "to you, sir," is a manner of stating a price with which one is still uncomfortably familiar, realising that the formula confers one of the compliments which few seek and fewer still appreciate. That village people prefer those who discard all social distinctions is not borne out by personal impressions. While detesting the upstart or snob, they despise decadence in any form and expect every man to maintain his accepted status. They are often quicker in detecting the "bounder" than people in a higher walk of life, and there is no surer indication of a man's class than the manner in which the village speaks of him. Strong friendship is possible and frequent between men in different walks of life, but only when neither assumes the other's position. Even as in dress, contrast is preferable to a bad match, so the best friends are those who tacitly accept disparity in taste, outlook and standard.

Social inequality in marriage is neither sought nor encouraged. "I call it proper *himpudence* for the likes of she to have aught to say to my boy" was the opinion expressed by our old charwoman when a certain young lady in the district was "carrying on" with her postman son, "impudence" in the vernacular having a meaning for which the dictionary supplies no word. It might best be defined, perhaps, as behaviour inconsistent with position, the word "rude" being the Devonian equivalent of "impudent" in the generally accepted sense.

Wonder is often expressed as to how villagers earn a living, since to the casual observer sources of employment or income appear so circumscribed. In Cornwall and Devonshire this problem is of comparatively modern date, for until the beginning of this century there were the mines already described, tin, copper, arsenic, etc., to which all who wanted work in the surrounding districts naturally gravitated. There was also the woollen industry, and in many villages iron smitheries whose hand labour supplied all the simple agricultural implements in use. Wool has gone and iron is going, and there is now only one smithery of the original type left in Devonshire.

This is an old-world institution, carried on at Sticklepath, near Okehampton, in the same setting and with the identical equipment in use when the business came into being about 1812. The premises occupy the site of an old grist mill, much of the original building being still in use, and stand near the banks of the river Taw, the good genius of the works, from which the stream is separated by the picturesque old Quaker burying-ground where "the rude forefathers of the hamlet sleep" within sound of the anvils at which so many of their hard-working lives were spent. Since its inauguration, this interesting survival of Devon's industrial past has been in the hands of one family, Messrs Finch Bros., and throughout its career has carried on a busy trade in iron tools of every description, from the homely Devon "tetty-chopper," otherwise potato slicer, to scythes, sickles, "browse-hooks," pitchforks and even horse-shoes. The equipment consists of a large water-wheel, the power for which is supplied by a leat drawn from the river Taw; an old-fashioned trip-hammer, rotary saw-benches and several anvils, the tools being forged by hand, and of such durability that some of the first to leave "the Foundry" are still in use today. Indeed a "Finch tool" has the reputation of never wearing out, and only needs replacement when lost or stolen. Although officially West-country, the firm's market is extensive, and a new resident in the village, bringing garden implements from Kent, found that the tools bore the local smithery brand.

In an article published by *Country Life* in January 1944, I gave a detailed description of this institution, following which the visitors, to say nothing of letters and orders, who arrived from various parts of the country testified to the interest still taken in Devonshire rural craft. This industry, like so many, is inevitably handicapped by competition with wholesale manufacture, and largely owes its survival to the maintenance of its high standards. It has outlived the local copper mines, the great Oxenham lime quarries and the comparatively modern tinning experiments on the Upper Taw, for which adventure it provided most of the tools, and still its hammers continue to ring, although swung now almost exclusively by men who have grown grey under the old "Foundry" roof.

Now with the demand for road metal continually increasing, a certain number of men are absorbed by the various stone quarries and other highway work. It also goes without saying that a large proportion of countrymen are farm labourers. Apart from these sources of employment, however, a considerable part of the population remains unaccounted for. In country phrase, "folks live on one another," local money passing from hand to hand like a communal tool. Convention demands the support of local industry, and there are few needs that a village cannot supply. Indeed, in old country life the principle worked very simply, and up to a certain point does so to this day.

The carpenter, cobbler or blacksmith did the farmer's repairs and bought the farmer's produce. The charwoman scrubbed out the village shop and laid out her earnings over the counter. Each petty trader or craftsman, from the chimney-sweep upwards, becomes directly or indirectly another's customer. Apart from a few work-shy individuals, there is little unemployment. It is not a case of finding work, but finding the man to do it. In this village, even before the war, a jobbing gardener or carpenter was almost unobtainable, there being no apparent successor to old Aubrey Tucker, then already well advanced in the seventies. The demand for farm labourers has long exceeded the supply. There are few professional hedgers today, and scarcely a young man who knows how to dig or lay one. Mr Wickett tells me that he now does the essential part of the work himself, if and when he can get anyone to cut off the wood and tie the faggots. The vastly increased number of bungalows and small "residences" has absorbed the demand for labour formerly monopolised by the big houses of the past. Most villages, also, nowadays cater for the summer visitor, even cottages finding room for this form of emolument, sometimes described as the housewife's harvest. Again, there are few labourers who do not run a side-show of some sort apart from the letting of rooms, which is always regarded as the wife's perquisite. One gardener in this village who works a day a week for half a dozen houses is a "bee-master," and has a considerable local market for his honey. Another, similarly employed, has a car for hire, demand for which increased so rapidly that it soon developed into whole-time employment for himself and a brother. Many farm labourers are also small-holders. Others keep poultry, almost everyone pigs. Unless there are too many young children it is the rule rather than the exception for the wife also to be employed, either in part-time domestic service or in laundry work at home. Until the present phase there has been no lack of domestic employees in country districts, girls preferring to remain near their own homes rather than seek bigger money in towns, home ties and loyalties being a strongly marked trait in the Devon character. Up to the present moment we ourselves have never experienced the necessity of advertising or applying for a maid: any possibility of a vacancy ensured an applicant upon the doorstep.

A few years ago, before the war with its sudden access of temporary affluence completely altered the situation, I asked a local doctor with a large country practice whether his working-class patients appeared to live comfortably. He replied without hesitation: "They have *plenty* of money, if that's what you mean. Don't ask me where it comes from. I only know that in any cottage you see a better wireless set than I can afford to buy, and there's no hint of want anywhere." My own experience is much the same. Some are better off than others, but cases of real need have always been incredibly rare, and the means whereby the cottager not only balances his budget but always seems to have money in hand when required often baffles the comprehension. To realise this one has only to attend a village auction sale and see the prices paid for entirely superfluous articles, such as an old gramophone or impossible picture, while it is a common occurrence to see village children in possession of expensive toys which were beyond one's own dreams at a similar age, and certainly cost more to buy than the entire weekly earnings of the father. I am told that the amount spent upon sweets alone in the local shops at normal times by the children is incredible.

One can only assume that the countryman's standard of life is simple, his wants and those of his family comparatively few, and this was once undoubtedly the case. Yet even so he bought the best. "Not any cheap tools there, lady," was Tucker's response to some chance remark of my wife's when he was emptying his basket of implements. When a local quarryman buys a new pair of boots, they are specially made for him by the village cobbler at a "special" price, which many people better placed financially would consider extravagantly high. No cottager will touch margarine unless compelled under rationing orders. His week-end dish of Devonshire cream was always the rule, and he never lacked the wherewithal for his pint of beer. Again, one would think that even doubled earnings would be swallowed by the new outlay that custom demands. Every village woman, or girl in her teens earning perhaps 30s. a week, regularly visits the nearest hairdresser for a permanent wave. Every bus to the town and cinema is crowded and every dance-hall packed to overflowing. "It isn't the money, madam; it's the coupons" announced the little maid who had never boarded a train, when the question of new clothes arose. As it is now, it has always been, the entire position being purely relative. The "widow's cruse" must have found its way into most Devonshire homes, for even if no relation can be traced between apparent income and obvious expenditure, there always seems to be money in the purse and tea in the pot.

One cannot conclude this sketch of village life without a glance at some of the old crafts, which, indispensable as they still seem, are none the less dying out, not for lack of custom but for lack of men to carry them on. The only man in this village who would sweep a chimney—at his own price—is now aged seventy-six, has just undergone a serious operation, and is never likely to sweep another. That competition for such work should not be keen will surprise nobody, but it is merely another example of "nor the ploughing neither." It may be very good for the householder to remove his own soot, but if the surgeon, the dentist and the midwife all objected to undertake work which cannot always be pleasant, the chimney-sweep himself might be at a loss for lack of their services.

The sweep, however, is not as apt an example of an old Devonshire workman as the hurdle-maker, already described, or the far more frequently encountered furze-cutter, he being one of those who, like the genuine but not the conventional stone-cracker, often adopted his calling because he preferred its independence to regular work, or had not specialised in anything else. His equivalent today would probably be a rabbit-trapper, one of the few professions at which village rolling-stones often succeed in gathering moss, and again by some unaccountable method can usually find means with which to procure the very considerable outfit. The furze-cutter's, like the hedger's, was a solitary job, hard but up to a certain point skilled, for there is easier stuff to cut than gorse and little more difficult to bind. He worked on the breaches or moorland with the wild life of the countryside for company, and his job has no appeal to the mechanically minded, sociable youth of today. The last professional furze-cutter that I knew was a native of Bewley Down, a very old man who lived alone in a one-storied cabin which could not have existed, one would have thought, anywhere save in Ireland. Outside the most picturesque, inside the dirtiest dwelling in East Devon, it did not long survive the occupier, who met a fearful end, as if to demonstrate that even furze-cutting can prove dangerous. Setting fire to some waste brush, he accidentally ignited the entire brake, and endeavouring to extinguish it, was caught by the flames and burned to death before anyone was aware of the accident. More than thirty years have passed since "old Jimmy set hisself afire," as the local version of the tragedy went, and many gorse faggots were bound after his time, but I doubt if any representative of his class is enrolled today on the National Register.

There is still the cobbler, for while people wear boots these need repair, and the local man is usually preferred to his rivals in the nearest town, his work being thorough because done by hand, his interest more personal. And scarcely less dispensable, to date, has been the blacksmith, there being still farm-horses to shoe and implements which require repair. It is, however, fortunate that the farm-horse has little future, for with the passing of the present generation of blacksmiths, mostly middle-aged or elderly men, the craft seems likely to be lost for lack of apprentices. Formerly, every smith had his understudy. Those days are gone. I have not seen a young man at work in a forge for many years, and am told that none can be found to adopt the calling. The work is hard, trying, dangerous up to a point, and owing to its limitations entirely lacking in modern appeal. The same applies to the village thatcher, once an institution, and, incidentally, the best paid man in the parish. True, slate, tile and, in the case of too many buildings, the unreservedly hideous corrugated iron have replaced the picturesque but admittedly uneconomic thatch. None the less, the demand for the few remaining thatchers is steady, and doubtless more of this roofing would be used but for the difficulty in getting the work done. However that may be, the thatcher, like the blacksmith, is one of the older generation, and although at the moment I know of a boy who is working with his father and intends to become a thatcher in his turn, the exceptional character of this instance certainly proves the rule. Incidentally he is the eldest of seven, all of whom, the father hopes, will follow his example. Whether this is too optimistic remains to be proved.

Old-fashioned thatchers provided most of their own equipment. Reed was the employer's province, also materials for making straw ropes and spars, but these the thatcher actually fashioned for himself as part of his craft, although latterly spars have been factory produced, like the carpenter's boards, once sawn out by hand in the pits attached to every carpenter's shop. Attempts to revive the craft artificially have been made and lessons are given at agricultural colleges. The fashion may return, but practical objections render this unlikely. High wages can be earned, but make little difference. As with the chimney-sweep, the blacksmith and the farm-labourer, "it is not the money, madam," but in this case the work which fails to attract. If a man can make as much as he wants at some easier job, it is only natural that he should do so, and when, as at present, either man or woman can achieve this end even without full employment, choice of and indifference to work follows as a matter of course.

There was one pillar of village life who must not be overlooked. This was the policeman, a personage of considerable importance: the stout ally of anything representing authority or property; the natural enemy of small boys, petty pilferers and scroungers. He was a wonderful institution, worthy, and within his limitations competent and usually courageous. He was never afraid to tackle a tough, and I well remember the case of two constables who unwisely interfered with an armed poaching gang, with fatal consequences to one and serious injury to the other. Yet for all his worth, beneath his magic garb he was very much of a mere man—particularly if Devon born. He was an unsophisticated person whose skill in being at any place where entertainment coincided with duty amounted to genius. I knew one man whose beat invariably followed the line of a fox-hunt. He kept a very useful terrier which always slipped collar on hunting days, joining its master at any place where a terrier was wanted. There was the constable who was very fond of rabbit-shooting, and when a chance of ferreting occurred always happened to be on "night duty" just then, which left the day free. He had no licence. I remember another who turned the usually unpopular night round to profitable account, and when the moon was bright might be seen staggering home with appropriations from local woodricks on his back. As a rule, however, the village constable was a respecter of property, and certainly of persons, as when he held up the vicar, cycling home at dusk without a light, and hastily apologised upon discovering the offender's identity.

Very different is the modern policeman, whom the village seldom sees nowadays since the county council has "standardised" all police-stations, discarding the old cottages in favour of imposing erections built as far as possible from the villages where the policeman was most wanted. He moves now in other spheres, being a uniformed clerk working at the head office rather than a patroller of lanes and foot-paths; but while the principal bogey has been lifted out of the fruit-stealing urchin's life, the village has also lost a good old watchdog, whose bark was useful, whose bite hurt nobody.

The future of rural life presents problems which to the realist often appear insuperable, and nobody who retains any regard for England as we know it can anticipate the proposed urbanisation of the countryside without dismay. Urban amenities cannot be otherwise than utterly incompatible with quiet village conditions, for new wine bursts old bottles. There is more to be said about country life and people, however, and nostalgic reflections at this stage are premature.

CHAPTER XXII

FOLKLORE

"AND that bain't true, neither," was the unpromising remark with which a Cornishman opened a conversation when my wife and I were inspecting the famous stone known as "King Arthur's Quoit," near Tintagel, and the uninvited pronouncement was typical of the now sceptical, if once credulous, West-country outlook upon the entire subject classified as "folklore." There has been a sustained effort within recent years to revive its interest, or rather perhaps to bolster up a belief in its survival, and up to a certain point it is true that many curious ideas still exist among country-people. In this respect, as in many others, however, the substance is too often lost in the shadow, reality in convention. A neighbour of mine, an old gentleman, was a good deal bothered a few years ago by the tricks of a mischievous little village girl. He ambushed her at last, lecturing her effectively, then as an afterthought added that the Pixies would get her if she persisted in her ill-doings. This proved a tactical error. The village policeman, schoolmistress or her mother's slipper were recognised sources of danger, but threatened intervention by the "little people" lacked any realistic background. "Pixies? *Garr*! There bain't none," she retorted, tossing her own curiously pixy-like locks with restored confidence, and upon this unsatisfactory note the interview closed.

Of course, quaint ideas still prevail and quaint people still exist. Truth, even if unpopular, is none the less essential when describing existing conditions, and misrepresentation for sentiment's sake becomes not only misleading but foolish. Getting down to realities, one doubts whether the Pixy ever took concrete form in the minds of the eminently prosaic country-people, although, admittedly, the word often occurs in Devon nomenclature. It is also true that I first heard of him in Devonshire as a child, but not in a cottage or farmhouse. It was in the village rectory, from which I was conducted with the little boy of the house to say goodnight to "Echo," who functioned in a neighbouring field, and was introduced as "a sort of a pixy." It was in the manor-house or rectory nursery that Pixy, like most fairy characters, mainly flourished through the medium of the story-book. The Pixy was a back-number even in Baring-Gould's time, according to that writer, and one cannot but suspect that his date was always in the past.

The West-countryman is eminently superstitious, but his imagination works upon other lines, equally fanciful perhaps and quite as picturesque, but less childish. His dread of the supernatural is real and deep-rooted and usually takes a definite form. He has no fear of "wish hounds" or of the historic spectres who perambulate through every guide-book. He reads no guide-books, so has never heard of them. Upon the whole, however, country-people fear the powers of darkness generally more than any identifiable apparition. For some unknown reason the abandoned limestone quarries with their dark pools at South Tawton have acquired a sinister reputation, and few of the villagers will visit the place after sundown. Incredible as it may seem in a class that can only be described as unimaginative, they dread the dark solitude of the remote countryside—actually the world's safest place at such a time. Once when describing a short cut to my house through a great larch wood to a young man who was bringing some pigeons—necessarily after dark—he shook his head. "I should meet the Devil if I came that way by night," he declared, quite seriously, and he preferred to take an alternative route, two miles round.

Quite recently we employed a maid whose family lived in an isolated hamlet about three miles away. Being afraid to return alone after visiting her home on dark winter evenings, her mother invariably escorted her, but was then in no better case than the daughter, since three bogey-haunted miles stretched back to her own cottage. This difficulty having arisen once or twice, a nine-year-old sister was pressed into service to act as moral support to the mother upon the return journey, a companion of any age being regarded as a talis-man against the supernatural. Whenever the maid went

home, therefore, it involved a six-mile walk for two of her relations. The labour of love was not only cheerfully undertaken, however, but regarded as a matter of course, the wildest weather proving no deterrent.

Belief in witchcraft has diminished considerably during the past quarter of a century. Within my own time it was strong, however, and is only passing with the old professors of the craft. Ability to exercise the black art was a useful asset when conducting business or soliciting a favour. Whether people with whom a recognised witch had dealings believed in the dark craft or not, few cared to subject themselves to its influence, and undeniably curious things happened. Stories akin to those told by Hawker and his contemporaries may seem fantastic, but whether due to coincidence or anything else, many of them appear to be true, at least in the underlying facts.

In the Torridge valley lived a village crone who, apparently, could not resist trying her skill upon any likely subject. When quite senile she was taken by her daughter to visit the Rector, through whose yard they were passing when some little pigs caught the old woman's eye. "Oh, the pretty dear!" she exclaimed, pointing at one, which promptly rolled over as if shot, within full view of the Rector, who himself told me the story, adding that the pig never got up again. The daughter, distressed but not surprised, admonished her parent as she might a child. "I never thought you'd ha' done it, mother, to *Parson's* pig."

During my own residence in this village there was an old woman who spat upon the doorstep of a neighbour with whom she had quarrelled. "Take that," she remarked pleasantly, and however impotent she may actually have been, the remainder of that man's life was a long tale of catastrophe, attributed by the villagers to "Mary Anne's ill-wishing." That same old lady's saliva possessed both good and evil properties, it would seem. A cottage child who at one period suffered from sore eyes, bad enough to necessitate continuous absence from school, met the witch in the lane behind my house. Her eyes attracted notice, were examined—much to the little girl's terror—and finally spat upon. She rushed home to her mother, who, realising the

18*   273

situation, sternly forbade the child to wash her face, in order that "Mary Anne's spell" might work. The cure was immediate and complete.

In West Devon if an old woman suspected of witchcraft was seen going down a lane, nothing would induce anyone wittingly to walk that way until somebody else, rushing in unaware where angels feared to tread, had taken the same course, the idea being that the witch would certainly have marked a line which would bring misfortune to the next individual who crossed it. When some unfortunate person had passed and incurred the ill-luck, everyone else was free to proceed as he pleased. The attitude, indeed, much resembled that of a local Home Guard, who, as we listened one night to the drone of German aircraft passing overhead, complacently remarked: "As long as they *do* pass, us needn't trouble."

Upon the Cornish border, indeed, fear of the black art was so real that people who believed themselves "overlooked" would go to almost any lengths to avert the consequences. The approved remedy was a counter-charm which only a white witch could supply. A witch, incidentally, might be of either sex, the term "wizard" being unknown in Devon. I know various people who well remember a man in Exeter, a famous witch, who drew clients from as far afield as the Tamar valley, some of sufficient social status to visit him in a carriage and pair. A Bradworthy woman who had contracted a tumour on her thigh, and attributed the growth to the malice of a neighbour, visited this man, who told her that her supposition was correct and specified the ill-wisher. Counter-measures were unnecessary, she was assured, certainty of origin being sufficient to break the spell. She went home quite satisfied, and the tumour, about which at any rate there had been no doubt, disappeared as completely as if it had been a wasp-sting. It was her nephew who told me the story in this room, only a few weeks ago.

The white witch functions to this day, but now purely as a witch-doctor in the literal sense, his department being to heal skin diseases and wounds or, particularly, to remove warts, in which the procedure adopted varies curiously. An East Devon farmer tells me that for years he suffered from this disfigurement on the backs of his hands, until one day he happened to visit an ironmonger's shop in Tiverton. The proprietor who served him noticed the warts and offered to cure them, declaring that he possessed the ability, but was quite unable to account for it. In the farmer's words: "He just rubbed my hands with his own and said that would be enough. Before I got home, all the warts were itching, and within a week or two every one had gone. I've never had one since," he concluded. He also tells me that his son, when a child, suffered from glandular swellings on his neck. These caught the eye of a gypsy woman who treated them in precisely the same manner as the ironmonger did the warts. "They'll go now," she pronounced, as she passed her hand over them—and they did.

Rather different, though equally successful, appears to be the method of a local wart specialist. A neighbour of mine, originally a confirmed sceptic, having been cured himself, sent his daughter, suffering from the same trouble, to try her luck. The man offered to purchase the warts for a copper coin, which is part of the customary formula, and told the girl that they would disappear within three weeks, an estimate which proved correct. She tells me that they have never returned. Why the spell should take three weeks to work is a point upon which no light has been shed. Whether it clarifies or complicates the problem to a medical man is another question. Apart from the token coin—usually a halfpenny—paid for the warts, no money passes in the transaction. Of the legal position, I lack knowledge. It is stated, however, that if the witch accepts remuneration, the spell is broken—although a present at some subsequent date is not refused.

A charm to stop bleeding, mentioned in *Dartmoor in all its Moods*, is more widely used than I was aware when writing that book. Mr Wickett often speaks of a man who practised it freely in this parish, and to demonstrate his powers once offered to arrest the flow of blood from a pig while actually being killed. Wickett rejected the offer, being unwilling to have his meat spoiled in order to establish the merits of any charm—which actually amounted to an admission of faith in its potency.

I make no attempt to account for all these occurrences, and express no opinion upon them, actually having none. They certainly happen, and even the ample cloak of coincidence cannot be stretched to cover everything.

One might mention other instances attributed to witchcraft, but less unaccountable. Once, years ago, while walking home I came upon a distinctly unusual group, consisting of a neighbour's mare lying flat on the road but still attached to the gig which she should have been drawing; a couple of onlookers; and the mare's owner, who stood regarding his prostrate servitor with complete resignation. To my inevitable enquiry, he calmly replied: "As far as I can see, sir, my mare's dropped dead in the road, and I bain't surprised neither." Knowing the mare, the only matter for "surprise" in my opinion was that she had remained upon her legs so long. The owner, however, had other reasons, it would seem, for expecting the disaster. He had been involved in a dispute with an acquaintance reputed to possess the evil eye, and trouble before reaching home was promised him. It was at this juncture that the old mare suddenly staged a most unexpected "come-back." Possibly the potency of the spell had worn off or, more probably, she had recovered her wind. Anyway, with a flounder and scramble, she regained her feet and started homewards, while the man, whom nothing would have induced to reboard the trap, trudged behind, entertaining me—since I considered myself beholden to see him home—with lurid tales of the evil eye and his intention to square accounts with its supposed possessor at their very next meeting.

In that same district—it was East Devon, near that almost incredibly primitive and picturesque area known as Bewley Down—another and less accountable incident occurred. Upon the Down, neighbour to old Jimmy the furze-cutter, lived another of the same profession, but possessing a more sinister reputation. Dirty, ugly, untrustworthy, surly and unsociable, it was inevitable that the evil eye should have been added to his other qualities, and he played up to the rôle. Early one morning he was caught setting snares by a small-holder, whom, in the course of a not very amicable interview, he promised to knock down before the day was over. The younger man, thinking little more about it, proceeded with his work, and a few hours later was picked up unconscious, having been stricken with a sudden mysterious illness which was never diagnosed, and for which his previous and subsequent robust health entirely failed to account. Neither he nor any of his friends ever doubted that "old Boots," as the furze-cutter was called owing to a singularly unbecoming style of footgear, had "overlooked" him, nor could anyone suggest a plausible alternative. Thirty years later I still hesitate to pronounce upon the case, coincidence seeming scarcely more acceptable than the local interpretation.

The precise stage in life at which a man or woman became a witch, the essential qualifications and their acquisition, together with the source from which they were derived, seem to be obscure points. Nor is it clear how a reputation for proficiency in this line becomes established. It would seem that unpopularity or eccentricity—the latter going a long way towards incurring the former—was one of the main essentials. Even so, many peculiar old crones who seemed to comply with all the requisites escaped the stigma, and it must be admitted that there was seldom smoke without some fire. The reputed witch usually practised witchcraft, or at least made some profession of doing so, and whatever may have happened when burnings or duckings were the custom, I have never known a case in which such a person—and there have been several—suffered any form of persecution or even ostracism. Upon the contrary, unless considered actively malignant, they were not regarded with avowed dislike, but treated rather as specialists and, above all, persons to be propitiated.

The attitude adopted towards such things by intelligent and educated people within my own experience was scarcely one of belief, but rather that of accepting the *status quo*. My late "Squarson" uncle, of whom more will be said, included the "charming" of sick animals among the numerous offices which he performed for his parishioners. Like them, he regarded the gift seriously, but was unwilling to talk about his methods, in case, as he once remarked to me, the "virtue" should go out of him. He was a scholar, an Oxford M.A., shrewd, level-headed, a keen naturalist and sportsman, the best shot in the district, and perhaps one of the most outstanding West-countrymen of his type and period. Although not a native, he took such firm root in the soil of his adopted county that its spirit became his own, the outlook and ways of the people his ways, and there was scarcely a branch of folklore with which he was not conversant or to which he did not conform, consciously or otherwise. Quite as a matter of course he accepted all the conventions which the old Devonian observes in his everyday life without questioning the why or wherefore, and in this respect he differed little from most natives of the county, no matter what their class.

Some years ago, when unaccustomed to Devon ways and ideas, my wife sent some blankets to the local washerwoman, mother of one of the maids, by whom a message was brought asking whether it would be convenient to wait until the month—which happened to be May—was out, thus avoiding the risk of "washing away one of the family." This remains a prevalent superstition, and upon the story being repeated to a Devonian lady friend, she immediately exclaimed: "*I* wouldn't wash a blanket in May on any account"; and that is the attitude to most of the rules laid down by folklore. Few admit belief, but most conform.

The prohibition list is long and varies with each district. Upon the Cornish side both magpie and raven are regarded as particularly unlucky, whereas elsewhere they attract little notice. The "weeping" note of a robin still distresses a Devonian, and I was once assured by a retired lawyer, of all people, that one should not tame these birds, since "they are very unlucky." "If you hurt a robin, you get the king's evil," declared Winifred, whose mother objected to washing the blankets; and when asked to define this malady, she could only add: "I don't know what it is, but that's what you get if you pull out young robins." For obvious reasons we did not discourage further circulation of the idea.

Peculiar notions concerning birds and animals are too many to be enumerated. Most unaccountable, possibly, is the belief that a snake cannot die before sundown, even if chopped into pieces. The fear of reptiles, indeed, irrespective of species, amounts almost to an obsession, particularly on the eastern side of the county. May kittens are seldom kept, solely upon account of the convention that they bring snakes into houses. Many superstitions concerning animal life, plants and weather are not, of course, essentially Devonian, being equally prevalent in other counties. Indeed, the weather lore of the countryman is simple, every locality and one might almost say every parish having its own special indications. Here, when upland cattle descend to the village and "the wind goes back to Dartmoor," we know what to expect, for wild weather follows the cattle downwards as a storm follows the petrel. If the hill mist drifts towards Belstone we know that the day will be clear. If it rolls towards Throwleigh there is little hope. One maid, brought up by a grandfather who had been the last old-fashioned shepherd in the locality, was full of field and weather lore, gleaned from the old man over his cottage fire. She read the signs with remarkable accuracy from the river's "cry" or from the stars, which she sometimes described as too "thick" for fine weather or frost, and her predictions rarely proved at fault. If suddenly consulted upon the immediate prospect, she would run to the door, from which a view of the smoke from Mary Anne's chimney could be obtained. If this infallible indicator blew across the village street the picnic-basket might be packed. If it blew towards "granfer's cottage," farther down the valley, expeditions were discouraged. Why that particular smoke possessed prophetic properties more than our own never transpired. Possibly the maid had ideas on the subject, for she took the witch very seriously, since it was upon her sister's eyes that the old lady had spat.

Until within the last few years no cottager and very few farmers possessed a barometer. I have seen the initial acquisition of many, and one neighbour still calls to consult mine before cutting his grass or uncovering a rick. To this day, however, the more primitive country-people remain a little contemptuous of barometers, as innovations and unreliable at best. The maid who consulted the river, stars and smoke, if told that the glass was rising would shrug her shoulders with the comment: "Going up to fetch the rain, I expect." One old die-hard, exasperated at the persistent and, in his opinion, unjustifiable optimism of a newly bought aneroid, hurled the discredited instrument from his back door during a heavy rain-storm, saying: "Go out into the court and see for yourself."

As a rule the old-fashioned field labourer finds "me rheumatics" the surest weather prophet, even as he prefers the time-honoured sack to the most up-to-date mackintosh. None the less, sacks are becoming unfashionable as articles of apparel, and despite the scorn of weatherwise young women or disgruntled old agriculturists, the barometer has now found its way into many cottage homes, while, in these days, more farmers base their policy upon the forecasts issued from the Meteorological Office than upon the direction of the mist which clouds High Dartmoor. No matter which oracle he consults, however, the farmer's attitude towards the weather is more or less fatalistic. He regards it as one of the uncertainties of life which his calling requires him to face, and actually he grumbles far less than many people to whom sunshine or rainfall make no material difference. "Seedtime and harvest shall never fail" is a proverb which found frequent expression in old rural Devonshire, and the vicissitudes of a season are accepted as incidental.

The days of incantation and ritual upon the land have now given place to a more practical outlook, although there are still gardeners of the older generation who sow their seeds in conformity with the moon phases. This applies also to old customs and ceremonies, few, if any, of which have survived the introduction of machinery, with which the social side of agricultural work for the most part disappeared. There could be no more "colting" of learners at sheep-shearing or mowing assemblies, since there was no longer any gathering or any learner to "colt." One has often seen "sweet hay" made, even in the near past, but today there are few village girls around whose "permed" heads the hay-ring, which entitles the holder to a kiss, has ever been placed. She no longer goes to the hayfield, her help, which was at least the pretext for her attendance there, now being superfluous, sweep, elevator and swath-turner doing the work once performed by volunteers.

Again, an age-old ritual such as "Crying the Neck"

became incompatible with the mechanised harvest-field. One doubts whether there lives in Devonshire today a man who ever saw the "Neck" cried, this being, of course, the much-described ceremony of twisting the last few ears of corn into a shape supposed to represent the "Corn Spirit," whose capture was thus effected amid the acclamations of the entire company. There can be little doubt that the custom had lost its significance long before it lapsed. It is hard to believe that the stolid farm-labourer of even a hundred years ago held many ideas concerning the Corn Spirit, or that the formula "We hae 'un," triumphantly "cried" upon the occasion, conveyed any more to those who used it than "Nuts and May" or "Tom Tiddler" to children. The oldest harvester of my day was far more interested in the last rabbit, and the rite was probably observed with no idea of its import. An obvious survival of the practice, as described to me by Mr Wickett, who frequently took part in it, persisted at Bradworthy until well into the present century. There, the last sheaf of the season was hoisted, as soon as bound, upon a high pole in the middle of the field, where it remained until the final waggon had been loaded. Its removal intimated the end of harvest, and the custom being general, there was keen competition among local farmers for the distinction of being the first to lower this symbolic standard. In this case no outcry acclaimed the capture of the Corn Spirit. The shouting was reserved until the substance rather than the shadow was safely in hand. As the last load trundled into the rick-yard, a cheer unlike anything else heard on the land arose, proclaiming "Harvest home." It sounded for miles across the Plain of Devon on a still August evening, to the discomfiture of other gangs, which had hoped for priority in making the announcement.

Parochial functions, not necessarily connected with the land, continue in many localities. As already mentioned, at Kingsteignton, Holne and Buckfastleigh, annual ram-roastings still take place, the proceedings, happily shorn of their former horrors, being kept alive, like the Helston Furry, as quaint old institutions. Many villages still observe a patronal "Revel," celebrated by athletic sports and usually horse-racing, which until the outbreak of the last war constituted the great parochial event of the year. There, too, within my own time featured the village step-dancer, the ring of whose hob-nailed boots on the waggon floor will seldom be heard again, for his descendant is lighter shod and prefers dancing of a different type.

So with old Devon generally, its pixies, its witches, its Corn Spirits and the many picturesque if mythical figures which passed across the stage, made their bow and evade recall. The Devon of the present is full of charm, but one cannot put back the clock, and even as the countryman of today would look foolish in a smock or the "maiden," as she is still called, something of a back number if attired in a flannel petticoat and sun-bonnet, so change must be accepted—even in Devonshire.

CHAPTER XXIII

VERNACULAR

MANY country-people are bilingual. One has known employees who spoke embarrassingly correct English when addressing the master or mistress, yet relapsed automatically into equally perfect vernacular if talking to their own friends or relatives. Indeed, the ingenuity with which a remark made in ordinary English can be adapted to local idiom is incredible and sometimes disconcerting. An intimation conveyed through the medium of a Devon-bred domestic that one does not encourage professional mendicants at the door would probably be given some such rendering as: "Maister says he don't have no dealings wi' the likes o' thee"; and one is sometimes entertained or annoyed, as the case may be, by the crude expressions for which one is given credit. When premature activities upon the part of my wife after an illness caused a relapse, the little Devonshire housemaid, Winifred, repeated my comment on the subject thus: "Maister, he says to I, ' 'er didn't ought to ha' went out,' " which rendering I hoped would be regarded as a translation rather than a verbatim report.

Pure Devonshire vernacular, said to be derived from the old Wessex speech of King Alfred's court, remains a language rather than a brogue, its peculiarity lying in distinctive words, curious adaption or turn of phrase. Apart from a certain softening of vowels and the letter f, there is no accent, or at least nothing that can be compared with the Somersetshire burr, the Cockney or Midland twang or the unmistakably broad vowels of the North. A Scot or Londoner who took up residence in the West would talk as such to the end. A Devonian who went north or east would soon lose all distinctive speech, since it was never so pronounced. A local girl—incidentally, the weather-wise housemaid described in the last chapter—married a Yorkshire miner a few years ago, and went to live at Wombwell. She returned a Yorkshire woman, scarcely intelligible to her relatives.

True Devon is of all dialects the least comprehensible to a stranger. Personally, I have never experienced any difficulty in understanding a North-countryman, whereas my wife, Yorkshire-born, still finds it impossible to follow many old Devonians. The genuine thing when first I heard it, in the Torridge valley as a child, was Greek to me, the rapidity, which is one of its main features, being the stumbling-block rather than the actual words. But most puzzling of all, perhaps, is the use, or rather misuse, of many ordinary words to which an entirely local interpretation is attached. When a Devonian announces that his neighbour's behaviour "made him wicked," he does not mean that it caused him to transgress against any accepted standard, but merely that it aroused his anger. If this amounted to much the same thing in the opinion of people who deprecate strong language, the similarity was accidental. A Devonshire man is never surprised, he is "frightened"; while his cattle are not teased by flies but "terrified." A true representative of the old generation speaks of "touching flesh" rather than of shaking hands, and any rubbish is referred to as "old trade." An insane person is "mazed," while anyone bedridden is a "bed-lier." "Comical" stands for touchy; "ignorant," mannerless; "old," crafty; "false," shy; "brave," impressive; and the list of adaptations might be prolonged almost indefinitely. "Don't he holler bravely" was the somewhat doubtful compliment paid to my late uncle's preaching upon his first appearance in the pulpit of his North Devon parish, where he subsequently worked for fifty years as parson, patron, lord of the manor, farming his own glebe as well as acting in the capacity of medical and legal adviser to his rural flock.

Many words still retain their pure old English meaning. The adjective "proper," which is perhaps more widely used than any other Devonshire expression, is employed in its Shakespearian sense. "As proper men as ever trod upon neat's leather" (*Julius Cæsar*) survives today in the Devonian's "a proper gentleman," "a proper job." Weather is described as "proper 'ot" or "proper cold," whilst a remark such as a "nice" or possibly "wet morning" is corroborated by the terse rejoinder "Proper!" The word, perhaps, may best be translated as "perfect of its kind." The Devonian in far more instances than might be supposed sets great store upon what he considers correct procedure in any given circumstance, and great offence may be caused by one who unwittingly fails to act "in the proper manner"—an exceedingly comprehensive expression.

In addition to the unusual application of ordinary words, there are, of course, names peculiar to the Cornish peninsula, if not to Devon exclusively. Few people who have not lived in the West-country would know the article classified as a "maund," although quite familiar with a potato basket. Most visitors at a farmhouse would rush to the window if told that the old "stag" was in the garden—only to see an ordinary barn-door rooster. A "chap" in Devonshire is not any mere male, but a young unmarried man. If still in his teens he is a "boy-chap"; if past middle life and still unwed, an "old-boy." "Widow," like "witch," is a descriptive term applied to either sex, but if specification is necessary, "widow-man" or "widow-woman," as the case may be, is used to avoid mistake.

Since natural history has been taught in the schools, a great many of the old names for animals and plants have fallen into disuse. A native septuagenarian, a keen naturalist, who has lately returned to the village after working as a gardener in Hampshire, commented upon the change to me in a recent "tell"—to use another colloquialism. "Years agone," he said, "we never talked of a wren. It was always a 'cutty,' same as a blue-tit was an 'acymal' and a yellow-hammer a 'gladdie.' " His brother, incidentally, was my old moorman friend John Bennett, from whom I learned many of the old names given in *Dartmoor in all its Moods*, such as "golden carenna" for the goldcrest and "firetail" for the red-start. In my own time "cutty" was more prevalent in East Devon, where a mole was unknown except as a "want" or a weasel as a "vairie." There, however, a stoat was always a stoat, whereas west of the Exe it is nothing but a "stottie." In the east a viper is invariably an adder, but is unknown by that name in the west. A badger has long ceased to be a "grey" or "graye," as recorded in old parish registers, but the hedgehog remains a "fuzzypig" to the older people;

while the wasp is still an "apple-drain" and it will be long before wood-lice can be anything but "sow-pigs." Quite recently the schoolmaster occupier of a neighbouring garden complained of the abundant "hemmets," with such emphasis on the *h* that for the moment I failed to follow him. "Emmet" is one of the old words that dies hard. A lizard is an "ebbit"; a minnow, a "biddlehead"; the dragonfly, a "horse-stinger." The expressive "dumbadore" for cockchafer is self-explanatory, if not onomatopœous. Many of the smaller wild creatures are not recognised in the vernacular, because unidentified. The harvest-mouse, for example, was unknown until classified by Gilbert White, and to the ordinary countryman any rodent smaller than a rat is just a mouse, with the exception of the dormouse, commonly called a "seven-sleeper," while any creepy-crawly thing is a "bittle." When shooting, I once heard a green woodpecker which clattered out of a thicket instead of the expected pheasant comtemptuously dismissed by a beater as "an old bird else," and other species quite as common are no less vaguely defined.

The same vagueness applies also to floral nomenclature, in which considerable confusion is common. Laburnum is often called "weeping willow" by country children, to whom, also, foxgloves are "poppies"—possibly by reason of the favourite pastime of blowing out the bells and then "popping" them, as one would a paper bag. I have also heard, though less frequently, the appropriate name of "proud ladies" for these same plants. The popping of seed-pods clearly explains the name "snap-jacks" for the greater stitchwort, while its alternative, and equally common Devonshire designation, "whitsuns," has already been explained in Chapter XX. Only a few years before the war, upon a summer evening, I was accosted in a quiet lane by a young courting couple and asked to settle an argument as to whether the stitchwort in the girl's hand was "Star of Bethlehem," as she maintained, or "whitsuns," as her more unsophisticated companion seemed to think. Star of Bethlehem, bachelor's-button and red-robin are names bestowed indiscriminately upon a variety of plants, the consequent confusion being great. "Chimney-sweeps," for herb-robert, again refers to seed-pods, showing accurate observation of wild plants, and the use of the ancient Anglo-Saxon word in its form "aggles" or "eagles," for haws, has been mentioned elsewhere.

Garden irises are "blue daggers" and white lilac "Prince of Wales's feathers," while peony remains the old-fashioned piony of Culpepper. But with "higher education" these names are rapidly disappearing, and while writing this I am constantly being asked by children, aged from twelve to fourteen, to verify wild flowers which they have been instructed to collect for a school competition. Undoubtedly it speaks well for the modern science teacher that no child from this particular senior school, to which our elder village children are daily conveyed, has referred to *Geranium robertianum* as chimney-sweeps or red-robin, but called it, most punctiliously, herb-robert. A few more years, and doubtless the smallest child will know it only by its Latin name, and much colour will have faded from everyday village speech.

Native talk is by no means lacking in poetic phraseology, although this, of course, has been exaggerated by novelists, and renderings on the stage or over the air acquire an inevitable artificial ring. The genuine countryman is never flowery, but creates his atmosphere merely with a picturesque idiom or expression. The true touch is too often lost by elaboration. The rustic does not describe the twilight as "when the dimpsy darkened down." He would say: "It was getting a bit dimpsy like," dimpsy actually being an adjective and not a noun. He refers to the early mist as "the pride of the morning," while dawn is "daylight"; as distinct from the commonplace daylight as "the reds" from an ordinary sunrise. "Dawny," by the way, means green, and is usually applied to insufficiently dried hay, but perhaps one of the most attractive touches when heard in the rough tongue is the allusion to birds' nests as "nesties," this being a general expression in old Devon.

A writer upon West-country life was lately criticised for making characters refer to one another as Baker X, Butcher Z, or any other title that indicated calling. In fact, he was quite correct. In many villages every man is still so distinguished, his profession being as inseparable from his name as that of a doctor or member of the forces. Indeed, like a medical man or army officer, he is often addressed by this title alone, as "Keeper," "Shepherd," or "Landlord." In our own parish, for instance, we have, addressed and spoken of as such, Parson B., Tailor H., Butcher D., Shoemaker W. and Baker E., while Farmer B. and Farmer W. are two well-known personalities, although officially designated Maister to W. and Maister to A. One resident who combined his occupations was wont to remark that Farmer B. would not get far without Draper B.—his alternative self.

When a man has no profession or rank, if one of the class erroneously described as "leisured," he is usually awarded the appellation of "Squire." The secretary of an East Devon village cricket club with which I often played, once entered a subscriber named Rodd as Mr Squirod, the prefix "squire" being inseparable in his mind from the plain surname. When a man is known simply as "Mister," no further interest need be taken in him. The designation proclaims him one of the stranded fish who have no place in country life.

The white farmhouse, with its thatch and cob, so general throughout Devonshire

Chapter XXIV

NOMENCLATURE

Surnames have always constituted a blind spot in village mentality. Even long familiarity does not remove inability to get them right, and this inhibition accounts for much variation in the rendering of names originally identical. Most common of dialectic change retained is the insertion of the vowels *a*, *i* or *e* into names which correctly lack them. This is characteristic of the soft slurring or lengthening of words in the Devon vernacular, heard in such common mispronunciation as Dartymoor and Chagyford, although these have not attained permanent adoption. In such typical names as Widecombe, Sharpitor, Maddaford, Westaway, Reddaway, Wonnacott, Westacott, Ellacott and Endacott, an inserted vowel has become permanently incorporated between the adjective and noun forming the original descriptive name—the wide coombe, sharp tor, the red way, the end cot and so on.

Cot or *cote* is among the commonest suffixes, others being *beare* and its variants, *hayes* and its variants, *worthy*, *tun*, *coombe*, *bury* and *leigh* or *ley*. One comes across groupings of similar names in different parts of the county; certain basic formations being prevalent in one district while totally absent in another. The *Nymet* group in the centre of the county has been mentioned in Chapter VI, also the frequency of the *Hayes* class in the Axminster area and East Devon generally. *Cotes*, increasing from Mid-Devon northwards, are almost unknown in the South Hams.

Like most derivations, these names are to a large extent word-pictures of the past, when the earliest Damnonian colonisers, Saxon, Celt or even Neolithic man—who has, however, left no traceable linguistic legacy behind him—laboured with rough tools to carve out from the thickly forested countryside a small plot as dwelling-place. Here, then, was established the first humble individual cot, possibly that of hunter or swineherd, an oasis in the surrounding

The Erme Valley with Sharp Tor in the background

woodland. These ever-predominant woods have left an indelible imprint upon Devon place-names in the numerous *beares*, *beres* and *beers*, all derived from the A.S. *bearu*, a grove or wood. In the neighbourhood of two small Mid-Devon villages, Hittisleigh and Spreyton, situated among the remains of what was once extensive forest, it is interesting to find a large group of *beares* typifying the original nature of the countryside. The word Spreyton itself emphasises this, its meaning being simply "clearing or settlement amongst the brushwood," from the A.S. *spray*, "twiggy," a root seen again in Sprydon Forest in East Devon. Around Spreyton, roughly within an area of half a dozen square miles, are Beer Ford, a crossing of the Troney in a thickly wooded coombe, and seven farms: North Beer, South Beer, Bowbeer, Big Beer, Trundlebeare, Colybeare and Coursebeare. In Spreyton village there are families named Beer and Connibeare. Two other characteristic farm names upon the fringes of the same parish are Nethercott—always pronounced and frequently spelled Narracott—and Yendicott, a survival of the original "yonder cots," actually identical with the more usual Endicott. The cots and cotes have deviated very little from their early conception as the smallest type of holding, for they are still confined almost exclusively to farms—enlargements of the first little plots—and to surnames denoting their first inhabitants.

After the isolated cot came the rather more ambitious effort, equivalent to the present-day small-holding, the Saxon *worthig*, surviving in the numerous names ending in *worthy*. These are particularly prevalent in North Devon—Holsworthy, Bradworthy, Alfardisworthy and Woolfardisworthy, the last two being characteristically slurred again in the vernacular to "Ollsery" and "Woolsery." The *worthy* might be considered a one-family farm in contradistinction to the community settlement or *tun*, which in varying forms of *ton* and *don* has become also our present-day "town." In the eighth century husbandry was being increasingly developed by the Saxon, whose enlarged clearings, supporting several families, became a feature of the countryside, and about 600 of these early *tuns* or settlements survive in Devon place-names—Seaton, the sea-settlement; Crediton, settlement on the Credy; Cheriton, church farm; Glendon, the valley farm. The preceding of *ton* by *ing*, as in Alphington and Kilmington, denotes a rather more important homestead, approaching the manor type.

The *manneriums*, or manors proper, however, were of later date, but developments of a more modern kind were emerging from these first simple agricultural settlements. There are about twenty Bucklands in Devon whose names, for the most part, are usually accorded the obvious interpretation of the "lands of the buck or deer." Certainly the woods of Devonshire abounded with deer in those days, and in the case of Buckfast, for example, whose old name was *Buc-faesten*, the deer's fastness, and whose monastic foundation is too old for recorded date, this may be considered the correct derivation. It seems more probable, however, that the Bucklands in general were the *boclands*, or lands "booked" by charter and granted under the Domesday Survey of 1086 to certain people—knights, barons, or sometimes ecclesiastical bodies —to be held under the king. These *boclands* were smaller estates than the actual demesnes of a manor, comparable, perhaps, to the "squire's acres," and upon them there soon arose the *sele*, or hall, residence of the land-owner, record of which is preserved in such names as Zeal Monachorum, house of the monks, and South Zeal.

One degree higher was the *wic*, a nobleman's house or manor, and in its numerous variations of *week*, *wyke*, *wick* and *wyche* it is encountered in most parts of the county. In this district alone we have North Wyke, West Week, Wickenden, East Week and Week, all farms, originally spelled *Wyke* or *Wyck*, the first three containing distinctive features in the way of old panelling, fireplaces and armorial bearings, which proclaim them as having been dwellings of importance in the past.

Attached to the *sele* or *wic* was the *barton*, an enclosed courtyard in which were housed ricks and general stores, for every lord farmed his own land with the help of his villeins living in the vills and cots. Barton has survived as the name of homesteads all over Devon, and there are few parishes in which there is not at least one farm called The Barton or some combination, such as Walter Raleigh's home, Hayes

Barton, in East Budleigh parish. In some districts today the farmyard is still spoken of simply as "the court" or "the barton," the rickyard being the "mow-barton," particularly in eastern parts of the county, thus taking us directly back through the centuries to Saxon times.

The preponderance of Saxon names, of which all the foregoing are examples, is very great, indicating an occupation so complete that, with a few exceptions, even the names used by the dispossessed Britons lapsed into oblivion. It must also be remembered that it was to the Saxon husbandman that agriculture owed its inception, and it was but natural, therefore, that his creations, the cot, worthig, ton, sele and wick, should bear his designation. Thus a large part of the explanation of nomenclature is simply a story of settlement wrested from the wild, improved, enlarged and built upon, while other enclosure names have been similarly developed—the nymets, hayes, hams, stocks, stowes and leighs. *Stowes* are usually connected with saints, Jacobstowe, Petrockstowe, Bridestowe, the places of Jacob (St James), St Petrock and St Bride (Bridget). *Leigh*, from the A.S. "a clearing," is a very common base from which comes the old-fashioned "lea," a meadow, still used as an agricultural term today in "ley fields." Buckfastleigh is the old ley or pasturage of the abbey, and Gidleigh, the clearing of Gytha or Gydda, probably King Harold's mother, a wealthy lady who was one of the largest Devon land-owners in the eleventh century, holding eight estates in the county.

As might be expected, the few Celtic names that remain are those of natural landscape features, hills, valleys and rivers, the highest percentage being found among the latter. All the larger rivers retain their British names, most being derived from the same Celtic root, *ta*, "water," which appears in Tamar, Tavy, Taw and, as R. N. Worth considers, also under a less recognisable form in Torridge and Teign. Dart has the same Celtic origin as Derwent, from *dwr*, again denoting water, and means "oak-tree river." Axe and Exe too have watery derivations, as also have the many "Yeo" streams, although their root may be found in the A.S. *ea*. Okement is of doubtful origin, but is generally considered to lack any connection with the obvious "oak." Clyst is usually interpreted as "clear."

The seven Walla Brooks and also, perhaps, the Walkham, upon Dartmoor, have a choice of two derivations, some authorities finding the root in the Celtic *huella*, "workings," in reference to the tin streamings; others that it lies in the A.S. *wielle*, "spring," according to whether they hold the opinion that a few Celtic names survive on Dartmoor, or consider them entirely lost.

Several Dartmoor streams bear the somewhat misleading suffix "lake," especially in the Erme basin, whose tributaries are Drylake, Redlake, Hook Lake and Left Lake. The significance of "lake" here is "rivulet," from the Celtic *lakka* or A.S. *lacu*, a root seen again in our word "leak" and probably also "leat."

Without entering into discussion whether Celtic nomenclature does or does not survive upon Dartmoor in view of the supposition that British and Saxon occupation could never have coincided, it may be stated that "tor" is probably a Celto-Saxon formation from the Welsh *twr* and the A.S. *torr*. Coombe, the most common suffix after tun, similarly derives from the Welsh *cwm* and the A.S. *cumb*. Cleave, however, is the A.S. *cleof*, "cliff," which is its correct meaning, although it has come to be applied to the valley itself rather than to its containing cliff walls. Distinct from "tor" as a projecting rock pile is the Celtic *dun*, "hill," which besides having given its name to Dunmonia (Damnonia) is seen in Cosdon, Dunnabridge and Dunsford, among many others, and, as already mentioned, the word Devon itself is of Celtic origin, Deuffnaint (Dyfnaint), the land of deep valleys.

Certain place-names remain as a Roman legacy, notably, apart from the camp and street types such as Exeter (Exceastre) and True Street, those indicating roadways. Such are Oldway, Straightway, Orway, Bromridge, Harepath and Sticklepath, the first part of the latter word deriving from the A.S. *stiegel*, "steep." Invasions by Danes and other Norsemen, though frequent throughout the early centuries, were more in the nature of raids, and one would scarcely expect, therefore, to find their "mark" left upon Devonshire place-names to the same extent as in the northern counties. Lundy, Isle of Puffins, whose chequered history is given in Chapter III, is pure Norse. Fingle, geographically a typical Devonshire coombe, is nevertheless distinguished by a name equivalent to a northern *ghyll*; and similarly the little Becky stream, near Manaton, with its popular "falls," masquerades as a North-country *beck*.

At the time of Domesday there were 900 manors in Devon, these being naturally subjected to a considerable amount of confiscation and general reshuffling. Some estates were enlarged and promoted to manorial dignity; others enclosed from waste land later. Thus most of the old manors bear names of post-Conquest date, usually compounded with that of the feudal lord. Royal manors are recognised by the prefix, as in Kingskerswell held by William I, and land-owning ecclesiastical bodies recorded by such names as Bishopsteignton, Newton Abbot and Abbotskerswell. Robert Herrick's parish, Dean Prior, has no double ecclesiastical significance, but merely denotes the dene, or valley, belonging to Plympton Priory in the eleventh century. A further example of medieval manorial names is the three Sampfords, Courtenay, Peverell and Spiney, the first word in each case meaning simply a sandy ford—crossings of the rivers Taw, Lynor and Walkham, respectively—and the second the feudal owners. The same formation is seen again in the old Raleigh estate, Withycombe Raleigh, that of the Pomeroys in Berry Pomeroy and many similar instances.

The name Ash in varying forms and combinations occurs throughout Devonshire, the greater proportion deriving from the personal name spelled variously Ayshe, Aysche, Eysche and Esse, very prevalent among post-Conquest manor holders.

Even in this incomplete sketch of Devon nomenclature, where only the simpler name types could be mentioned, there are controversial points, but to pursue the subject further is beyond the scope of this work. Devon surnames call for little comment, the larger proportion being derived from place-names. There is also, of course, the occupational group in which, as might be supposed, we find reference to the bearer's connection with some old industry, particularly the wool trade, though, curiously enough, none, as far as I have been able to discover, suggestive of tinning or mining generally. Tucker, Weaver, Webber and Woolcombe (wool-comber) all occur in early documents, and if Crocker, Copplestone and Carew were all at home when the Conqueror called, according to early records, a certain Wulf-weard Webba was equally in residence less than fifty years later, and was shortly followed by Richard le Touker—possibly an ancestor of our old friend Aubrey Tucker.

BIBLIOGRAPHY

Devon Association Transactions; J. J. Alexander: LXIV, p. 539; LXV, p. 363; LXVI, p. 270; LXVII, p. 399; R. N. Worth: x. p. 276.
The Place Names of Devon. Gover, Mawer and Stenton.
Victoria History of Devon.

Chapter XXV

HUNTING THE STAG

Devonshire hunting, like everything else in the county, possesses a character peculiarly its own. That the historic chase of the red deer stands in a class apart need scarcely be mentioned. There is nothing else quite like it. That modern conditions have to a great extent altered everything also goes without saying. None the less, the atmosphere of "Red Deer Land" remains unique, and there are few people who can remain insensible to its special charm. It is, of course, in the mere presence of the red deer rather than in the actual pursuit of them that the interest lies for the naturalist-sportsman. That stags mean stag-hunting in some shape or form is a logical sequence, and in Devonshire, or indeed anywhere in the British Isles, wild red deer exist for no other purpose than sport. Whether this takes the form of stalking or hunting is immaterial from a humanitarian point of view. Mere interest would never suffice to preserve them upon anything approaching the present scale, sport alone serving the dual purpose of preservation and control. Should political pressure or a wave of popular emotionalism ever lead to the extermination of our largest and most decorative animal, the loss to the county would be so great that its reintroduction would probably follow, but at the cost of replacing the natural with the artificial.

Behind the wild red deer of Exmoor and Devon is a story so old that it has no beginning. We know that the first recorded pack of hounds was inaugurated three centuries ago, and kept by the Forest Ranger at Simonsbath, but theirs were not the first hunting cries that woke the echoes of the coombes. As early as the reign of Edward II, the Sheriff of Devon was instructed to aid the efforts of two yeomen who were sent with "twenty-four running dogs" and nine greyhounds to procure a supply of venison for the king's table. Even prior to the Norman Conquest, Exmoor was a royal hunting-ground, Saxon Edgar setting so high a value upon the deer that he accepted an annual tribute of 300 wolves' heads from the county of Devon in lieu of other taxation, the wolf being considered highly destructive to the herds. Again, in the reign of Edward III a number of landed gentry were arraigned at Bridgwater for allowing their cattle to trespass upon the special pasturage of the deer, whose importance had not diminished during the intervening centuries. Indeed, the wild red stag of the West has been a national asset and his chase an institution since the earliest records of our existing fauna can be traced. "Sylvan war" has formed the background of his long history, and he has successfully contended with every type of hunter, from Nature's hound, the gaunt timber wolf; the "running dog" and shaggy greyhound of the Norman foresters; the staghound pack of the Elizabethan and subsequent period; down to its representative of our own time, the glossy, tuneful-tongued animal which in reality is a foxhound. After stag-hunting had ceased to be the special province of royalty or Crown officials, it was carried on during a considerable part of the eighteenth century by the Acland family and later by members of many other old West-country houses. The list of Masters is too long for enumeration, but can be found in any hunting directory. A comprehensive history of this hunt will also be found in *The Devon and Somerset Staghounds*, by E. T. Macdermot.

In the actual technique of the sport, little has changed since Whyte Melville wrote his *Katerfelto*, or when, at a later date, Fortescue produced his incomparable *Life of a Red Deer*. The country still produces hounds as good as those which Abner Gale and Garnet followed, with intent so different, upon their splendid horses, black and grey. Devon hills still breed stags as gallant as Fortescue's antlered hero, whose spirit passed out into the dark mountain pool, responding to the invitation of the stream which "called him so kindly that he could not but obey."

"Again the scented morning and the fair September sky
  And the sound of the horn o'er the purple moor as the hunt
    comes sweeping by,"

wrote one who in a single couplet drew a vivid word picture of stag-hunting, and the hills and coombes of the country are never more shrouded in mist-wraiths than haunted by the picturesque scenes and figures which the long pageant of the centuries has produced.

Stag-hunting, with its history, tradition, colour and pathos, remains an institution, and if the great crowds which assemble to view the proceedings during the late summer months may be regarded as any criterion, its popularity has in no way declined. That the field during this period should have developed into something of a car and cavalry parade was inevitable, and applies equally to fashionable fox-hunting. Such conditions, however, concern Somerset more than Devonshire, the historic Cloutsham meet and others scarcely less famous taking place on the eastern side of the county boundary. Indeed, a considerable part of Red Deer Land actually lies in Somerset, and were the deer confined to Exmoor and its immediate surroundings, as many people seem to imagine, Devonshire's share would be very limited. In reality they have penetrated far more deeply into the western than the eastern county, having followed the course of the Exe to Tiverton and thence westwards to the Taw, whose numerous tributary valleys they have explored to the fringes of Dartmoor, which many have crossed from time to time to reach the Tamar valley and Buckland woods, a certain number lying for short periods upon the Moor itself. They have never re-established themselves for any length of time either on or beyond the Moor excepting those which latterly have reached the afforested areas west of Okehampton.

The main stronghold of these outlying deer, if so they may be termed, has been for many years the extensively wooded country between Crediton and Chumleigh, an area which, elastically considered, covers a considerable part of central Devon. This country has been hunted since 1896 by the Tiverton Staghounds, which, although quite independent of the Devon and Somerset, act as an auxiliary to the premier pack, supplementing its efforts when requested. Originally founded by the Amery family, these hounds were handled most efficiently for many years by the Yandle brothers, who were responsible for most of the field work, and combining natural woodcraft with lifelong experience, preserved a high standard of sport. It is not an easy country to hunt, and owing to their extending range and unequal distribution, the habits of the deer, when hunted, have altered considerably within recent years. At one period a stag, roused in the Chumleigh or Chawleigh district, almost as a matter of course pointed for the Exe valley, by far the greater number of runs ending in that historic stream, usually in the Chain Bridge locality between Bampton and Tiverton. Latterly, however, big rings rather than long points became the rule. Deer showed an indisposition to quit the locality in which they were roused, and proved harder to kill in consequence, change being more frequent.

Several years ago a certain number of deer gravitated to the Cornish border, but, as already stated, their western movement was not maintained, although they are now tolerably plentiful in the broken country stretching in a north-easterly direction from Okehampton. An increasing tendency to take this line has developed on the part of deer presumably reared on the farther side of the Taw, this river forming a rough boundary beyond which they are seldom sought. I have known runs from the Chumleigh or Lapford district as far west as the Torridge and Okement, terminating in each case with the escape of the deer at dusk and the benighting of hounds and hunters almost as complete as that which overtook Jorrocks and James Pigg at the end of their first great "bye." The ability of both deer and foxes to extend their efforts with the closing day is an interesting point to which very little attention has been paid. Account for it as one may, they undoubtedly seem to acquire new powers as darkness falls, and out of numerous runs which have extended into the night, I can think of few within personal experience which have ended otherwise than successfully for the hunted.

Big fields have never been a feature of the Tiverton hunt upon the western side of their country. Their atmosphere is eminently workmanlike, and their following consists mainly of keen hunters. Cars have outnumbered horses within recent years, but the occupants of these consist almost entirely of hunting people, a large percentage of whom are farmers and old sportsmen of a type rarely seen outside Devonshire nowadays.

That war-time hunting was a mere travesty of the sport as normally conducted need scarcely be mentioned, nor could any purpose be served by describing purely temporary conditions. The Devon and Somerset Hunt has survived many vicissitudes, and the next few years will probably decide the future of both deer-hunting and the deer itself. One can only emphasise that unless preserved for sport it is too eminently destructive an animal to be tolerated in any agricultural county for sentiment's sake, and the North Devon herds would soon share the fate of those which formerly ranged Dartmoor and were exterminated about 1780 at the request of farmers, mainly in the Tavistock area.

The object of this work is rather to present actual conditions than to express personal opinions. Concerning the long and bitter controversy upon the whole subject of stag-hunting, my own views have been fully stated in a previous book, *Field Philosophy*, while E. W. Hendy in his *Wild Exmoor throughout the Year* has more to say upon the subject. Wonder is sometimes expressed that any animal-lover can countenance field sports, but for my own part I can only say that regard for wild creatures has always induced me to defend hunting both in print and over the air, long practical experience in sport and its alternatives having removed all doubt upon the subject. Since this, however, might be considered a distinct statement of opinion, and therefore a quick departure from a policy just avowed, I should remove this impression in the recent words of one downright old countryman: "I don't *think* so. I'm sure of it."

BIBLIOGRAPHY

The Devon and Somerset Staghounds. E. T. Macdermot.
Devon Association Transactions, XXXIX, p. 267, J. F. Chanter.

CHAPTER XXVI

HUNTING THE FOX

WHILE Devonshire's stag-hunting is unique, her fox-hunting in many respects also differs from that of most counties. This is mainly due to the rough character of the country, which entirely eliminates the steeplechase element and, upon the high moors, renders the proceeding more closely akin to the Lakeland methods, although there is no longer any fox-hound pack which is not followed upon horses.

The general character of the hunting varies considerably in different parts of the county and includes almost every condition except those which people accustomed to the Shires would consider ideal. Once when the Taunton Vale Foxhounds had a long run into East Devon, the huntsman asked me whether much of the country resembled that which we were negotiating. Upon being told that it was characteristic, he emphatically declared: "Then I'm glad I haven't got to ride over it." When a former Master of the Cattistock in a similar case, attempted to follow his hounds field by field, he fell at three successive fences and abandoned the effort. Apart from a few stone walls around the moors, double-banks predominate; there is also a great deal of wire, while much of the bogland is impassable. Rough country, however, always means a wild, tough breed of foxes, and hunting of the type that can only be described as "natural." Except in East Devon, where earths are so numerous and deep that no fox could be kept above ground many minutes without a certain amount of "stopping," very little of this work is done. The size of the coverts for the most part prevents any mobbing of cubs, and hounds find, hunt and—if they can—kill their foxes with very little outside help.

Behind Devonshire fox-hunting there is neither the long history nor tradition that some counties can claim. The country as a whole was too wild and undeveloped until a comparatively late period. It was yet another case of extremes; and while some districts remained eminently primitive, others were so highly cultivated that foxes had been practically exterminated long before orthodox hunting became fashionable, and throughout Devonshire, even to the present day, there remain extensive areas which have never been more than sporadically hunted.

The conditions which prevailed in old Devon might well have suggested the opening chapters of *Handley Cross*, although the picture was probably true of many counties half a century or so earlier. However that may have been, the old cob-riding sportsman, so realistically depicted by Surtees, had many western representatives within my own memory, while Michael Hardy with his home-made pack could have been found without difficulty, needing only the accident of a popular song to acquire the romantic fame of John Peel. The most outstanding figure of this type was undoubtedly the famous Rev. "Jack" Russell, Vicar of Iddisleigh, who starting his pack in 1827, became a pioneer of fox-hunting in Mid-Devon. At one period he hunted practically the entire district from Torrington to Bodmin, and his personality still invests the country over which he exercised so wide an influence for half a century.

There were other less famous but equally picturesque figures, each representing the conditions of his time. Attached to the premises of many old Devonshire country houses one may still see the dilapidated relics of primitive kennels, where the Russell or Hardy of the district kept the sporting little harrier pack with which he hunted anything that the locality could provide. There was Pinsent Matthew of Rydon, also Jack Mitchell of Hayne, who, hunting in country never drawn by foxhounds with a private harrier pack, the property of his father—another sporting parson of the old school—achieved one of the greatest runs of the nineteenth century. Finding a travelling fox late in the day at Spillcombe, under which Honiton Tunnel now passes, his hounds, unaccustomed to a quarry of this straight-necked description, were quickly led into country of which neither they nor their huntsman had any knowledge. Past Up-Ottery, over the wilds of Otterhead, Brown Down and Castle

Neroche, they steered a hard course into Somerset, and well after dark, then far up the Taunton Vale, Mitchell, who for long had been following only distant sounds and stray scraps of information, stood alone, benighted and completely lost, with nothing but empty fields and woodland around him. As a forlorn hope, he sounded his horn, the long notes of which echoing over the deserted country were for a while the only response, until through the silence came the most welcome reply possible—the light, unmistakable patter of hounds' feet splashing up a wet lane towards him. One by one the staunch little harriers materialised out of the night, and, not knowing what else to do, exhausted man, horse and pack headed for home, which they reached the following morning. The story had a sad sequel, for the horse, an old favourite, did not survive the experience. News travelled slowly in those days, and some time elapsed before the story got round that a mysterious pack of hounds had killed a fox one night in a farmyard near Hatch Beauchamp, disappearing again into the darkness before full investigation could be made. No record of this run, the point of which could not have been much less than twenty miles, was ever published to my knowledge. I have only mentioned it as a back-glimpse of old Devonshire hunting, depending largely upon memory which cannot now be substantiated, for Mr Mitchell died some thirty-five years ago, and he must have been a septuagenarian when he told the story to me, then an interested boy.

The actual beginning of any particular hunt is almost impossible to determine, there being few parts of the country in which a nucleus of hounds has not been privately kept and could not be claimed as forerunners of others since established. For the present purpose, which is to enumerate countries as recognised today, it will only be necessary, therefore, to state the actual conditions as they have developed within the past century or so or since the date when existing boundaries were determined.

Apart from the Devon and Somerset Staghounds, the Tetcott appears to be the oldest Devonshire hunt now in existence, dating as it does from early in the eighteenth century. Since gaps occur in its record, however, it must yield first place for continuity to the Cotley, which shows an unbroken history since 1796. Although famous as a fox-hunting pack, the Cotley Hounds are actually old English "lemon-pie" harriers, which, originally established by T. Dean and hunted by a relative, T. P. Eames of Cotley, have remained under successive masterships in the Eames family until the present day. They are kennelled on the Cotley estate, just within the Devon boundary, in which county they mainly hunt. These hounds, once hunting fox and hare impartially, with an increasing tendency towards fox as time went on, acquired a high reputation under the mastership of the late E. Eames, who seldom went by any other name than "Mr Edward" among the country-people. Carrying the horn from 1886 until 1931, his fox-hunting country extended roughly from the Somerset border to the sea, embracing also a section of West Dorset, since taken over by the Seavington Hunt. Generations of careful breeding had brought the hounds to a high standard of efficiency, and prior to about 1918, when a virulent distemper epidemic almost wiped out the old strain, their prestige was unrivalled. The present Master is Major F. P. R. Eames, a great-nephew of the late Edward, and during his absence upon military service the pack, almost for the first time in its long history, was taken out by a professional, until whose acquisition at the outbreak of war nobody but an Eames had as much as whipped in to the pack within living memory.

One anecdote at the expense of the Cotley might now be told, since the grass has long been green over the episode and, alas, over most of those concerned in it. It happened during Edward Eames's time, when one good-scenting February morning the Rev. J. Milne, the famous Cattistock Master, came out by special invitation to see what sport Devon's oldest hunt could show. The meet was on Stockland Hill, near Honiton, and the first fox went quickly to ground, to bolt with equal readiness in the company of another chance occupant which proved to be a traveller from the Somerset side, and after this alien went the pack. At first he took the line which a resident would have chosen, and never doubting that he would make the almost invariable point, which was a favourite wood near Up-Ottery, straight for that covert by an

Dartmoor ponies

approved short cut galloped the field, including Master and staff. Being a stranger, however, the fox did not realise what was expected of him, and deciding to go home, doubled sharply and set his mask resolutely for his own country. One or two people only noted the sudden turn, but among these, as it happened, was the distinguished visitor, who, not knowing the customary line, had taken his own. Long before the sages of the hunt—too wise for once—had discovered their mistake, it was irretrievable. The hounds, meanwhile, had not been idle, and after a two-hour run which included a ten-mile point, eventually lost the fox on their own Master's lawn, attended throughout, cast when necessary, and finally kennelled by Mr Milne. The discomfiture of the greencoats could scarcely have been more complete or Fortune more capricious upon a "special occasion."

The south-east corner of the county is held by the Axe Vale, another pack of fox-hunting harriers always staffed by amateurs. This country, while containing the lush vale of the Axe, is in the main stiff, hilly and riddled with great earths, which also present a problem on the Cotley side. Throughout its early career the mastership of these hounds, inaugurated in 1885, was held for many years by Mr J. Scarborough, well-known sporting West-country names such as Pape, Head and Broom being also associated with the hunt. Upon the whole the Cotley and Axe Vale have much in common, and the status of these two harrier packs, together with the general conditions under which they are carried on, is, I think, unique, at least in southern England.

The period during which the sporting little Axe Vale pack came into being appears to have been one of general reshuffle of Devonshire hunting, for in 1890 the East Devon Foxhounds, whose country adjoins the Axe Vale on the western side, was established by Colonel J. A. Garrett. The neighbouring Silverton, the only Devonshire foxhound pack whose followers wore green uniform, is also the youngest hunt, dating only from 1906, when it was instituted by Mr H. F. Brunskill. Much of the pioneer work was done by a later Master, "Archie" Pape. He was the founder of the now highly popular Stoke Hill Beagles, and for several seasons also hunted a nocturnal pack of badger-hounds, whose cry

20*

Dartmoor

at dead of night often awoke the stillness of the chines and wooded coombes of South Devon.

As compared with the Silverton, the story of the adjoining South Devon Hunt might be regarded as ancient history. A continuous record of this pack can be traced from 1827. Prior to the reinstitution of the Mid-Devon, this country absorbed one of the largest areas in Devon, including all the magnificent sporting ground from the Exe valley to the East Dart, the western half of Dartmoor being hunted by the pack which still bears its name. The list of South Devon Masters is long, but in 1915 the management passed into the hands of Messrs W. and H. Whitley, the latter carrying on with one season's interlude until 1936, when the revival of the Mid-Devon led once again to the division of the country.

Dartmoor was not affected by the shortage of foxes which followed the first world war. Upon the contrary, the supply exceeded the demand, and for several years the situation was eased by Mr Raleigh Philpotts, who hunted the country north of the Moreton Hampstead–Princetown road with a private auxiliary pack, at first for a few weeks only to reduce cubs, but subsequently for the greater part of the season. The sport which he showed led to an increasing demand for the restoration of the Mid-Devon pack, which had closed down about 1916, and after an interval of twenty years this hunt was eventually revived under the mastership of Major A. C. Arden, ably seconded in the field by his wife. The hounds now occupy the old Mid-Devon kennels at Furlong. Major Arden is a natural huntsman with a keen eye for a fox, and working single-handed at times, has kept the country going under conditions of remarkable difficulty.

The cream of the Mid-Devon country lies between Throwleigh and Postbridge, where broad sweeps of heather, broken only by occasional stone walls, stream gullies and bog, provide excellent riding ground. Most difficult is the Belstone and Okehampton district, extending from the upper Taw to the West Okement valley. This is a mountainous region, including the highest ground in southern England, with vast clitters flanking the steep hillsides, only negotiable in good weather, and bounded by the formidable peat-veins over which hunting is impossible. Into this country, subject to sudden mists and rendered impassable by bog, hounds may disappear and with astonishing suddenness. It was here that the Eggesford pack was once lost for several days, and the end of many a run which terminates on the great wastes, with only, perhaps, a grimly observant raven for witness, is never known. Much of it has seldom been drawn since the days when Mr Raleigh Philpotts actually met at Cranmere Pool and followed his hounds over the peat on foot. Latterly there has been little necessity to seek foxes so far out on the wilds, where they can only be hunted with difficulty. The supply on the fringes has proved sufficient, and it is from the precincts of civilisation that valid claims for damage emanate.

A notable increase of foxes followed the initiation of the Mid-Devon Hunt, this being partly attributable, no doubt, to a natural revival which occurred with local variations throughout Devonshire generally, from the Cotley country on the far east almost to the Cornish border. Upon Dartmoor it was so pronounced that drawing frequently proved un-necessary, upon several occasions within my own observation a fresh fox being viewed away before one actually in hand could be broken up.

The Dartmoor Hunt has suffered a severe blow through the loss upon active service of Commander C. H. Davy, whose twenty years of outstanding mastership brought a well-earned reputation to the beautiful pack of hounds which he had built up. At the outbreak of war the Dartmoor was the largest pack in Devonshire, numbering fifty couples and hunting four days a week. The hunt inherits a long sporting tradition from its initiation about 1827 by Mr J. Bulteel, and in many respects the country can have altered very little since the days described by Davies, when Trelawney brought his "brilliant pack" to Over-Brent, to be followed through-out a characteristic Dartmoor run by men whose names still linger in the west.

Both in the Dartmoor and Mid-Devon countries afforesta-tion schemes have been responsible for new heavy cover upon a large scale. Upon the open Moor, however, the rocks alone provide strong holding, from which foxes cannot always be dislodged, although at times they bolt from terriers like rabbits before a ferret. Many lie in the heather, a certain number being "stub-bred," but more are found on the bogs wherever rushes grow above water level, and a different technique from that employed in woodland hunting is required when drawing for them, a good moorland pack fanning out to cover a wider area. Rocks abound in the Dartmoor country, but the deepest peat-veins lie farther to the north. Hounds occasionally run through these, however, as far as Hangingstone and Cranmere, for the hill fox is no more a respecter of boundaries than any other. Good points are common, and cover calculated to slacken pace is almost entirely absent. Scenting conditions being good, Dartmoor runs are therefore fast as a rule.

Much of Dartmoor is also hunted by harrier packs, of which the Haldon upon the south-east can claim the oldest record, dating from 1759. There are, too, the Dart Vale, Modbury and South Pool Harriers, although the latter scarcely touch the Moor itself. On the western side is Mr Spooner's hunt, once the Lamerton and later the Spurling Harriers. The pack, which also hunts foxes, became known as Mr Spooner's when bought by him in 1913, and was later taken over by Miss Sylvia Spooner, who, combining the offices of Master and huntsman, was probably the first lady to try her hounds against Dartmoor foxes. This pack, after a period of committee management, is now hunted by Mr Stanley Roose.

The country lying north-west of the Dartmoor, some of which is technically within the Lamerton boundaries, is hunted very little. It includes the wilds of Fur Tor, Tavy Head and the peaty region between the Ammicombe and Rattle Brook. The main Lamerton country stretches westwards into Cornwall, and it is not, therefore, an exclusively Devonshire hunt. Originally divided, it became one country in 1853, and in 1920 was taken over by the late Master, Captain G. Babington, who until 1939, acting as his own huntsman, worked the country upon a three-day-a-week basis, with an occasional bye, which is a considerable achievement with twenty-six couples of hounds.

North of the Lamerton lies the Tetcott, Devonshire's oldest fox-hunting country as far as records can be traced, some of it, as in the case of the Lamerton, extending over the

Cornish border. This country has undergone various changes, and as now constituted is divided between two packs, the Tetcott and South Tetcott, the final division having been effected in 1919. All recent South Tetcott history is told in the memoirs of Philip Back, whose reputation among West-country huntsmen was unsurpassed. His connection with the pack dated from 1886 and continued until his death a year or so ago. Few packs have enjoyed or earned a better prestige than the South Tetcott, or Scott Browne's, as it was more generally termed thirty years ago, when Back was in his prime and supported in the field by Ned Chapman, whose long subsequent service with the South Devon is also a matter of history. The story of the hunt has much in common with that of the Tetcott, and like its southern neighbour, the Lamerton, the sport which it shows is of the type to enjoy which man and horse must do their best, and hounds *hunt* their foxes from start to finish. There is little earth-stopping. Foxes are stout and wild, and the extensive afforestation area at Halwill has provided them with a stronghold in which the hunter is at a distinct disadvantage.

The Tetcott, as distinct from the "South," is an eminently sporting country comprising most of the upper Tamar and the rough moorland stretching to the Atlantic coast. This hunt owes much of the good sport which it has shown during the past quarter of a century to the efforts of its former Master, Dr F. A. King, whose standing among England's amateur huntsmen is high. Dr King exercised a wide personal influence in the country, and being also a medical practitioner, a humorous convention prevailed among his farmer patients that foxes must be scrupulously preserved in case undesirable ingredients got into their medicine!

With the Stevenstone, as known today, one reaches the Jack Russell country, or the North Devon, as originally founded by him in 1827. Apart from the post-war establishment of the Torrington Farmers' Hunt, the country has altered little, geographically or otherwise, since Russell's time, and the general description of the Lamerton and Tetcott Hunts apply equally to the Stevenstone.

Bounded on the south and west by the Mid-Devon, the South Tetcott and the Stevenstone, lies the Eggesford country, in many respects the stiffest in Devonshire, as it contains more than its share of deep valleys, big banks, heavy cover and extensive areas of wild, rough land over which hounds can only be followed with difficulty—if at all. Records of hunting in this country extend as far back as 1798, and in the early days of the fifth Lord Portsmouth, the real founder of the Eggesford Hunt, an enormous country was covered by the great pack, which, prior to the building of the present kennels in the same locality, was kept at Eggesford House, forming one of the finest hunting establishments ever seen in Western England. The premises included stabling for seventy horses, and six-day-a-week country at one time extended from Exmoor to Dartmoor. At the close of Lord Portsmouth's long mastership in 1890 a period of change ensued, the pack being twice placed under the management of a committee. In 1901, however, Mr G. Luxon, another of Devonshire's great amateur huntsmen, took charge for some twenty years. Mr Luxon stood high in the category of those who can best be described as "classics of the hunting-field" and his name, like that of Jack Russell, Philip Back, Dr King and Edward Eames, will for long remain inseparable from the country in which he figured. His period is still referred to by those who followed him— all veterans now—as "Old Master's time," and comparison with him in Devonshire is regarded as high tribute. After his death, he was succeeded by Major Upton, a North-country sportsman, Jack Lyne, who had acted as kennel-huntsman during the greater part of Luxon's period, now carrying the horn. Major Upton took office under difficult conditions. In 1922, the war having depleted both the pack and its finances, fresh stock was not only scarcely obtainable but priceless. He went to Rugby, ostensibly to buy at least the foundation of a pack, and returned with one couple, for which he had been obliged to pay £300, the total sum at his disposal. Persevering, he eventually restored the pack, but had to contend with the unparalleled shortage of foxes, which applied to many hunts at the time, but was particularly acute in the Eggesford country, not abundantly stocked even before the war. Bert Wills, the present huntsman, who then whipped in to Jack Lyne, tells me that his first eight cubbing mornings with Major Upton proved blank. These difficulties were overcome, however. A fine pack was built up, and after Major Upton's successor, the late Mr Martin, had been compelled to resign his successful mastership, to the general regret, Captain J. Baron Lethbridge took charge until the outbreak of the 1939 war. He showed great sport during his term of office, being a skilful huntsman with considerable experience of West-country conditions, and upon his resignation in 1940 the management of the pack once again passed to a committee, with Bert Wills now occupying the post of huntsman. After more than thirty years of service with the Eggesford, there is no more popular figure than "Bert" in the Devonshire hunting-field, and one could not pay him a better tribute than to say that throughout this long period I have never heard a word to his disparagement. His loyal support of the huntsmen under whom he successively served was on a par with his own conscientious efforts in that capacity.

The sudden increase of foxes reached its peak about 1935, and was not only helpful in restoring the Mid-Devon, but led to the temporary formation, until 1940, of a supplementary Eggesford pack, known as the North Eggesford. It hunted the northern portion of the old Eggesford country, which, incidentally, enters "Red Deer Land" upon this side, and is also hunted by the Tiverton Staghounds. Part of the Eggesford ground is worked by the Hatherleigh Harriers, a sporting little old-English pack which, when the war brought its inevitable difficulties, relieved the Eggesford by transferring its efforts from hares to foxes. These hounds were for some years hunted by Captain Budget, who resigned the mastership in 1949.

The Dulverton foxhounds, as now constituted, came into being in 1875, when a part of Lord Portsmouth's country was ceded of Mr Froude Bellew. As with the Tiverton and Exmoor, the Dulverton country reaches into Somerset, but on the Devonshire side contains all the conditions characteristic of the county. The hounds were taken over by the present Master, Lord Poltimore, in 1920.

The Tiverton is mainly a Devonshire hunt, only a very limited area extending over the Somerset border. Since the original boundaries were defined, prior to 1841, the country has not been subjected to the various adjustments which occurred so frequently elsewhere, the hunt being associated for many years with the Amery family. In the Dulverton, Tiverton and Exmoor countries one may see fox-hunting in its most picturesque setting, the Exmoor being the only Devonshire pack, if not the only one in southern England, whose country consists almost exclusively of moorland. This hunt is indeed most appropriately named, since the Exmoor foxes are its special game, and the heathery slopes and coombes of this romantic region provide the setting for its activities. The Exmoor began their history in 1869 under the original name of "Stars of the West," and since starlight usually brings hunting to an end this seems to provide an appropriate note upon which to conclude this summary of Devonshire fox-hunting.

The history of fox-hunting is, in the main, a history of periods, each of which was characterised by the prevailing conditions and produced its own type of man. Had the hard-bitten sportsman of the nineteenth century revisited the scenes of his former exploits before the war he would probably have desired nothing so much as a quick return to the happy if shadowy hunting-grounds, which, presumably, are closed to the numerous "abominations" which render the life of the modern M.F.H. a burden to him. During the emergency period, however, many would have found conditions much as they left them; packs reduced to a mere retention of the fittest; the car problem as little in evidence as though it had never been; scanty fields composed only of the keenest; and hound meal, though scarce enough, no harder to obtain than was the money with which to provide it in the tough, strenuous and often straightened old days. Once again the hunter homeward hacked his weary way upon the horse which had carried him throughout the day; nor was it then difficult to find the Master-huntsman who himself fed his hounds and bedded down his horse before attending to his own creature comforts.

The pleasure of present-day sport is certainly tempered

with toil, which goes far to prove the value set upon it. Subscription lists are reduced, but so are expenses, and I know
of no Devonshire pack that, to date, has been obliged to close
down upon financial grounds. As long as one can remember,
the worst threat to hunting has always been apprehended
from new agricultural policies, but in this county it is
primarily a sport of the agricultural classes, and upon their
attitude its future depends. That the farming community
generally is well disposed towards hunting there can be no
doubt, since in an eminently democratic county such as
Devon no pack of hounds could carry on for a month without
its support, and the satisfactory position of many hunts at
this critical time is largely due to the unsolicited and unosten-
tatious help of its land-occupiers.

CHAPTER XXVII

DEVONSHIRE'S FAUNA

BEASTS

THE sport of a county introduces the wild animals which it maintains, and the geographical distribution of the red deer, Devon's and England's largest mammal, has already been sketched. The elementary natural history of any creature is the same in the West-country as elsewhere, subject only to the effect of environment on habit. Devonshire deer, for example, differ from those of the Highlands in that they are mainly woodland creatures, living not upon mountain sides but in an agricultural country, and through long custom have become dependent upon cultivated crops for their food. The stout wire fences which protect tillage in the Exmoor district have not followed the western trend of the deer, and throughout much of the country into which they have penetrated the fat of the land is at their disposal. They are wasteful rather than voracious feeders and, like reindeer, never clear as they go. A stag might not eat more than half a dozen swedes at one meal, but he would probably nibble and uproot a cartload, and his trail through a turnip-field is devastating. He also possesses a pig's passion for potatoes, which he "lifts" more effectively than a man with a mattock, and should a herd discover a potato-plot, the owner of that crop will be saved the labour of harvesting it. Indeed, though wild enough, the red deer of Devonshire are self-supporting animals, and their existence today is proof of the high sporting value set upon them by the agricultural community.

This species is not the only wild deer of Devon. Upon the county's eastern fringe the roe is plentiful, having increased notably within the present century. Though not strictly indigenous, the West-country strain having been reintroduced into Dorset, the extension of its range was so gradual and natural that the roe may now be claimed as a native of

Devon. It is most numerous in the Axminster and Hawkchurch district, where Devon mingles with Dorset so imperceptibly that it would be hard to decide the "nationality" of
the boundary deer.

Although mischievous in young plantations owing to its
trick of barking saplings, like a rabbit, it is less destructive
than other species, and attempts at control have not been very
serious or sustained. In themselves exquisite little creatures,
roe deer should considerably beautify our fauna, but so
furtive is their disposition that even the most painstaking
observer seldom obtains a glimpse of them. Being mainly
nocturnal feeders, they waste their charms upon the un-
appreciative starlight, which is regrettable, since it lessens
the interest which would otherwise be taken in an exceedingly attractive little animal. Even the badger attracts more
notice, as his presence cannot be concealed, but while the
badger's earthworks are conspicuous although his person
may be hidden, so secluded is the life of the roe-buck that he
might live and die without a human being setting eyes on
him. Again, to lay hands upon a badger when once his fortress has been located is often, unfortunately, too easy. To
get hold of a roe-buck in the type of country which he
haunts may prove a task beyond the efforts of a well organised
battue, and the fact that few countrymen know a roe deer by
sight proves the success of his self-effacing policy. When
disturbed they often run in pairs, and gliding along the same
runway like twin sprites, disappear as quickly as possible
into the green shadowy world which is their home. Dis-
regarded as it is and scarcely even read, Nature's book contains no prettier passage than the life story of these woodland
fawns, disliked by the huntsman because they tempt his
hounds to riot, by the forester because they bark his trees, and
ignored by the naturalist because "one never sees them."

Very different in most essentials is the fallow deer, now
well distributed in the wild state throughout southern and
eastern Devon, owing its re-establishment mainly to
"escapes" from various parks. This species, differing from
the roe in its larger size, dappled hide and palmated antlers,
is the least shy of all English deer, partly, no doubt, upon
account of its semi-domesticated ancestry, even as pheasants,

315

which may have been wild for generations, are less timid than game birds into whose history no artificial touch has crept. Fallow deer are much bolder than either of their relatives and have no objection to displaying themselves from a discreet distance at any hour of the day. Although insignificant as compared with a red stag, a fallow buck can look quite impressive when he stands in bold relief upon a hillside, his broad antlers agleam in the sunlight, and there is more than a hint of pageantry in the passing of a herd across a woodland glade, each animal a picture of grace as with effortless stride and almost mechanical uniformity it maintains its place in the long file.

Bold as he is, the fallow deer has proved very well able to take care of himself, and since, like the roe, he knows the value of heavy cover, his numbers latterly have also increased far beyond anticipation. Habitually insidious, polygamous and gregarious, the fallow deer is a successful coloniser, and a community becomes established within a surprisingly short period. In Whiddon Park, near Chagford, a few years ago there existed a herd of about eighty animals the origin of which was quite unknown. Stragglers have lately appeared on northern Dartmoor in the Fernworthy area, where the extensive afforestation would doubtless encourage others, were feeding facilities more attractive. The Haldon district has been well stocked for many years, while between the Axe and Exe the increase has created a problem which local farmers have endeavoured to tackle by means of organised drives with shotguns posted at vantage points—a proceeding concerning which the less said the better, the obvious difficulties of the case alone excusing, if scarcely justifying, much of which one has heard. Stories of maiming and mutilation are reminiscent of the three years on Exmoor when controlled hunting was in abeyance, from 1825, and atrocities committed with shotguns and blunderbusses created a scandal.

All considered, Devonshire, with her wood and moorland, wild coastline and estuaries, probably possesses a more varied fauna than any county south of the Tweed. Within these boundaries most of Britain's remaining mammals still exist, or have survived until within living memory. In coombes which harbour the red deer and the shadowy roe the badger is deeply entrenched, occupying more often than not earth fortresses so old that their history cannot be traced. Among the wild homes of England there is nothing quite like these great ancestral sand-earths, and the most remarkable, as regards extent and antiquity, may be seen in the south and east of the county, where many of the precipitous chines or sandy ridges are honeycombed with cavernous burrows from end to end. It is a curious thought that while Briton, Saxon and Roman were throwing up their fortifications to resist foreign attack, even more ancient inhabitants of the country, the rabbits, badgers and foxes, were also digging themselves in, preparing for a longer struggle with the eventual masters of the soil.

Some years ago a contributor to a sporting periodical when discoursing upon fox-mange advised "the destruction of every infected earth." Clearly he knew little of West-country "batches," where the eradication of burrows would often involve the quarrying out of an entire hillside. The immense depth of a great main earth can only be estimated by the amount of soil which generations of tunnelling have brought to the surface, and even this only represents comparatively recent work, since the rains of every winter carry quantities of loose material away. Even so, an imposing pile of sand or foxmould mounts to the entrance of each hole, like a flight of steps to a mansion door, and anyone knowledgeable in such matters will form some idea of the strength of these burrows from the fact that the yapping of the most "talkative" terrier soon becomes inaudible when following a fox or badger into the heart of the earth. The badger certainly owes his existence today to the many impregnable holts from which he cannot be ejected. Holt is the expression generally, if erroneously, applied to the underground abode of badger, fox or otter, a mere rabbit-hole being always a "bury."

Upon clay soil I have seen no holt that can be compared with the great sand burrows, and consequently the badgers of West and Central Devon fall much easier victims to their persecutors. During recent years there has been a definite infiltration of badgers into the Dartmoor coombes, some penetrating to the heart of the Moor itself, where measures for their complete protection should certainly be taken. The unsuitability of the soil for extensive excavation has prevented them, as it has always prevented rabbits, from digging themselves securely into the hillsides. Like the foxes, however, they have, instead, availed themselves of the great clitters, but whether the rocks would provide sufficient warmth to comply with the badger's standards of comfort is another question. However that may be, only a limited number hibernate upon the Moor, where they are most commonly found in spring or autumn when upon the move. That he will ever establish himself there in strength seems improbable, since, if the country attracted him, there was nothing to prevent him from taking possession long ago. He has always haunted the outskirts, as old parish records of bounties paid for his destruction clearly prove, and clitters which provided impregnable stronghold for foxes would afford equal sanctuary to a badger. If never abundant on the Moor, it was a case of would not rather than could not live there, and climate seems to be the most probable reason for this neglect of an apparently invaluable refuge.

It is also, of course, a matter of food supply. When the badger emerges from his winter sleep, gaunt and ravenous, the lowland coombes are full of newly born rabbits, upon whose nests he descends with avidity, thus providing the agriculturist, who despite propaganda has regarded rabbits as a profitable sideline, with a pretext for waging war upon the badger. As long as I can remember I have heard this excuse advanced, nor can its pertinence be denied if the preservation of rabbits is desired. Upon the other hand, there is scarcely a farmer who, even if he dislikes rabbits, does not encourage the destruction of this natural ally. Among the country-people the badger has few sympathisers. He is more unpopular than the fox, for whom a certain amount of consideration is shown. Should it be necessary to dig out a fox, many voices are raised demanding fair play for him. Should the earth produce a badger, as often happens, rarely does he find a champion, although far more deserving of consideration. For him it must be instant death or the infinitely worse fate of the bag and subsequent torture. I have always remembered an incident at Inwardleigh, when a badger, accidentally unearthed, was released by order of the Eggesford M.F.H., Mr Martin. He lumbered away up a rough slope, and after him went the thwarted mob, yelling as if demented.

It is curious that whereas cock-fighting has long been prohibited by law, the far more cruel practice of bagging and baiting badgers is not only widely practised but arouses little comment and less protest. Were a fox or deer despatched by such means in the hunting-field, outcry and prosecution would follow, yet the maltreatment of badgers provokes no enquiry, creates no scandal. The sturdy, brave, inoffensive creature is not only the object of anybody's brutality, but is regarded as outside the rules of ordinary sportsmanship.

At the beginning of the past century, the few foxes which existed in the county fared little better, the methods employed against them being much the same. Their scarcity is proved by the limited number of claims for the payment made from parish funds to the fox-killers of the period. Were a similar policy adopted today, a special rate would be required for the purpose—as long as the fox supply lasted. That foxes should have been virtually exterminated over wide areas is not surprising, and but for reintroductions, made in some cases more than a century ago, there would be none in Devonshire today. Their decline during the 1914 war and subsequent phenomenal recovery was mentioned in the last chapter. They are not as numerous now, and doubtless they will continue to decrease if present practices persist, although not necessarily to the low level reached in 1918, the original stock having been more abundant. For many years the Moor has been their principal stronghold, mainly because they escape the arch-enemy of Devonshire foxes, the rabbit-trapper. Upon the lowland, hundreds perish each year in gins, many miserably, since it is not unusual for a fox to escape—if so it may be termed—with the trap still fastened to his pad. In such cases, death, though sure, is slow and weeks may elapse before starvation or blood-poisoning eventually brings release. The condition in which trapped foxes are found while still alive will not bear description. Yet the steel gin still has influential supporters.

Upon the Moor the fox is at least immune from traps.

The need for food effects the downfall of most wild animals, however, and even as deer forage upon cultivated land and become unpopular, so Dartmoor foxes follow the rabbits, which are always more numerous on the confines, and there get into trouble. The true hill foxes which live far out on the wilds mainly subsist upon the animals that die there, and upon such fare mountain cubs are reared. The home of a litter upon a remote hillside is strewn with gruesome remains, mostly mutton, much of which must be brought from a considerable distance, dead sheep not being "that thick" even upon Dartmoor. Fox-cubs, however, possess not only healthy appetites but precocious dispositions. Born to be hunters, they embark upon their natural vocation at a very early age, and I have watched tiny things emerge from the earth, and after cutting a caper or two, set off with a comically purposeful air to hunt for themselves.

Before the trapping system became so general, the rabbit problem was not very urgent in Devonshire, polecats, stoats and weasels providing a natural system of control. The polecat has gone, the last of which I heard being trapped on Allen's Down farm, near Spreyton, in 1925. That the stoat should remain as abundant as he is proves unusual tenacity, his ferocious energies being mainly devoted to rabbit slaughter and the consequent treading of the rabbit's gin-infested paths. Studying the records of a local trapper, I find that during the past quarter of a century he had taken upon an average thirty stoats each season, and allowing no more than one rabbit a day to every stoat, the significance of such calculations requires no comment.

The stoat and weasel position is paradoxical. We wage war on the weasel race and grumble at the "rabbit plague." When weasels are numerous, we deplore the massacre of innocents, and one can but wonder what sort of world would emerge were the striking of a wild-life balance left entirely to man. Nature in her own way has always solved the problem and provided general abundance. Man, certainly, has his place in the natural scale, but nobody could regard the wholesale trapping system now in practice throughout Devonshire as Nature's method of control. It was tragic that the passing of the law to prohibit the setting of gins in the open should have

Isolated hawthorns, growing among ling and bracken, are characteristic of Dartmoor's vegetation

coincided with the outbreak of war, thus providing its opponents with means to negative both its purpose and effect.

The wild rabbit has been the object of a particularly bad press within the last few years, his extermination, even upon waste land, being strongly urged. If this end is indeed desirable, nothing is better calculated to effect it than the present high price of rabbits, trappers or land-occupiers being thus induced to catch as many as possible instead of leaving the customary stock. This, together with the general meat shortage, has already brought about a scarcity in some localities, and one is now confronted with the palpable absurdity of people keeping tame rabbits and buying hay with which to feed them.

The genuine countryman, accustomed to deal with the irrepressible rabbit at first hand, is often puzzled at the vehemence of the campaign to exterminate this "pest." Under ordinary circumstances the matter rests between the animal and the man whose crops it raids. Speaking from a wide general experience, I have yet to meet the practical farmer who is unable to cultivate his fields properly upon account of rabbits, or to protect his corn and roots against their depredations. Failure in either respect would be regarded as mere incompetence among his fellows, like inability to safeguard his other interests. It will usually be found that the man who objects to rabbits contrives to get rid of them. Upon the whole, complete elimination of rabbits is the last thing that the ordinary farmer desires, and he complains even more bitterly of any real scarcity. He does not want his produce demolished and takes preventative measures, but he likes to have a crop of rabbits also, to be harvested in early winter before the young wheat appears, and in Devonshire at any rate he contrives to get it both ways.

The problem seldom assumes any magnitude upon highly cultivated land, where rabbits have long been discouraged as a matter of course. Generally speaking, they are numerous upon rough ground only, and at times like the present undoubtedly provide a self-producing source of unrationed meat to supply a public need. When it is remembered that the normal consumption of rabbits, according to some

Hartland, Devon's most remote village

estimates, approaches the nine-figure mark, its importance as a national asset cannot be dismissed as negligible. The extent to which rabbit has always figured in the countryman's bill of fare is not perhaps fully realised. It appears upon every table, from that of the squire to the cottager, and is certainly missed when unobtainable. "To see all they rabbits running about an' I can't pick the bones o' one o' them" was the heart-felt plaint of one labourer who had been unlucky with his snaring, and he would have considered the grievance even more serious had there been no rabbits to catch.

It was not my original intention to devote so much space to the rabbit, but when describing the fauna of a county, its principal animal problem could not be entirely overlooked. From rabbits there follows automatically the question of hares, whose status might be summarised in one word, "local," and they have certainly decreased in Devon during the present century. They show a marked partiality for certain areas, or more probably, certain soils. It may be coincidence, but I have never found many on sandy slopes, a preference for moister herbage being a possible reason. They appear to like clay lands, but here again is no rule, since one could mark culm areas of many square miles in extent where hares have never been known. A few are still found on the lower slopes of the Moor, but seldom far out, this, once again, being a matter of suitable food.

To begin a survey of our "ground game" with the "deer poem" and descend to as low a note as rats and mice seems something of an anti-climax. The importance of an animal, however, does not necessarily coincide with its size. Mr Wickett always declares that he would sooner have rats in a rick than mice, while a gamekeeper I knew had a proverb of his own coining: "Rats is the worst thing out." Since this entailed precedence over foxes, badgers and cats, to mention only a few of the names upon his long black list, it seems clear that inches bore no relation to eminence. All considered, however, I think that such small fry as rats, mice, moles and voles may be taken for granted, as sparrows among birds or buttercups and daisies as specimens of our flora. Admittedly, the tiniest creatures are often the most attractive, and it is unfortunate that man's interests should be so directly at variance with those of the little furred people who inhabit the under-world, the sprites of the earth comprehensively classified as "vermin." Between man and most rodents no truce is possible, being incompatible with civilised or artificial life. The countryman's confirmed and incorrigible hostility towards the hedgehog, most innocuous of British quadrupeds, is quite unaccountable, however, the animal being not only harmless but even serviceable, as anybody who has kept one in a garden is aware.

The survival of the hedgehog in Devonshire is mainly attributable to his hibernating habits, which keep him out of harm's way during the greater part of the trapping season. Even so, gins claim a tragic toll, and the "fuzzypig" has certainly lost ground in the battle for existence. About twenty years ago, before the fox multiplication occurred, hedgehogs also staged a revival upon a minor scale. Knowing our interest in wild life, neighbours often bring in any odd creature that comes to hand, and during that period the number of hedgehogs that literally rolled up on the doorstep became quite embarrassing, involving, as it did, the surreptitious restoration of the captives to their native haunts. We do not discourage this practice, which saves the lives of many animals, as it never occurs to the countryman to spare anything. Harmful or otherwise, from his point of view, "it bain't no good." A day or two ago a neighbour told me that he had killed fifty shrews in his garden. When asked what harm they did, he replied: "I can't see they do aught, but the old wall's full o' them." In brief, they were there, and he destroyed them as a matter of course. Incidentally, his shrews were more innocuous than mine, which spoiled an excellent bed of strawberries this summer by drilling holes, large enough to admit their little snouts, into the hearts of the fruit. This is the only instance of their harmful activities within my experience.

More than three decades have elapsed since the red squirrel, abundant throughout Devonshire until about 1910, went down almost overnight, like leaves at the nip of a premature frost, and the lost status has never been regained. Formerly their nests in the tree-tops aroused no more comment than mole-hills on a rough pasture. Their chatter was as familiar a sound in the woods as the green woodpecker's call. Now, there are many country-people of the younger generation who have never seen a squirrel, and the interest with which an isolated pair is regarded testifies to the scarcity of the species. One must, however, emphasise the fact that, as far as Devonshire is concerned, the disappearance of the red squirrel had not the slightest connection with the spread of the grey, which has never yet reached the county, except for a few introduced into one or two parks and to the Stoke Canon district, near Exeter.

Whether future afforestation schemes will help the squirrel or finally defeat its full recovery remains to be proved. A lover of conifers, he is unpopular in young plantations, but at the moment his scarcity should save him from organised destruction, and in the course of time the growing woods should provide him with protection, if he does not increase too rapidly in the meanwhile. Of the latter there seems to be little immediate prospect, although he has certainly embarked upon the upward grade. He was always better represented in the east of the county, and there his recovery is most marked.

The red squirrel's charming understudy, the dormouse, is another animal into whose life story one would like to enter more fully. It reads like a fairy-tale in the woodland book, and unlike most pretty stories has the additional attraction of truth. Even the countryman cannot resist his charm, which is unfortunate, for while a "seven-sleeper" is the one furred creature which nobody dreams of destroying, the temptation to pull out the wonderful little nest and inspect the occupant is more than hedger or woodsman can withstand, and the dormouse, still sleeping, is transferred to the labourer's pocket, to be taken home as a curiosity or pet for the children. No animal sleeps like a dormouse, and being nocturnal— the only essential in which he differs from the squirrel— even during the summer he passes the daylight hours in slumber so profound that nothing short of the removal of his nest will wake him. Even a hibernating hedgehog is conscious of noise or vibration in his vicinity. One which for some years passed the winter in our woodshed always made his presence evident by agitated breathing while anyone was at work in the shed. His "whazing," as the gardener would call it, waxed in volume as the disturbance proceeded, until it became as loud as the singing of a kettle, but subsided almost instantly when silence was restored. That he "slept yet heard" and that apprehension entered his dreams was evident; but I doubt whether a bursting bomb would cause a dormouse to draw one deep breath, unless his nest were blown to pieces. If taken from his bed while heavily asleep, he snuggles down in the warmth of a captor's hand, and reclosing his eyes—if he ever opened them—curls himself into a somnolent ball, one place being as good as another as long as it is comfortable, and sleep at any price, anywhere, being all that he asks of life.

I have said nothing about animals whose complete banishment from the county appears to be final. The last marten that I can trace appears to have been destroyed in the Axminster district about fifty years ago, and of the wild cat there is no positive record. One trapped about 1923 was probably an "escape," and most of the "cats" for which bounties were paid, according to old registers, were doubtless domesticated animals which had taken to the woods.

There remain only the creatures which inhabit our streams and coasts, and they are few. One cannot entirely omit the Atlantic seal, although Devon's claim to this splendid maritime beast for inclusion in her fauna might be contested. He may occasionally come to shore among the rocky fastnesses of Hartland, but I do not think he often breeds east of Beeny Beaches. Devon with her many rivers, few of which are fouled or commercialised, is probably better stocked with otters than any other county. Seldom seen except by fishermen, and not very often even by them, its presence may remain unsuspected for a long while until betrayed by some chance circumstance, as when a local farmer recently discovered mauled trout upon the banks of a quarry pool near South Tawton. Once in a lifetime, perhaps, the occupier of a riverside farm becomes an astonished spectator of an otter love-chase, or a procession of suitors filing like a huge brown snake along the hovers under the banks, and it was with the characteristic luck of the stranger that a Pioneer officer, billeted in the district and paying his first visit to the Erme that summer, was entertained for half an hour by a dog otter paying court to a coy sylph of the stream upon a grassy bank overshadowed by waterside willows.

The overland wanderings of otters are extensive. They will follow any brook to its source, and occasionally make short cuts over high ground from one stream to another. One was killed on the road between South and North Tawton a few years ago, nowhere near water. This is unusual, however. Trappers seldom get hold of them, except with intent at their landing-stages, which proves that their terrestrial activities are mainly confined to low-lying marshy land where there is little trapping. Within my own experience, more have been caught in snares than in gins, casual wires for rabbit or hare being set upon ground over which the wholesale trapper cannot work profitably.

What the position of the otter would be without sport is a debatable question. Upon the smaller streams, where fishing is not seriously preserved, he would probably increase. Upon the main trout and salmon rivers, where riparian rights are at a premium, his extermination would doubtless be demanded. All considered, it is probable that otter-hunting preserves the species, particularly on big water, where few are killed by hounds but could be easily destroyed by other means. The Devonshire rivers are hunted by three packs, the Culmstock, the Dartmoor and the Cheriton, and since fishermen complain that too many otters still harry the trout and salmon, it seems clear that more drastic "control" would be exercised but for the hounds. At present, with two packs in abeyance, otters have taken full advantage of the respite to augment their population, particularly upon the Teign, always a "sporting" river. One has heard good accounts of otter-hunting on the Teign in the days when hounds met soon after sunrise and hunted the trail over the dew-soaked meadows, followed only by a few keen spirits who had never heard of cars and came out for sport alone. One anecdote might be repeated against the Cheriton Hounds, who, meeting at Steppes Bridge, drew upstream, the river here flowing between wooded slopes which at that time harboured a small herd of red deer. These, unfortunately for the hunters, had visited the river at dawn. The pack, composed largely of draft staghounds, hailed the fresh line as a familiar friend. Before anyone realised the situation, they were away, and spent the next day or two exercising the deer around Mid-Devon. The sequel was more interesting. The deer had for a long while constituted a problem among local farmers, and the Steppes Bridge incident suggesting hounds as a remedy, a harrier pack which had occasionally hunted stag was requisitioned to drive the valley, while all the inhabitants who could be pressed into service turned out for the occasion, armed, like the early Home Guard, with shotguns or anything upon which they could lay hands. Every deer-path was covered, and it only remained for the hounds to drive the herd to the waiting guns. Unfortunately or otherwise, according to point of view, the deer declined to cooperate. All broke back, heading for quieter woodland, while the "sportsmen," nerved for the occasion by deep draughts from the cider-jar, emptied their guns at everything that came along. Four foxes and three men were brought to earth, no record of unimportant "sundries" being preserved.

That occurred fifty years ago, and red deer no longer tempt otter-hounds to riot on the banks of the Teign. The otters are there, however, and doubtless they are also regrouping their forces on the Exe, Axe, Taw, Torridge, Tamar and, most notably, the Dart, upon whose romantic waters the enthusiastic otter-hunter finds his brightest dreams realised.

CHAPTER XXVIII

BIRDS

1. MAINLY IN THE GARDEN

My riverside garden, with its outlook on pasture, tillage, moor and woodland, might be regarded as an observation point from which most of Devonshire's birds are seen, excepting those which never abandon coast or mud flats. This particular spot is singularly adapted for the purpose, since the deep gorge down which the Taw rushes in tumultuous haste here provides a natural passage from the hills to the lowland; while the valleys of the Taw and Dart, which from their common starting-point virtually bisect the county, form a direct migration route from coast to coast.

Our list of genuine garden birds would not be particularly impressive as compared, for example, with that achieved by the South Devon ornithologist Mr W. Walmsley-White, who, in his own grounds at Budleigh Salterton, has recorded 104 species. If, upon the contrary, we include all that may be seen or heard from the windows or the summer-house in which I now write, few of our inland birds would be absent. Now and again a hoopoe works its way up or down the valley. Harriers, hen and Montagu's, and an occasional peregrine falcon or short-eared owl pay a brief visit, and once a rough-legged buzzard rested within easy view on the hillside, spreading his plumage in the sunshine as though to facilitate identification. These, however, are mere "ships that pass," and it is from residents and our regular summer migrants that we derive most interest and pleasure.

In the hanging wood upon which we look, with the river and one little field between, the raven has nested for more than twenty years, in a giant spruce whose growth has now left the nest far below its original position in the crown. Within view, nest also the buzzard, sparrowhawk, kestrel, carrion crow, magpie and jay, woodpecker (green and spotted), nuthatch and small birds innumerable. Upon the river-bank below the tennis-court the woodcock lodges among the waterside alders. Snipe drum overhead in the twilight. The barn owl patrols our outbuildings, to the consternation of the swallows which nest on the rafters. The little owl's note can be heard, and the tawnies create nightly discord in an old yew where missel-thrushes gorge on the autumnal berries, and finches, green and gold, build during May and June. The course of the stream, which the moorhen haunts, marks also the heron's line of flight to the Moor, and the creaking of his long wings as he passes over the lawn is a very familiar sound. The curlew, too, uses our airway in spring, tuning his flute as he sights his domain spread wide below, and sometimes doing us the honour of choosing the near moorside for his summer quarters.

Inclining over the river stands a great poplar, freely used by jackdaws, crows and woodpigeons. In the thorn hedge which forms our boundary the blackcap, willow warbler, whitethroat and chiff-chaff sing, and amongst the stonework at its base wagtails, pied and grey, rear their broods. In autumn that same tall hedge attracts passing flocks of long-tailed tits which drift like leaf-flurries amongst the mellowing greenery. Its high-walled bank, stumps and crevices, has many occupants, some of whom seldom wander far from the garden which caters for all their needs. Within three feet of my papers is a little wooden tray upon which chaffinches, thrushes, tits, hedge-sparrows and robins compete for crumbs, and my train of thought is constantly disturbed by their bickerings, two robins occasionally going so far as to quarrel upon my knee.

Martins build under the eaves of a long barn, and swifts scream like distracted spirits around the house at dusk. There are also those rival claimants for holes in the masonry, blue-tits and starlings, while the house-sparrow and ubiquitous blackbird, like rats and mice on the animal list, go without saying. The sparrow has a uniformly "bad press," but apart from his predilection for dust-baths on newly sown ground and his truly gutter-snipe habit of nipping off blossoms for pure mischief, as it would seem, I find him far less destructive in the garden than various birds which are popular. The chaffinch, who insists upon pulling up seed-lings, can easily be frustrated by pea-guards. The bullfinch is not common enough to do much damage. The terrors of our garden are blue-tits and blackbirds: the one regarding green peas as sown for his special benefit, the other falling upon fruit of every description. From a gardener's point of view, no comparison can be drawn between the blackbird and song-thrush. If given the choice between a strawberry and a snail, there is little doubt which the thrush would select, and when he does assail fruit he is a far less greedy feeder than the blackbird, nipping off and eating his berry cleanly, while a blackbird spoils scores without finishing any. A thrush does not necessarily lack resolution in ill-doing, however. The other day, when my wife was trying to per-suade a semi-tame one to vacate the raspberry cage, he deliberately settled on a bush near the opening made for him, selected the finest berry within reach, and flew out with it firmly grasped in his beak.

In this garden we can keep neither fruit nor peas unnetted, while in those of neighbours upon either side no trouble is ex-perienced. By contrast, during the first ten years of residence here I lost no produce at all, and privately regarded the com-plaints of others as exaggerations. Around my home in East Devon, again, the only birds that raided peas were jays. Here, jays abound, but attack no peas, this applying even during a curious influx of the birds about 1938, when they might even be seen in little flocks upon the cornfields.

It is far from my purpose, however, to enlarge upon the damage done in a garden by birds which constitute its prin-cipal charm, and were these confined to purely unoffending species, the list would be reduced to hedge-sparrows and robins, with spotted flycatchers and goldfinches where these are to be found. Here we are not lucky enough to have nut-hatches or woodpeckers on the premises, and in the case of "bigger fowl," the crows, sparrowhawks, rooks, jackdaws and magpies, we are divided between the interest which they bring and concern for the smaller feathered friends who are always with us. There are birds resident in the garden who have proved more than able to take care of themselves. In a laurel thicket immediately below the leaning poplar, our missel-thrushes had their nest this summer, and regarded every crow, rook or jackdaw which alighted in the poplar as a menace to their growing brood. Perhaps they were justified. At any rate they left nothing to chance, and the clatter of black wings alighting in the tree was the signal for the occupants of the laurels to arise and offer battle, which the prospective robber invariably declined.

The story of that nest ended dramatically. In the early stillness of a Sunday morning, a period when all village life is in abeyance, we were aroused by an appalling clamour under the windows. The cause was soon apparent. The young missel-thrushes, still in the bobtail stage, were out upon the ground, and over one stood a magpie, with beak and wing warding off the savage swoops which the parent birds were launching at him. I hurried out to interfere, but quite unnecessarily. The magpie was already heading for cover, and after him into the mists of the morning which still over-hung river and valley went two grey furies, whose aim upon this occasion appeared to be "not victory but conquest." The rescued fledgling, when interviewed, made it apparent that he required no first aid, and after collecting the scattered family, I left the situation to be dealt with by the parents upon their return.

Unfortunately, few birds possess either the courage or prowess of the missel-thrush, and tragedy is frequent, par-ticularly when the strategic as well as physical advantages lie with the robber. Just outside our cob-walled fruit-garden stands the grand oak previously mentioned, a parish orna-ment but doubtful blessing as a neighbour. Its immense shadow steals over the growing crops at sunrise and persists until reluctantly withdrawn some hours later. Its wide-ranging roots burrow deeply under our soil, and its branches provide an excellent base from which feathered marauders devise and launch operations against the garden. No seed can be sown, no fruit can ripen, no little bird can visit its nest on wall or standard fruit tree unobserved from the giant oak, where feathered bandits in varied guise mount guard for the purpose. There rooks assemble, hold their droll consulta-tions, and like members of a mothers' meeting, or any other village gathering, miss nothing even while they talk. There rest sparrowhawk, crow and jay; but it is the cold, discriminating eye of the magpie that we have most cause to fear. Blame for recent disaster to the nests of pied wagtail, chaffinch, song-thrush and spotted flycatcher has been laid at his door, and although he may not always have been guilty, he has certainly earned his bad name.

One inevitable consequence of the enlarged scope which quick transport has given to ornithological study is the comparative neglect of common birds, whose habits are quite as interesting as those of rarer species. It is characteristic that while we accumulate and publish elaborate data concerning birds which the ordinary reader has never seen, nobody as yet has fully mastered the life story of the common wren. He is singing to me at this moment, doubtless near one of his many nests. Around the back premises alone, at this moment, there are five of which we know, all used, as far as can be judged, by one pair of birds. Three are under cover, one in ivy against the house, and the fifth in a cluster of raspberry canes. This and two of the others, respectively built under the back-door porch and just inside the stable— once requisitioned by the army as an "ablution-house"—are new this summer. The ivy nest is three seasons old, while the remaining one, built between two beams at the woodshed entrance, has an eleven-year history behind it. Here the first brood was reared this summer, while the second was hatched above the ablution bench on the foundation of an old swallow's nest, the other three continuing unoccupied.

Unlike any other bird with which I am acquainted, the wren keeps its many nests not only in perennial repair but also in regular, if periodical, occupation. They serve as roosting-places at all times of the year, and uncompleted structures are frequently visited, being obviously reserved for future use. This policy of treating them as homes rather than temporary nurseries is probably the reason why so many are built, facilitating a change of quarters as circumstances require. The habit of roosting under cover also enables the wren to live at higher altitudes than other birds, and he is therefore found upon the high Moor in dead of winter and during the hardest weather, when even the larks and meadow-pipits have sought less rigorous conditions.

He is not, however, the only bird which builds several nests before making a final selection for first use. A pair of swallows which took possession of a spare bedroom in a friend's house this summer started to build upon the picture rail in all four corners, and the practice only corresponds with the alternative eyrie policy followed by larger birds which occupy lifelong breeding-places. Choice of accommodation enables a wren to be independent as well as indecisive, and a laying bird will sometimes abandon an incomplete clutch which has attracted attention to make a fresh start in one of its reserve nests. The "cock-nest" theory undoubtedly originated from failure to observe that such structures, although temporarily abandoned, are eventually lined and used, the truth being that the wren does all elementary work in advance, completing or repairing as required.

We have never experienced the doubtful privilege of a cuckoo's egg in any of our garden nests, although the first cuckoo of the present season was reported as having alighted on our tennis-court. We were called out in the chill of a late March evening by a lady friend who had witnessed the arrival and vehemently repudiated any suggestion of mistaken identity. When challenged to describe the suspect, she replied that it was something like myself, "rather long and grey," and so, woman-like, secured the last word.

The cuckoos of our immediate neighbourhood keep mainly to the Moor, and we seldom get them very near houses, although they may be heard from dawn till dusk. The bird reaches this district as a rule with the swallows, about April 21st. He attains full voice as the hill winds lose their harshness, and then his contribution, misnamed "song," considerably strengthens the limited moorland orchestra. A few years ago, at the head of Belstone Cleave, I was indebted to four cuckoos for a wonderful musical entertainment. The birds had gathered in a group of wind-bitten hawthorns, which, silhouetted against the misty blue of the distant in-country, provided an effective background. It might have been a rehearsed performance, for while all four birds participated, each timed his note to follow that of another with astonishing perfection of tone and pitch, the effect being that of a well modulated chime of bells, and as they rang one change after another it seemed hard to believe that chance alone produced such novel music.

There is another wild concert held upon the high Moor, and unrecorded because seldom heard. This is the twilight chorus of skylarks, which attains full volume in early June, and is peculiar to those rare moorland nights when the windless, fragrant air seems palpitant with life and sound, when the glow-worms light up and fox-cubs play, when nobody thinks of sleep because charged with a mysterious vitality. When dusk falls upon this enchanted world, the larks, the meadow-pipits, the wheatears, and all the little hill birds draw near their nesting-places, but not to roost as yet. There is a spirit abroad on the darkening landscape to which expression cannot be denied, and mounting—only a short distance now, for there is no sun to call him skywards—the lark ripples into a song that daylight never hears, for the still evening air imparts to each note an outstanding clarity and volume. Through the purple gloom the melody rings as the birds draw closer to one another, until all the larks upon the hillside seem to be gathered within a narrow circle of song. High aloft, the snipe, the "hoolet of the bogs," is circling under the dim stars. No eye can detect his ethereal form, much less follow his aerial gambols, but one is conscious of a vague intermittent thrumming which quivers through the twilight and mingles with the riot of song as though stringed instruments, touched now and again by an invisible bow, awaited their turn to tune in, when night, closing down, at last reduces the larks to silence. No moorland bird is silent during this, the grand finale to a "perfect day." Even the old red grouse mounts a boulder and sends his longest call rolling over the heather without giving thought to the pricked ears of the listening vixen, who may turn such indiscretion to account before the stars are bright.

But since I have wandered from the garden to the moorland and the red grouse has thrust himself into notice, it might be as well to allow him and the larger birds of the county a section to themselves.

BIRDS

2. OF MOOR AND WOODLAND

MORE than three decades have now elapsed since the consignment of red grouse, entrusted with the task of colonising Devon's highlands, emerged from crate and hamper to survey the new land, so like and yet so different from the heathery sweeps that overlook loch, burn and the grey expanses of the North Sea.

It would be a long story to recount in full the fortunes of this little "expeditionary force," embarked upon a cause which many experts, basing their predictions on past experiment, regarded as hopeless. The struggle proved unending, and up to a certain point the venture must be considered a failure. Yet neither the pessimist who thought the country unsuitable nor the optimist who dreamed of the day when grouse-trains bound for the west would steam out from Paddington or Waterloo were entirely correct. True, the latter rosy picture remains imaginary, and must continue so under existing conditions. Upon the other hand, the sturdy invaders from the north, like Rollo's conquering bands, have demonstrated that their empire recognises no traditional boundary line. For this exclusively British bird, Britain can provide a home wherever suitable altitudes can be found. Moorland is moorland and heather remains heather, no matter whether its pollen drifts along the banks of the Tavy or the Tees, and if afforded the same measure of protection, there can be no reasonable doubt that the red grouse would be as plentiful upon Dartmoor as upon any Scottish heath were corresponding facilities available.

It cannot be denied that actually the stock has dwindled to a remnant. At the moment the birds are most numerous upon the upper Dart, that is to say, the country most directly under the eye of authority. Speaking for the wilder moorlands, and particularly the mountainous district extending from Okehampton in the north to Tavistock and Princetown, at a rough computation one pair might be found to a thousand acres, yet meagre as this well might seem, the tenacity with which this remnant persists, despite incessant persecution, indiscriminate destruction of the heather, and the constant activities of natural enemies, indubitably proves their ability to multiply were the struggle less unequal.

Whether or not the red grouse will eventually outstay the indigenous blackcock remains to be proved. The survival of either species will depend entirely upon what measures, if any, are taken in the future for their preservation. Excepting the afforested areas, blackgame—the "old sort," as the country-people call them—have practically disappeared from Dartmoor, and whereas they were formerly common on the rough land around Sampford Courtenay, I have heard of none on the in-country for many years.

When walking through Central or Northern Devon, the stranger is surprised at the abundance of rapacious or predatory birds, as compared with the avifauna of other counties. This is due not only to the virtual disappearance of the game-keeper, but also to the wild nature of the country, which affords stronghold to all hard-pressed creatures. Wood-pigeons are not particularly plentiful, the land being too sparsely cultivated, and good roosting-places such as fir or larch plantations neither frequent nor extensive, if one excepts the newly afforested areas, as yet in their infancy. The bulky nest of the magpie is conspicuous everywhere, particularly in hawthorn spinneys or poised like a pigeon-cote high in the crown of a birch sapling. In the bigger hedgerow trees the dark blot of the carrion crow's nest is often visible against the background of sky or distance. In midsummer, the mewing of young sparrowhawks and buzzards fills the woods, and the jay's scream sounds from the thickets, often accompanied by the fretful grunts of a tawny owl whose dormitory the blue-winged busybody has ferreted out. Within the last few years the monotonous cry of the little owl has added a new voice to the wild babel, for this insidious little alien has made strong headway in the west, where nobody, to date, has taken very much notice of him. Although now outnumbering the barn owl in this locality, he is not so often seen, for while the white owl patrols the hedgerows freely in the gloom of a winter afternoon, the little brown bird is less conspicuous. The farmers have not the same objection to him as to the crow and magpie. He raids

Old cob and thatch at Cockington

neither their chicken-coops nor laying-boxes, and in justice to a much accused species it must be said that here we have found no evidence of his destructiveness to small-bird life, and unless he evinces worse tendencies than he has hitherto displayed, one is inclined to adopt the view that "second thoughts" concerning the little owl have corrected a previous error.

Birds of a feather are much the same wherever they occur, and since about 270 species have been recorded in the county of Devon, to describe them all would require a weighty volume. The difficulty lies in drawing a distinction between local or ecological and purely general interest, and this applies particularly to birds of the coasts. One might devote chapters to the multitudes of waders or wildfowl which throng the Exe estuary from September to April, but no species being peculiar to Devon's tidal waters, a detailed description would be superfluous. Since the gannet abandoned Lundy, we can no longer claim this spectacular bird as a breeding species, the island being now mainly famous for its puffins. Apart from Lundy, we have no great general nesting-place for ocean birds, comparable with Lye Rock, off Tintagel, and other Cornish islets. Devonshire can claim only one colony of the black-headed gull. The black-backed gull on the whole prefers the Cornish cliffs; and, generally speaking, the bird life of our coastline, with its gulls, cormorants, oyster-catchers, divers, kestrels and occasional peregrines, is much the same as elsewhere.

Devon might, however, be considered the southern home of the curlew, and the Cornish peninsula generally as the woodcock's main winter resort south of Ireland. The woodcock, of course, is not perennially with us. We do not hear his whirring love note, nor witness any of the remarkable doings which have won him such controversial fame. Generally speaking, as the curlew arrives the woodcock goes, and is not seen again until the beginning of October, when an advance party, probably consisting of birds reared in the British Isles, precedes the main southward movement a month or so later. From November to March, distribution throughout the central and western parts of the county is widespread, with a tendency to become denser when nearing

An example of modern thatching at Kennford, near Exeter

the Cornish border, the reason for the latter circumstance being purely geographical. The migratorial urge is naturally south-west, and a continual drift in that direction, being more or less checked by the sea, ensures the greatest abundance along the Atlantic seaboard.

With the curlew the situation is reversed. He visits our moorlands to raise his brood, which he hurries away to the estuaries with discourteous haste almost before the young have attained full wing power. Alone among our larger birds possessing a voice that is both far-sounding and eminently musical, the curlew is no mean contributor to the charm of our marshes. As the first cuckoo suggests summer, so the curlew's call announces the spring early in March. He invites the fisherman to prospect the water, the gardener to plant his early crops, but his voice high in the blue during late July has a melancholy association, for it means that summer has passed its prime, that days are already shortening, and that essentially summer birds, having taken the best that the year can offer, are now leaving us to witness its decline.

While here, the curlew is not primarily a Dartmoor bird. Although nesting on the confines, he does not follow the resident snipe into the farthest recesses of the hills, and is far more numerous on the in-country marshes, where his main habitat might be summarised as the Culm area. A quarter of a century ago he was unknown east of the Exe, but within the past decade he has extended his breeding range to the Somerset and Dorset boundaries, his sudden discovery of this new terrain being as noteworthy as his previous neglect of it.

It might be interesting to mention that the curlew penetration into East Devon coincided with a marked withdrawal of the nightjar from that entire region, which had long been famous as the veritable home of the species. In no other part of England have I found anything that could compare with the nightjars of East Devon as they were at the beginning of the present century. Anywhere in the Bewley Down district, for example, on a midsummer evening the throbbing purr of the nightjar vibrated from every quarter of the compass. Like small-bird song in a lowland spinney, it filled the dusk, and the birds themselves, hawking, sporting in air or resting upon stumps and rails, were so common that they aroused no more interest than a passing woodpigeon. So numerous they were that when moving to the centre of the county, where perhaps a pair monopolised a parish, one missed their churring at nightfall as a Londoner misses the sound of traffic, and their sudden decline from remarkable abundance to comparative scarcity has been one of the many curious "freaks" which have marked the natural history of the county.

Among the country-people the nightjar is an unrecognised species, being always confused with the landrail, which is curious, since until the landrail's decline they knew both birds very well. The rustic does not as a rule confuse his species, being in general more reliable than the enthusiastic recorder. He may have his own name for a bird, but he knows the bird to which he refers. Usually, also, he is good at identification, and no country lad, for example, would mistake the nest of a carrion crow for that of a raven, which I find is a most common error among public-school ornithologists.

The raven must not be overlooked, his position in Devonshire being probably unique as far as English counties are concerned. Ravens have now advanced along a great part of the British coastline, but in this county he is quite as much a bird of the inland, having staged a notable "come-back" during the last twenty years, and now nests not only on the cliffs but in many disused quarries, woods and latterly upon the Dartmoor tors.

In 1922 the only known breeding-place of the raven in Mid-Devon was Meldon Quarry. I could now enumerate sixteen eyries within a ten-mile radius, and doubtless there are others which have escaped notice. Five of them are, or were, in trees, one being a lone hedgerow Scotch pine. A notable increase of ravens was observed about 1936, and for the succeeding three or four seasons, during which period there was scarcely a tor of any eminence upon northern Dartmoor upon which a nest might not be found. The most picturesque was upon grand and desolate Fur Tor—an old eyrie mentioned in previous works, and probably the first established on the Forest after the raven "renaissance." The most interesting is on Lints Tor, a lonely little rock guarding the pass through which the West Okement escapes from Cranmere. Its remarkable feature is the diminutive size of the tor, the nest being little more than eight feet above ground, although a circuitous ascent is necessary to reach it. That eyries should escape detection and annual pillage could scarcely be expected. They are regularly plundered, and I have mentioned localities without reserve, since there is no secrecy to be observed. The Lints Tor nest is unique, however: an ornithological curiosity; and measures to preserve it should certainly be taken in the event of Dartmoor becoming a National Park. It has been used for nineteen years, although robbed as many times. Unfortunately, the extension of the artillery range has led to the destruction of two rock eyries, a flagstaff having been erected on Fur Tor, in the very pile where the ravens built, and another on Waterton, where not only the raven rock was utilised, but the crevice which had always contained the nest.

An injured raven brought in to me was introduced as "one o' they Dartmoor birds," and the Moor is the recognised habitat of this species. Its abundance there, like that of the carrion crow, is largely due to the dead sheep, which naturally attract scavenger birds and beasts. It is unnecessary to deal at length with accusations brought against both the raven and the mountain fox by moorland farmers. "Incidents" occur, of course, but no British bird or beast is a habitual lamb-killer, although all carnivorous animals— including every sheep-dog—prey upon carcases, particularly those of lambs. Lifelong experience has produced no reliable evidence of anything approaching an extensive departure from this rule.

Ecologically the carrion crow upon Dartmoor is scarcely less interesting than the raven, mainly upon account of his nesting habits, which again are unique. There are no high trees, so the crow, if he wants to rear his brood within easy reach of food, must adapt himself to existing conditions, and people accustomed to regard the nest of this bird as one of the least accessible are astonished to find it placed in some dwarfed mountain-ash or oak overhanging a stream, or in a mere "withy-bush" encircled by bog, which alone prevents the discoverer from reaching the nest without lifting a foot from the ground. Upon the banks of Taw, Teign, Tavy, the northern Walla Brook, the Redaven and the Fishcombe Water there are trees not more than ten feet high in which the bulky nest of the crow may be seen. Blacktor Beare and its extensions are full of them. Upon the Walla Brook is a hawthorn in which I have seen three at one time, of varying ages; and upon the northern slope of West Mill, beside the Moor Brook, is a crow-tree so tiny that the nest fills its crown, like a good cauliflower. Upon the fringes they often select low bushes, even when bigger trees are near, such builders being, presumably, Moor-bred birds whose standards are low. It should be added that they never nest upon the tors, these being regarded as the raven's special property.

Dartmoor is the winter home of the golden plover, the "whistling plover" of the county. Foraging flocks of these birds visit most of the higher ground north of the Moor, particularly the Whiddon Down area, over which much of the moorland atmosphere still lingers. It is not considered a summer resident, although remaining to breed upon exceedingly rare occasions. Mr Vesey-FitzGerald, when Editor of the *Field*, recorded two nests near Two Bridges. During winter they frequent the high Moor, being most plentiful on the great northern ridge supporting Yes Tor and High Willhayes. The first flights arrive about the middle of September—earlier than is stated in some books of reference—and with the first April sunshine the return movement is in full swing. Then great formations of birds, reduced indeed as compared with old-time standards, but still immense flocks, pass northwards, filling the air with their tuneful cries and the rush of innumerable pinions. The spring moorland can offer no more impressive sight than that of golden plover on the wing. By contrast their arrival in autumn is unspectacular. Although the seasons are reversed, the plover resemble swallows in their coming and going, the former unheralded and almost surreptitious; the latter announced by frenzied preparation and rehearsal, culminating in a grand take-off.

While the whistling companies pass northwards, the summer population of the moorland assembles. As though blown in by a snow-shower from the south-east, with the flakes still adhering to his plumage, the wheatear appears. The reed bunting, whinchat, sedge-warbler and sandpiper take possession of their accustomed localities. The stonechat wanders farther up the rocky hillside, and a clear, far-sounding pipe announces somewhat monotonously that Dartmoor's most outstanding summer bird, the ring-ouzel, has also returned. He may claim this distinction, being the only indigenous Devonshire bird whose range is restricted to Dartmoor and Exmoor, and since the greater part of the latter habitat lies upon the Somerset boundary, Dartmoor is his principal Devonshire haunt and, indeed, his main stronghold in southern England. The nest of the ring-ouzel may be found in any moorland valley above the 1,000-foot level. The bird may breed at a lower altitude, but personal observation has never established an instance. A bank beside a stream is a favourite site, but I have found nests upon high ridges nowhere near water. Since they rear two broods in a season, one cannot but wonder that they are not more numerous. Upon a rough estimate, one pair might be allocated to every three miles of stream, and meagre as this representation may seem, a continuous tendency to decrease has been noted over a long period of years. Strong families are raised, but of these an unduly large majority never return to the Moor. This raises many questions to which, as usual in such cases, satisfactory answers cannot be found. One point is clear, however. If this bold mountain bird must be reckoned among the losers in the race for survival, the causes of his decline lie elsewhere than upon Dartmoor which to the ring-ouzel has always been a land of plenty and comparative peace.

When first I became acquainted with the country west of the Exe, the bird which caught my eye above all others was the buzzard, then slowly fighting its way back to a numerical status little anticipated by the most sanguine. Devonshire can claim full credit for the recovery of the buzzard since her rough woodland, which in effect amounts to natural forest, enabled the bird to regain a foothold and build up a substantial stock. True, the occupation of the entire county has only been completed within the last few years, but already pioneers of an eastern movement are making their way through Dorset, and Devonshire will probably gain the distinction of having restored a banished species.

Here the buzzard is regarded as a woodland rather than a cliff bird. Although he cruises freely over Dartmoor, where he has assumed the duties of the exiled kite, he never competes with the raven for house room on the tors or ventures to use the lowly sites accepted by the crow. Now and again one finds or hears of an eyrie at no great height above ground, particularly in North Devon, but, generally speaking, no tree is too high for the buzzard, and his nest is the least accessible in our woods today.

Now probably the most numerous and certainly the most conspicuous of our rapacious birds, he has become as essential a feature of the Devonshire landscape as the golden eagle was once inseparable from Highland scenery. He is the more decorative, since, unlike many hawks, he is gregarious up to a certain point, particularly in spring, when eight or ten of these splendid birds may be seen cruising in wide circles, often at a vast height and sometimes above the clouds themselves. Compared with the buzzard, even the kestrel is an aeronaut of a far inferior order. From our summer-house overlooking the wood where both species breed, we can watch adults and young upon the wing, but while comparison is interesting, no question of competition arises.

Family hunting parties of kestrels are common upon the late summer moorland, where, as autumn steps in, they are occasionally joined by passing harriers attracted by the prospect of good hawking. Devon's effort to restore Montagu's harrier, as she restored the raven and buzzard, has not been so successful. One nest only was recorded in 1943, as compared with several in previous years, and this despite every effort upon the part of the DEVON BIRD-WATCHING AND PRESERVATION SOCIETY to ensure protection. No harrier has taken advantage of Dartmoor's wild spaces for many a year, and it is to be feared that birds of this order have failed to appreciate our amenities, at least for nesting purposes.

With Montagu's harrier begins the list of our failures,

happily short and in most cases confined to species whose decline is general. They comprise the landrail, now exceedingly rare except upon migration; the merlin, whose efforts can only be described as sporadic; and the wryneck, of which few occurrences were recorded in recent reports of the Society. This is an insignificant debit when set against the acquisition of the nightingale, which has penetrated as far west as Northam; the arrival in Devon of the Dartford warbler; and the increase of the goldfinch and great spotted woodpecker. An added cause for gratification is the ever-widening interest in ornithology which the DEVON BIRD-WATCHING AND PRESERVATION SOCIETY has done much to foster. This is a keen society with a membership of 300 to date, the list including many well-known naturalists. In its early days it benefited from the services of its honorary secretary, the Rev. F. C. Butters, whose former vicarage in the enchanted Stockland valley is ideally placed for wild-life study. Mr Butters combined tactful administration with an extensive first-hand knowledge of the county, its inhabitants and fauna, and his untiring and valuable work has been widely appreciated. The Society was inaugurated in 1926, and a year later, upon the death of Mr Allen, the founder, the Presidency passed into the capable hands of Dr E. Ward, succeeded by Mr S. Gibbard, with Mr E. H. Ware as secretary.

The cause of wild-life preservation and research in Devon and Cornwall has also been considerably furthered by the *Western Morning News*, whose ex-Editor-in-Chief, Mr Jas. L. Palmer, has always taken an active interest in the natural history of the west, and given the powerful support of his columns to all efforts made on behalf of the county and its fauna.

Distressing from the ornithologist's point of view was the felling of our woods and the occupation for military purposes of places such as Braunton Burrows and Slapton Ley. In such matters, however, we need not be unduly pessimistic. The dispossessed woodland birds will find new nesting and roosting-places. I do not think that any of our eighteen heronries have fallen before axe and saw, and when quiet is restored to Braunton Burrows the wild will reclaim its own.

The high cliffs of North Devon
A Dartmoor coombe—haunt of the ring-ouzel, wheatear and golden plover

Devon may not be the aviary of England, but her avifauna is abundant and distinctive, and although poorer perhaps in bird life than was once the case, there is good reason to hope that her present considerable wealth may be conserved, if not increased.

Foxgloves: the "proud ladies" of Devonshire
Statue of Charles Kingsley at Bideford

CHAPTER XXIX

WHERE WILD FLOWERS BLOW

So me account of moorland plant life has already been given, and the county in general is adequately covered by various scientific publications, from the old *Flora Devoniensis* of 1829, by Jones and Kingston, down to the 1939 *Flora of Devon*, by the Rev W. K. Martin and Gordon Fraser. The later work is particularly comprehensive, every "escape" and variety being listed, including, for example, over forty violets alone. Any attempt at a full categorical list of the county's wild flowers is, therefore, not only beyond the scope of this limited volume, but unnecessary. It is proposed, however, to substitute two or three "flower pictures" characteristic of the Devonshire landscape.

As early as February in a mild season, primroses appear along sheltered hedgerows, and before they have reached perfection river-banks are yellow with wild daffodils, the "Lent lilies" of the country-people. Joy of springtime, these flowers are plentifully distributed, especially along the valleys bordering Dartmoor, where in a normal season Taw, Okement and Teign daily attract hundreds of visitors, who do not depart empty-handed. I have seen that particularly famed area lying between Steppes and Clifford Bridges picked out so cleanly within a few hours that not one bud remained. Some years before the war, indeed, "Daffodil Expresses" were being advertised by railway companies as an inducement to West-country trips, and results may be left to the imagination.

There remain, however, the less accessible spots, which afford more lingering enjoyment, but even here competition is keen, and for some inexplicable reason people who normally seldom stir beyond their doorsteps will walk miles over rough lanes and fields to gather daffodils. "Boy chaps" who remain perennially indifferent to other wild flowers hurry through work on a Sunday morning, jump on their bicycles, and return with huge bunches, which for a week or so blazon forth in jam-jars in every cottage window.

To come upon a mile or so of open field or riverside which has escaped the despoiler, where water tumbles between banks pale with daffodil and primrose, is one of Devon's fairest scenes. To complete the green and yellow colour pageant, and itself resembling nothing so much as an animated blossom, that first and loveliest butterfly of spring, the sulphur yellow Brimstone, darts on swift wings into a canvas already crowded with beauty. That similar scenes should have inspired the haunting lines of Shakespeare, Herrick and Wordsworth is but inevitable tribute to the universal appeal of the daffodil in its natural setting. Nor has the primrose failed in its poetic appeal, and the "primrose path," synonym of perfect happiness, might well be typified by a Devonshire lane in springtime.

Once the year has embarked upon its flower-set course, with celandine, primrose, Lent lily and wood anemone, the successive months are progressively colour-filled. Sometimes it is the hedge-banks that have burst into gaiety after an April shower, or a wood become blue overnight with myriads of wild hyacinths; or again a cliff-top in early summer may present a display of flowering plants rivalling those of a cherished garden.

I have always retained a vivid impression of one such picture on the North Devon cliffs. The rugged coast, stretching south-west from Hartland Point, confronts the full force of the Atlantic storms, yet summer makes an early appearance in these coombes—Speke's Bay, Welcombe and Marsland Mouth—which gash the great cliffs and hurl their streams down sheer rock ledges to pebbly beaches below. Upon an early May day beneath a blue and white-billowed sky, we came upon a small grassy plateau extending to the edge of a 400-foot precipice. Upon this exposed spot, entirely unprotected from the sweeping sea winds, a brilliant carpet of blossom, colour and fragrance halted our steps. Here within fifty square yards sixteen flowering species were counted, massed in such a manner amongst the grass that they imparted the effect of a mosaic patterned upon a green background. There were tufts of pale sea-pink and white sea-campion; mauve patches of dog-violet and the deeper purple of bugle; bright celandine and delicate primrose; tall spikes of red sorrel pushing up among the humble daisies and golden dandelions. Germander speedwell contrasted its bright blue with the white blossoms and glaucous green of scurvy-grass. Bird's-foot trefoil grew beside the little creeping tormentilla, pink lousewort and the vivid yellow, green and red of spurge. Most attractive of all, perhaps, were the blue-mauve patches of the dainty spring scilla, whose faint aromatic scent mingled with that of wild thyme trodden underfoot.

Although so common, sea-pink, or thrift, with its great blossoming cushions, is itself worth a visit to the coast in early summer. No carefully planned artificial rockery could surpass the loveliness of these wild boulder gardens where Nature had appropriated the old grey walls which run along the cliff-tops. One such, bounding the entire length of a small enclosure, was so enveloped in thrift that its foundation could only be surmised, no stones being visible. Here and there the pink hue was relieved by a mass of white sea-campion, and in just one spot, by the vivid contrast of the trefoil's red and yellow flowers, the entire effect heightened by a skyscape unbroken by tree or bush, with the brilliant green, purple and white of the sea beyond.

To this wonderful florescence might be added that of the deep, intersecting "mouths" where bluebells, "lords-and-ladies," marsh marigolds and primroses flourished luxuriantly in damp shelter, while white and gold drifts of late blackthorn and gorse in full perfection rioted up the steep slopes.

Gorse in both its forms, the spring and autumn flowering, is certainly partial to the western peninsula. Its abundance was commented upon nearly three centuries ago, when the observant Gerard, journeying through Devonshire, described the furze thus:

> "The greatest and highest that I did ever see do grow about Excester in the West parts of England, where the great stalkes are dearly bought for the better sort of people, the small thorny spraies for the poorer sort."

The latter part of this statement is puzzling, for one cannot conceive that West-country people ever had need to *buy* gorse, which could always have been theirs for the gathering. Gather it they certainly did, for "vuzz" has always figured largely in Devonshire rural economy. Corrugated iron has replaced it as thatching or building material, but a nice bushy "Vuzz-stick" is still a common sight upon the cottage or farmhouse doorstep, where it does duty as boot-scraper-cum-doormat. Happily, too, the aromatic scent of gorse, redolent of almond, rising on the hot air of a May afternoon, is an annual recurrence. Fascinating, also, is the "popping" of the ripe pods, like miniature rifle-fire, in July sunshine when blossoms have changed to tawny orange. Then, only an observant eye is able to distinguish the dainty Green Hairstreak butterfly, green beneath and tawny above, presenting a perfect camouflage as it rests among the browning flowers and young shoots whose colouring it exactly reproduces.

Typical of that large area stretching from Dartmoor northwards to the coast are the swampy fields known to botanists as *molinia moor*, from the characteristic coarse grass which forms huge tussocks in the muddy ooze. The flora of these marshes, referred to by the farmer as "rough bottoms," differs considerably from that of the Dartmoor peat-bogs. Here, early in the year, shiny red shoots of young birch scrub and the yellow catkins of bog-myrtle are effectively contrasted against the pale withered grass-humps. Between them, like dark pancakes, lie the flat leaf-tufts of the marsh thistle, from which later will rise the handsome purple flower-stem, sometimes to a height of between five and six feet. Under summer sunshine the warm, humid air has a greenhouse atmosphere, and where it is possible to thread a course along the drying mud, various swamp-loving plants may be noticed. Marsh marigolds, plentiful in some districts, are scarce in others, such as this, but the two commonest orchises, *mascula* and *maculata*, are plentifully sprinkled between pale bevies of milkmaids or cuckoo-flowers, red rattle, valerian and tall, shaggy hemp agrimony.

Memory recalls another summer-day picture of one such "bottom," hot and redolent of crushed mint. The whole sun-dried area was ablaze with golden fleabane, over which in the quivering heat haze danced a host of dark-winged ringlet butterflies. In autumn these open marshes produce larger and more luscious blackberries than are to be found elsewhere, for moist feet and a hot head are ideal conditions for some of the 160 varieties of *rubus* assigned to the county of Devon. At this season the bottoms present one of the last floral displays of the year, for in late September and October they are sheeted with the dark purple blue of the devil's-bit scabious. Viewed in mellow sunshine against a typical background of flaming birch and deep autumnal sky, the richness of the gold and blue colouring is arresting.

Although this is the final flower picture, Devon's gay hues have by no means faded from the landscape. Moorlands are a-sheen with the copper of decaying bracken. Woods acquire a special beauty in early November, canopied in autumn tints above a host of bright-capped fungi. Hedgerows retain the scarlet of their berries until Christmas, December being more often than not a mild, open month of gradually fading splendour. Only for a brief period after the New Year does Nature appear to be enjoying a well earned rest. Yet before January is passed she is awake again, swinging the "lambs'-tails" on the hazel bushes and pushing up the sun-faced celandines to begin once more her tireless task of filling the year with beauty.

CHAPTER XXX

LITERATURE AND LEARNING

HAD the *Victoria History of Devon* ever been completed, it would have comprised six large volumes, and the impossibility of compressing so wide a range of subjects into the present book must be sufficiently obvious. The last few chapters have been mainly concerned with country life and natural history, but much that one would have liked to include has unavoidably been omitted. I have not, for example, mentioned the long-established gypsy settlements of the west, but Mr Vesey-FitzGerald's recent authoritative book, *Gypsies of Britain*, leaves little to be said about Romany life in any part of England. Entomology has not been touched, but this subject, again, is exhaustively treated in the one published volume of the *Victoria History of Devon*. Of shooting and fishing also little has been said. In Devonshire, however, neither is sufficiently distinctive to merit space in a work not primarily concerned with sport, and, indeed, since the introduction of the trapping system, shooting throughout the county has been mainly notable for its deterioration. There remain ecclesiastical, cultural and scholastic developments to be considered. Each of these subjects offers almost unlimited scope for study, as manifested by the many works already published, and notably by the papers contained in the *Transactions* of the Devon Association.

Founded in 1862, this Association may undoubtedly be considered as holding primary place among county societies for its valuable and exhaustive research, which has covered every possible field of Devonshire interest. Indeed, anyone who can study the complete annual records, containing papers contributed by specialists, has access to a Devonshire encyclopædia of the most accurate and comprehensive nature. Among the earlier Presidents of this body we find such distinguished names as William Pengelly (1867), the geologist responsible for the Kent's Cavern and other archæological research; Charles Kingsley (1871); the Bishop of Exeter, later Archbishop Temple (1872); Baring-Gould (1896); and approaching our own day, the astonishingly versatile father and son, R. N. and R. Hansford Worth, to the latter of whom I am indebted for permission to make use of some of the authoritative matter so painstakingly acquired through their combined efforts. The results of their exhaustive investigations upon so great a variety of subjects may be considered a lasting contribution to Devon's store of knowledge.

The intellectual development of the county, of course, originated, like its commerce and industry, in the monasteries. The monks were the instructors, the architects, the librarians; and the monastic settlements the centres of general information, medical, theological and technical. At the Dissolution, twenty-four ecclesiastical institutions were suppressed in Devon, ten of these being classified as "greater monasteries," that is to say, possessing an income of more than £200 per annum. Of these, five were Cistercian: Buckfast, Ford, Newenham, Dunkeswell and Buckland, which was the last to be founded. Three were Augustinian, Plympton, Hartland and Canonsleigh. Torre Abbey was Premonstratensian, while the one Benedictine settlement at Tavistock, although not the oldest—Buckfast claiming seniority—was the most influential. For a considerable period it exercised a despotism almost equal to that of the Stanneries, a state of affairs which more than once required special diocesan action to control the arbitrary powers assumed by autocratic abbots.

As the Cistercians specialised in commerce, so the Benedictines were reputed to be the most learned order in Europe, and to Tavistock Abbey belongs the distinction of introducing the first printing press seen in Devonshire. This was set up in 1525, and from it issued Devon's first two books, *The Boke of Comfort*, a translation from Boethius, and nine years later *The confirmation of the Charter perteynynge to all the Tynners wythyn the Country of deuonshyre*. The original MS. of the latter was presumably lodged in the abbey, where

The home of the Red Deer on the Somerset border of Exmoor

also lay the Charter of Disafforestation, concerning which a good deal has already been said.

After the Dissolution, Devonshire printing fell into abeyance until about 1683, when, according to the earliest reliable evidence, it was revived in Exeter, and from that date developed rapidly, the first West-country newspaper, the *Exeter Mercury*, being issued in 1714. Various publications followed, Exeter at this early period keeping well ahead of Plymouth, whose first periodical, the *Weekly Journal*, appeared in 1721. Exeter maintained her journalistic supremacy for the greater part of a century. In 1860, however, Plymouth produced the *Western Morning News*, which steadily increased its circulation until, under the recent editorship of Mr Jas. L. Palmer, it has attained a standard seldom reached by a provincial publication. During the great aerial bombardment of 1941, when Plymouth was subjected to five heavy raids in nine nights, the *Western Morning News* maintained publication of its two daily papers under almost incredible difficulties. Working from practically the only building in the street that remained standing, the staff surmounted loss of transport, paper, photographic apparatus, gas, electricity and water, not one issue of either the *Western Morning News* or the *Western Evening Herald* failing to make its customary appearance. By a curious turn of circumstance's wheel, the *W.M.N.* press was subsequently removed to Tavistock, where for three years the principal publication of the modern west was produced in the same environment as had witnessed the birth of printing in Devonshire.

From journalism one passes automatically to literary personalities, the earliest of whom, as might be supposed, had an ecclesiastical connection. Taken chronologically, Winfrith of Crediton, canonised as St Boniface, takes priority, his epistles, written during his missionary career in Germany from 718 to 755, being noteworthy upon account of their early date rather than for any literary value.

More important was the work of Leofric, Bishop of Exeter, who, prior to his death in 1072, established and tabulated his remarkable collection of MSS, which, says E. H. Pedler, "was the earliest catalogue of an English

23   353

library now known to exist." Of this collection a certain number found their way to the Bodley Library at Oxford, which also possesses two copies of *The Boke of Comfort*. This famous library was opened in 1602, its founder Thomas Bodley being a native of Exeter. The city now possesses only one of Leofric's original MSS, that being the *Exeter Book*, or *Codex Exoniensis*, considered to be one of the most valuable Anglo-Saxon documents in England.

After Leofric, few literary notabilities appear until the Elizabethan period of general revival, the only outstanding exception being Miles Coverdale, another Exeter bishop from 1551 to 1553 and the well-known translator of the Bible. Elizabeth's reign produced George Peel, the dramatist, and, of course, Sir Walter Raleigh, with his varied works, and during this period were born the poets William Browne and Robert Herrick, the former a Devonian by birth, the latter by adoption, holding the living of Dean Prior from 1649 to 1662 with a short interim.

From Boniface to the present time Devon has been indebted to the Church for many of her literary men. In addition to those mentioned, there were Prince, Polwhele, Kingsley, Bray, Rowe, Moore, Baring Gould and Thornton —all Devonshire incumbents. This list includes three of the county's recognised historians, Polwhele, Rowe and Moore, and to these must be added Hooker, Pole, Westcote, Risdon and Izacke, while the excellent works of Crossing must not be omitted. Excluding living authors, such as Eden Phillpotts, who are self-evident, the most outstanding novelists have been Kingsley, Blackmore, Oxenham and Baring-Gould, and considering her picturesque background, Devon seems entitled to a more prominent place in classical fiction. It is also noteworthy that a county possessing so extensive and varied a fauna has not produced its Gilbert White, and it fell to Charles Dixon, whose heart was never in the west, to publish some of the first ornithological works of mainly Devonian interest.

Few Devonshire writers were educated in the county. It was assumed that Raleigh, who remained at home until sixteen years old, received local tuition, but there is no evidence that he attended any educational establishment. Even the poet Coleridge, although his father was headmaster of Ottery Grammar School, obtained a presentation to Christ's Hospital, and Blackmore's six-year association with Blundell's is by way of an exception. It might be interesting to add that the same school can also claim two writers of the present day, Sir J. Squire and E. W. Hendy, and its share of literary or ecclesiastical figures with a West-country association is considerable. A famous contemporary of Blackmore was Frederick Temple, successively Bishop of Exeter, London, and Archbishop of Canterbury. Archbishop William Temple was born at Exeter Palace, a Devonian father and son thus achieving the unprecedented distinction of occupying the Canterbury See.

Another Blundellian who became distinguished in a very different field was Jack Russell, like Blackmore proceeding from Tiverton to Exeter College, Oxford. As its name suggests, this college has a particular West-country association, for, together with the ancient grammar-school of Ashburton, it was founded in 1314 by a Devonian prelate, Walter Stapledon, Bishop of Exeter. Ashburton School is probably the oldest institution of the kind in Devonshire, if not in the west, considerably pre-dating that of Ottery St Mary (1545), Okehampton (1610) and South Molton (1682), to mention only a few of the long-established grammar-schools. Many, as Bideford, for example, were founded in the sixteenth and seventeenth centuries or during the woollen boom, but exact dates are lacking in most instances.

Equally noteworthy are the county's modern educational establishments. Seale Hayne and Dartington Hall are both colleges promoting agricultural science and experiment, the latter occupying the site of an ancient manor now appropriately devoted to the development of Devon's oldest industry. The University College of the South-West, founded in 1865 upon modest lines by the City of Exeter Council, was incorporated as a University College in 1922, since when its growth and general development have been extensive. Of outstanding importance is the Plymouth Laboratory of Marine Biology, this being the headquarters of the M.B. Association of the U.K., founded in 1884 under

23*

the Presidency of T. H. Huxley, the first laboratory buildings being opened four years later. A great deal of invaluable research is undertaken by this institution, which also possesses a first-class library of scientific literature.

The political history of Devonshire is mainly passive, nor, with the exception of Pym, a native of Tavistock, does the list of the county's celebrities contain an outstanding legislator. Plymouth can boast the honour of returning the first woman M.P., while the recent Liberal Member for South Molton, Mr George Lambert (now Viscount Lambert), occupied the seat, with one short break, from 1891 until the dissolution in 1945, so attaining the position of seniority in the House upon the retirement of the late Earl Lloyd George. Apart from the few big towns, however, Devon is not a politically minded county, and her rural population upon the whole remains as remote from party strife and trade disputes as her countryside from the general march of progress. "I haven't never voted and bain't going to, unless by doing so I could drown the whole blasted issue of 'em," was the political outlook expressed in one emphatic sentence by old Aubrey Tucker, and this retrogressive "school of thought" finds many adherents among the country-people.

And with this final reference to old and still primitive Devon, the book must close, upon a not inappropriate note perhaps, for in spite of inevitable innovation the Devonshire of today is old-world still, and fundamental must be the changes that take place in England before this, the fairest of her western shires, loses the unique character and atmosphere which even in the twentieth century invest the very name of Devonshire.

INDEX

357